THE ABC'S OF FORTRAN PROGRAMMING

Michael J. Merchant

Wadsworth Publishing Company, A Division of Wadsworth, Inc., Belmont, California

Computer Science Editor: H. Michael Snell
Editorial Associate: Jenny Sill
Production Editor: Anne Kelly
Art Director: Kate Michels
Designer: Rick Chafian
Cover Designer: Albert Burkhardt

Printed in the United States of America

3 4 5 6 7 8 9 10—83 82 81 80

Library of Congress Cataloging in Publication Data

Merchant, Michael J
The ABC's of FORTRAN programming.

Includes index.
1. FORTRAN (Computer program language)
I. Title.
QA76.73.F25M45 001.6′424 78-24198
ISBN 0-534-00634-5

Contents

Note: Small boxes before section titles indicate optional sections.

Preface to the Instructor

FORTRAN is an easy language to learn. Most students can learn to write a FORTRAN program in a few weeks. Learning to write a good FORTRAN program, however, is another matter. Too often the student leaves a first course in programming unprepared to tackle a real programming problem.

The ABC's of FORTRAN Programming has two goals. The first is to teach the basics of the FORTRAN computer language, plainly and simply. The second is to help the student put this knowledge to work in solving problems with a computer.

In addressing the first goal, the text concentrates on the mainstream of the FORTRAN language. A few topics, such as P scaling factors and BLOCK DATA subprograms, have been omitted entirely because the beginning student has almost no use for them. Other topics, such as computed and assigned GO TO statements, are of very limited use to a beginning student and so are included in Appendix B. The philosophy of this text is that it is better to give the student a basic set of tools with instructions for using them well, than to provide every conceivable tool and leave the student bewildered by such an excessive variety.

In addressing the second goal, the book provides numerous examples of complete programs. These are all short and easily understood, but they illustrate essential principles in realistic applications. There are no examples concocted to illustrate a syntactic point in a context that would never be used by a good programmer. Many of the exercises also ask the student to write a complete program and run it on the computer. Such active participation is the only way to really grasp the subject.

This book can be used either for a short course on FORTRAN or for a full semester's introduction to programming. Material that is not essential for a basic understanding of the FORTRAN language is included in *optional* sections (indicated by small boxes in the margin), which you can cover selectively, depending on the time available and the interests of the students. Two optional modules on programming style and structured programming give practical advice on how to write a program.

The text does not assume that students have any previous computer experience. Chapter 1 introduces the concepts of an algorithm and a program, and explains how an algorithm is represented by a flowchart. Students familiar with these topics can omit Chapter 1 or use it as a quick review. Chapter 2 gives an overview of the FORTRAN language. Chapter 3 explains how programs are run on a computer and describes how to set up a FORTRAN job. Finally, Chapters 4–10 present a gradual, thorough introduction to FORTRAN programming.

No knowledge of mathematics beyond basic algebra is required. FORTRAN programming can be useful to anyone, not just to mathematicians and scientists; all the examples in this book are nontechnical and self-explanatory.

List-directed input and output statements are used in the early chapters. Most FORTRAN compilers (and WATFOR and WATFIV in particular) allow these forms, and they greatly simplify the details of reading and writing data. If you prefer, however, students can study the optional section in Chapter 2 on formatted PRINT and READ statements and use these forms throughout the book.

I would like to thank Mike Snell, of Wadsworth Publishing Company, for his encouragement. While the responsibility for any deficiencies in this text is my own, I am sincerely grateful to the following for their many helpful comments on the manuscript: Henry A. Etlinger, Rochester Institute of Technology; William L. Harrison, Oregon State University; Lansing Hatfield, Lawrence Livermore Laboratory; Charles E. Moulton, Beaver College; Linda T. Moulton, Montgomery County Community College; Ronald G. Sykora, E. G. & G., Inc.; and Collin J. Watson, University of Oklahoma. I also thank Janet Churchey for her excellent typing. Finally, to my wife Nancy, for her help, and my daughters, Kristina and Vanessa, for their patience, my special thanks.

Preface to the Student

You are about to begin an exciting experience: learning to program, to command a general-purpose machine capable of any kind of calculation or symbolic manipulation and of following your instructions at the rate of a million operations per second. This machine is a computer. The trick is getting the computer to do what you want, and that is what programming is about.

Of course, you can use a computer without being a programmer. Credit card transactions, checking accounts, automated payroll systems—these are familiar computerized activities that touch our lives daily. Directly or indirectly, most of us deal with computers hundreds of times each year. But the fun part of dealing with computers is writing your own programs. When you can do that, the computer becomes *your* tool, doing what *you* want, and you will be able to use it to do things you could not possibly do alone.

A word of encouragement: Programming is not difficult. It can be learned by anyone who has the patience to do so. I have heard the opinion that programming is only for people with mathematical minds. Nonsense. Anyone who wants to learn and has the patience to practice the skill can become a good programmer. Computers *are* useful for solving mathematical problems; but a knowledge of mathematics is not essential for understanding programming. Computers are also useful in business data processing, social sciences, applied engineering, and dozens of other fields, including just having fun. This book has examples drawn from many fields. However, the text does not assume any special knowledge of the fields, and no mathematics beyond basic algebra is required.

A word of caution, however: Programming is not easy. This is not a subject to be learned the night before an examination. Nor do you learn programming by passively reading and memorizing. What you will be learning is not just a collection of facts but a way of thinking, a way of approaching a problem, a way of inventing a program to achieve a desired result through using the FORTRAN language. This requires practice and active involvement. By the time you have finished Chapter 3, you will be running programs on the computer. From then on, writing programs of increasing difficulty and complexity and running them on the computer will be the most important things you do to learn FORTRAN programming.

Do not expect this skill to come effortlessly. Programs rarely work on the first try. Careful thought, analysis, and perseverance are required. You can expect some frustration, but you can also look forward to an immense pride and satisfaction when your program works.

A word about attitude: There is a tendency for beginners to personify the computer—jokingly, but only half so, to think of it as an antagonist who is out to thwart the programmer. Students often remark to each other, "Do you know what that stupid computer did to me?" What they mean is that their program did not run due to a programming error. They rarely say, "I made the most amusing mistake." Instead, they say, "That darn computer did it again." Students sometimes regard programming as a contest between themselves and the computer. Be assured that the computer is quite impersonal and derives no satisfaction from your errors. It is neither intelligent nor malevolent and has neither creativity nor common sense. It does exactly what your program says to do, nothing more. You cannot casually dash off a successful program any more than you can hastily pen a great poem.

Learning to analyze and correct errors requires logical thinking, which can be fun. But if programming is regarded as a hit-or-miss enterprise, it is bound to be difficult and frustrating. Some students try to get a program to run successfully by making random changes in the program and submitting dozens of variations to the computer, hoping that one will work. Even if this method succeeds in getting their homework done, the students are missing the point.

The real enjoyment of programming is in knowing that your program works because you understand it. Answers to selected exercises are provided at the end of this book, and you will profit from comparing your solution to a problem with the answer given here (although there is never just one solution to a programming problem). Ultimately, though, you must be the judge of your own work. When you are applying FORTRAN to your own problems, there will be no answer in the back of the book. The only way you can be sure of your program is to understand thoroughly the FORTRAN language and the basic programming principles you are using. Write your program carefully, making sure you know the reason for each step. Then test the program with trial computer runs to ensure that you have not made any mistakes. Your goal should be to understand the subject so well you do not need to look in the answer section to see if your program is correct. When you can program with that confidence, the computer will truly be your servant.

In many ways, programming is a science. It requires a precise expression of a procedure in unambiguous language, subject to strict rules. But there is also an element of art, for programming is an intensely creative process. To start with a problem statement and build a program requires imagination and intuition. Sometimes, a clever, well thought-out program is a truly beautiful expression of intellect and understanding. The excitement and satisfaction of inventing such a program is no less than that felt by the artist who paints a beautiful picture or chisels a sculpture from stone.

This is what you can look forward to. You will be learning neither pure art nor pure science. I like to think of it as a craft; like the artist's brush, the computer is a tool. The more skilled you become in the craft of programming, the more intricate and polished your creations will be. With these thoughts in mind, let us begin.

1

Algorithms, Programs, and Flowcharts

You will learn in this book to program a computer in the FORTRAN language. This chapter explains what a program is and how it is represented by a diagram called a flowchart.

Computers

If you have access to a computer system, have someone explain its parts and show you how to run programs on it. The computer may seem complicated, but you can program it without knowing a great deal about its inner workings, just as you can operate a television set without knowing how it is built.

In some ways, a computer is like a hand calculator. The program instructions are like the keys you press on a calculator: They tell the machine what to do. Unlike a hand calculator, however, a computer can process nonnumeric data, such as symbols and alphabetic characters, as well as numbers. For example, in compiling a telephone directory, a properly programmed computer sorts all the names and prints them in alphabetical order. We can define a **computer** as *a machine that can process data by following a list of program instructions.*

What kind of instructions can you give in a program? It would be convenient just to say, "Computer, solve the following problem!" and watch the machine obey. Unfortunately, computers can obey only very simple commands. Every computer has an **instruction set**, consisting typically of one or two hundred commands calling for operations it can perform electronically. All these commands fall into one of seven categories: computation, input, output, storing in memory, recalling from memory, comparison, and program control.

COMPUTATION. A computer can do arithmetic. You can write a program instruction telling the machine to multiply, for example. As with a calculator, the actual multiplication is done electronically. A typical large computer can multiply two numbers in one millionth of a second.

INPUT AND OUTPUT. You can also instruct a computer to read in data. Data to be read by a program is called **input data**, or simply **input**. To tell the machine to read, you use an **input instruction** in your program.

On a hand calculator, you enter numbers by pressing the keys. On a computer system, you might use punch cards instead. You first type the data on a keypunch machine, which has a typewriterlike keyboard. The keypunch is not part of the computer itself, but the punch cards it produces are put in the computer's **card reader**. An input instruction in your program tells the card reader to read a punch card.

When you want your program to write out results, you use an **output instruction**. For instance, you can instruct the machine to print results on a **line printer**. Data written by a program is called **output**.

You will probably use only the card reader and line printer at first, but several other devices are used for input and output. Each type has some advantages that make it suitable for certain applications. A computer **terminal** has a keyboard that you can use to enter data directly without using punch cards. Some terminals have a **cathode ray tube (CRT)** display similar to a television screen. Instead of printing results on paper, you can have your program write on the CRT screen. **Magnetic tape** is used for both input and output. Large volumes of data can be recorded very compactly on magnetic tape. Although the data on tape cannot be read directly by a person, it can be read by a computer program for further processing. For example, a commercial bank might run a program each day to record the day's transactions on a magnetic tape. At the end of the month, another program could read the tapes and print statements for the customers. Other common media are **magnetic disk**, **paper tape**, and **microfilm**.

STORING AND RECALLING FROM MEMORY. You can also instruct a computer to *store* or *recall* data from its **memory**. The computer memory is nothing like a human memory; it is just a device for storing data electronically. Many hand calculators have a memory key that lets you save a number. For instance, in a constant percentage problem, you might store a percent figure in memory. Each time you need to use the figure, you can recall it from memory rather than reentering it on the keyboard. This is exactly how a computer memory works. The difference is that instead of a single number, the computer memory can store thousands of numbers.

Each memory location has a unique **address**, which is a number used to distinguish it from other memory locations. Think of computer memory as a sequence of mailboxes with a different address on each one. Each mailbox can contain one item of data. A program instruction might say, "Store the number 5.2 in address 1001." Later in the same program, an instruction might say, "Recall the contents of address 1001."

A computer terminal has a keyboard for input and a display screen for output.

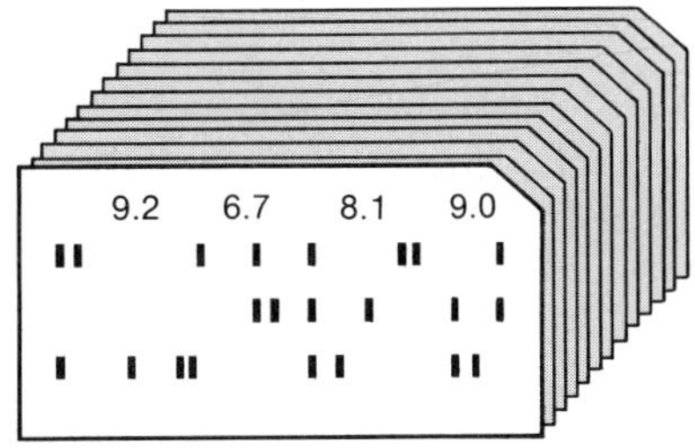

Punch card input is prepared on a keypunch and read on a card reader.

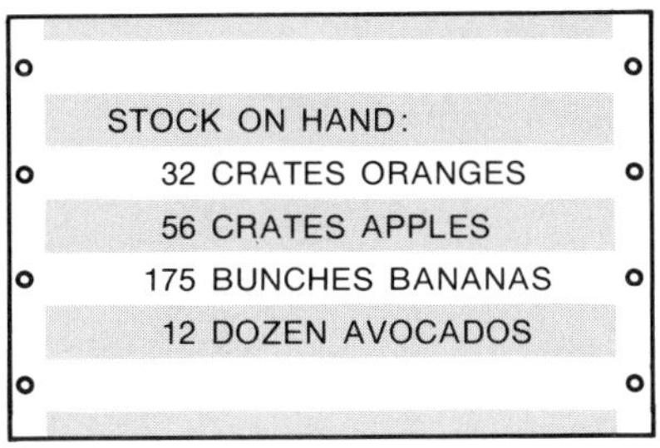

Printed output is produced on a line printer.

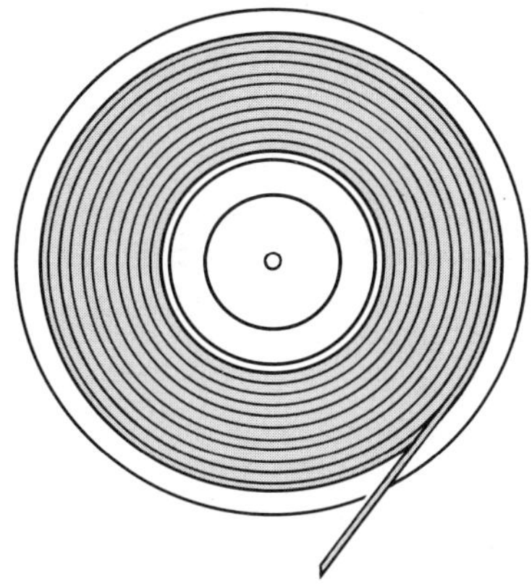

Magnetic tape is used for both input and output.

Figure 1.1 Some devices used for input and output.

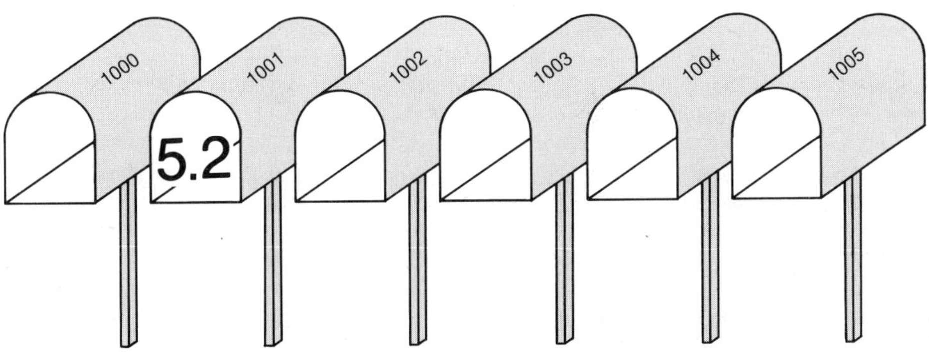

Figure 1.2 You can think of computer memory as a sequence of mailboxes, each with its own address. The instruction "Store 5.2 at address 1001" stores the data 5.2 as the contents of mailbox number 1001.

COMPARISON. Another type of instruction is a **comparison**. This instruction tells the computer to determine whether two numbers stored in memory are the same, or whether one number is greater or less than the other.

PROGRAM CONTROL. The last type of instruction is used for **program control**, which means telling the computer what to do next. This is like an instruction on a tax form that says, "If losses are shown on both lines 12 and 13, go to Part IV." You can use a program control instruction, for example, to tell the machine to repeat a procedure over and over again.

Program control instructions are often combined with comparison instructions. For example, some computers may have a single instruction meaning "Go to Step 1 if the number in address 1010 is greater than zero." Together, comparison and control instructions give a computer the capability to make elementary decisions.

A few more specialized types of instructions exist, such as determining when a card reader is empty. Basically, however, the operations summarized in Table 1.1 are all a computer can do. Writing a program means using these seven kinds of instructions to tell the computer how to solve your problem.

Table 1.1 Types of Program Instructions*

Instruction Type	*Function*	*Example*
Computation	Add, subtract, multiply, etc.	"Add 1 and 2."
Input	Transfer data from some device into memory	"Read a punch card."
Output	Transfer data from memory to some device	"Print the contents of memory address 2000."
Storing in Memory	Save data for later use	"Store the number 5.2 in address 1001."
Recalling from Memory	Retrieve stored data	"Recall the contents of address 1001."
Comparison	Determine whether one number is less than, greater than, or equal to another	"Is the number in address 1001 greater than zero?
Program Control**	Specify which instruction to do next	"Go to Step 1."

* Every computer has an instruction set, consisting typically of one or two hundred basic instructions. These are the building blocks of which all programs are composed. There are seven general types of instructions.

** Program control instructions are often combined with comparison instructions.

Algorithms and Programs

Before you can write a program to solve a problem, you must devise a method of solution expressed as a step-by-step procedure. Such a procedure is called an **algorithm**.* For

* The word *algorithm* comes from the name of a Persian textbook author, al-Khowârizmî (c. 825).

example, to determine whether an integer number is even or odd, you can use the following method.

Algorithm A

1. Divide the number by 2, obtaining a quotient and a remainder.
2. If the remainder is 0, then the number is even.
3. If the remainder is not 0, then the number is odd.

A different algorithm for the same purpose is the following.

Algorithm B

1. Look at the last digit of the number.
2. If the digit is 0, 2, 4, 6, or 8, then the number is even.
3. If the digit is 1, 3, 5, 7, or 9, then the number is odd.

Having decided on the method to be used, you need to express the procedure in a computer language such as FORTRAN. *A program is an algorithm written in a computer language.*

In Chapter 2 we begin our study of the FORTRAN language itself, and in Chapter 3 you will learn how to run a program on a computer. In this chapter we are concerned with how to write an algorithm.

People are usually imprecise in giving instructions to each other. A simple instruction such as "Go to the store for a loaf of bread" requires hundreds of decisions to carry out: Should you go out the front door or the back door? Should you turn left or right? Where is the store? Where is the bread? Should you buy a large loaf, or small? Whole wheat, sourdough, or caraway rye? When you write an algorithm for a computer, you must include every such detail.

Suppose you want to solve a math problem using a calculator. You do not have a calculator, but you have a friend who does, so you call her on the phone to ask for help. She is not at home, but her young brother, who knows very little math, offers to work the calculator if you will tell him exactly what to do. Now you must specify how to solve your problem using instructions that are so precise and unambiguous that he cannot possibly misinterpret them. You might say, "Enter the number 56.2, press the plus key, enter the number 475.3, press the plus key, enter the number 11.63, press the equals key, and tell me the answer." This is an algorithm, expressed in English.

You can imagine how hard it would be to tell someone on the phone how to do a really complicated computation. It is hard in English (or any natural language) to convey complex algorithms that involve many decisions. A useful way of expressing such algorithms is to draw a flowchart.

Flowcharts

A **flowchart** is an easy-to-read diagram of an algorithm. You will probably find it useful to make a flowchart as a first step in writing a program. When the flowchart is done, it will serve as a guide for writing FORTRAN statements.

Each instruction in a flowchart is enclosed in a box, and you use different shapes for different types of instructions. A parallelogram means an input or output operation

(Figure 1.3), and a rectangle means a computation (Figure 1.4). To indicate the order in which the instructions are performed, you connect the boxes with arrows. For example, Figure 1.5 shows a flowchart for a procedure to compute and print the value of 2 + 2. The "Start" oval shows where the procedure begins, and the "Stop" oval shows where it ends.

Figure 1.3 A parallelogram represents an input or output instruction.

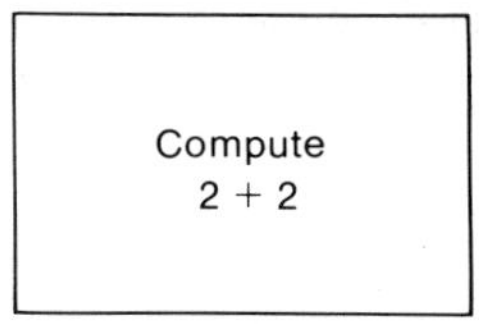

Figure 1.4 A rectangular box represents computation.

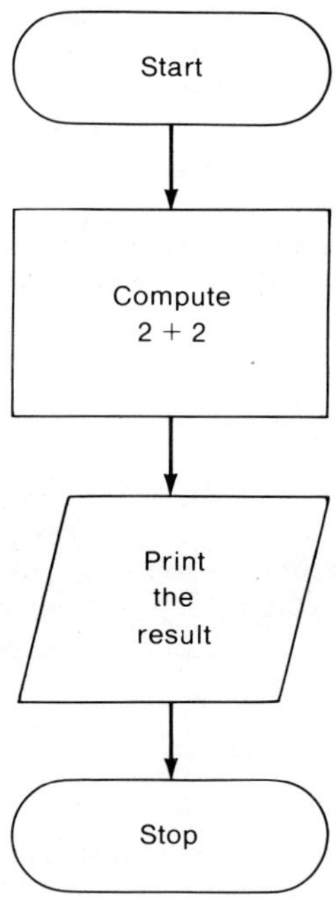

Figure 1.5 Arrows connect the boxes to show the order in which to carry out the instructions.

EXAMPLE 1. A friend has offered to bake cookies for your birthday if you will explain how to make them. Draw a flowchart to describe the cookie-making process. Figure 1.6 shows a flowchart for this procedure. Of course, this is not a computer algorithm, but it illustrates the use of flowcharts in representing processes.

Since the recipe in this example consists of a sequence of instructions that are performed in order, you might just as well have written the instruction in a list, as in a cook book.

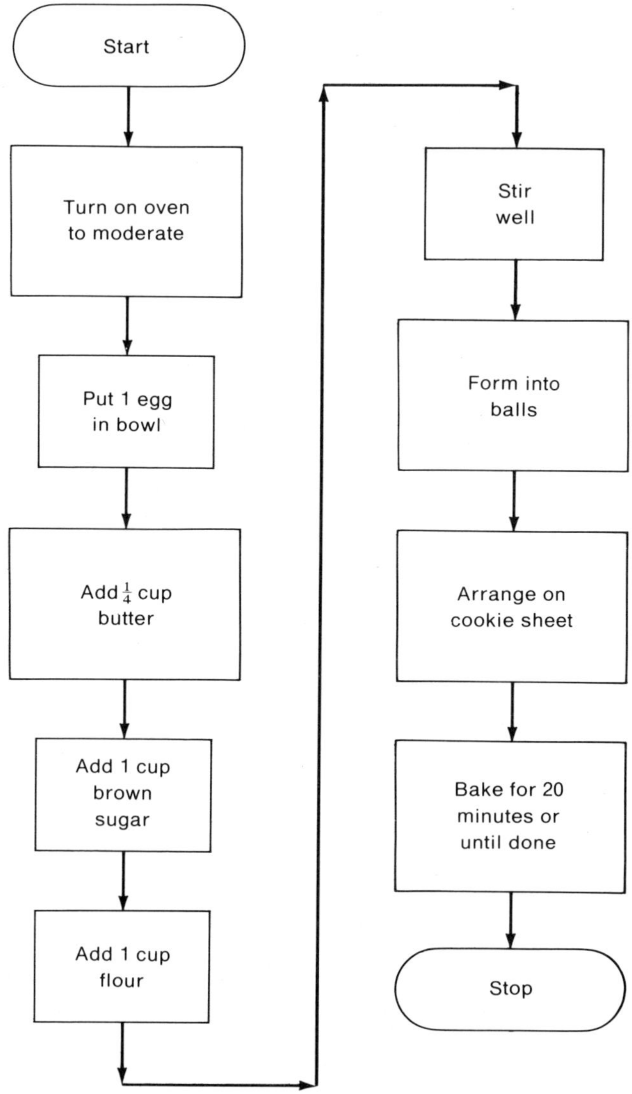

Figure 1.6 Recipe flowchart.

However, many algorithms require choosing among alternate courses of action, and a flowchart is especially suited to diagramming such a procedure.

You represent a decision in a flowchart by a diamond, as in Figure 1.7. A single arrow comes into the diamond, but two (or possibly three) arrows go out of it. This indicates that the path to be followed depends on the answer to the question written in the diamond.

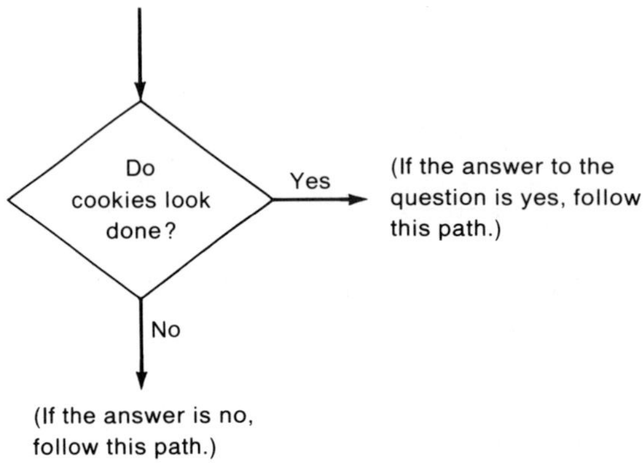

Figure 1.7 A decision.

EXAMPLE 2. The recipe flowchart contains the box shown in Figure 1.8. You can use a decision diamond to give a more detailed description of this process. In words, the process is this: Put cookies in oven, close oven door, wait 18 minutes, open oven door, see if cookies look done, take them out if they look done, otherwise close oven door and check again in 2 minutes.

Figure 1.8 A general instruction like this can be made more detailed, as in Figure 1.9.

Figure 1.9 shows the corresponding flowchart. In this flowchart there is more than one possible path since the decision has two possible outcomes. If the cookies do not look done, your friend will have to wait 2 minutes, open the oven door, and see again if the cookies look done. This is an example of a **loop**: a set of instructions that is repeated until some condition is attained. In this case, you have no way of knowing how many times your friend will have to go through the loop. The cookies may be done after 18 minutes. On the other

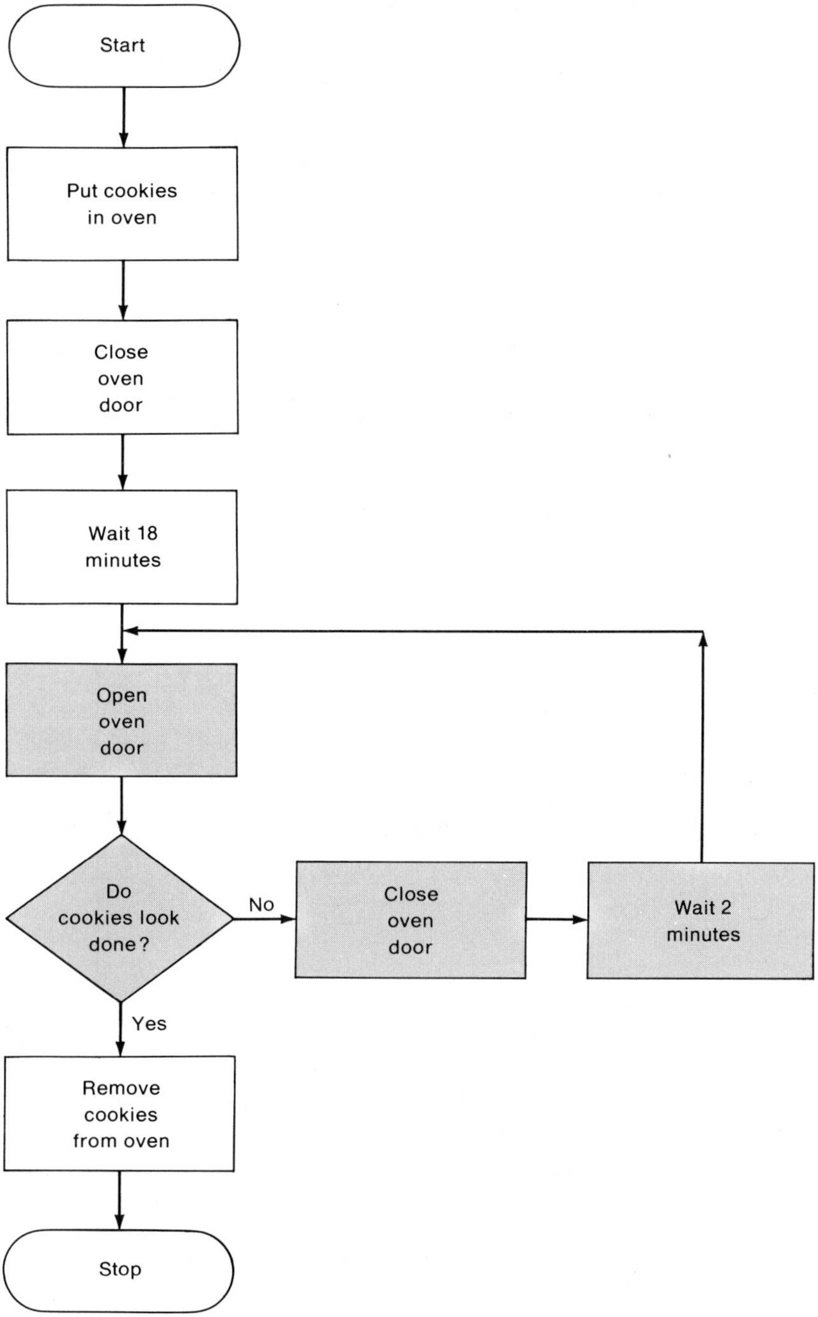

Figure 1.9 Cookie-baking flowchart with a decision diamond for determining if cookies are done. The shaded boxes form a loop—a set of instructions that is performed repeatedly until the question in the decision diamond is answered "Yes."

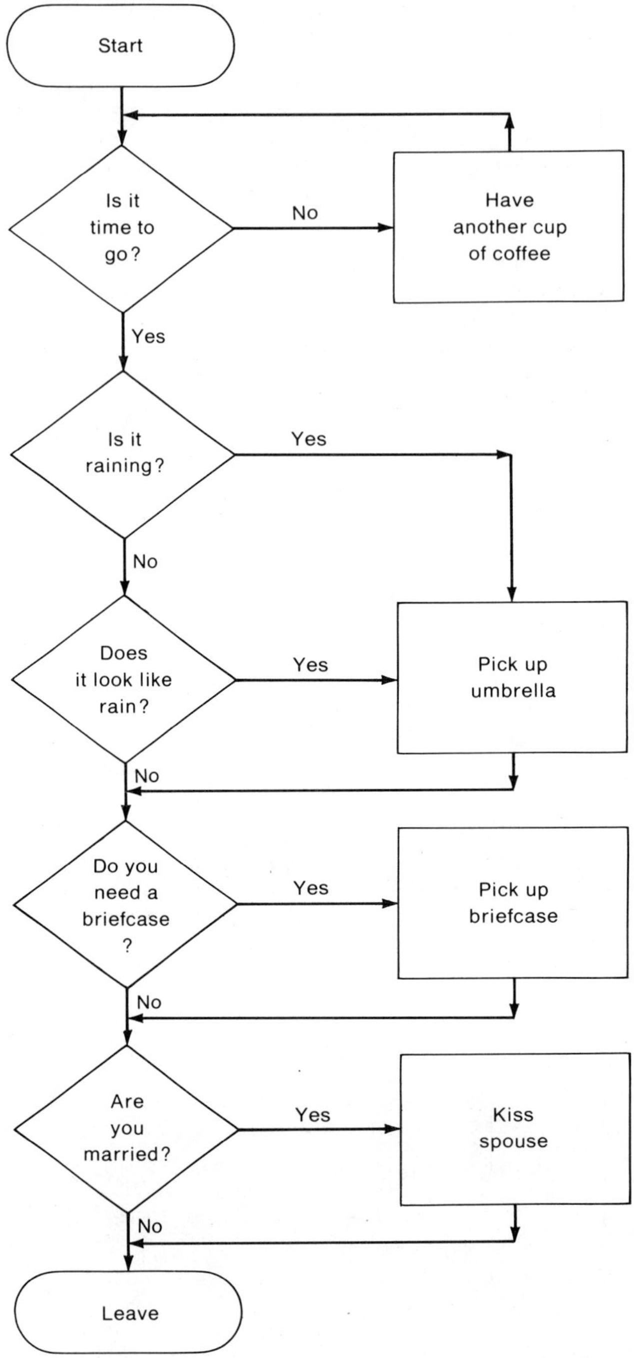

Figure 1.10 Procedure for leaving house in the morning.

hand, if your friend has forgotten to turn on the oven and follows the procedure faithfully, he will continue to open the oven door every 2 minutes, forever. This is called **getting stuck in a loop**. When writing a procedure for a computer, which has no common sense, you must take care that this cannot happen. *A correct algorithm must eventually terminate.*

EXAMPLE 3. A flowchart may contain many decisions and many possible paths. Figure 1.10 shows a general procedure for leaving the house in the morning, indicating several decisions that must be made. The first decision ("Is it time to go?") controls a loop. You keep drinking coffee and checking the time until it is time to go. The other decisions do not control loops, but simply determine whether or not you follow some instruction.

Examples 1 through 3 illustrate the general idea of flowcharts. But when writing an algorithm for a computer, you must write in each flowchart box an instruction that a computer can follow. Let us consider in more detail just what these instructions are.

Variables

Data can be processed only after it has been stored in the computer memory. As you have seen, each memory location has an address of its own. The actual structure of memory varies slightly among different computers, but here you can assume that the memory locations are numbered consecutively and that each location can contain one number or symbol. Figure 1.11 depicts a part of memory. The numbers 1001, 1002, . . . are the addresses, and the numbers inside the boxes are the contents of the memory. Thus, the contents of address 1003 is the number 762.333.

Address	Contents
1001	11
1002	0
1003	762.333
1004	2
1005	0.666667

Figure 1.11 Each memory location stores a value. The addresses distinguish different memory locations from one another.

When writing flowcharts (and FORTRAN programs), you rarely refer to the actual memory addresses. Instead, you use **variables**. A variable is just a name for some memory location. As in algebra, you denote a variable by a letter such as X or Y. You can also use a whole word for a variable name: WEIGHT or TAX, for example. Figure 1.12 represents a portion of memory assigned to five variables: A, B, C, X, and Y. The **value** of each variable is the contents of the memory location. In the figure, the value of Y is 0.666667. It really does not matter which addresses are used for the variables; the important thing is that each variable corresponds to some unique memory location.

Variable	Contents
A	11
B	0
X	762.333
C	2
Y	0.666667

Figure 1.12 You will generally use variables, instead of addresses, to refer to memory locations. The *value* of a variable is the contents of the memory location.

The operation of storing a value in memory is represented by an equal sign (=). When you write

X = 2

this means to store the value 2 in the memory location named X. The variable X will contain the value 2 until you assign it some other value.

You always use a variable name to the *left* of the equal sign to tell where to store the data. To emphasize that the value is stored in the variable on the left, some people use an arrow (←) to indicate a storing operation, and would write

X ← 2

The equal sign and the arrow mean the same thing: The value of the variable on the left is replaced by the value on the right. We will be using the equal sign in our flowcharts, as this is how the storing operation is written in FORTRAN.

To the right of the equal sign, you can put a variable instead of a number. For example,

X = A

means to recall the value of the variable A and store it as the new value of the variable X.

You can also write a flowchart box such as

X = A + B + 1

This means to recall the values of the variables A and B, add them, add 1 to the sum, and store the result in the variable X.

In general, you have the following:

Flowchart Rules

Rule 1: Computation, recalling from memory, and storing operations are represented in a flowchart by a rectangular box of the form

variable = *expression*

where *variable* is a variable name, and *expression* is some mathematical expression. This means to recall the values of the variables used in the expression, carry out the computation, and store the result in the variable to the left of the equal sign.

In writing algorithms, the concept of a variable and the use of the equal sign have a slightly different meaning than in ordinary algebra. Consider the instruction

$$X = X + 1$$

As an algebraic equation, it makes no sense. In a flowchart, however, we are not saying to solve an equation for an unknown X; the instruction means simply to add 1 to the value of X and store the result back in X.

Variables are also used in input and output operations. When you tell the computer to read a number, the number must be stored somewhere. An input operation must tell which variables are to be used to store the numbers read. Thus, an instruction might say, "Read the next card and store the two numbers on it in the variables A and B." For brevity, however, the flowchart could simply say, "Read A, B" (Figure 1.13). Similarly, an ouput operation writes the value of a variable. An output instruction might say, "Print out the values of the variables X and Y." The flowchart would say, "Print X, Y" (Figure 1.14).

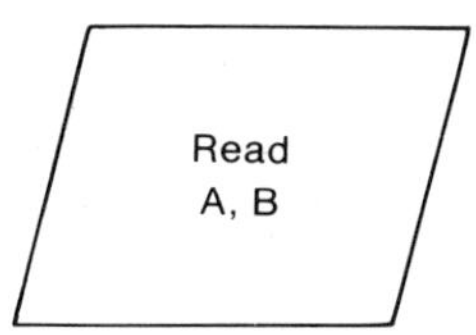

Figure 1.13 Input instruction: The variables tell where to store the data.

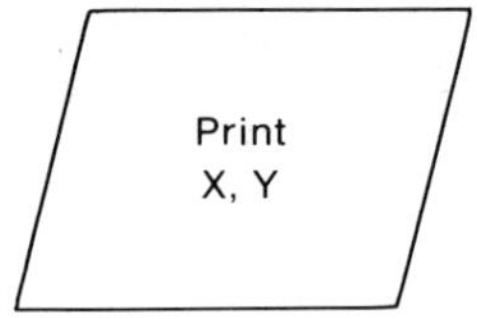

Figure 1.14 Output instruction: The values of the variables are printed.

In general, you have:

More Flowchart Rules

Rule 2: An input instruction is represented by a parallelogram of the form

where *list* is a list of variable names. This means to read data and store the values in the variables.

Rule 3: An output instruction is represented by a parallelogram of the form

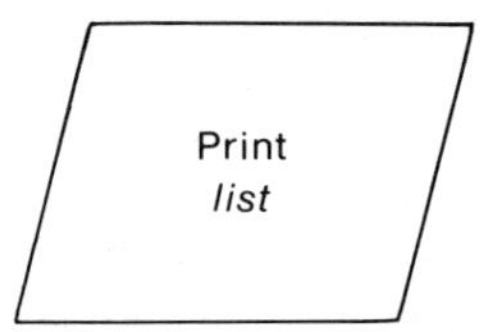

where *list* is a list of variable names. This means to write out the values of the variables.

Decisions

You have seen that a diamond-shaped symbol represents a decision in a flowchart. Only elementary decisions are possible on a computer. A program can choose only one branch or another based on an arithmetic comparison of two values. For example, Figure 1.15 means to compare the values of the variables A and B. If A is less than B, follow the left branch from the decision box; otherwise, follow the right branch. This same decision could also be written as shown in Figure 1.16.

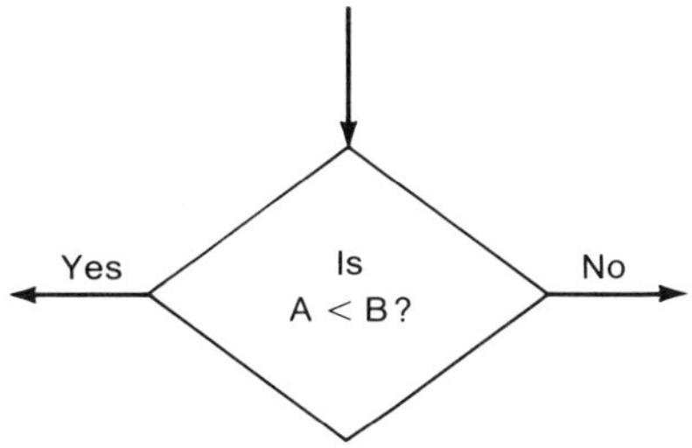

Figure 1.15 A decision selects a branch based on a comparison.

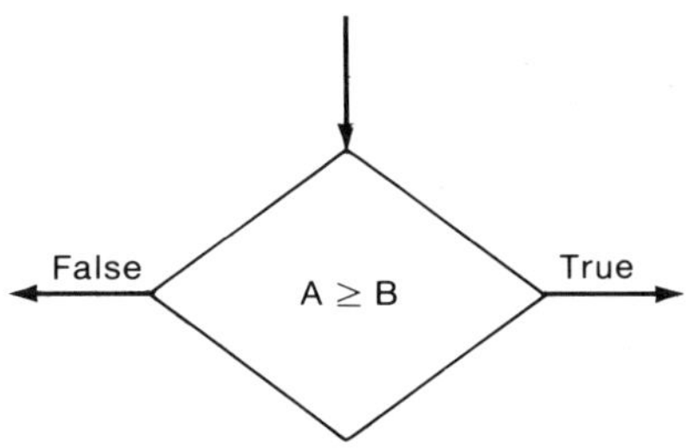

Figure 1.16 Another way to write the same decision.

As another example, the decision diamond shown in Figure 1.17 means to follow the bottom branch if N is equal to L − 1; otherwise, follow the right branch. The T and F stand for "True" and "False." Of course, you can also write this as in Figure 1.18.

Sometimes you may want to select among three possible branches, depending on whether one result is less than (<), equal to (=), or greater than (>) another. Figure 1.19 shows how to do this.

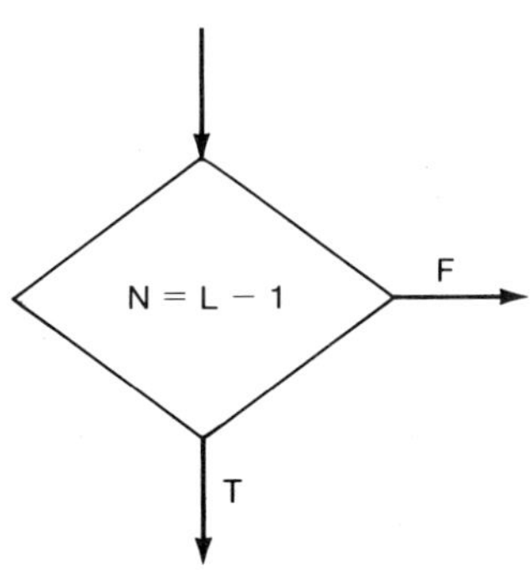

Figure 1.17 T and F stand for "True" and "False."

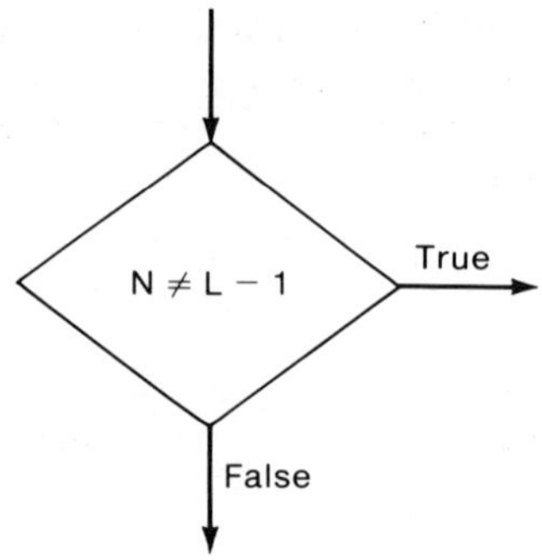

Figure 1.18 Another way to write the same decision.

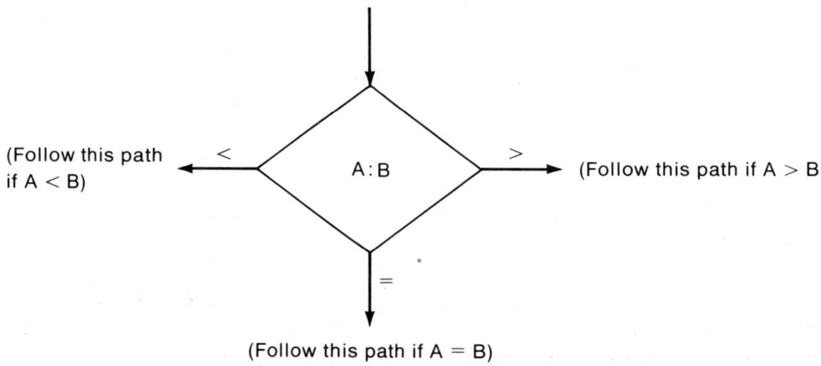

Figure 1.19 A comparison with three branches. The symbol A:B means "Compare A to B."

In summary, you write a decision in a flowchart according to the following:

Another Flowchart Rule

Rule 4: A decision is called for in a diamond-shaped box:

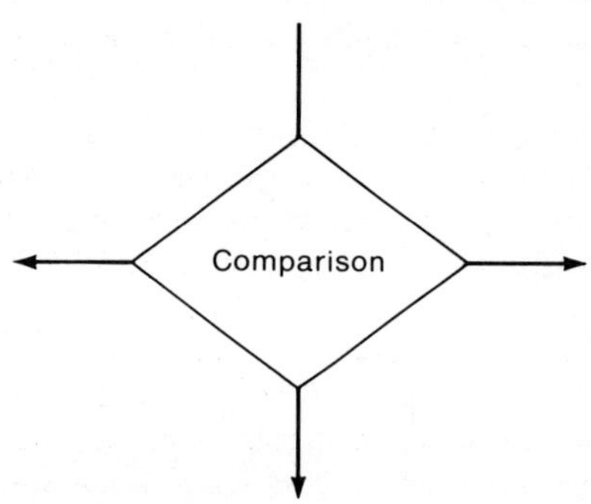

Inside the diamond, we write a comparison of two quantities which may be numbers, variables, or expressions. There may be two or three arrows coming out of the diamond, but there must be one path to follow for each possible outcome of the comparison.

You can usually represent a decision several ways. The three decision diamonds of Figure 1.20 are equivalent. The important thing is that inside each diamond two quantities are compared, and that one of the branches is followed out of the diamond, depending on the result of the comparison.

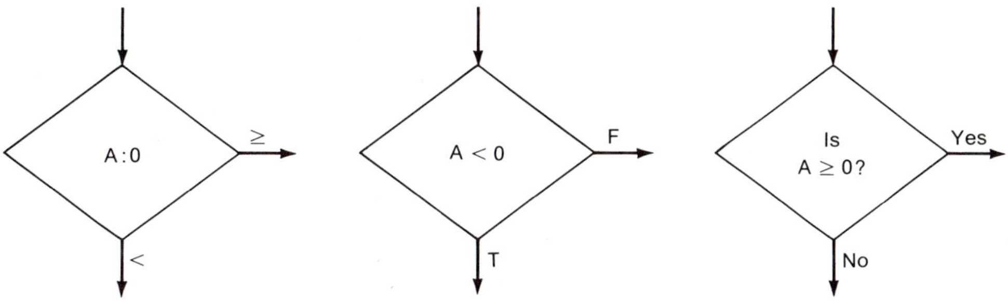

Figure 1.20 Three equivalent ways of writing a decision.

EXAMPLE 4. John Doe & Sons' Department Store has computed the total monthly sales for each month of the previous quarter. The general manager now wants to know the average monthly sales for this three-month period. Flowchart a procedure that will find this average.

Suppose the data is prepared on punch cards with one month's sales per card. There are three cards, so three input operations will be done. The first input operation reads the amount of the first month's sales and stores it in the variable A. The second and third input operations read the second and third month's sales figures into the variables B and C. The average, X, can then be computed by the formula

$$X = \frac{A + B + C}{3}$$

The last instruction in the flowchart will be to output the value of X. Figure 1.21 gives the solution. This is a simple procedure, since there are no decisions involved.

EXAMPLE 5. Suppose that instead of monthly sales figures, the manager in Example 4 had the amounts of each day's sales for the previous year and wanted the average daily sales. Then there would be 365 data cards, each containing the amount of one day's sales (for simplicity, assume that Doe's is open every day of the year and that it is not a leap year).

One possible solution is to expand on the idea of Example 4 and use 365 different input boxes with 365 different variables. That would be horribly tedious. Fortunately, there is a much better way, which makes use of a flowchart loop. The solution is shown in Figure 1.22.

You use a variable SUM that stores a running total of sales read so far. The basic idea is to read the amount of one day's sales into the variable X, and then add X to SUM. This

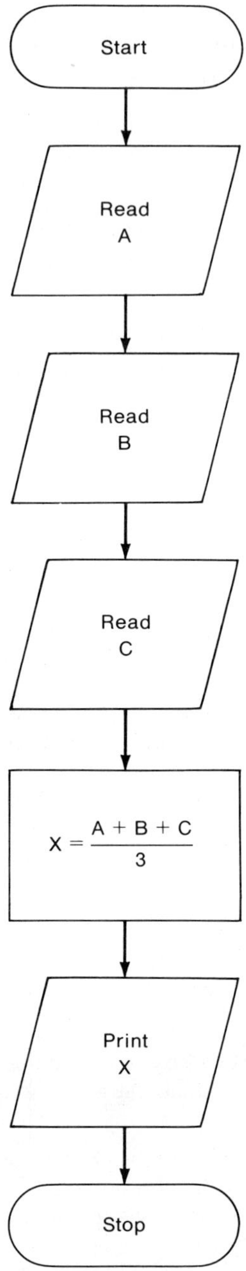

Figure 1.21 Average of three numbers.

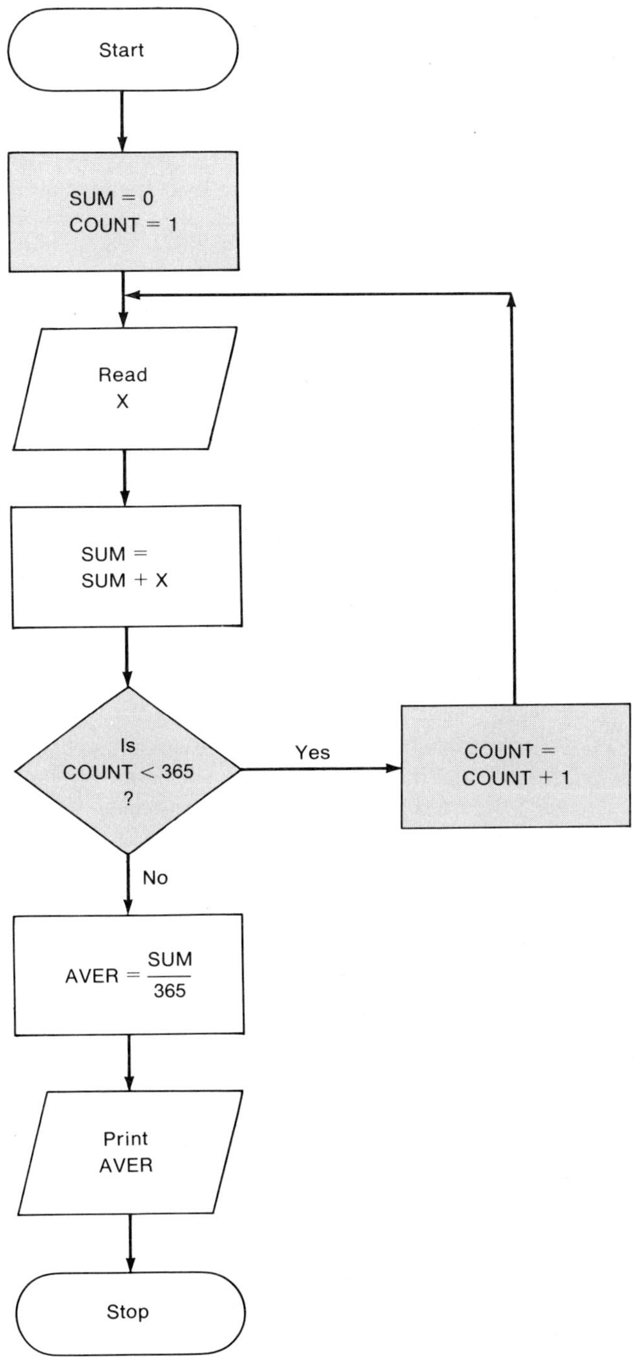

Figure 1.22 Procedure to find the average of 365 values. The variable COUNT (see shaded boxes) is used as a counter to control a loop.

process forms a loop which is repeated for all 365 input cards. Then SUM is divided by 365 to give the average, which is printed.

To make sure the process is done once for each input card, another variable, COUNT, is used to COUNT the number of times the computer goes through the loop. We call a variable used in this manner a **counter**, and each trip through the loop is called an **iteration** of the loop (to "iterate" means to do again). The decision statement is used to **break out of the loop** after all 365 values have been read. Notice that each time through the loop you must add 1 to the value of COUNT. This is called **incrementing** the counter. Also, be sure to assign a value to SUM and COUNT before beginning the loop. This is called **initializing** these variables. If you forgot to initialize SUM, the instruction SUM = SUM + X would be meaningless, since SUM has no defined value.

To save space, a single flowchart box has been used to initialize SUM and COUNT. If several similar, related instructions are to be done in sequence, you can write them in a single box.

EXAMPLE 6. Actually, the flowchart in Example 5 is not a very good solution to the problem because the procedure works only for finding the average of 365 numbers; it is of no use in finding the average of 30 numbers or 52 numbers, for instance. Since designing a procedure is time-consuming, you will usually want your procedures to be as general-purpose as possible. With a little extra effort, we can generalize Example 5 into a general procedure to find the average of any set of numbers.

One approach would be to count the input cards and replace the number 365 in Figure 1.22 with the actual number of cards to be read. This would work, but it would be better to design a flowchart that would not have to be changed every time. It would also be nice if you could get the computer to count the input cards for you (after all, the computer can count just as well as we can). In fact, it is quite easy to do both these things.

Instead of looping until COUNT = 365, the procedure will loop until there are no more cards to be read. This is determined by including a decision diamond right after the input parallelogram. The condition "End of data?" is true if there were no more data cards when the input operation was done. If this condition is false, the program loops.

Initially, we set COUNT = 0. (Compare this with Figure 1.22, in which we initially set COUNT = 1.) On each iteration of the loop, we add X to SUM and add 1 to COUNT. By tracing through the flowchart, you can see that at the beginning of the loop (before the "Read" instruction is executed), two things are always true: COUNT is equal to the number of data values that have been read, and SUM is equal to their sum. When the procedure leaves the loop because there is no more data, COUNT is equal to the total number of data values, and SUM is equal to the sum of all the data values. We can compute the average simply by dividing SUM by COUNT, and we will store this result as the new value of SUM so that we can print it. We could use a different variable for the average, but there is no need to, since after the average is computed, we no longer need to use the old value of SUM.

There is one minor point to consider: What happens if there are *no* data values? COUNT is zero in this case, and we would not want to divide by zero, since that is an undefined mathematical operation. Instead, we just skip this step and go on to print the values of COUNT and SUM. (The value printed for SUM, in this case, is its initial value: zero.)

You should try to design procedures so that they work even in exceptional cases, such as when there is no input data. This practice makes procedures easier to check out and to use on a computer, as you will appreciate when you begin running programs. Figure 1.23 shows the complete flowchart.

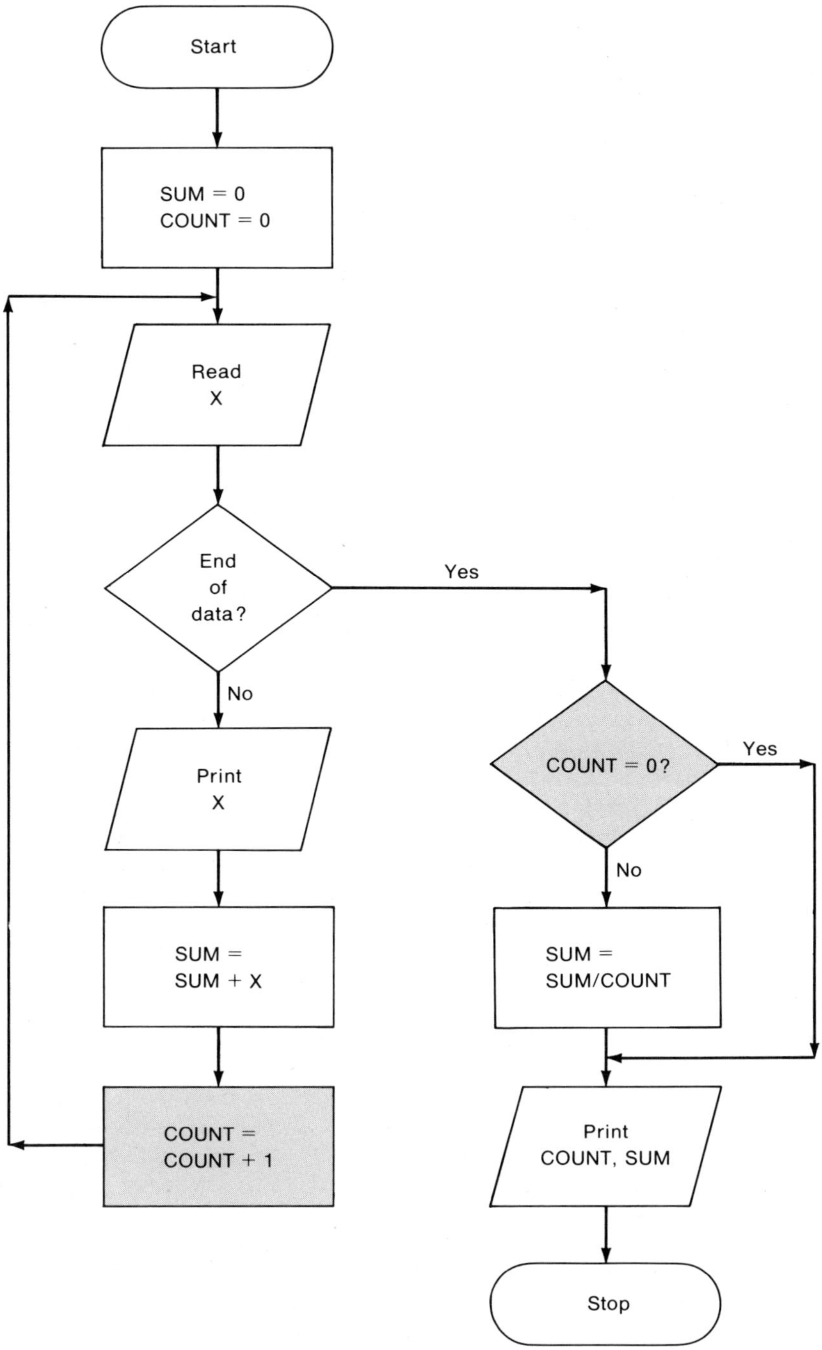

Figure 1.23 Procedure to find the average of a set of numbers. The variable COUNT is a counter, which is incremented in the shaded box on the left. When the shaded diamond is reached, SUM is equal to the sum of the input values and COUNT is the number of input values.

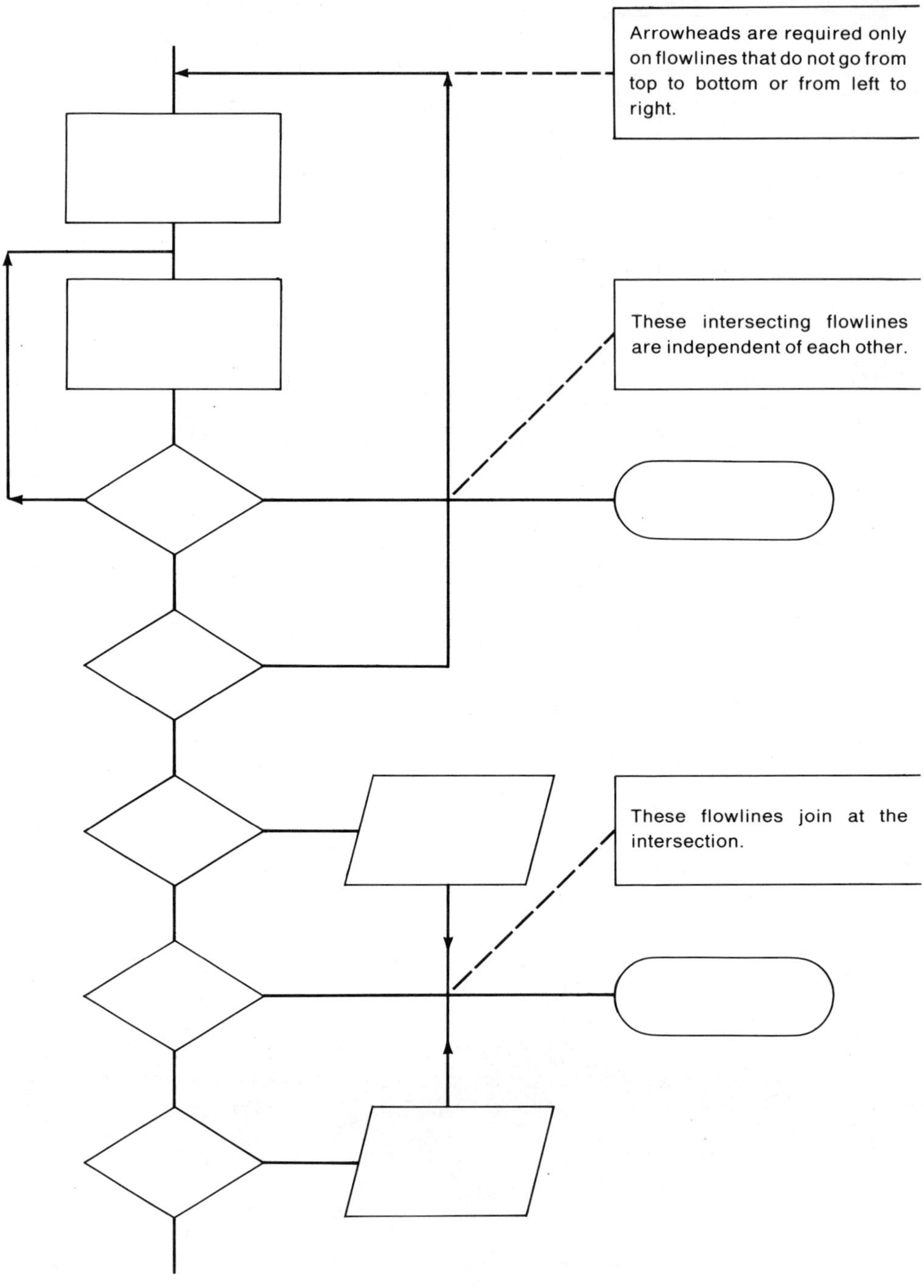

Figure 1.24 Flowchart conventions.

The "Print" instruction in the program loop was also included to make the procedure easier to use on a computer. By printing the value of each number after it is read, you can make sure that you prepared the input data correctly. This practice is called **echoing**, or **echo checking**, the input data, and it is usually advisable unless there are too many data values to read.

■ Flowchart Style*

Flowchart symbols and their use have been standardized by the American National Standards Institute (ANSI). This standardization helps flowcharts to be an effective tool for communication among programmers. A flowchart should be arranged so that the main line of flow goes from top to bottom. When a flowline goes from top to bottom, or from left to right, the arrowhead is optional, as illustrated in Figure 1.24. There is no ambiguity in a flowchart like this. The rule is simply to follow the lines from top to bottom and from left to right unless otherwise indicated by arrowheads. You might find it less confusing simply to put arrowheads on all lines of flow. Both methods are widely used.

Figures 1.24 and 1.25 show how comments can be indicated in a flowchart by using an open rectangle with a dashed line. The commentary is not part of the process represented by the flowchart; it simply gives an additional explanation.

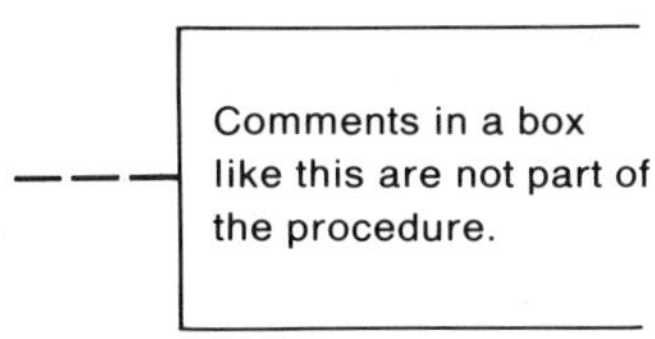

Figure 1.25 Comment box.

Flowlines can cross. Unless arrowheads indicate otherwise, crossing flowlines are independent of one another. If flowlines are supposed to join, arrowheads can be used to indicate the intended flow. This also is illustrated in Figure 1.24.

Crossing flowlines, though standard practice and useful in certain situations, can make a flowchart confusing and should be avoided if possible. One alternative to crossing flowlines is to use a **connector**, which is a small circle with some identifier in it. When a flowline comes into a connector, it means to go to a matching connector. In Figure 1.26, the right branch out of the first decision diamond goes to a connector. This means to go to the connector above the first input parallelogram.

EXAMPLE 7. The Cacophony Music Company has computerized its checking account. For each check written during the month, a punch card is prepared. The first number in the

* Small box in margin indicates optional sections.

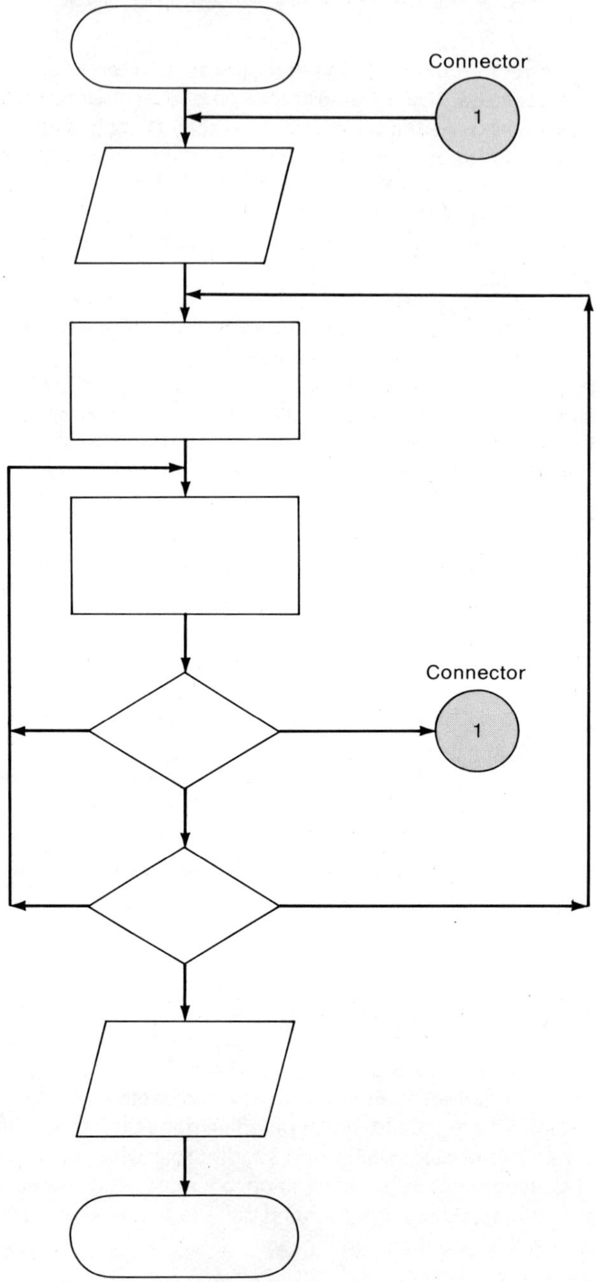

Figure 1.26 Crossing lines can be avoided with a connector. When the bottom connector is reached, it means to continue at the top connector, just as though these points were connected by a arrow.

card is the code number 0, meaning that this is a check. The second number in the card is the amount of the check. A punch card is also prepared for each deposit to the account. For a deposit, the code number is 1. This is punched on the deposit card, followed by the amount of the deposit. At the end of each month, the check and deposit cards are arranged chronologically. In front of all of them is placed a card with a code number 2 followed by the previous month's balance. Flowchart a procedure that will read these cards and print a running total of the balance. A sample of the output is as follows:

PREVIOUS BALANCE		\$415.63
CHECK	\$ 20.00	395.63
CHECK	11.18	384.45
DEPOSIT	100.00	484.45
CHECK	82.46	401.99

According to the statement of the problem, the first card will always be the previous balance. Thus, the first step is to read a card and store the amount as the balance, which we will call B. It is a good idea to check this by making sure the first card has a code number 2. We will use a variable C for the code number. The decision box of Figure 1.27 can be used for checking.

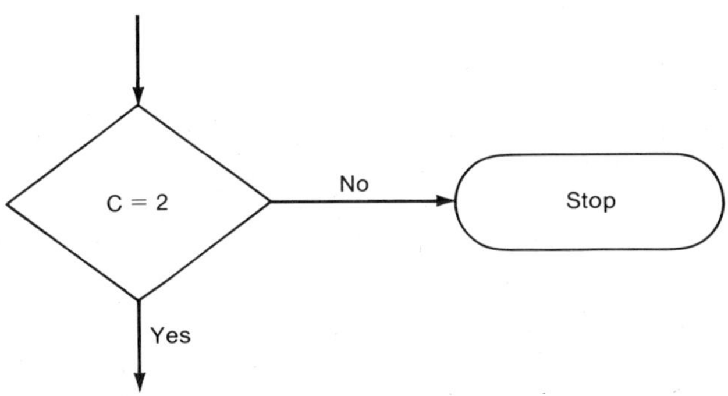

Figure 1.27 To make sure the first card has the previous month's balance, you check the code number and stop if it is not a 2.

After the first card, the procedure is the same for each card; this will be the main loop in the procedure. From each card, the computer reads the code C and the amount A. If the code is 0, then this is a check; so the computer *subtracts* the amount A from the balance B and prints the word CHECK followed by the values of A and B.

When you learn about output statements in FORTRAN, you will learn how to describe the exact format of each print line. For the purpose of a flowchart, however, you can skip this detail and simply use an output box, as in Figure 1.28. If the code is 1, then the card is

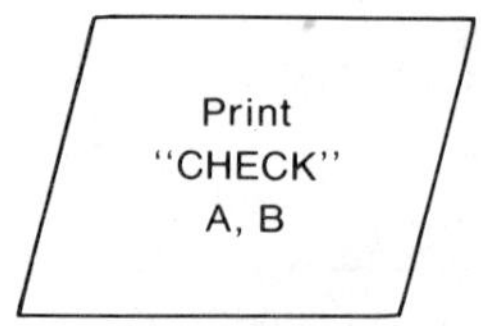

Figure 1.28 An output box.

a deposit and the amount A is *added* to B and the word DEPOSIT is printed instead of CHECK.

Suppose the checking procedure in Figure 1.27 shows a 0 or a 1 on the first card, and the program stops. You will not know why it has stopped unless you program the computer to print an error message before stopping, as in Figure 1.29. The same kind of error message can be programmed into the main loop, as in Figure 1.30. You could even have the computer print an error message and then ignore the invalid card. The person running the program then has the option of either correcting the output by hand or running the program again. With the latter method, all the erroneous cards (not just the first one) will be reported.

Like the output box, the input box in this example gives no details of how to read the variables C and A. They could be in any format on the input card. In fact, they would not even have to be on the same card. A complete FORTRAN program would have to be more precise, but the flowchart does not have to go into that much detail.

Another detail that has not been spelled out is how to determine when you have reached the end of input data. We will use a decision diamond to test for the condition "End of data?" This procedure is shown in Figure 1.31.

This flowchart is still ambiguous, since it does not tell exactly how to determine when the end of input data is reached. On many computer systems, the end of input condition is determined automatically, sometimes as part of the "Read" instruction itself. Unfortunately, there is no standard way of doing this: Each computer system is a little different. An alternative method, which we will often use in the FORTRAN programs in following chapters, is to include a special data card at the end of the data. For instance, in this example you could

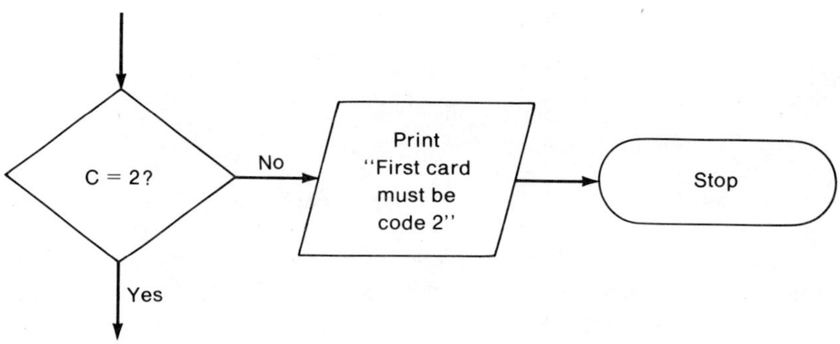

Figure 1.29 When a program detects an error, it should print an error message.

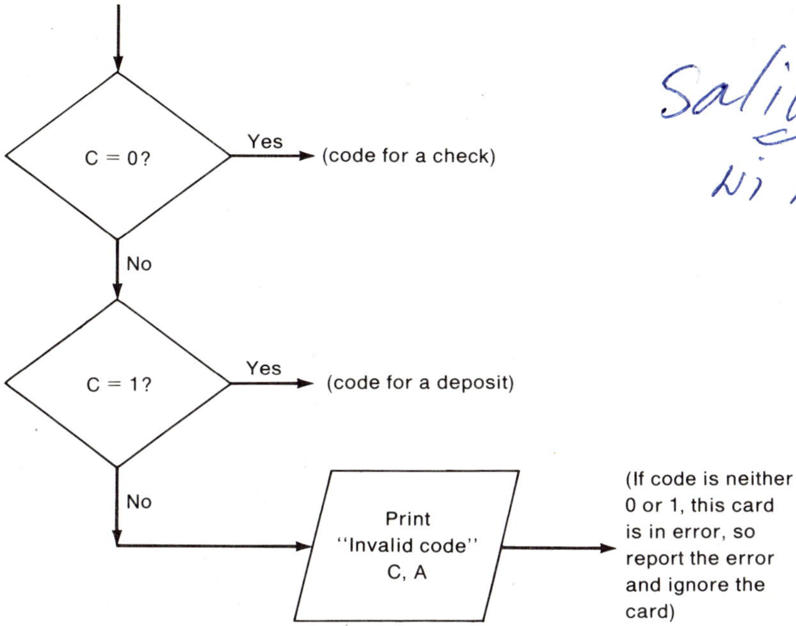

Figure 1.30 In the case of an invalid code, the program can print an error message and then proceed to the next data card.

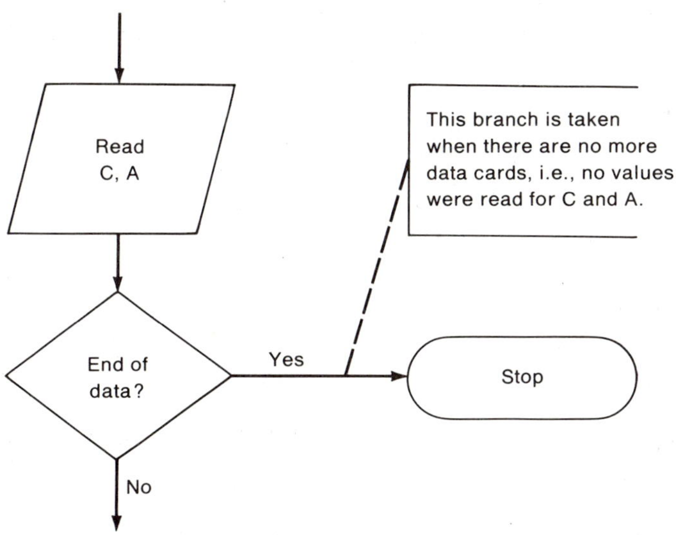

Figure 1.31 The "End of data?" condition is true if no values were read by the "READ" instruction.

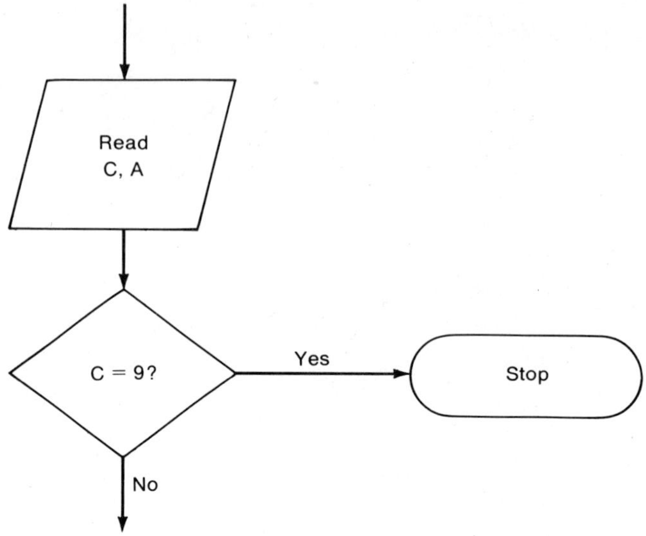

Figure 1.32 An alternate way to check for the end of data is to include at the end of input a card with some special value.

add a data card at the end having a code 9 in it and test for the end of data, as in Figure 1.32. The complete flowchart for Example 7 appears in Figure 1.33.

EXAMPLE 8. The Bellemorte Insurance Company sells life insurance policies in multiples of $5000. The monthly premium depends on the age of the insured, according to Table 1.2. Flowchart a procedure that reads a client's age and amount of coverage and prints out his annual premium.

Table 1.2 Bellemorte Life Insurance Premiums

Age	*Monthly Premium (Per $5000 Coverage)*
Under 20	$ 2
20 to 29	5
30 to 39	12
40 to 59	17
Over 59	25

This procedure consists mainly of a chain of decisions. Let A be the age and M the monthly premium per $5000. You test to see if $A < 20$. If so, then you set $M = 2$ and branch to the calculation of the annual premium. Otherwise, you see if $A < 30$. If so, you set $M = 5$.

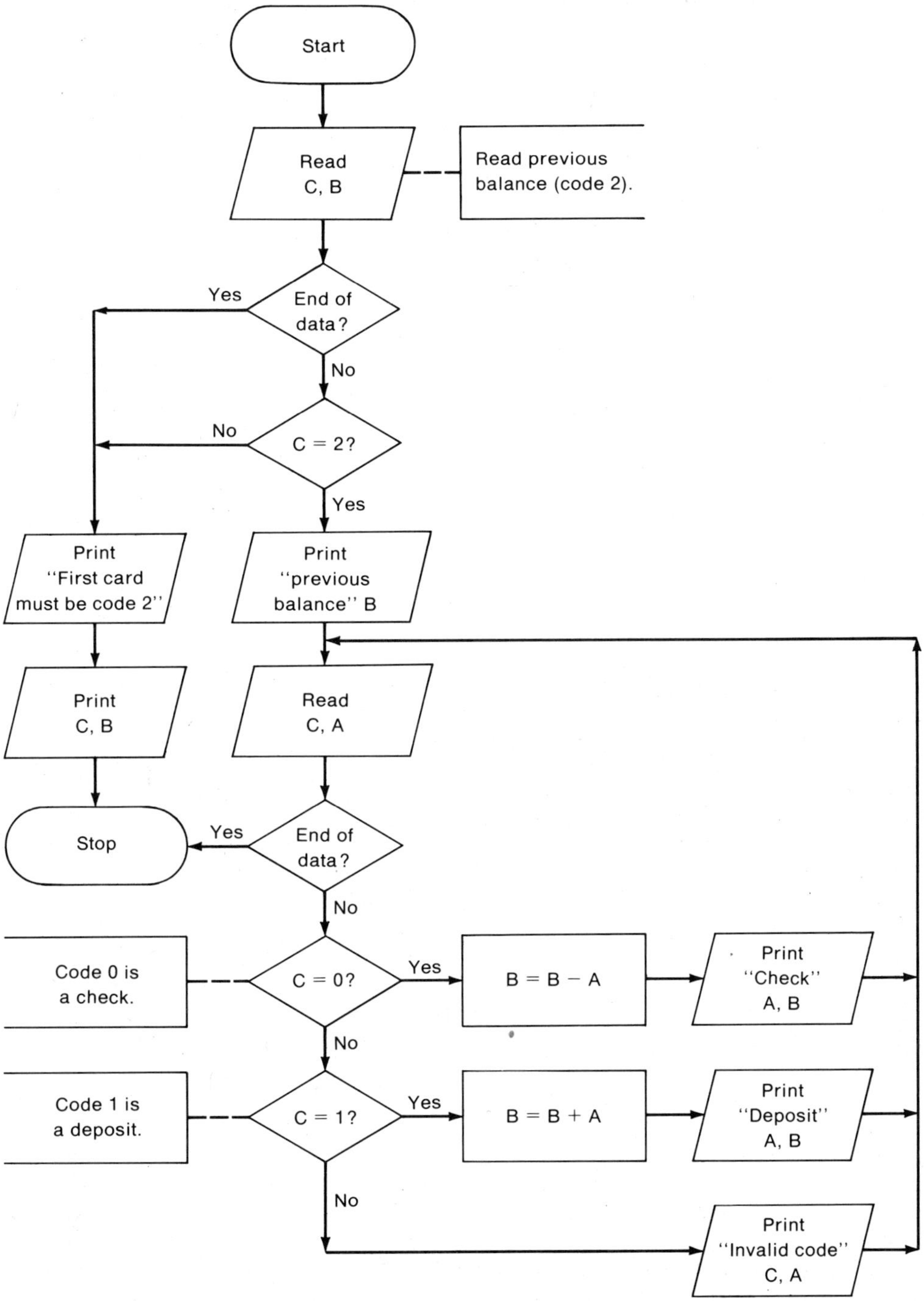

Figure 1.33 Checkbook program.

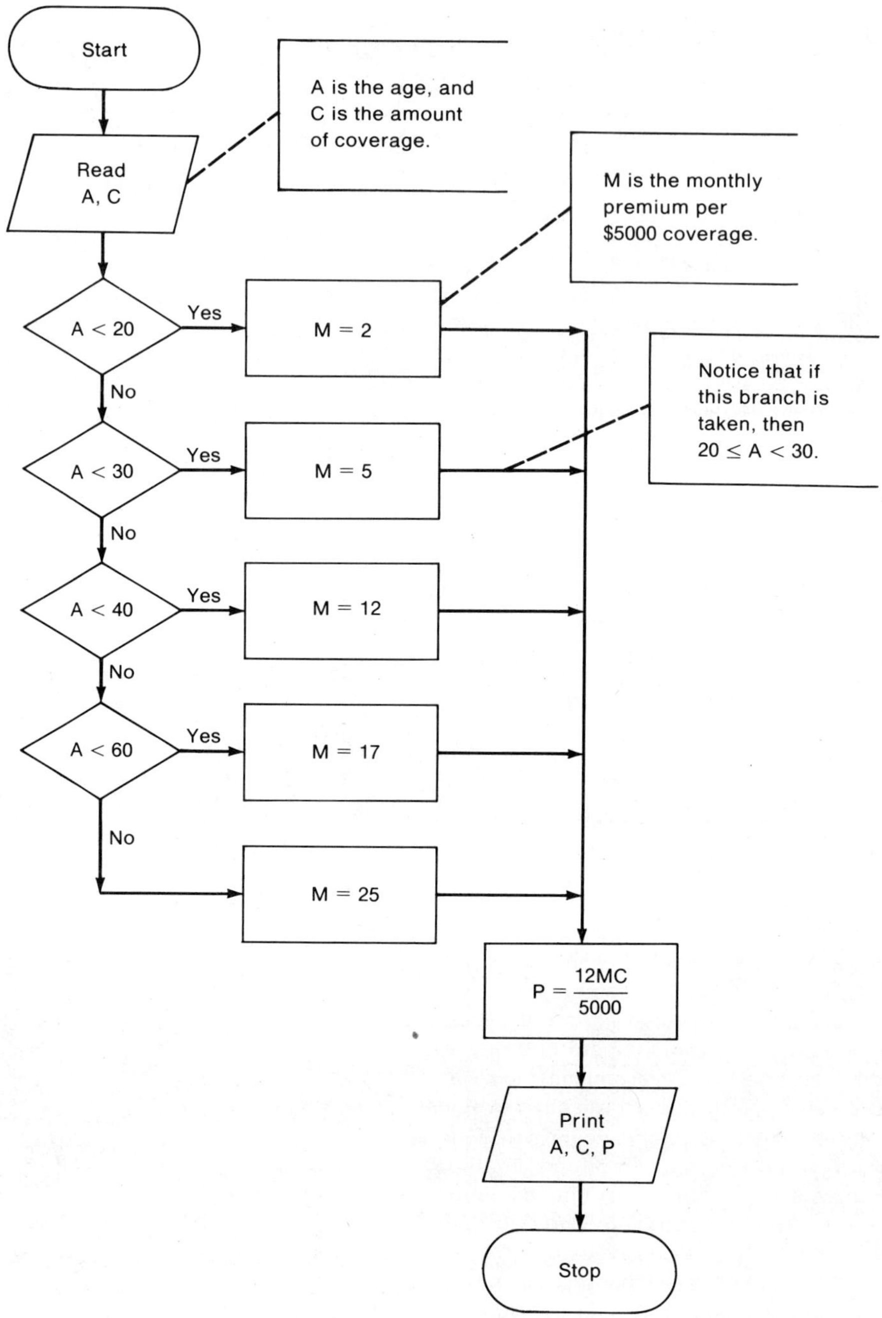

Figure 1.34 Insurance program.

Note that if the first test fails and the second test succeeds, then A must be between 20 and 29 (inclusive). If the client's total coverage is C, then the annual premium, P, is computed from the formula

$$P = \frac{12MC}{5000}$$

The flowchart is given in Figure 1.34.

The examples in this chapter have demonstrated the concept of an algorithm, and its representation by a flowchart. The flowchart can be a valuable tool to the programmer. The examples shown so far may be misleading in presenting only the finished flowcharts. In practice, several attempts are usually required during this creative phase of program design. Often, the first version of a flowchart is only a rough outline, with very general instructions in the boxes and many details omitted. This is especially true when you begin a large project. These first drafts can be successively refined to produce a final flowchart.

Exercises

In the following exercises, a description is given of some action involving one or more decisions. Most of these cannot be programmed on a computer, but they can be represented by a flowchart. For example: If the sun is shining, walk to work; otherwise, take a taxi.

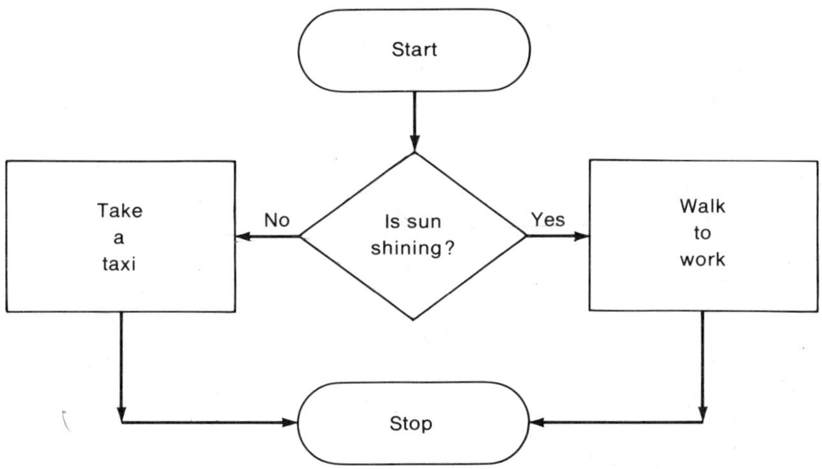

There may be more than one way to describe the process in a flowchart. Try to make a flowchart that is clear and unambiguous.

1. Look outside. If it is raining, stay home; otherwise, go for a walk.
2. Read the thermometer. If the temperature is below 60°F, put on your sweater. If the temperature is below 50°F, put on your coat, too. Go to the store.
3. You are approaching a cross street in your car. Slow down. Read the street sign. If this is Main Street, turn right. Resume speed.

4. If it is noon and you are hungry, go to the cafeteria. If it is noon and you are not hungry, go to the snack bar. If it is not noon, but between 8 A.M. and 5 P.M., continue working. If it is before 8 A.M. or after 5 P.M., relax.

5. If it is baseball season, then if there is a game on television, watch it; otherwise, read the sports news. If it is not baseball season, then if there is a movie on television, watch it; otherwise, read a book.

6. If the sun is shining and the sea is calm, go sailing. If the sun is shining and the sea is not calm, go to the beach. If the sun is not shining, stay home.

7. Brand X sells for A cents per pound. Brand Y sells for B cents per ounce. Buy the brand that is cheaper.

8. A tank of gasoline holds 20 gallons. Gasoline costs C cents per gallon. The tank is P percent full. If filling the tank will cost more than D dollars, get gas; otherwise, do not get gas.

9. You have a measuring cup and an empty bowl. The bowl has a capacity of N cups for some whole number N. Fill the measuring cup with water. Pour it into the bowl. Repeat this procedure, counting the number of cups, until the bowl is full. Print out N, the capacity of the bowl.

10. There are three weights labeled A, B, and C. Two of them are the same. The other is heavier. Suppose you have a balance. Put A on one side and B on the other. Print out whether A, B, or C is the heavy weight.

11. This is the same as Exercise 10, but now you know that two of the weights are the same and the other is either heavier or lighter. In two weighings on a balance, find the odd weight and determine whether it is heavier or lighter than the other two. (*Hint:* First weigh A against B; then weigh A against C. There are six possible outcomes.)

12. Flip a coin until it comes up heads. Print the number of times you flipped the coin.

13. Roll a die. If it comes up 1 or 2, print "You win." If it comes up 3 or 4, print "I win." If it comes up 5 or 6, roll it again.

14. If the temperature is below 70°F and you are not wearing a sweater, or if the temperature is at least 70°F and you are wearing a sweater, then adjust the thermostat.

15. In the game of Twenty-One, a player draws cards from a deck and tries to get a hand in which the total value of the cards is as great as possible, but not greater than 21. Face cards count as 10, aces can count as either 1 or 11, and all other cards count as their face value. One way to play is this: Keep drawing cards until the total value of your hand is greater than or equal to 17. Draw a flowchart for this procedure. Your flowchart should include an input box with the instruction "Draw a card," and it should compute the value of a variable HAND, which is the total value of your hand. When your hand is complete, print the value of HAND if it is less than or equal to 21; otherwise, print "Too many." (*Hint:* To decide whether aces should count as 1 or 11, let BASIC be the basic value of your hand, obtained by counting aces as 1, and let ACES be the number of aces in your hand. You can compute the value of HAND if you know the value of BASIC and ACES.)

16. What number is printed by the procedure in the following flowchart?

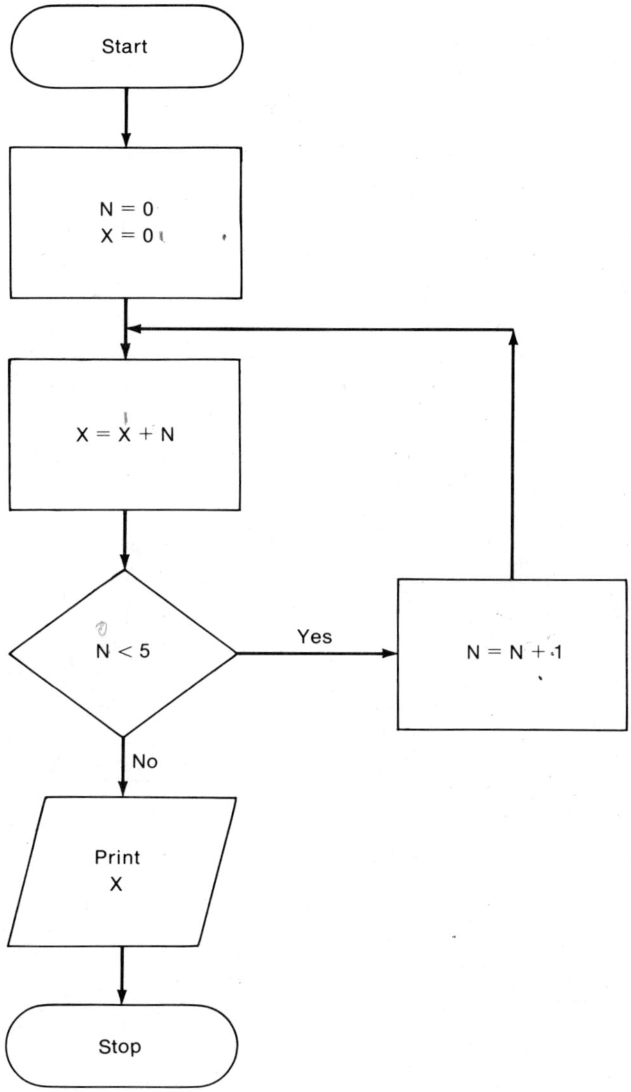

17. What general formula is computed by the algorithm of the flowchart in Exercise 16? Can you generalize the flowchart?

18. What values are printed by the algorithm shown in the flowchart?

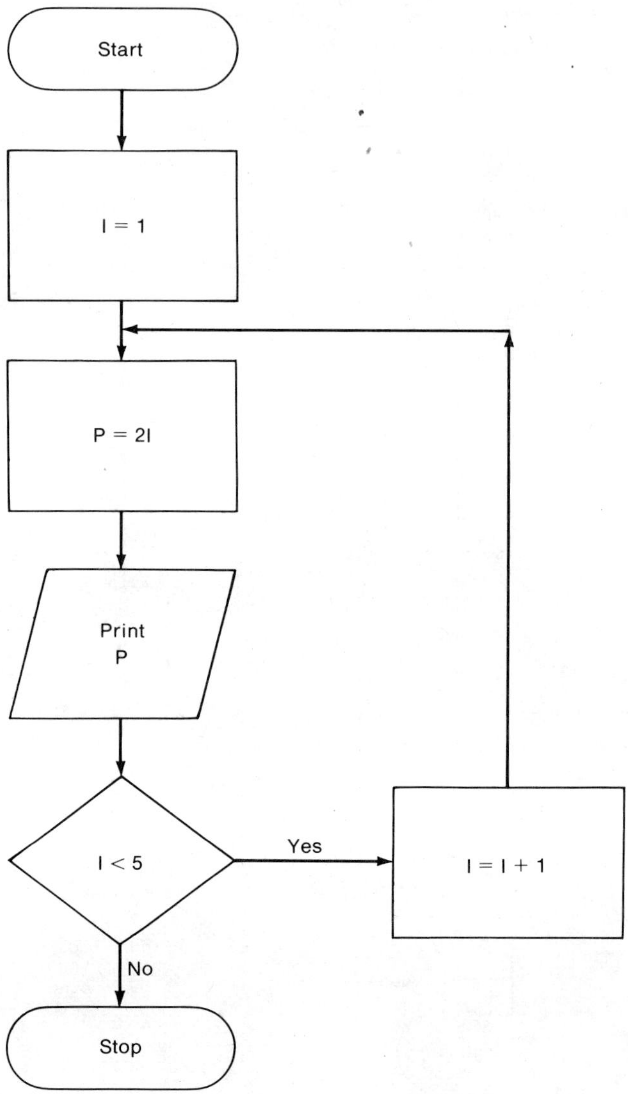

19. In general, what numbers are printed by the flowchart in Exercise 18? What happens if the initial value of I is 0? If the test is changed to I $\leq$ 10, what is the last value printed?

20. Suppose the value read for N is 6. What numbers are printed by the algorithm flowcharted here? What general formula is represented?

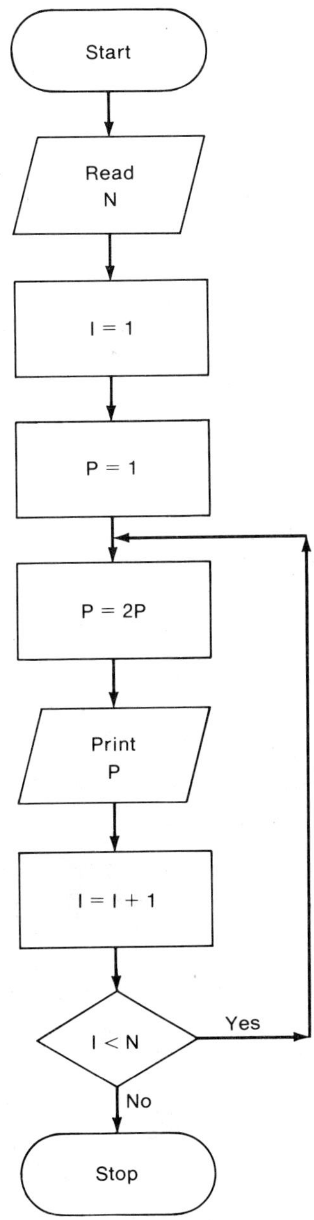

21. For A = 1, B = 3, C = 2.5, what value is output by the algorithm shown in the flowchart? For A = 1, B = 1, C = 2?

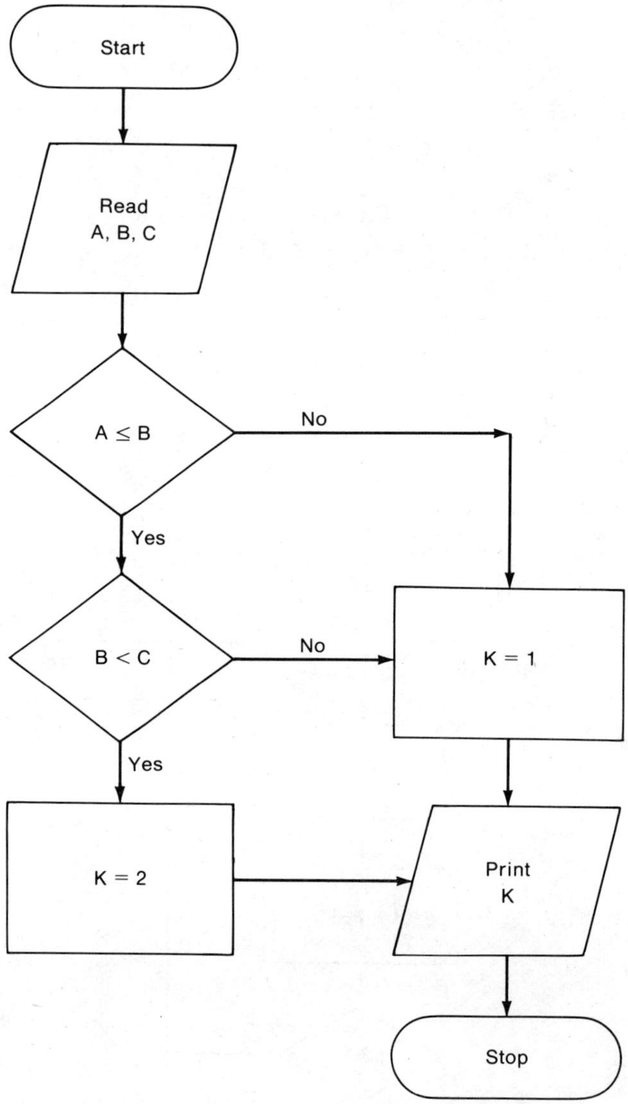

22. What does the flowchart do? What is the output for N = 2, X = 4? For N = 4, X = 2?

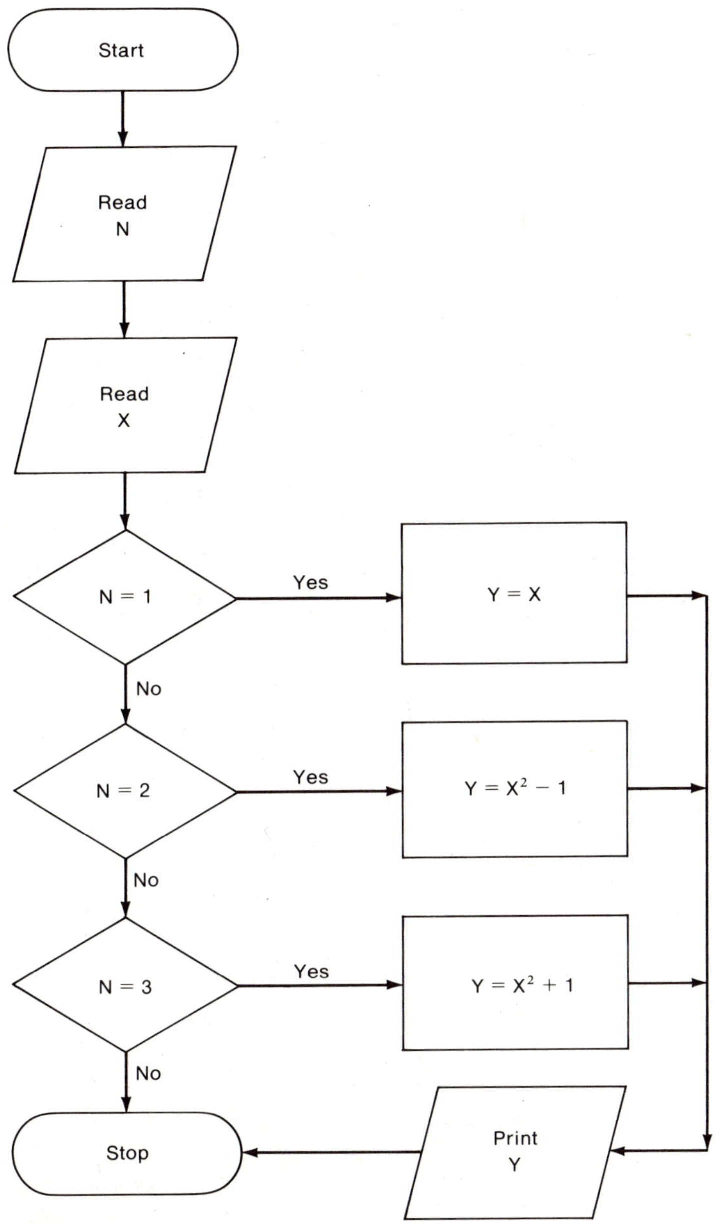

23. What is the output from the process represented in the flowchart, assuming the input is 5? What if the input is 3.6?

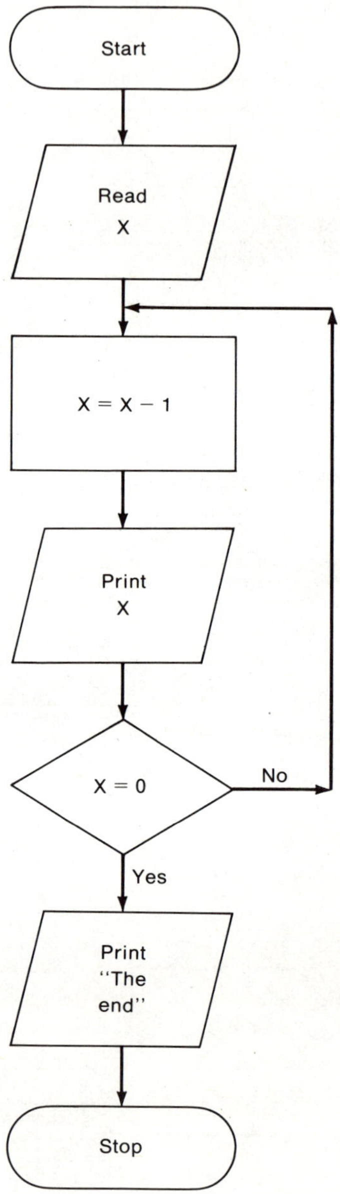

24. What is the output represented by the process in the flowchart, assuming the input is 3?

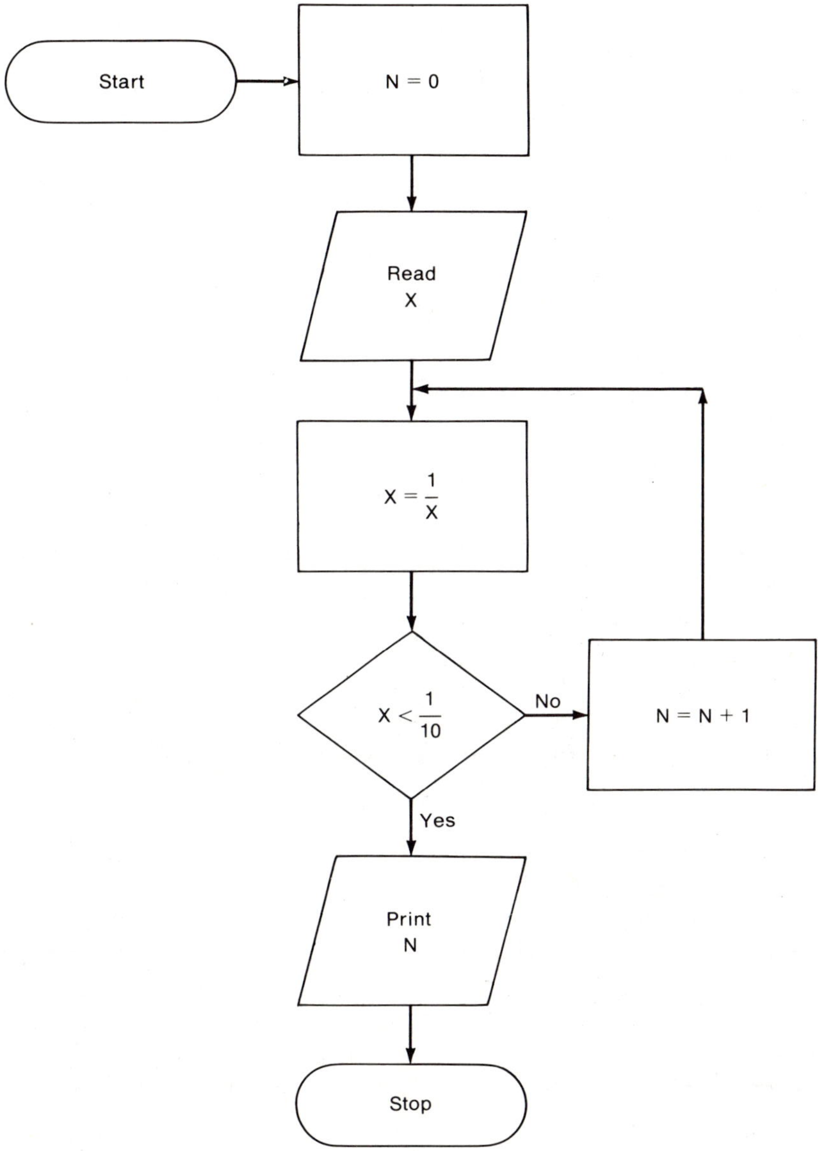

25. What is the value of N printed by the process shown in the flowchart?

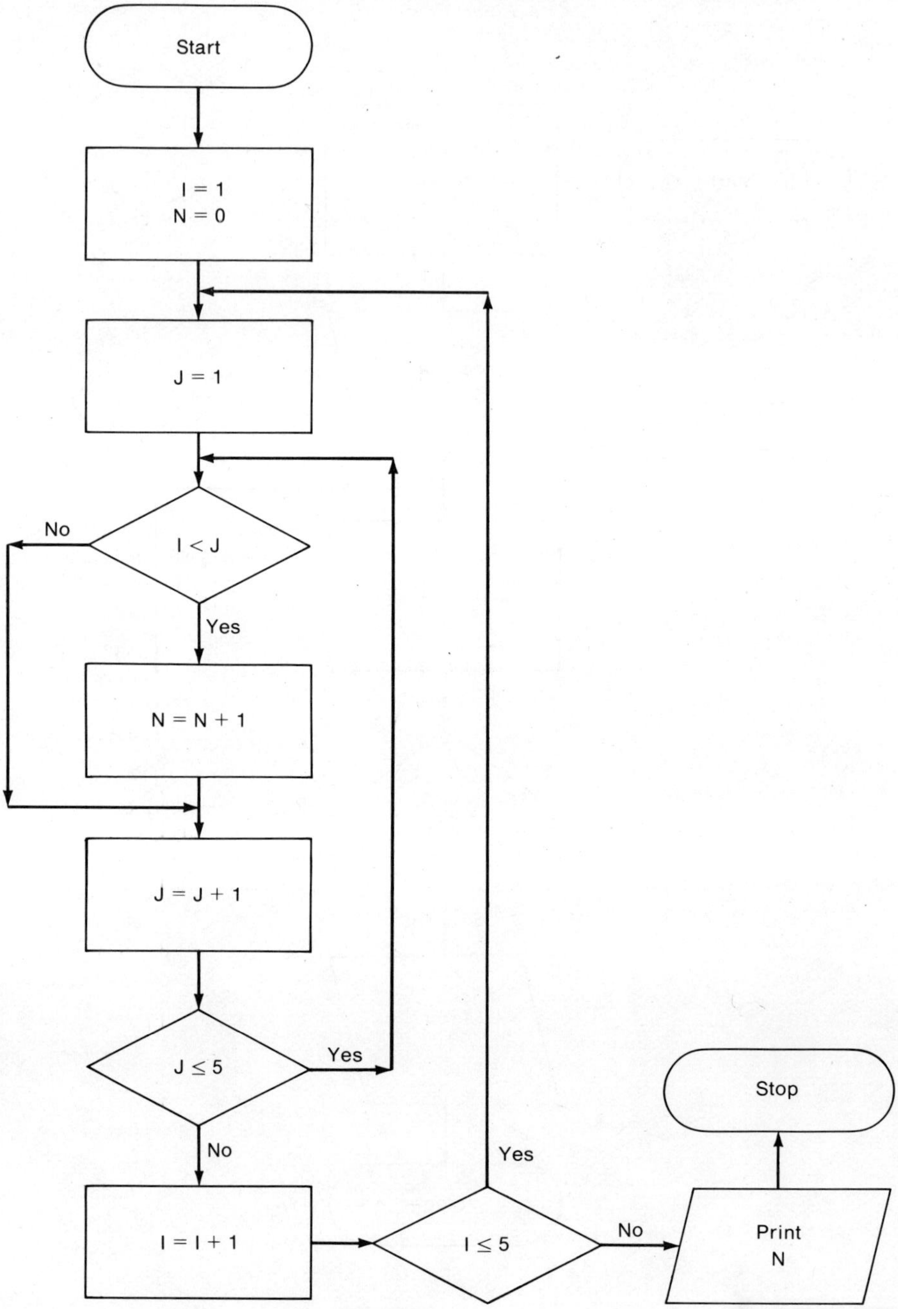

26. Construct a flowchart:
    Read X
    If X is negative, stop
    Set N = 0
    Add 1 to N until N is greater than X
    Print N
    Stop

27. Construct a flowchart:
    Read R
    If $R < 0$, stop; otherwise set $A = \pi R^2$
    Print A
    Stop

28. Construct a flowchart:
    Read A
    Read X
    If X = 0, print A, then stop
    Otherwise, subtract X from A and go back to read another X

29. Construct a flowchart:
    a. Read N
    b. Let X = 1
    c. Print X
    d. Let X = X + 2
    e. If $X < N$, go back to step c
    f. Stop

30. Construct a fowchart:
    a. Set P and N equal to 0
    b. Read X
    c. If X = 0, print P and N, and then stop
    d. Otherwise, if X is negative, add 1 to N
    e. Or if X is positive, add 1 to P
    f. Go back to step b

    In words, what is the output from this program?

2

Introduction to FORTRAN

The flowchart, useful as it is, is only a diagram. Before you can actually run a program on the computer, you must write the procedure in a computer language such as FORTRAN.

FORTRAN is a standardized language. Like the flowchart symbols you have been using, FORTRAN standards are prepared by the American National Standards Institute (ANSI). This means that a program written in standard FORTRAN can be run on just about any computer system. There are inevitably a few minor variations in the language from one installation to the next, and you may occasionally need to consult the reference manual for the particular computer system you are using. But standard FORTRAN is basically the same everywhere, and the FORTRAN language presented in this book applies to just about any computer system.

WATFOR and WATFIV are common versions of FORTRAN used on IBM 360/370 systems. They include standard FORTRAN statements as well as several useful features (such as list-directed input and output) that are not part of standard FORTRAN. We shall point out these differences as we go along. Unless otherwise noted, WATFIV statements are also valid in WATFOR. Other computer manufacturers have versions of FORTRAN that are very similar to WATFIV.

Compared to ordinary English, FORTRAN is a simple language. A program consists of a series of **statements**, each one written on a separate line. There are only a few types of statements in FORTRAN, just as there are only a few types of computer instructions. In this chapter you will learn some basic FORTRAN statements and see how to combine them to make a complete program. Later chapters will cover these statements in more detail.

The Assignment Statement

The name FORTRAN comes from FORmula TRANslation, which is significant because mathematical formulas can be written in FORTRAN in almost the same way as they are in ordinary algebra. In Chapter 1 you wrote formulas in a rectangular flowchart box. The corresponding type of FORTRAN instruction is called an **assignment** statement. An example is:

```
X = A + 1.0
```

This means to recall the value of the variable A, add 1 to it, and store the result in the variable X.

The form of the assignment statement is the same as we have been using in flowcharts:

variable = *expression*

This statement instructs the machine to compute the value of the expression on the right of the equal sign and to store the result in the variable on the left of the equal sign.

In algebra, there are many ways of writing a formula. For example,

amount = 7% of principal

or

$A = 0.07$ times P

or

$$A = 0.07P$$

In FORTRAN, there are specific rules for writing formulas. You might write this formula as:

```
A = 0.07 * P
```

You always use an asterisk (*) to denote multiplication in FORTRAN. For instance, if you want to multiply 2 times X, you write this as 2*X; not 2X, as in algebra.

Addition and subtraction are denoted by a plus and minus, as usual. The statement

```
C = A + B - 1.0
```

means to add A and B, subtract 1, and store the result in the variable C.

To denote division, you always use a slash (/). The statement

```
Y = A/2.0
```

means to divide the value of A by 2 and store the result in Y. In algebra, we often indicate division by a fraction such as:

$$P = \frac{A}{A + B}$$

A FORTRAN statement is written on one line, so you cannot write a fraction on two lines like this. But you can use parentheses to group terms and write this formula as:

```
P = A/(A + B)
```

This statement means, divide A by A + B and store the result in P.

Raising a number to a power is denoted by a superscript in algebra, as in the formula for the area of a circle:

$$A = \pi r^2$$

In FORTRAN, raising to a power is denoted by two asterisks (**). You would write this formula as:

```
A = 3.1416 * R * * 2
```

The expression R**2 means "R squared." Greek letters are not allowed in FORTRAN, so you substitute an approximate value such as 3.1416 for π.

Table 2.1 summarizes the FORTRAN symbols for mathematical operations.

Table 2.1 FORTRAN Symbols for Mathematical Operations

Operation	*FORTRAN Symbol*
Addition	+
Subtraction or negation	−
Multiplication	*
Division	/
Exponentiation (raising to a power)	**

In algebra, you usually use letters for variables; in FORTRAN, you can also use words. For example, you can compute the area of a circle with the statement:

```
AREA = 3.1416 * RADIUS * * 2
```

Variable names should be words of six or fewer characters. Table 2.2 gives more examples of assignment statements.

Table 2.2 Some FORTRAN Assignment Statements

Statement	*Meaning*
A = 0.0	Store the value zero in the variable A
A = 1.2 − R	Subtract the value of R from 1.2 and store the result in the variable A
X = A + B	Add the values of A and B and store the result in the variable X
C = 2.0 * A	Multiply A by 2.0 and store the result in the variable C
D = A/B	Divide the value of A by the value of B and store the result in the variable D
QUANT = (A + B)/2.0	Add the values of A and B, divide the result by 2.0 and store the result in the variable QUANT
CHANGE = 100.0 * A/(B − A)	Multiply 100.0 by the value of A, divide by the value of B − A and store the result in the variable CHANGE
TOTAL = 2.0 * TOTAL	Multiply the value of TOTAL by 2.0 and store the result in the variable TOTAL

The PRINT and READ Statements*

To write out results on a line printer, you use a **PRINT** statement similar to the output instructions you have been using in flowcharts. An example is:

```
PRINT, X
```

This statement means to print out the value of the variable X.

In general, you write the word PRINT, followed by a comma, followed by a variable. You can print the value of one variable, as in the example just given, or you can print the values of several variables with a single PRINT statement. In this case, you put a comma between the variables to be printed, as in the following example.

```
PRINT, A, B, C, X, Y
```

This statement writes the values of all five variables on one line of output.

Some versions of FORTRAN (including WATFIV) allow titles to be printed with a PRINT statement. Instead of a variable name in the PRINT statement, you can write a string of characters enclosed in single quote marks (')**, and the characters will be printed on the

* In this section we introduce the WATFIV forms of PRINT and READ; your instructor may modify these slightly.

** On some computer systems, double quote marks (") are used instead.

output. For example,

```
PRINT, 'X = ', X, 'Y = ', Y, 'TIME = ', T
```

This might produce the output:

```
X = 5.2 Y = 11.0 TIME = 100.0
```

If you are printing only a title, you don't need any variables at all in the PRINT statement. The following statement might be used to write a heading at the beginning of some output.

```
PRINT, 'ANNUAL RAINFALL DATA'
```

You use a **READ** statement to read in data. For example,

```
READ, X
```

means to read a value from a card and store the value in the variable X. Every time a number is read in, its value is stored in a variable. The READ statement tells which variables are to receive the values read. You can read a single value or you can read several values, as in the following:

```
READ, A, B, C
```

This means to read three values and store them in the variables A, B, and C.

Data to be read is keypunched on cards which are placed at the end of the FORTRAN program. In the next chapter you will see an example of how to prepare data for a program.

The PRINT and READ statements used here are called **list-directed** PRINT and READ statements. You will see later another form, called the **formatted** PRINT and READ, which gives you more control over the format of the data to be printed or read.

Some computer systems have a slightly different form for list-directed PRINT and READ statements: You put an asterisk (*) after the word PRINT or READ and before the comma. For example:

```
READ*, X, Y
PRINT*, 'THE ANSWER IS', Q
```

On some timesharing systems, the word ACCEPT and TYPE are used in place of READ and PRINT, as in the statements:

```
ACCEPT*, X, Y
TYPE*, 'THE ANSWER IS', Q
```

The PRINT and READ statements used in this book follow the forms used on WATFOR and WATFIV systems.

The STOP and END Statements

In your flowcharts, you indicated the end of a procedure with a stop box:

The corresponding FORTRAN statement is the **STOP** statement, which you write simply as:

```
STOP
```

This instructs the computer to terminate your program. Most likely, the computer will then begin running someone else's program; that is all done automatically by the computer's operating system.

Each FORTRAN statement is written on one line (that is, on one punch card or on one input line from a terminal). Together, the lines form a program. The computer carries out the instructions one after another in the order in which they are written (unless you tell it otherwise, as you will see later). The last line in any program must be an **END** statement, which is simply a line that says:

```
END
```

Do not confuse the STOP and END statements. STOP is an instruction that tells the machine to do something: to stop running. END is not an instruction to the computer but just a statement that is required as the last line of every FORTRAN program to indicate the end of the program.

EXAMPLE 1. Three common ways of measuring temperature are the Fahrenheit, Celsius, and absolute scales. If you know the temperature in degrees Fahrenheit, you can find the Celsius temperature using the formula

$$C = \frac{5}{9}(F - 32)$$

The absolute temperature (often used in scientific work) is found by adding 273.16 to the Celsius temperature. Write a program that reads a Fahrenheit temperature and prints it out with its Celsius and absolute equivalent.

A flowchart for this procedure is shown in Figure 2.1. The first step is an input operation that reads a number and stores it in the variable FAREN. The next step is to calculate the Celsius equivalent from the formula just given. You can use the following FORTRAN assignment statement:

```
CELS = (5.0/9.0)*(FAREN - 32.0)
```

This means to subtract 32 from the value of FAREN, then multiply by $\frac{5}{9}$ and store the result in the variable CELS. There is a reason for writing the fraction as 5.0/9.0, rather than just

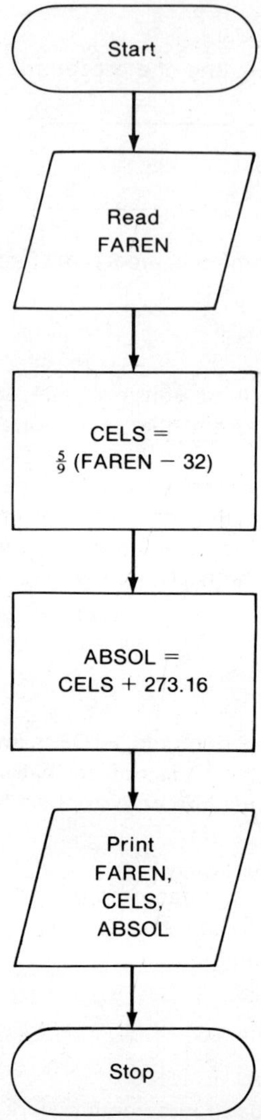

Figure 2.1 Temperature conversion program.

5/9; we will explain that in detail in Chapter 4. You compute the absolute temperature with another assignment statement and assign the result to the variable ABSOL:

```
ABSOL = CELS + 273.16
```

You can write out the values of the three variables with the statement

```
PRINT, FAREN, CELS, ABSOL
```

Finally, a STOP statement terminates execution, and an END statement indicates the end of the program. Here is the complete program.

```
READ, FAREN
CELS = (5.0/9.0) * (FAREN - 32.0)
ABSOL = CELS + 273.16
PRINT, FAREN, CELS, ABSOL
STOP
END
```

The GO TO and IF Statements

In flowcharts, you use an arrow to indicate the next instruction. In FORTRAN, statements are executed in the order in which they are written, unless you indicate otherwise. One way to change the order of executing instructions is with a **GO TO** statement. Here is an example:

```
7       READ, X
        PRINT, X
        GO TO 7
```

Notice the 7 to the left of the READ statement. This number is called a **statement number** (or **statement label**). The particular number 7 has no special significance; we could have used any other number. The important thing is that 7 is the same number that appears in the statement:

```
GO TO 7
```

When this GO TO statement is executed, it branches back to statement 7, the READ statement. Thus, the three FORTRAN statements have the effect shown in the flowchart in Figure 2.2.

In general, you can write a statement number to the left of any statement except the END statement. The statement number can be any positive integer number. To branch to the statement from any part of your program, you can use a GO TO statement with the same statement number.

A decision is programmed in FORTRAN with an **IF** statement. This statement causes the program to execute some statement or not to execute it, depending on the outcome of a comparison. An example is:

```
IF (A .EQ. B) STOP
```

This means, "If A is equal to B, then stop." The corresponding flowchart is shown in Figure 2.3

More generally, you, can write a logical IF statement of the form

IF (*A* .EQ. *B*) *statement*

Flowchart:

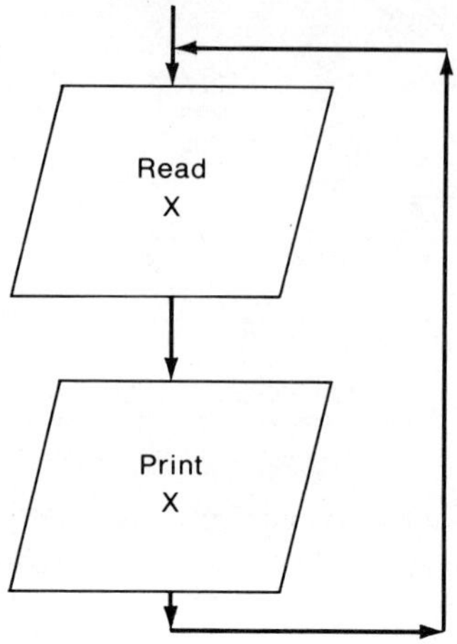

FORTRAN statements:

```
7       READ, X
        PRINT, X
        GO TO 7
```

Figure 2.2 The GO TO statement transfers control.

Flowchart:

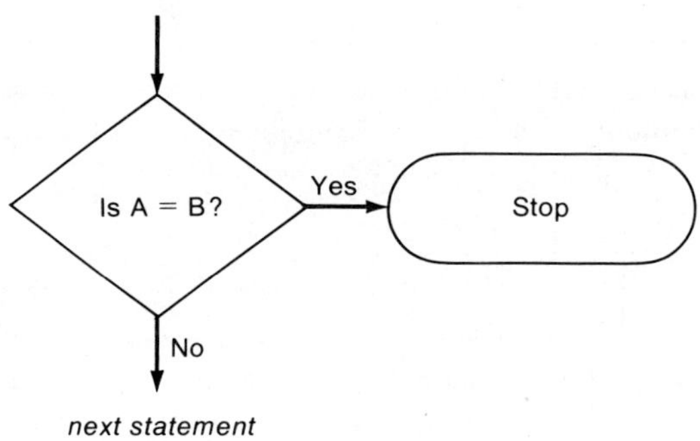

FORTRAN statement:

```
IF (A .EQ. B) STOP
```

Figure 2.3 A decision is programmed with an IF statement.

where *statement* is any FORTRAN statement (with a few exceptions we will mention later). *A* and *B* can be numbers, variables, or expressions. This means, "If *A* is equal to *B*, then execute *statement*; otherwise, do not execute *statement*."* The corresponding flowchart is shown in Figure 2.4.

Notice that there are periods on each side of the letters EQ; these are required. In addition to writing .EQ., meaning "equal to," we can use .NE., meaning "not equal to." For example,

```
IF (N .NE. 10) GO TO 7
```

* When we write part of a FORTRAN statement in italics, as we have done in this example, the part in italics represents a general class of statement or expression (i.e., *statement* represents any FORTRAN statement).

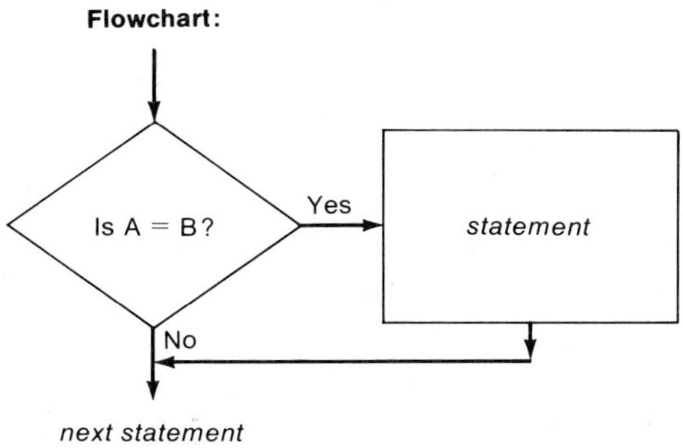

FORTRAN statement:

IF (A .EQ. B) *statement*
next statement

Figure 2.4 An IF statement causes some statement to be executed or not executed, depending on the outcome of a comparison.

This means, "If N is not equal to 10, then GO TO statement 7." There are symbols for other comparisons as well: .LT. for "less than," .GT. for "greater than," .LE. for "less than or equal to," and .GE. for "greater than or equal to." Table 2.3 gives some examples.

Table 2.3 Examples of IF Statements

Statement	*Meaning*
IF (X .EQ. 0.0) STOP	If X is equal to 0, then stop.
IF (X .NE. 0.0) STOP	If X is not equal to 0, then stop.
IF (N .LT. LAST) GO TO 7	If N is less than LAST, then go to statement 7.
IF (N .GT. LAST) GO TO 7	If N is greater than LAST, then go to statement 7.
IF (A .LE. B) PRINT, X	If A is less than or equal to B, then print X.
IF (A .GE. B) PRINT, X	If A is greater than or equal to B, then print X.
IF (X .LT. 0.0) X = −X	If X is less than 0, then set X equal negative X.

EXAMPLE 2. Suppose you have a deck of data cards with one number punched on each card. Write a program to read all the cards and print the numbers.

The program will have a loop that reads one card and prints the number read. To break out of the loop, you need some way of determining when the computer has read the last card. One way is to incude at the end of the data an extra card with some special value. For instance, suppose you know that all the numbers are greater than 0. You can include an extra card containing the number 0, and use a decision in the program to stop if the number read is 0.

The flowchart for this procedure is shown in Figure 2.5.

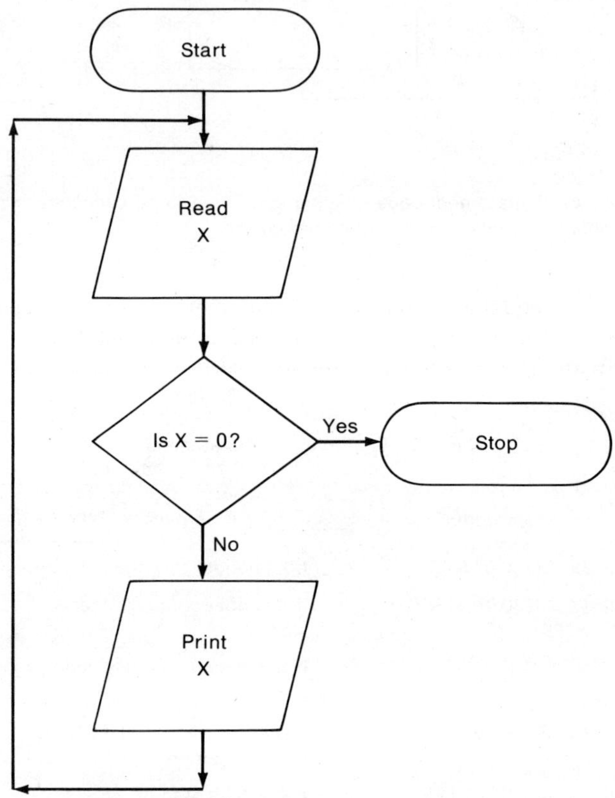

Figure 2.5 Flowchart for Example 2: Read and print a list of numbers, stopping when 0 is read.

Here is the FORTRAN program.

```
10      READ, X
        IF (X .EQ. 0.0) STOP
        PRINT, X
        GO TO 10
        END
```

EXAMPLE 3. In Example 6 of Chapter 1, we drew a flowchart for a procedure to find the average of a set of numbers. Write a FORTRAN program for this procedure.

You can base the program on the flowchart developed in Chapter 1 (page 20) with one modification: You need some specific way of determining when you have reached the end of data. As you will see later, there are several ways to do this in FORTRAN.* One way that is easy to program is to include at the end of the input an extra card containing some special data value. For instance, you can use the value −9999.0 to mean "End of data." After the "Read" instruction, check to see if the value read was −9999.0. If not, proceed through the loop. When the value −9999.0 is read, break out of the loop and compute the average of the numbers read (not including the last value, −9999.0). You could do this with the statement

```
IF (X .EQ. -9999.0) GO TO 20
```

Or, you can use the equivalent statement

```
IF (X .EQ. ENDATA) GO TO 20
```

where ENDATA is a variable to which you have previously assigned the value −9999.0. This is purely a matter of style. The latter statement makes the program a little easier to understand. It would also make the program easier to modify if you decided to use a value other than −9999.0 to represent the end of data.

As another matter of style, variable names such as SUM, for the sum of the values (and for the average), and COUNT, for the number of values, are recommended. Since variable names in FORTRAN can be words as well as single letters, it is a good idea to choose words that help you remember what the variable stands for. Figure 2.6 shows the revised flowchart. The following is the corresponding FORTRAN program.

```
      ENDATA = -9999.0
      SUM = 0.0
      COUNT = 0.0
10    READ, X
      IF (X .EQ. ENDATA) GO TO 20
      PRINT, X
      COUNT = COUNT + 1.0
      SUM = SUM + X
      GO TO 10
20    IF (COUNT .NE. 0.0) SUM = SUM/COUNT
      PRINT, COUNT, SUM
      STOP
      END
```

* See page 177 for a discussion of the END = option of the READ statement.

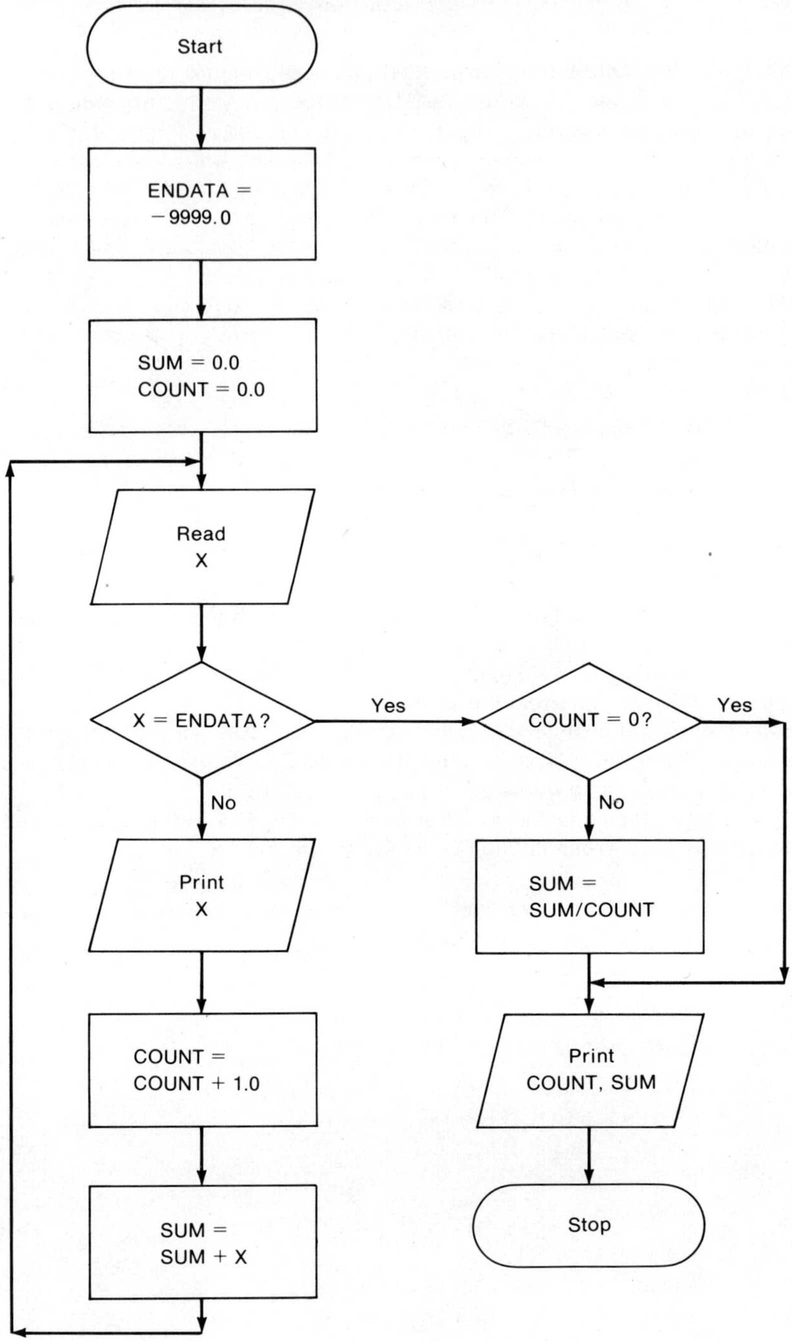

Figure 2.6 Flowchart for Example 3: procedure to find the average of a set of numbers.

Table 2.4 summarizes the FORTRAN statements covered so far. In the next four chapters we will discuss these in detail and see more examples of their use. Chapter 3 explains how you prepare a program on cards and what happens when you run a program on the computer.

Table 2.4 Summary of FORTRAN Statements Covered in This Chapter

Type	*Purpose*	*Example*
Assignment statement	Perform a computation and store the result in a variable	VALUE = 2.0*X − Y/3.0
READ statement	Read in numbers and store them in variables	READ, I, J, K
PRINT statement	Write out the values of variables	PRINT, Y, ANSWER
STOP statement	Terminate execution of the program	STOP
GO TO statement	Branch to some other statement (identified by a statement number)	GO TO 77
IF statement	Compare two expressions and conditionally execute some statement	IF (N .GT. 10) X = 0
END statement	Cause no action, but necessary as the last statement in a program	END

Introduction to Formatted PRINT and READ Statements

Some computer systems do not provide the list-directed forms of the PRINT and READ statements we covered earlier. In this case, you can use a different form of these statements, called the **formatted PRINT** and **formatted READ**. We will cover these in detail in Chapter 6, but a brief introduction will serve for now.

An example of the formatted PRINT statement is

```
PRINT 100, X, Y
```

The X and Y here are variable names, just as in the list-directed PRINT. The number 100 before the first comma is the statement number of a **FORMAT** statement which specifies how the values of the variables X and Y are to be printed. In this case, we will use the statement

```
100     FORMAT (1X, F10.3, F10.3)
```

The 1X and the F10.3 in this statement are called **field descriptors**. Chapter 6 will cover these in detail.

The formatted READ statement is similar to the PRINT. An example is

```
      READ 700, A
700   FORMAT(F10.3)
```

These statements read a value into the variable A under the control of FORMAT statement number 700.

The FORMAT statement, by itself, does not *do* anything; it only tells the PRINT or READ statement how to print or read the values. You can put the FORMAT statement right after the PRINT or READ statement that uses it.

Until we have covered the details in Chapter 6, you can use formatted PRINT and READ statements by following a few basic rules.

Rules for Basic Use of Formatted PRINT and READ Statements

Rule 1: Use a different FORMAT statement number in each PRINT or READ statement in your program.

Rule 2: Following the PRINT or READ statement, include a FORMAT statement with the same statement number you used in the PRINT or READ.

Rule 3: Within the parentheses of the FORMAT, write a list of field descriptors, separated by commas. If the FORMAT is for a PRINT statement, begin with a 1X field descriptor. If it is for a READ statement, omit the 1X field descriptor. Include one F10.3 field descriptor for each variable in the PRINT or READ.

You will need one additional rule, the meaning of which will become clear when you get to Chapter 4, where you will see that there are two kinds of variables: real and integer. Thus far, you have been using real variables. For integer variables, there is a slight modification.

Another Rule for Basic Use of Formatted PRINT and READ Statements

Rule 4: When you are printing or reading an integer variable, use an I10 field descriptor in place of F10.3.

EXAMPLE 4. Using the formatted PRINT and READ statements, you can rewrite the program of Example 3 as follows.

```
      ENDATA = -9999.0
      SUM = 0.0
      COUNT = 0.0
10    READ 15, X
```

```
15    FORMAT(F10.3)
      IF (X .EQ. ENDATA) GO TO 20
      PRINT 16, X
16    FORMAT(1X, F10.3)
      COUNT = COUNT + 1.0
      SUM = SUM + X
      GO TO 10
20    IF (COUNT .NE. 0.0) SUM = SUM / COUNT
      PRINT 25, COUNT, SUM
25    FORMAT(1X, F10.3, F10.3)
      STOP
      END
```

Exercises

1. Which of the following are valid FORTRAN statements?
   a. X = 1.0 + 2.0
   b. 3.0 = D
   c. ANSWER = W times 2
   d. GO TO 5
   e. IF (X = 10.0) STOP
2. Give a definition of the following:
   a. Statement
   b. Variable
   c. Statement label
   d. END statement
   e. GO TO statement
3. What is a FORTRAN statement to stop the program if X is a negative number?
4. What is a FORTRAN statement to jump back in the program and execute statement number 100?
5. Can there be more than one STOP statement in a program? Can there be more than one END statement in a program?
6. Make a flowchart for the following program.

```
      X = 1.0
      PROD = 1.0
10    PROD = PROD * X
      X = X + 1.0
      IF (X .LE. 8.0) GO TO 10
      PRINT, PROD
      STOP
      END
```

7. Make a flowchart for the following program.

```
        READ, VALUE
        IF (VALUE .GT. 0.0) GO TO 20
        VALUE = -VALUE
 20     PRINT, VALUE
        STOP
        END
```

8. The program in Example 2 (page 51) prints out the value of each number that it reads. Change the program so that it prints out *two times* the number it reads (for example, if it reads the number 3, it should print out 6).

9. In the program for Example 3 (page 53), what is the purpose of the statement

   SUM = SUM + X

   What is the purpose of the statement

   COUNT = 0.0

   Do you think this statement is really necessary? Suppose that the input data for this program consists of the numbers 2.0, 4.0, 6.0, 8.0, 10.0, −9999.0. What will be the value of the variable A just *before* statement 20 is executed? What values will be printed by the program?

10. Following the model of Example 3, write a program that will read a set of numbers and print out the *sum* of the numbers. Have the program keep reading until it reads the number 9999. Thus, if the input numbers are 1, 2, 3, 4, 9999, the program should print out the number 10 (= 1 + 2 + 3 + 4).

3

Running a Program

Now that you've seen what the FORTRAN language is like, let's consider the steps you go through to run a program on the computer.

Preparing Your Program

Each FORTRAN statement is written on a separate line. If you use a keypunch to prepare your program, you type each line of the program on a separate card. This has to be done in a certain format. Figure 3.1 shows a card punched with the letters A through Z, numbers 0 through 9, and the special characters (+, −, etc.), that can be used in forming FORTRAN statements. The printing on the card is for the convenience of the programmer; the computer senses only the holes. If you are preparing your program on a computer terminal, the program is stored directly onto some storage device in the computer. The principle is the same whether using cards or a terminal: Each line begins a new FORTRAN statement.

The punch card has 80 **columns**, so you can type up to 80 characters on a single card. The columns are numbered 1 through 80 from left to right. Many computer terminals have 80 "columns," although the exact number depends on the particular model. Columns on a terminal are not numbered as on a punch card, but you can think of each line as having 80 characters (including blanks) numbered 1 to 80 from left to right.

A statement must be prepared in a certain format. You type the statement in columns 7 through 72 of the line. Columns 1 through 5 are used for the statement number. Column 6 indicates a continued statement. Columns 73 through 80 are not used by FORTRAN; you can leave them blank or use them for whatever you want. They could contain a number, for example, so that the cards can be put back in sequence if they are dropped.

You may find it helpful to write your program on a coding form, such as the one shown in Figure 3.2, which has the columns marked on it. Blank spaces are ignored by FORTRAN, so

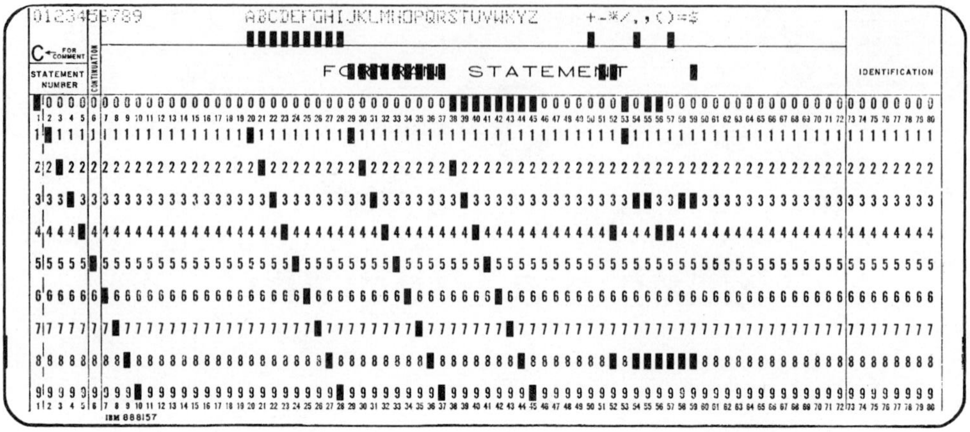

Figure 3.1 A punch card, showing the legal FORTRAN characters. Each character is represented by a pattern of holes. (*Note*: the hole codes for special characters may be different on some computer systems.)

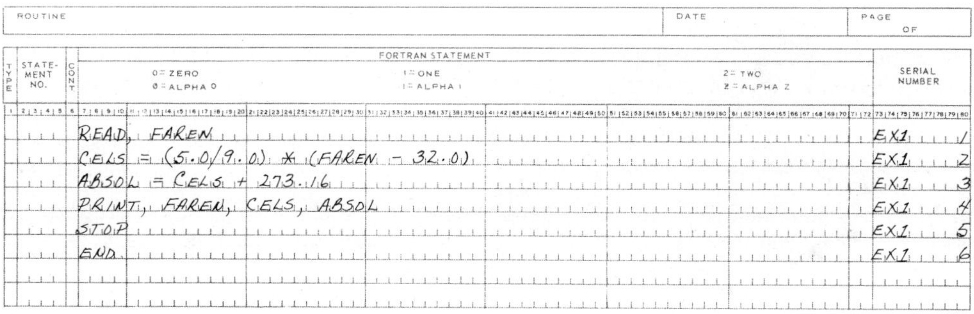

Figure 3.2 Columns are numbered on a FORTRAN coding form.

you can use them wherever you want to make the program more readable as long as the statement is punched somewhere in columns 7 through 72.

In Figure 3.3, the first two statements are equivalent. The second one has several blank spaces, which tend to make it more readable to the programmer, but its meaning is exactly the same as the first statement. Similarly, the last four statements in Figure 3.3 are equivalent. The first of these is the easiest to read (for the programmer), but the spacing of the last three does not alter their meaning. Since the spacing is arbitrary within most FORTRAN statements, it is frequently not necessary to use a coding form when writing a program.

Sometimes a FORTRAN statement is too long to fit on a single line. In this case, the statement can be continued on the next line. A statement is continued by placing any nonblank character other than 0 in column 6 of the second card. This is the only thing

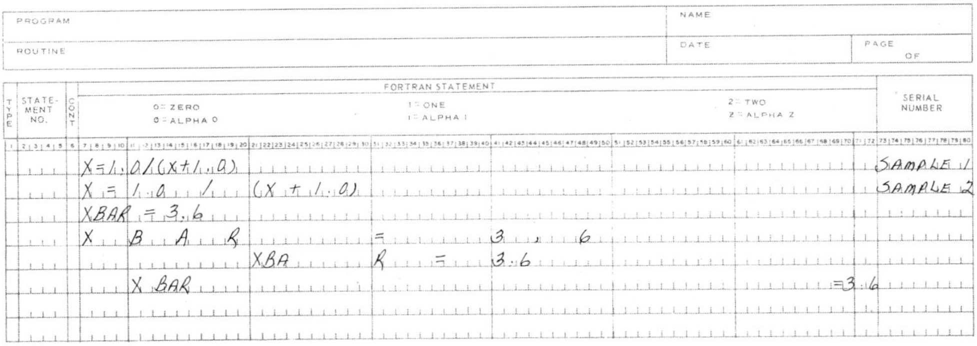

Figure 3.3 Blank spaces can be used in a FORTRAN statement with no effect on the meaning.

column 6 is ever used for in FORTRAN. You can use any nonblank, nonzero character to indicate a continuation. It is preferable to use a dollar sign because there is little chance of confusing it with part of the statement, as you might if a digit were used. The statement can be broken anywhere, but for clarity it is best to break it at some natural place such as at an arithmetic operator. You'll find your programs more readable if you indent the second line of a continued statement several spaces. A statement may be continued on more than two lines. If a line has a nonblank, nonzero character in column 6, then columns 7 through 72 are considered to be a continuation of columns 7 through 72 of the previous line. Some programmers number continuation lines with consecutive digits in column 6, with the first line having a zero or a blank in column 6. Figure 3.4 shows a two-line statement. Standard FORTRAN allows up to 19 continuation cards in a statement. Some versions of FORTRAN, including WATFIV, allow a maximum of five continuation cards.

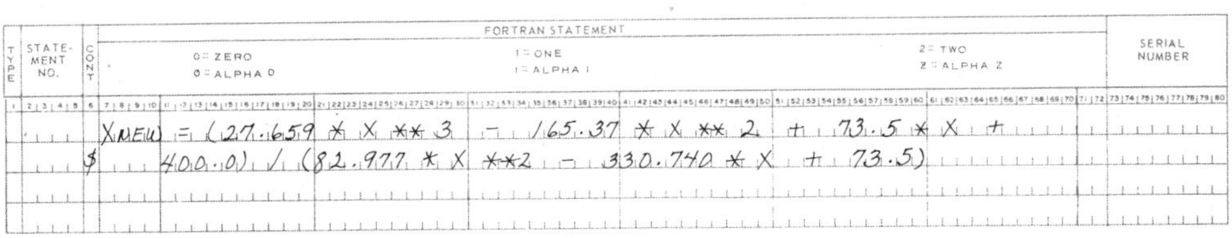

Figure 3.4 A continued statement: If column 6 is not blank or zero, the rest of the line is a continuation of the previous line.

Any line with the letter C in column 1 is a **comment line**. Comment lines are ignored by FORTRAN; they have no effect on the program. It is a good practice to use comment lines to explain what your program does or how it works. Such comments will be very helpful when you are reading the program or making changes in it. This is especially true when you are writing long programs, which may take several weeks to complete. Comments will also be invaluable to anyone else trying to read your program. Figure 3.5 shows examples of comment lines.

```
C THIS IS AN EXAMPLE OF A COMMENT LINE.
C---------A COMMENT CAN HAVE ANYTHING ON IT.
C---------THE ONLY RESTRICTION IS THAT A LETTER C IS IN COLUMN 1.
C
C     FORMULA FOR GROUP 6
      TARRIF = 1.635 * QUAN + 17.9
C
C     FORMULA FOR GROUP 7
      TAR = 1.62 * QUAN + 15.0
C     COMMENTS CAN COME ANYWHERE IN A PROGRAM EXCEPT
C     BETWEEN CONTINUATION LINES OF A STATEMENT.
```

Figure 3.5 Comment lines.

A FORTRAN statement does not have to have a statement number (or label), but if it does have one, the number is punched in columns 1 through 5. You can punch the statement number starting in column 1 or you can precede the number with one or more blank spaces. Spacing is not important as long as the number is punched somewhere in columns 1 through 5. Figure 3.6 shows some examples.

```
C     STATEMENT LABELS ARE PLACED ANYWHERE IN COLUMNS 1 - 5.
   10 X = X + 1.0
   20 D = 2.0 * AID
76543 W = 1
13    BRAVO = X + Y
C     SPACING OF THE STATEMENT LABEL IS NOT IMPORTANT.
C     THE FOLLOWING STATEMENTS ARE EQUIVALENT.
123   N = N / 2
1 2 3 N = N / 2
 123  N = N / 2
  123 N = N / 2
C     BE CAREFUL NOT TO PUT THE STATEMENT LABEL IN COLUMN 6
```

Figure 3.6 Statement labels (also called statement numbers) are punched in columns 1 through 5.

The following rules summarize the format of a FORTRAN statement.

Rules for Writing FORTRAN Statements

Rule 1: A FORTRAN statement is formed from the capital letters A through Z, digits 0 through 9, and the special characters = + − * / ( ) , . $ and blank. Most versions of FORTRAN, including WATFIV, allow the apostrophe (') also.

Rule 2: A statement is written anywhere in the range of columns 7 to 72, inclusive. Blank characters may be used freely to improve the appearance of the program.

Rule 3: A line with the letter C in column 1 is a comment line. It does not affect the execution of the program.

Rule 4: A statement label of from one to five digits may be placed anywhere in columns 1 through 5 of a statement. If a statement is continued onto more than one line, the label goes in the first line of the statement.

Rule 5: A continuation line is any line with a nonzero, nonblank character in column 6. Columns 7 through 72 of such a line are considered a continuation of columns 7 through 72 of the previous line.

Rule 6: Columns 73 through 80 of each line are ignored.

EXAMPLE 1. In Example 3 of the last chapter (page 53), we wrote a program to find the average of a set of numbers. Figure 3.7 shows this same program written on a FORTRAN coding form, with some comments added.

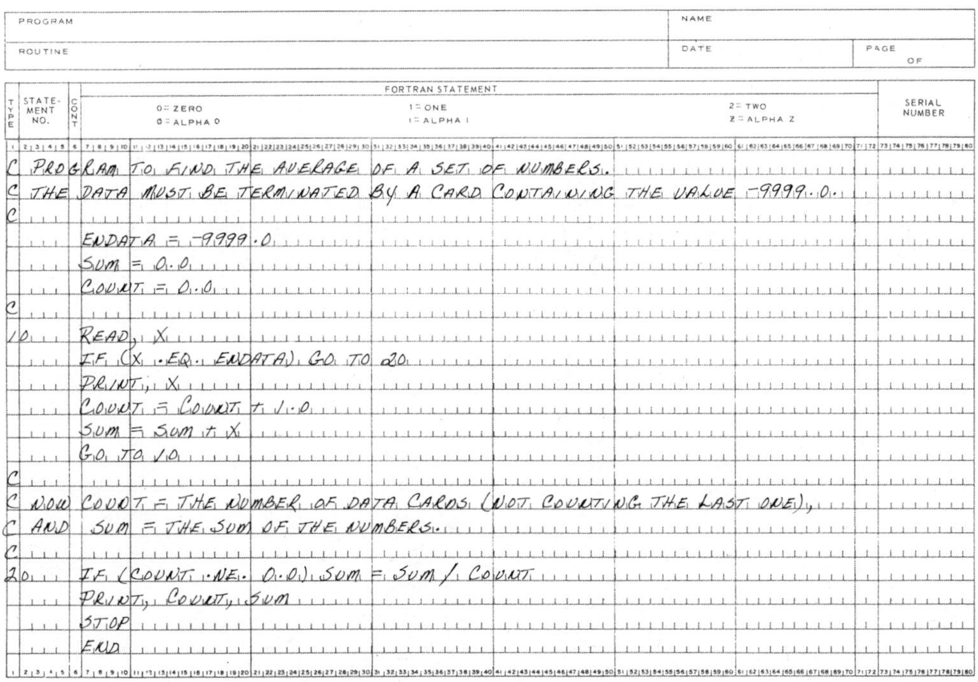

```
C PROGRAM TO FIND THE AVERAGE OF A SET OF NUMBERS.
C THE DATA MUST BE TERMINATED BY A CARD CONTAINING THE VALUE -9999.0.
C
      ENDATA = -9999.0
      SUM = 0.0
      COUNT = 0.0
C
10    READ, X
      IF (X .EQ. ENDATA) GO TO 20
      PRINT, X
      COUNT = COUNT + 1.0
      SUM = SUM + X
      GO TO 10
C
C NOW COUNT = THE NUMBER OF DATA CARDS (NOT COUNTING THE LAST ONE),
C AND SUM = THE SUM OF THE NUMBERS.
C
20    IF (COUNT .NE. 0.0) SUM = SUM / COUNT
      PRINT, COUNT, SUM
      STOP
      END
```

Figure 3.7 A FORTRAN program written or a coding form.

Preparing Your Data

The cards on which you keypunch your program are called **program cards**. If your program does any input operations, you will also need a set of **data cards**, which are the punch cards containing the values to be read. If you are using a computer terminal rather than a keypunch, you may enter a line of data directly on the terminal, rather than punching a card. The principle is the same.

You put all your data cards together at the end of your program. Each time your program executes a READ statement, a new data card is read, and the values are stored in the variables specified in the READ.

An easy way to keypunch your data is to put one number on each data card. For the list-directed READ statement we have been using, it doesn't matter what columns in the card you use. You can begin in column 1 of the card, or you can leave some blank spaces in front of the number if you like. If the number to be read is negative, you keypunch a minus sign in front of the number. Do not leave a blank space after the minus sign. That is, you can keypunch the number −12 as

```
-12
```

but *not* as

```
-  12
```

The statement

```
READ, A, B, C
```

says to read three numbers. You could provide three data cards, with one number on each card, or you could put all three numbers on one card, with a blank space or a comma (or both) separating the numbers. Thus, if you want to read the numbers 11, 12, and 13 for A, B, and C, you can keypunch three data cards:

```
11
12
13
```

or just a single data card:

```
11, 12, 13
```

or, without the commas:

```
11 12 13
```

A whole number can be keypunched with or without a decimal point. Thus, the number 2 can be punched on a data card as

2.0

or just as

2

If the number is not a whole number, you must punch it with a decimal point. The number $3\frac{1}{2}$ is keypunched

3.5

The number $\frac{1}{3}$ must be approximated by a decimal fraction such as

0.333333

We shall see in the next chapter that some variables are allowed to have only integer values. When reading a value for one of these integer variables, the number must *not* be keypunched with a decimal point.

■ Setting Up Your Job Deck

In addition to your FORTRAN program and your data cards, you will need some **control cards** to tell the computer system to run your program. Control cards are used, for example, to tell the computer that you are running a FORTRAN program rather than a program written in some other language, such as COBOL. Each computer system has a control language of its own. You will need only a few control language statements to run a FORTRAN program. Your instructor or your computer center can tell you the exact statements to use. Write them down on the page labeled NOTES in the back of this book.

The control cards together with the program and data cards comprise the **job deck** which you submit to be run on the computer. Again, the exact format of the job deck depends on the particular computer you are using, but typically you will put a few control cards in front of your program cards, followed by your data cards, as shown in Figure 3.8.

EXAMPLE 2. One week in July, the high temperatures in Cleveland were 78.2°F, 76.9°F, 76.0°F, 80.1°F, 79.1°F, 77.4°F, and 78.5°F. Set up this data so that the program of Example 1 can find the average daily high temperature for the week. The data cards are shown in Figure 3.9. Notice the eighth card with a negative number on it. This is needed for the program in Example 1 to detect the end of the data.

In this simple example, it doesn't matter what columns the numbers are keypunched in, as long as there is one number per data card. For more complicated data cards, you might

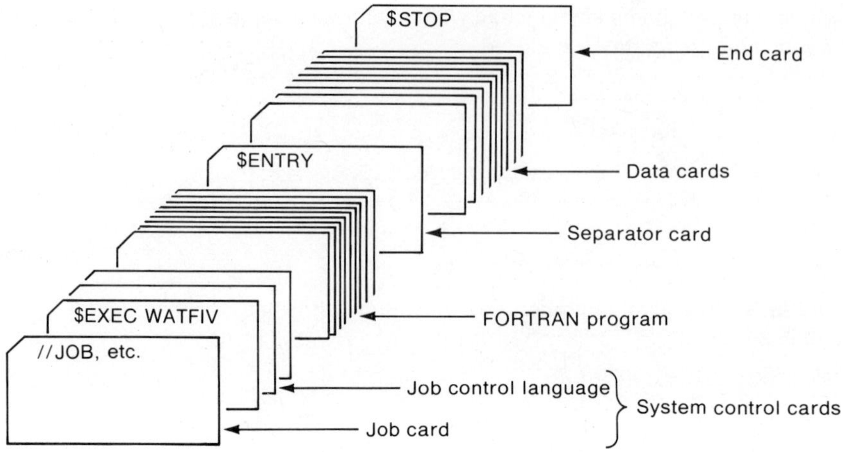

Figure 3.8 Typical job deck setup.

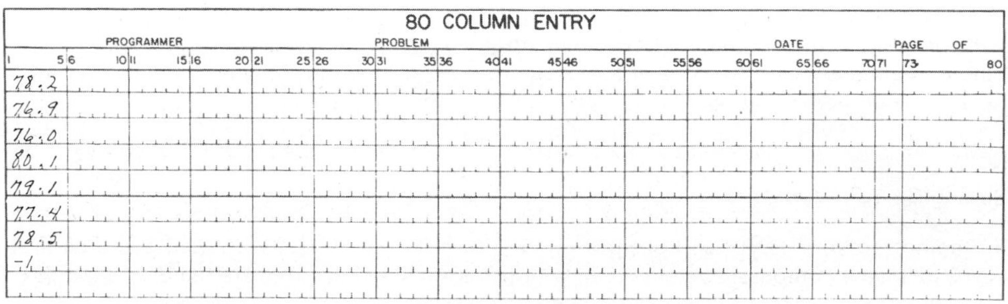
80 COLUMN ENTRY

PROGRAMMER PROBLEM DATE PAGE OF

78.2
76.9
76.0
80.1
79.1
77.4
78.5
-1

Figure 3.9 Data cards for Example 2.

find it useful to lay out the data on a coding form like the one shown in Figure 3.9. The input deck can be set up as shown in Figure 3.10.

Running Your Program

When the job deck has been properly set up, you can run it on the computer, and eventually you will get back your output listing. You need not be concerned with exactly what happens when your job is run, but in order to understand your output, you should be aware that there are two main steps in running any FORTRAN program: **compilation** and **execution**.

Compilation is the process of translating your FORTRAN program into machine language instructions, which will be stored in the computer memory. This is done by the FORTRAN **compiler**, which itself is actually just a big program. During compilation, the computer will print a listing of your program. It may also print a **cross-reference map**, which is a table giving information about your program, such as the names of the variables you

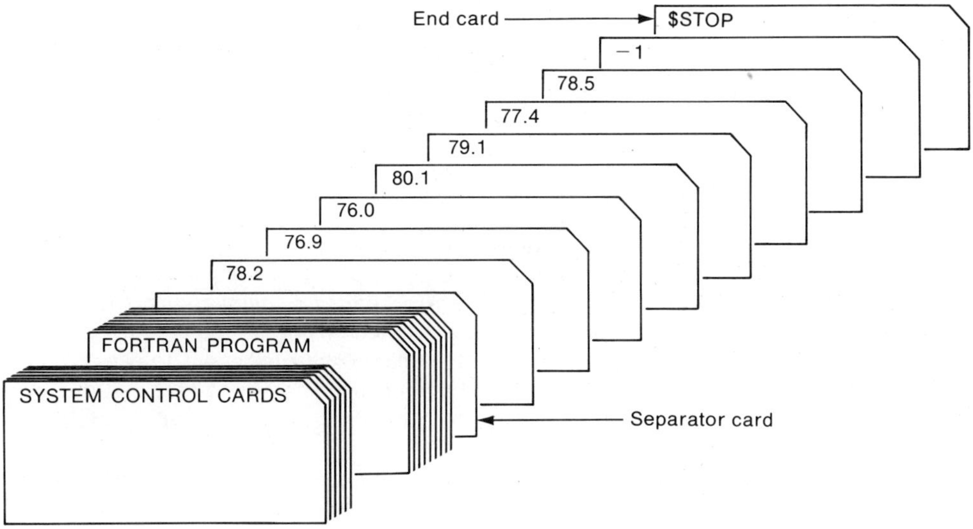

Figure 3.10 Input for Example 2: The exact form of the system control cards, separator card, and end card will depend on the particular computer system you are using.

used in the program. If the compiler detects any errors in your program, it will print an **error listing** to help you find and correct the errors.

If the compiler does not detect any errors in your program, the program begins execution. This is the step in which your FORTRAN instructions are actually carried out. It is during the execution that READ and PRINT statements in your program read in your data and print out your results.

Figure 3.11 shows the parts of the output produced by a typical computer system.

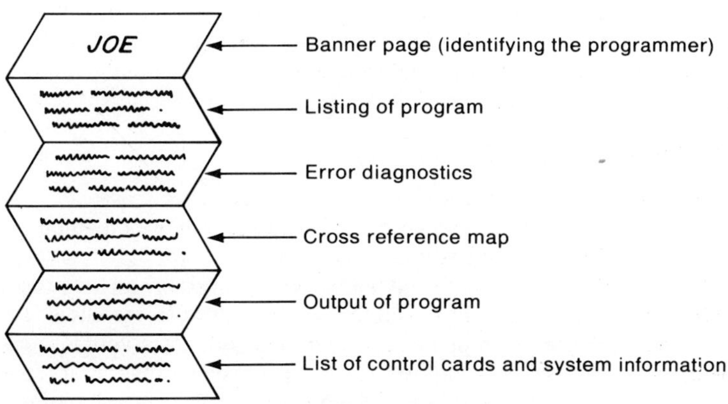

Figure 3.11 Typical output format.

Errors and Diagnostics

It is a fact of life that programs frequently contain mistakes. There are several things that can go wrong. The program may have statements of incorrect form; something that violates one of the rules previously given, for example. The statement

```
W = 2K + 3
```

is incorrect because 2K is an illegal variable name. Probably, the programmer intended to write 2*K instead of 2K. Having no "common sense," FORTRAN is merciless and simply marks the statement to be in error. This kind of error is called a *compilation error* because it is detected by the compiler. An error message is listed on the printout and the program does not execute. These error messages are called **diagnostic** messages: They help you to diagnose the problem. Learning to understand diagnostics is an important part of a programmer's education. The compilation error in this example is a **syntax error**; the statement has an illegal syntax (form).

Another type of error is an **execution error**. This happens when a program compiles correctly and begins execution but then tries to do something impossible. Consider the statements

```
N = 1
M = 5 + K/(N - 1)
```

These statements are valid FORTRAN statements and so could be part of a valid program. But when the computer tries to execute the second statement, it has to divide K by zero. Since division by zero is undefined, most computers would halt and display some sort of error message. It is up to the programmer to read the error message and figure out what happened. This process is known as **debugging**, and programmers typically spend half their time doing it. (It pays to be careful when writing the program in the first place.)

The worst kind of error is when a program compiles and executes all the way through but produces the wrong answers. We say it is the worst because it is usually the most difficult type to diagnose and correct, since no error messages at all are printed out. Frequently in such cases, the programmer has made a mistake in basic reasoning about the problem. Consider the following example from a student program to compute the circumference of a circle.

```
C = 3.2426 * D
```

This is a valid statement; but, due to a keypunching error, the wrong value of π was used. So, of course, the circumference was incorrectly computed, although the computer gave no hint of this. The only way to detect this kind of mistake is to proofread the program carefully and run it with some sample data for which the correct answers are known.

You will undoubtedly encounter all these types of errors in your programs; professional programmers do, also. It is important to realize at the outset that a program is not finished until it has been tested and found to work correctly. This seldom happens on the first try. Learning to find and correct "bugs" is just as important as learning to write programs in the first place. The best thing you can do along this line is to understand in detail what each statement does and what each error diagnostic means.

EXAMPLE 3. Suppose you keypunch the program in Example 1 and the data cards in Example 2, provide the necessary control cards, and run the program. Here are some things that might go wrong.

You get no output at all. May be you used the wrong control cards. One of the control cards tells the computer system to compile your FORTRAN program. If you make a mistake keypunching this card, the system does not even try to compile the program (much less execute it).

You get a listing of your program but no answers. Most likely there was a compilation error. For example, in keypunching the statement

```
IF (X .EQ. ENDATA) GO TO 20
```

you might have left off a period and keypunched it as

```
IF (X .EQ  ENDATA) GO TO 20
```

The FORTRAN compiler will recognize that this is an incorrect statement, and it will print an error diagnostic on your listing.

The program executes and lists all your data cards on the output, but does not print the average. A probable cause is that you omitted the last data card with a negative number on it. When the program reads the last data card, it adds the value to the variable sum, as it should, then returns to statement 10, which tells it to read another data card. Since there are no data cards left, the program cannot carry out this instruction, so it terminates with an execution error. Somewhere on your output listing there will be an error message that says your program ran out of data before it was through.

Your program executes normally and prints out all the numbers it should, but the average is wrong. In this case, you have to read the listing of the program and analyze what the program is actually doing. You can try **desk checking** the program: executing each statement "by hand" to see what answers you get. For example, if you accidentally left out the statement

```
SUM = SUM + X
```

then the program would always print out 0 for the average. If you trace through the program, you will find this mistake when you reach statement 20 and see that the value of SUM is 0.

Exercises

1. From your instructor or from the system reference manual, find out the job control language statements needed to run a job on your system. Write them down on the blank pages in back of this book. Also, obtain an access number for running jobs, and find out how to submit jobs and receive your output.

2. On a keypunch, locate the FEED key. Depress it twice. A card is now ready for punching. Hold down the NUM (numeric) key and punch the digits 0123456789. Press the space bar until the column indicator (the red arrow in the window) is at column 20. Punch all the letters A through Z in alphabetical order. Press the space bar until column 50 is reached. Punch the special characters + − * / . , ( ) = $. Press the REL (release) key, the REG (register) key, and the REL key again. Remove the card from the hopper. Compare your card with Figure 3.1. Are the holes the same? If not, did you forget to press the NUM key for some numbers or special characters?

3. John Van Winkle has discovered a remarkable machine which will allow him to be in a state of suspended animation. John has set the machine so that he will awaken in 300 years. Before beginning this experiment, John opened a savings account and deposited one dollar. The money earns 6% interest, compounded quarterly. How much money will John have when he awakes?
The formula is

$$A = \left(1 + \frac{0.06}{4}\right)^{4 \cdot 300}$$

The following program will compute this amount and print it. Punch up the program and control cards and run it.

```
C        JOHN VAN WINKLE PROBLEM
         A = (1.0 + 0.06/4.0)**(4.0*300.0)
         PRINT 10, A
10       FORMAT(10X, 'JOHN WILL HAVE', F15.2,
     $      1X, 'DOLLARS')
         STOP
         END
```

Be sure to punch the statements in accordance with the rules for preparing FORTRAN input.

4. If your program from Exercise 3 worked, identify the various parts of the printout, such as the program listing, the output, and the system information. How long did your job take to run (in actual computer time)? Why did it take so much longer to get your output back? Find out how to get a cross-reference map of symbolic names and addresses (if you did not get one with your run). Have someone explain it to you and tell you what it is used for.

5. The following program is supposed to compute the area of a circle having a radius of 6.9 inches.

```
           AREA OF CIRCLE
           R = 6.9
           A = PI(R 2)
      PRONT A
                STOP
```

This program has many errors: There is no C in the first column of the comment card, the variable PI is never assigned a value, the formula for A is not written correctly, the word "print" is misspelled and begins in the wrong column, and there is no END line. Punch the program exactly as it is written and run it on the computer. Look carefully at each of the error messages you get on your output. Try to determine exactly what caused each error message. If you come to one you do not understand, get someone to explain it to you. Now fix all the mistakes and run the program again.

6. Suppose you are playing a gambling game for a penny a game. You lose the first game. You and your opponent agree to make it "double or nothing" on the second game, meaning that if you lose again, you will owe 2 cents, but if you win, you will be even. You lose again. Again you go for double or nothing: Either you will owe four cents or you will be even. Suppose you continue this and lose 30 times in a row. How much money will you owe? The answer, in pennies, is 2 raised to the 30th power. The following program computes this number and prints it (as dollars). Punch the program and run it.

```
C       DOUBLE OR NOTHING
        X = 2.0 ** 30/100.0
        PRINT, X
        STOP
        END
```

7. This program reads data cards, which you can make up yourself. Each card contains one number. There may be any number of data cards. Each number must be positive, except the last one, which must be zero. The program will compute the square root of each number and print it. (Mathematically, the square root of a number can be found by raising the number to the $\frac{1}{2}$ power; the FORTRAN expression is X**0.5.) Find out from your instructor how to run a program with data cards. Keypunch this program and run it. Check the answers with a calculator.

```
C   PROGRAM TO FIND SQUARE ROOTS
103     READ, X
        IF (X .EQ. 0.0) STOP
        Y = X ** 0.5
        PRINT, X, Y
        GO TO 103
        END
```

8. Run the program in Exercise 7 with a negative number included in the input cards. Since the square root of a negative number cannot be computed (at least not in the ordinary way), what do you think will happen? Are there any error messages? If so, do they indicate the same kind of error you encountered in Exercise 5? What kind of error is this? Does the error message say what you thought it would?

9. Run the same program with the input cards

```
1.0
2.0
3.0
```

and no zero on the end. What happens? What kind of error is this? What statement was being executed when the error occurred?

10. Modify the program in Exercise 7 so that it will read a number and print out the square, cube, and fourth powers of the number.

4

Arithmetic

As we have seen, computation is done in FORTRAN with an assignment statement of the form

variable = expression

This chapter explains the rules for writing numbers, variables, and expressions.

Numbers

A number in FORTRAN is written as a string of digits, 0 through 9, and may have a decimal point and a plus or minus sign.

We distinguish between two types of numbers: **integer** and **real**. Integer numbers are whole numbers written without a decimal point, such as −2, −1, 0, 1, 2, 3. Integer numbers are used in calculations where only whole numbers are involved: For example, you will see in Chapter 8 that integer numbers are used for subscripts.

Real numbers are used when results may not be whole numbers. Real numbers can have a decimal fraction part as well as an integer part: for example, 4.6, −3.01, 999.0. Real numbers are always written with a decimal point, even if they are whole numbers; integer numbers are always written without a decimal point—that is the difference between them. The number 3 can be written as 3 or as 3.0. Without the decimal point, it is an integer number; with the decimal point, it is a real number.

The reason we distinguish real numbers from integer numbers is that they are stored differently in the computer memory. Real numbers are stored in a kind of scientific notation, in which each number has a fraction part and an exponent part. For example, in scientific notation, the number 25.0 is written as 0.25×10^2. As a real number in the computer memory, the fraction part, 0.25, and the exponent part, 2, are stored separately. The integer value 25 is stored as one number.

You may wonder why we bother with two different kinds of numbers. The underlying reason is that some numbers can be represented only approximately in a computer. For example, when you divide 1 by 3, the exact result is an infinite series of digits: 0.33333333 . . . . A computer memory can store only a finite series of digits, so this number would be rounded to an approximation such as 0.3333333. A typical computer provides seven-place accuracy, so this is not a serious restriction in practice. There are cases, however, where an exact whole number is required: for instance, in counting the number of times a program loop has executed. It does not make sense to say an instruction has been executed *approximately* four times; either it has been done exactly four times, or it has not. This is why we use two kinds of numbers: Real numbers are approximate; integer numbers are exact. You will see more examples of each type as we go along.

Tables 4.1 and 4.2 give some examples of integer and real numbers. The numbers are written in the usual way, with one exception: Commas are not allowed. Thus, the number 10,000 must be written without the comma as 10000. The exact rules for writing numbers in FORTRAN follow.

Rules for Integer Numbers

Rule 1: Integer numbers do not have a decimal point.

Rule 2: Commas are not allowed in numbers in FORTRAN. An integer number is made up of digits 0 through 9, and possibly an initial plus or minus sign. Blank spaces may separate parts of the number without affecting its value.

Rule 3: Zeros placed in front of a number do not affect its value.

Rule 4: A number may have a plus or minus sign in front of it to indicate whether it is positive or negative. If there is no sign, the number is taken to be positive.

Table 4.1 Some FORTRAN Integer Numbers

Arithmetic Number	*FORTRAN Integer Number*	
31.3	31 or 313	31.3 is not an integer; to make it a FORTRAN integer number, you must somehow write it without a decimal point
1,000	1000	No comma
−6.0	−6	Number must be written without decimal point
25	25	Number was already in integer form
+47	+47	Number was already in integer form
7	7 or 07 or 007	Leading zeros are allowed
1,000,123	1 000 123	Blanks are allowed

Rules for Real Numbers

Rule 1: Real numbers are always written with the decimal point. There is an integer part, a decimal point, and a decimal fraction part.

Rule 2: Commas are not allowed in numbers in FORTRAN. A real number consists of digits 0 through 9, a decimal point, and possibly an initial plus or minus sign. Blank spaces may separate parts of the number without affecting its value.

Rule 3: Zeros placed in front of or behind a real number do not affect its value. For example, 7., 7.0, 7.00, 07., 007., and 07.0 mean the same thing. The integer part or the fraction part may be omitted altogether. For example, 0.0, 0., and .0 are all ways of writing zero as a real number.

Rule 4: A number may have a plus or minus sign in front of it to indicate whether it is positive or negative. If there is no sign, it is taken to be positive.

Table 4.2 Some FORTRAN Real Numbers

Arithmetic Number	*FORTRAN Real Number*
1	1.0 or 1. or 1.00 or 01.0, etc.
26	26.0
1000	1000.
−16	−16.0
1,000,000	1 000 000.
+2	+2.0
0	0.0 or 0. or .0, etc.
8.2	8.2
$\frac{1}{2}$	0.5
$3\frac{1}{3}$	3.3333333 (We must use an approximation)
π	3.1416 (We must use an approximation)
$\sqrt{2}$	1.414 (We must use an approximation)

Integer numbers are also called *fixed-point* numbers because of the way they are stored internally in the computer: with the decimal point in a fixed place. Real numbers are also called *floating-point* numbers, a name derived from the fact that the computer can automatically align the decimal point when doing arithmetic with these numbers. The decimal point *floats* during computation. The term "real number" comes from mathematics, where it is used to distinguish ordinary numbers from the so-called imaginary numbers.

Variables

Remember that an assignment statement tells the machine to store a value in a variable. A variable is a name for a memory location, so executing an assignment statement changes the contents of the memory. Consider an example.

```
A = 1.2
B = 3.0
A = A + B
A = A + B
```

The first two statements give initial values to A and B. Representing a memory location by a box, the effect is shown in Figure 4.1a. The third statement means to recall the values of the variables A and B, add them, and store the result in A. The contents of A and B at this point are shown in Figure 4.1b. When the fourth statement is executed, the contents of memory are as shown in Figure 4.1c.

a.	A = 1.2 B = 3.0	Contents of memory:	A	1.2
			B	3.0
b.	A = A + B	Contents of memory:	A	4.2
			B	3.0
c.	A = A + B	Contents of memory:	A	7.2
			B	3.0

Figure 4.1 An assignment statement changes the value of a variable.

You use variables in FORTRAN in much the same way as in ordinary algebra, but there is a difference: An assignment statement is not an equation to be solved; it is an instruction that stores a value in memory. Here is another example.

```
A = 1.2
B = 3.0
A = B
B = A
```

			Contents of memory locations
a.	After the instructions: $A = 1.2$, $B = 3.0$	A	1.2
		B	3.0
b.	After the instruction: $A = B$	A	3.0
		B	3.0
c.	After the instruction: $B = A$	A	3.0
		B	3.0

Figure 4.2 Assigning a value to a memory location destroys the previous value. Thus, the instructions:

$$A = B$$

$$B = A$$

do *not* interchange the values of A and B, because the instruction

$$A = B$$

destroys the previous value of A. To interchange the values of A and B, an additional variable is needed (see Figure 4.3).

What are the values of A and B after these four instructions are executed? After the first two instructions, the values of A and B are as shown in Figure 4.2a. After the third instruction (A = B), the values are as shown in Figure 4.2b, and after the fourth instruction (B = A), the values are as shown in Figure 4.2c. You might think that these statements should interchange the values of A and B, but they do not. When you assign a value to a variable, the previous value is lost. Thus, the number 1.2 was erased from memory by the statement A = B. To interchange the values of A and B, you have to use a third variable to hold a value temporarily, as in the following statements.

$$C = A$$

$$A = B$$

$$B = C$$

Assuming that A and B are initially 1.2 and 3.0, the effect of these statements is shown in Figure 4.3.

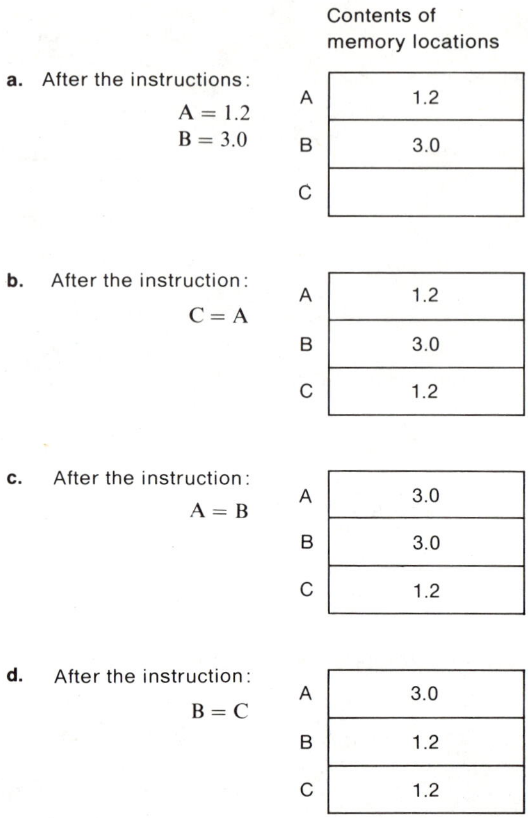

Figure 4.3 Three assignment statements are needed to interchange the values of A and B. The extra variable C is needed to store temporarily the old value of A.

In algebra you generally use a single letter for a variable. Thus, *X* and *Y* might be variables, and *XY* would mean *X* times *Y*. FORTRAN programs can be quite long and complicated; if we used only one-letter names, we would soon run out of possible variables. So a variable in FORTRAN can have a longer name such as RATE, ANSWER, COUNT. Specifically, the rules are as follows.

Rules for Naming Variables

Rule 1: A name consists of from one to six characters.

Rule 2: Only letters (A–Z) and numbers (0–9) can be used in the name. Special symbols such as + or / are not permitted as part of the name.

Rule 3: The name must start with a letter.

Table 4.3 gives some examples of correct and incorrect names.

Table 4.3 Examples of Variable Names

Some Correct Variable Names	
A	LETTER
I	ALPHA
MASS	WW7777
TAX	NNN
X1234	HELLO

Some Incorrect Variable Names	
IJKLMNOPQ	Too many characters
I + J	Illegal symbol
4H	Does not start with a letter
NAME.1	Illegal symbol
AMOUNTDUE	Too many characters

We saw that there are two kinds of numbers in FORTRAN: integer and real. We also have two kinds of variables. An **integer variable** can contain an integer number; a **real variable** can contain a real number. You can tell whether a variable is integer or real by the first letter of its name.

More Rules for Naming Variables

Rule 4: If the name begins with a letter I, J, K, L, M, or N, it is an integer variable.

Rule 5: If the name begins with a letter A through H or O through Z, it is a real variable.

Table 4.4 shows some names of each type.

It is a good idea to use variable names that mean something. If you need to use a variable to store a value of hours worked, call the variable HOURS instead of H or X. This will help avoid confusion as you use the variable throughout your program. Of course, if hours worked is an integer number to be stored in an integer variable, HOURS would not be an acceptable name. Common practice is to call it something like NHOURS. Another good practice is to avoid variable names that are too similar. If your program uses two variables for state tax and federal tax, you might call them TAX1 and TAX2. These are valid names, but it would be easy to confuse them. Better names would be STATAX and FEDTAX.

Table 4.4 Some Integer and Real Variable Names

Integer Variables		
I	JUMP	KOUNT
MAX	LIMIT	NTIMES
ISTART	KTR	N33
Real Variables		
A	X	ETC
B	ANSWER	P1
FORCE	DELTA	T2

In WATFIV (and some other versions of FORTRAN), variable names can have more than six characters. Only the first six characters are used in distinguishing different names, however. Thus, the variables LETTER, LETTERHEAD, and LETTERPERFECT are all names for the *same* variable: LETTER. In WATFIV, you can also use a dollar sign ($) in a variable name: J$J, ABC$$. In standard FORTRAN, this is not allowed.

Expressions

In an assignment statement, you write an **expression** to the right of the equal sign. An expression can be a number or a variable or a combination of these. As you have seen, there are certain symbols used to indicate the basic mathematical operations, as summarized by the following rule.

Rule for Expressions

Rule 1: Numbers and variables can be combined to form expressions using the symbols

+ for addition
− for subtraction or negation
* for multiplication
/ for division
** for exponentiation (raising to a power)

Spacing may be used freely and does not affect the meaning of the expression.

The minus sign can denote subtraction, as in the statement

```
Y = A - 1.0
```

or it can mean to change the sign of a quantity, as in the statement

```
X = -A
```

which means to take the negative of A and store it in X.

FORTRAN does not permit one mathematical operator to come right after another. For example,

```
A + / B
```

is an incorrect expression. If you ever need to use two operators in a row, use parentheses to separate them. For instance, to multiply X by the negative of WEIGHT, you *cannot* use the expression

```
X * -WEIGHT
```

but you *can* use the expression

```
X * (-WEIGHT)
```

Another Rule for Expressions

Rule 2: Two operators may not be placed together unless separated by parentheses. Note that the symbol for exponentiation (**) is considered to be a single operator.

Blank spaces are ignored in FORTRAN, so it does not matter whether you write

```
T = 2.0*(X + Y)
```

or

```
T = 2.0 * (X + Y)
```

or even

```
T   =   2.0   *   (   X   +   Y   )
```

The meaning is the same. Table 4.5 gives some more examples of FORTRAN expressions.

Table 4.5 Examples of FORTRAN Expressions

Algebra Form	*FORTRAN Expression*
profit − 10% of sales	PROFIT − 0.10 * SALES
$\frac{1}{x-1}$	1.0/(X − 1.0)
$\frac{1}{2}at^2 + vt$	0.5 * A * T ** 2 + V * T
$\frac{a-1}{b-2}$	(A − 1.0)/(B − 2.0)

In algebra, the expression

$$2x + 1$$

means to multiply x by 2, then add 1. It does *not* mean to add 1 to x, then multiply by 2. That is, it means

$$(2x) + 1$$

not

$$2(x + 1)$$

Similarly, in FORTRAN there are rules that specify in what order operations are done.

Rules for Evaluating Expressions

Rule 1: Parentheses may be used to group the terms in an expression. Any quantity in parentheses is evaluated before evaluating anything outside the parentheses.

Rule 2: Unless otherwise grouped by parentheses, all exponentiations are performed first; then all multiplications and divisions are performed; then all additions, subtractions, and negations.

Rule 3: Subject to Rules 1 and 2, expressions are evaluated left to right.

To see how these rules work, consider the statement

```
DELTA = A/B * C
```

This might seem ambiguous. Does it mean

$$\text{DELTA} = \frac{A}{B * C}$$

or

$$\text{DELTA} = \frac{A}{B} * C$$

Rule 3 says that multiplication and division are done from left to right. Thus, A is divided by B, then the result is multiplied by C, just as though you had written parentheses:

```
DELTA = (A/B)*C
```

As another example, the statement

```
W = 2.0*X + 3.0*Y
```

means the same as

```
W = (2.0*X) + (3.0*Y)
```

because of Rule 2, which says that multiplication is done before addition.

EXAMPLE 1. A retail merchant paid $357 for 75 toys. What is the average cost of each item, and what should be the selling price if it is desired to make a 20% profit?

In writing FORTRAN statements to carry out this computation, it will be just as easy to use variable names for the quantities involved as to use their numerical values. In this case, use real variables for all quantities. You could let A be the average cost, P the price, and so on. Here it is better to use longer variable names that give more indication of what the variables stand for. Let

UNITS	be the number of units
TCOST	be the total cost
PMARG	be the profit margin
UCOST	be the unit cost
PRICE	be the unit price

Now, the unit cost is the total cost divided by the number of units. The unit price, to attain a desired profit margin, is the unit cost divided by 1 minus the profit margin. This computation can be carried out by the following five FORTRAN statements.

```
UNITS  = 75.0
TCOST  = 357.00
PMARG  = 0.20
UCOST  = TCOST/UNITS
PRICE  = UCOST/(1.0 - PMARG)
```

FORTRAN statements are performed in the order in which they are written. So, when the fourth statement is carried out by the computer, the values of the variables TCOST and UNITS are already established by the first two statements. Similarly, when the fifth statement is carried out, the variable UCOST had a well-defined value, so the expression for PRICE makes sense. Note that it would be incorrect to write the formula for PRICE before the formula for UCOST, since the value of UCOST would then be undefined at the time the expression for PRICE was evaluated.

EXAMPLE 2 (COMPOUND INTEREST). A sum of money P (the principal) is invested at a rate of interest r. The interest is compounded annually for n years. At the end of this time, the accumulated amount A_n is given by the formula

$$A_n = P(1 + r)^n$$

Write a program to read values of P, r, and n and compute the value of the amount.

First, you must decide on names for the variables. A_n has a subscript, so it is not a legal variable name. There is really no need to use a subscript here. You can call the amount A or, better yet, call it AMOUNT. Likewise, you can use the names RATE, for the rate, and PRINCE, for the principal. The formula is written in FORTRAN as

```
AMOUNT = PRINCE * (1.0 + RATE) ** N
```

Here is a complete program to read values of PRINCE, RATE, and N and print them with the computed value of AMOUNT.

```
READ, PRINCE, RATE, N
PRINT, PRINCE, RATE, N
AMOUNT = PRINCE * (1.0 + RATE) ** N
PRINT, AMOUNT
STOP
END
```

Real and Integer Arithmetic

If an arithmetic expression involves only integer numbers and integer variables, we call it an **integer expression**. For example,

```
2 * LIMIT + 11
```

is an integer expression, since 2, LIMIT, and 11 are all integer quantities. When the computer evaluates this expression, the result will be an integer number.

If an arithmetic expression involves only real numbers and real variables, we call it a **real expression**. For example,

```
9.0 * FISH/SCALE
```

One difference between real and integer expressions is in the way division is performed. In integer arithmetic, a quotient is always an integer number, while in real arithmetic, decimal fractions are allowed. For example, the real expression

$$3.0/2.0$$

would be evaluated as 1.5. In integer division, however, the decimal part is truncated, and

$$3/2$$

is evaluated as 1. As another example, 10/(−3) is the integer −3 (the fractional part is truncated and the minus sign is retained).

Rule for Integer Division

Rule: When one integer expression is divided by another, any fractional part is truncated. The absolute value of the result is the greatest integer less than the absolute value of the true quotient. The sign of the result is the sign of the true quotient.

This property of integer arithmetic has some useful applications, as you will see later. It is a bit different from ordinary arithmetic. Consider the expression

$$(5 * 3)/5$$

This is evaluated as $\frac{15}{5} = 3$. However, if the parentheses are placed differently, as

$$5 * (3/5)$$

then the result is $5 * 0 = 0$, since $3.0/5.0 = 0.6$, which is truncated to 0 in integer arithmetic.

When an expression involves both real and integer variables, we call it a **mixed-mode expression**. An example of a mixed-mode expression is

$$2.1 + (17/5)$$

Here 17 and 5 are integer numbers and 2.1 is a real number. In this expression, first $\frac{17}{5}$ is evaluated in integer mode. The result is the integer value 3 (*not* 3.4). The computer cannot add the real number 2.1 directly to the integer number 3, so it converts the integer number to its floating-point equivalent 3.0, and then adds these two real numbers to get the real result 5.1. This example illustrates the following rule.

Rule for Mixed-Mode Arithmetic

Rule: If an addition, subtraction, multiplication, or division operation involves both an integer and a real number, the integer number is converted to real form, the operation is performed in real arithmetic, and the result is a real number.

This means that the statements

```
X = X + 1
```

and

```
X = X + 1.0
```

will have exactly the same effect.

While most versions of FORTRAN, including WATFIV, allow mixed-mode expressions, some FORTRAN compilers do not allow them.

Expressions involving raising to a power deserve some special attention. A real expression raised to an integer power is considered a real expression, not a mixed-mode expression. For example,

```
X**3
```

is a real expression, since it means the same as

```
X*X*X
```

Integer exponents should be used when raising a quantity to an integer power. To square the value of X, you should write

```
X**2
```

not

```
X**2.0
```

These may seem like the same thing, but these two expressions are evaluated differently. The second form is computed using logarithms, which is a comparatively slow method. The second form has one other drawback: It is illegal in FORTRAN to raise a negative number to a real power. So the expression X ** 2 (with an integer exponent) is legal whether X is positive, negative, or zero; but the expression X ** 2.0 (with a real exponent) will cause an execution error in the program if the value of X is not a positive number.

Type Conversion with an Assignment Statement

An integer variable must always contain an integer number, and a real variable must always contain a real number. As we saw earlier, these types of numbers are stored differently in the computer memory. You can use an assignment statement to convert an integer value to real, or vice versa.

For example, the statement

X = 34

says to assign an integer value to the variable X. Since X is a real variable, the computer will convert the integer value 34 to the real value 34.0 before storing it in X. Thus, the statements

X = 34

and

X = 34.0

have exactly the same effect.

You can also assign a real value to an integer variable, as in the statement

N = 7.3

Since 7.3 is not an integer, the computer discards the fraction part and stores the integer value 7 in N. Thus, the statements

N = 7.3

and

N = 7

have exactly the same effect.

In general, the rules for conversion are simply these:

Rules for Conversion in an Assignment Statement

Rule 1: When setting a real variable equal to an integer expression, the value is simply converted to real form.

Rule 2: When setting an integer variable equal to a real expression, the value of the real expression is converted to integer form by truncating the decimal fraction part.

Table 4.6 gives some more examples.

Table 4.6 Examples of Type Conversion

Assignment Statement	*Value Stored*
N = 7.9	7
KICK = −6.2	−6
K = −6.0	−6
LIMIT = 100.0	100
LIMIT = 100.001	100
X = 2 + 2	4.0
CROP = 2 * (3 + 1)	8.0
C = 7/3	2.0

FORTRAN-Supplied Functions

Some common mathematical functions, such as the square root, occur frequently in applications. To make things easier for the programmer, they are built-in features of FORTRAN. For example, the statement

```
Y = SQRT(T)
```

is a valid FORTRAN statement that sets Y equal to the square root of T. The SQRT function, for finding square roots, is supplied by FORTRAN, so you can use it in a program just by writing it as part of an expression.

A function in FORTRAN is always written as a **function name** followed by a pair of parentheses which enclose the **argument** of the function (the expression to which the function is applied). FORTRAN computes the **function value**, using the argument you give, and the function value is used in the expression just like a variable. For example, the statement

```
Y = 1.0 + 2.0 * SQRT(3.0)
```

means to compute the square root of 3.0, multiply it by 2.0, add 1.0, and store the result in Y.

The argument of a function can be any expression. To compute the square root of

T + 1.0, you can use the statement

Y = SQRT(T + 1.0)

There is one restriction on the argument: It must be of the correct type (integer or real). The SQRT function requires a *real* argument, so if you want to find the square root of 2, you write

SQRT(2.0)

not

SQRT(2)

since 2 is an integer number.

Another useful function is

ABS(X)

which finds the absolute value of the argument (the value converted to a nonnegative number). The argument must be a real number or expression.

The FLOAT function converts an integer value to a real value. For example, to set B equal to the real value 3.1 divided by the integer variable N, we can use the statement

B = 3.1/FLOAT(N)

The INT function is the opposite of FLOAT: It converts a real value to an integer value. For example,

N = 1 + INT(B/A)

means to divide B by A, convert the quotient to integer form by truncating the decimal fraction part, add 1 to the result and store in N.

A complete list of functions available in FORTRAN is given in Appendix A, along with the rules for using them.

Exercises

Write each of the following as a FORTRAN real number, accurate to at least six digits.

1. 1/10
2. 1,000
3. one million
4. π
5. $\frac{1}{3}$
6. 12,345
7. −1
8. zero

Write each of the following as a FORTRAN integer number.

9. 1,000

10. one million

11. negative one

12. zero

There is something wrong in each of the following assignment statements. Find the mistake.

13. X = 2.0 ÷ A

14. W + X = A

15. ENERGY = R * * − 2

16. ANSWER = (A + B * C

17. R = 2(N + 1)

18. AREA = 3.14 * R * * * 2

19. Q = (1.0 + A * (1.0 + B)

20. F = A * − B

State whether each of the following names is a valid variable name. If so, is it an integer or real variable? If not, what is wrong with it?

21. 123

22. TAXICAB

23. 7X

24. X7

25. L I M A

26. ADD

27. DATE

28. A.3

29. ONE

30. 2L

31. PI

32. PI/2

33. LETTER

34. A+B

35. A PLUS B

For each of the following FORTRAN expressions, write an equivalent algebraic expression.

36. A * * B/C

37. A/B/C

38. A * B + C * D

39. A + B/C + D

40. 1.0/X + 1.0

41. A * * B * C + 1.0

42. 2 * * (2 * N)/I * * 2

43. (1 + X) * * (− 1)

44. 4.0 / 3.0 * 3.1416 * 4**3

45. (A * D − B * C) * * 0.5

For each of the following algebraic formulas, write an equivalent assignment statement in FORTRAN, giving suitable names to the variables to comply with the rules.

46. $A = r^2$

47. $W = (x_2 - x_1)y^2$

48. $R = \dfrac{1}{\dfrac{1}{R_1} + \dfrac{1}{R_2} + \dfrac{1}{R_3}}$

49. $A = \frac{1}{3}bh$, where $h = d/4$

50. $V = \sqrt{x^2 + y^2 + z^2}$

51. The program in Example 2 (page 84) computes the amount of money resulting from a fixed investment with compound interest. A related problem is to find the amount of principal, PRINCE, that will provide a given amount, AMOUNT, when invested for N years with compound interest rate, RATE. Modify the program to compute this principal. Make up some sample data and run the program.

52. Modify the program in Exercise 51 to read not one but several data sets. Each data set is different value of AMOUNT, RATE, and N. Compute and print the corresponding principal, PRINCE, and repeat this procedure until reading a value of zero for N.

53. In a five-card poker hand, the number of ways of getting one pair of cards alike is

$$\frac{52 \cdot 3 \cdot 48 \cdot 44 \cdot 40}{2 \cdot 6}$$

The number of ways of getting three of a kind is

$$\frac{52 \cdot 3 \cdot 2 \cdot 48 \cdot 44}{2 \cdot 2 \cdot 3}$$

The total number of possible five-card poker hands is

$$\frac{52 \cdot 51 \cdot 50 \cdot 49 \cdot 48}{5 \cdot 4 \cdot 3 \cdot 2}$$

Write a program that computes and prints these three numbers. Also compute the probability of getting a pair (the number of ways of getting a pair divided by the number of possible hands), and the probability of getting three of a kind.

54. Write a program that reads two numbers, representing feet and inches. Multiply the number of feet by 12 and add the number of inches. Multiply the result by 2.54. This gives the equivalent measurement in centimeters. Print the two input numbers and the computed value. For sample data, use your own height, in feet and inches, to find out how tall you are measured in centimeters.

55. An architect is making a scale model of a building. She has a blueprint giving all the dimensions in feet, and she wants to know how many inches to make each dimension in the model. Write a program to read a scale factor and a set of dimensions. Divide each dimension by the scale factor and multiply by 12 to get the corresponding scaled dimension in inches. For each dimension, print the value as read and the corresponding scaled value. Continue the procedure until reading a data card containing a value of zero.

56. Write a program to compute the value N from the formula

$$N = X + 0.5$$

for X = 0.0, 0.1, 0.2, 0.3, 0.4, . . . , 4.8, 4.9, 5.0.
Print each X with the corresponding N. What do these numbers represent?

57. What is the output from the following program, assuming that the value used for F is 98.6?

```
READ, F
C = 5/9 * (F - 32)
PRINT, C
STOP
END
```

5

Control Statements

FORTRAN statements are executed one after another, unless you specify otherwise. You can change the order of execution with a **control statement**. In Chapter 2 you learned about three control statements: STOP, GO TO, and IF. We will review these now and see some more examples of how to use them.

The GO TO Statement

The **GO TO** statement transfers control to another statement in the program. To specify which statement is to be performed next, you use a **statement number**. A statement number (also called a **statement label**) is just a one- to five-digit number written in columns 1 through 5 of the line. Figure 3.6 (page 62) gives examples of statement numbers.

Any statement except an END statement may have a statement number. It is good programming practice to label statements only when necessary and to assign these numbers in increasing order. It is also good practice to skip some numbers between statement numbers. For example, number statements 10, 20, 30, and so on, rather than 1, 2, 3, and so on. Then if you change your program later, you can add a statement number and still keep the numbers in increasing order. These suggestions are not restrictions of FORTRAN, however; any numbers can be used in any order for statement labels. The only restriction is that no two statements can have the same number. In general, you have the following rules.

Rules for Statement Numbers and GO TO Statements

Rule 1: Any statement except an END statement can have a statement number of one to five digits.

Rule 2: No two statements can have the same statement number.

Rule 3: A GO TO statement has the form

GO TO *n*

where *n* is a statement number. It transfers control to the statement numbered *n*.

As explained in Chapter 2, blank spaces do not affect the meaning of FORTRAN statements. You can write GO TO as two words, or as one word (GOTO); they mean the same. Also, blank spaces do not matter in statement numbers. You can punch the statement number starting in column 1 or in some other column as long as the whole statement number is contained in columns 1 through 5.

The IF Statement

You program a decision in FORTRAN with an **IF** statement. For example,

```
IF (N .EQ. 10) X = 0.0
```

means to set X equal to zero if N is equal to 10. The general form is shown in Figure 5.1. When the IF statement is executed, the condition in parentheses is either true or false. If it is true, the statement following the parentheses is executed; if it is false, this statement is skipped.

Inside the parentheses of the IF statement you can write a **relational expression** of the form

A .op. B

where *.op.* is one of the relational operators listed in Table 5.1. You must always include the period around the relational operator.

Table 5.1 Relational Operators

Operator	*Meaning*	*Arithmetic Equivalent*
.EQ.	Equal to	$=$
.NE.	Not equal to	$\neq$
.LT.	Less than	$<$
.GT.	Greater than	$>$
.LE.	Less than or equal to	$\leq$
.GE.	Greater than or equal to	$\geq$

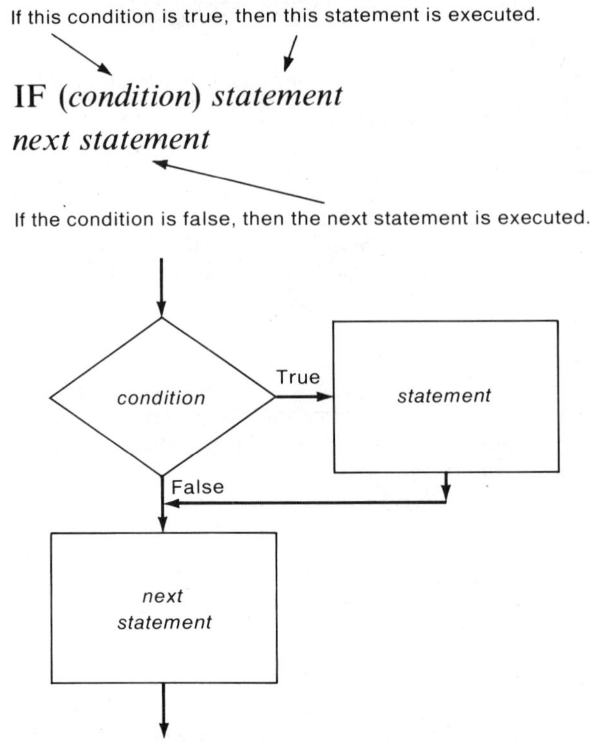

Figure 5.1a The IF statement and corresponding flowchart. If *Statement* is a control statement (e.g., STOP or GO TO), it may not transfer to *Next statement*; these cases are illustrated in Figures 5.1b and 5.1c.

IF (*condition*) STOP
next statement

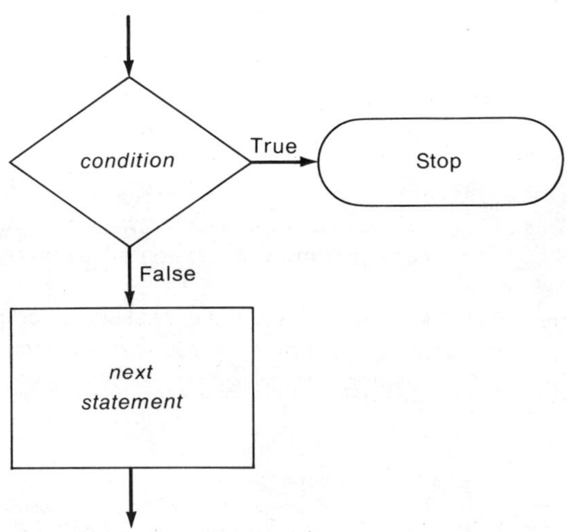

Figure 5.1b Flowchart for an IF statement containing a STOP instruction.

IF (*condition*) GO TO *n*
next statement

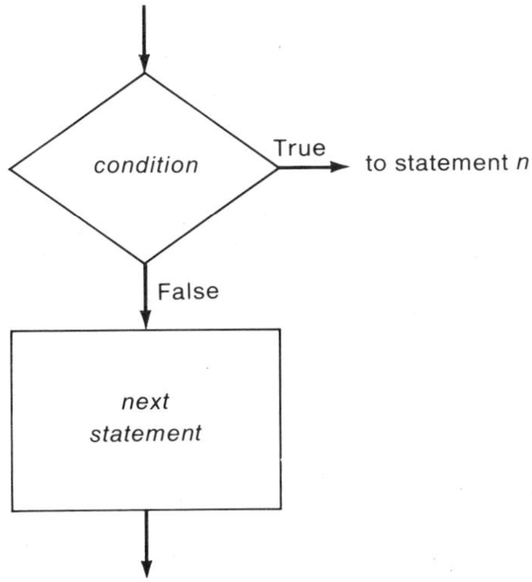

Figure 5.1c Flowchart for an IF statement containing a GO TO instruction.

As in all FORTRAN statements, the spacing is not significant; you can write

```
A.LT.10.0
```

or

```
A .LT. 10.0
```

or

```
A . LT . 10.0
```

The relation in an IF statement can compare any two expressions. Often you compare two variables, but you can compare more complicated expressions as well. Table 5.2 gives some more examples.

Some versions of FORTRAN require that the expressions compared in an IF statement be of the same type: For example, both must be real expressions or both must be integer expressions. Most FORTRAN compilers, however, allow expressions of mixed modes, and would accept a statement such as

```
IF (X .LT. N) GO TO 100
```

Of course, such a comparison can always be performed without mixing modes, as in the

Table 5.2 Examples of IF Statements

```
IF (JINX .LT. 100) GO TO 7
IF (100 .GT. JINX) GO TO 7
IF (X − 3.0 .GT. 0.0) STOP
IF (X .GT. 3.0) STOP
IF (N .NE. 0) W = 3.0 * X + 2.8
IF (A * D .EQ. B * C) GO TO 100
IF (ABS(X) .LE. 3.0) X = 0.0
```

equivalent statement

```
IF (X .LT. FLOAT(N)) GO TO 100
```

The statement that is conditionally executed by the IF statement must *not* be another IF statement. Thus, the following is not allowed:

```
IF (I .EQ. 0) IF (J .EQ. 0) STOP
```

Another restriction is that the statement conditionally executed must *not* be a DO statement (which will be explained in Chapter 7). Rules for the IF statement are summarized as follows.

Rules for the IF Statement

Rule 1: The form of the IF statement is

IF (*A .op. B*) *Statement*

where *A .op. B* is a relational expression and *Statement* is any executable FORTRAN statement other than an IF statement or a DO statement.

Rule 2: In the statement just given, *A* and *B* can be any arithmetic expressions. The relational operator should be one of the following

.EQ. (equal to)	.GT. (greater than)
.NE. (not equal to)	.LE. (less than or equal to)
.LT. (less than)	.GE. (greater than or equal to)

Rule 3: After *A* and *B* are evaluated, if *A .op. B* is found to be true, then *Statement* is executed; otherwise, *Statement* is not executed and control passes to the next statement in the program.

Rule 4: In some versions of FORTRAN, *A* and *B* are required to be of the same type; that is, both should be integer expressions or both should be real expressions.

EXAMPLE 1. Write a program that reads two numbers and prints the value of the larger one. One way to do this is shown in the flowchart in Figure 5.2. In words, the procedure is this: "Read A and B; if A is greater than B, print the value of A; if B is greater than or equal to A, print the value of B." Here is the corresponding FORTRAN program.

```
C     READ TWO NUMBERS AND PRINT THE LARGER
      READ, A, B
      IF (A .GT. B) PRINT, A
      IF (B .GE. A) PRINT, B
      STOP
      END
```

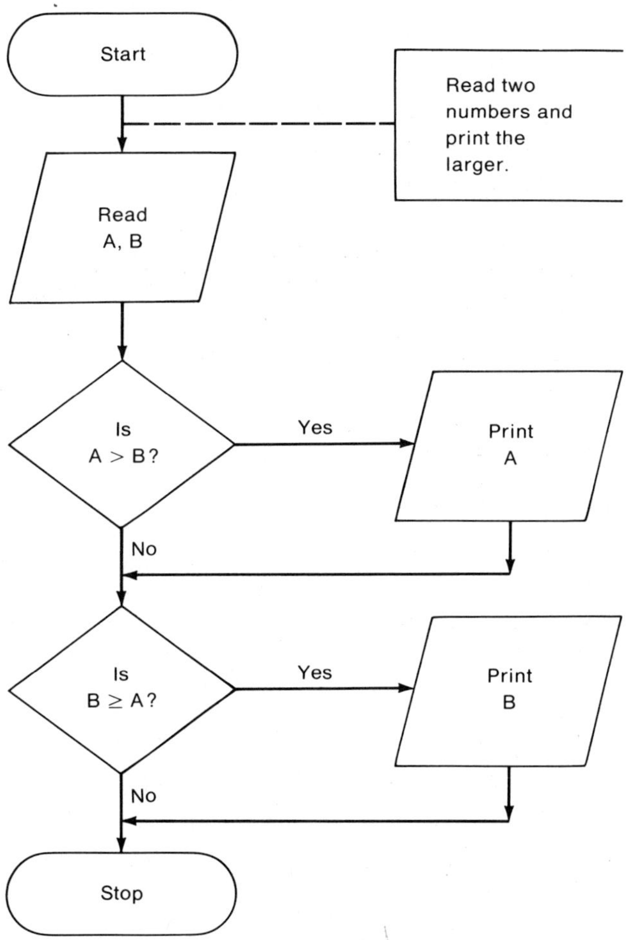

Figure 5.2 A procedure to read two numbers and print the larger one.

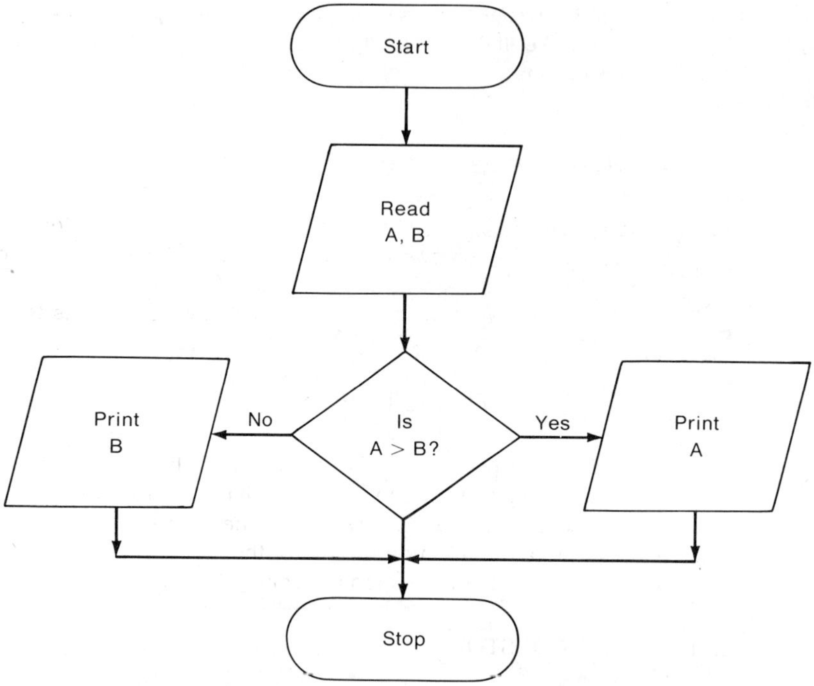

Figure 5.3 A procedure to read two numbers and print the larger one. This differs from the method shown in Figure 5.2 in that only one decision is used.

Figure 5.3 shows an alternate way to accomplish the same thing using a single decision. To program this in FORTRAN, you need two GO TO statements, as follows.

```
C   READ TWO NUMBERS AND PRINT THE LARGER
      READ, A, B
      IF (A .GT. B) GO TO 10
      PRINT, B
      GO TO 20
10    PRINT, A
20    STOP
      END
```

Logical Operators

What if you want your program to test if I is between 1 and 10? In mathematics, we usually write this condition as

$$1 \leq I \leq 10$$

There is a way to write this condition in FORTRAN, too. You use the **logical operator** .AND. as in the following IF statement:

```
IF (1 .LE. I .AND. I .LE. 10) STOP
```

This means to stop the program if 1 is less than or equal to I and I is less than or equal to 10.

Notice that the periods around the word AND are part of the symbol for the .AND. operator. You must always write the periods; if you forget them, the FORTRAN compiler will think you mean a variable named AND (with no periods).

The operator .OR. determines whether at least one of two conditions is true. Thus, the statement

```
IF (N .EQ. 1 .OR. N .EQ. 3) STOP
```

means to stop the program if N is equal to 1 or if N is equal to 3. In everyday speech, the word "or" sometimes means "one or the other but not both." For example, if someone says, "You can have soup or salad," it is generally implied that you cannot have both soup and salad. In FORTRAN, the operator .OR. means "one or the other or possibly both."

The operator .NOT. gives a condition its opposite value. Thus,

```
IF (.NOT. I .LT. J) STOP
```

means to stop the program if I is *not* less than J; in other words, it means to stop *unless* I is less than J.

Table 5.3 Logical Operators

Operator	*Use*	*True When*	*Example*
.AND.	P .AND. Q	Both P and Q are true	1 .LE. N .AND. N .LE. 10
.OR.	P .OR. Q	Either P is true or Q is true or both are true	N .EQ. 1 .OR. N .EQ. 3
.NOT.	.NOT. P	P is false	.NOT. I .LT. J

The three logical operators are summarized in Table 5.3. In general, these operators can be used in IF statements in accordance with the following rules.

More Rules for IF Statements

Rule 5: The condition in a logical IF statement can be any logical expression made up of relational expressions and logical operators.

Rule 6: If *P* and *Q* represent any logical expressions, then

$$P \text{ .AND. } Q$$

is true if and only if both *P* is true and *Q* is true.

Rule 7: If *P* and *Q* represent any logical expressions, then

$$P \text{ .OR. } Q$$

is true if and only if *P* is true, or *Q* is true, or both *P* and *Q* are true.

Rule 8: If *P* represents any logical expression, then

$$\text{.NOT. } P$$

is true if and only if *P* is false.

In Chapter 4, we listed rules for evaluating arithmetic expressions. One of the rules said that multiplication is done before addition. This means that the expression

$$A * B + C * D$$

is equivalent to the expression

$$(A * B) + (C * D)$$

Similarly, there are rules for evaluating logical expressions.

Rules for Evaluating Logical Expressions

Rule 1: Parentheses can be used to group parts of a logical expression.

Rule 2: Unless otherwise grouped by parentheses, the operator .NOT. is evaluated before .AND.

Rule 3: Unless otherwise grouped by parentheses, the operator .AND. is evaluated before .OR.

Rule 4: Unless otherwise grouped by parentheses, arithmetic operators (+, −, *, /, **) are evaluated before relational operators (.LT., .GT., and so on), and relational operators are evaluated before logical operators (.AND., .OR., and .NOT.).

These rules imply that the condition

```
.NOT. I .EQ. 5 .OR. N .EQ. 0
```

means the same as the condition

```
(.NOT. I .EQ. 5) .OR. N .EQ. 0
```

which is the same as

```
(I .NE. 5) .OR. (N .EQ. 0)
```

Rule 4 implies that the condition

```
0 .LE. N + 1 .AND. N + 1 .LE. LIM
```

means the same as the condition

```
(0 .LE. (N + 1)) .AND. ((N + 1) .LE. LIM)
```

EXAMPLE 2. A set of data cards contains exam grades. Each grade is an integer between 0 and 100, and there is one card for each student in the class. The last data card has a grade of −1, to signal the end of input data. Write a program that counts the number of grades that are between 91 and 100, between 81 and 90, and less than 81.

You can use three variables to count grades in the three ranges: NA will be the number of grades between 91 and 100, NB the number of grades between 81 and 90, and NC the number of grades less than 81. You start by setting each of these variables equal to zero.

Read each data card and store the number in a variable NGRADE. If NGRADE is between 91 and 100, you add 1 to NA. In FORTRAN, this is written:

```
IF (91 .LE. NGRADE .AND. NGRADE .LE. 100) NA = NA + 1
```

If NGRADE is between 81 and 90, you add 1 to NB with the statement

```
IF (81 .LE. NGRADE .AND. NGRADE .LE. 90) NB = NB + 1
```

Finally, if NGRADE is between 0 and 80, you add 1 to NC with the statement

```
IF (0 .LE. NGRADE .AND. NGRADE .LE. 80) NC = NC + 1
```

If NGRADE is greater than or equal to 0, repeat the process. Otherwise, print the values of NA, NB, and NC, then stop.

The flowchart in Figure 5.4 shows the complete procedure. Here is the FORTRAN program.

```
C   COUNT THE NUMBER OF GRADES IN EACH RANGE.
C   NA = NUMBER OF GRADES BETWEEN 91 AND 100.
C   NB = NUMBER OF GRADES BETWEEN 81 AND 90.
C   NC = NUMBER OF GRADES BETWEEN 0 AND 80.
        NA = 0
        NB = 0
        NC = 0
10      READ, NGRADE
        IF (91 .LE. NGRADE .AND. NGRADE .LE. 100) NA = NA + 1
        IF (81 .LE. NGRADE .AND. NGRADE .LE. 90) NB = NB + 1
        IF (0 .LE. NGRADE .AND. NGRADE .LE. 80) NC = NC + 1
C   STOP WHEN THE GRADE IS LESS THAN ZERO (LAST CARD).
        IF (NGRADE .GE. 0) GO TO 10
        PRINT, NA, NB, NC
        STOP
        END
```

EXAMPLE 3. Suppose you deposit \$100 in the bank and add \$25 each year, beginning one year from now. If you earn 5% interest each year (compounded annually), how much will you have on deposit at the end of 10 years? Write a program to print the amount on deposit at the end of each year.

Let AMOUNT be the amount on deposit. Initially, AMOUNT = 100. At the end of each year the interest payment increases this by 5% to 1.05 * AMOUNT. When you add the \$25 deposit, the new amount at the end of the year is calculated by

```
AMOUNT = 1.05 * AMOUNT + 25.00
```

This statement is the basis of a loop performed 10 times: once for each year. Also in the loop is a PRINT statement and a statement to increment a variable N that counts the number of iterations of the loop.

Figure 5.5 shows a flowchart for this procedure. Notice that we have written the test at the end of the loop. Here is the corresponding FORTRAN program.

```
        AMOUNT = 100.00
        N = 1
5           AMOUNT = 1.05*AMOUNT + 25.00
            PRINT, N, AMOUNT
            N = N + 1
        IF (N .LE. 10) GO TO 5
        STOP
        END
```

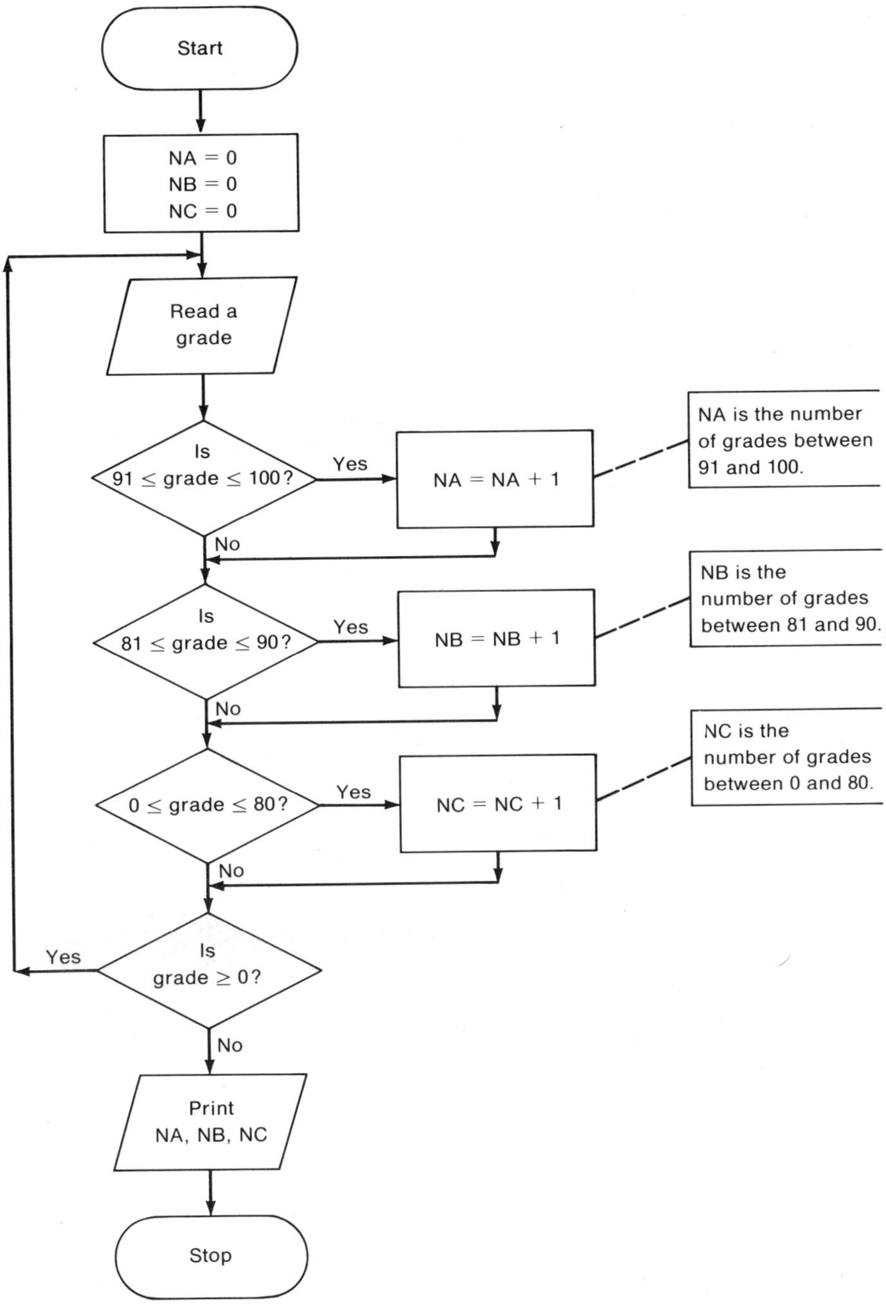

Figure 5.4 Procedure to find the number of grades in each range.

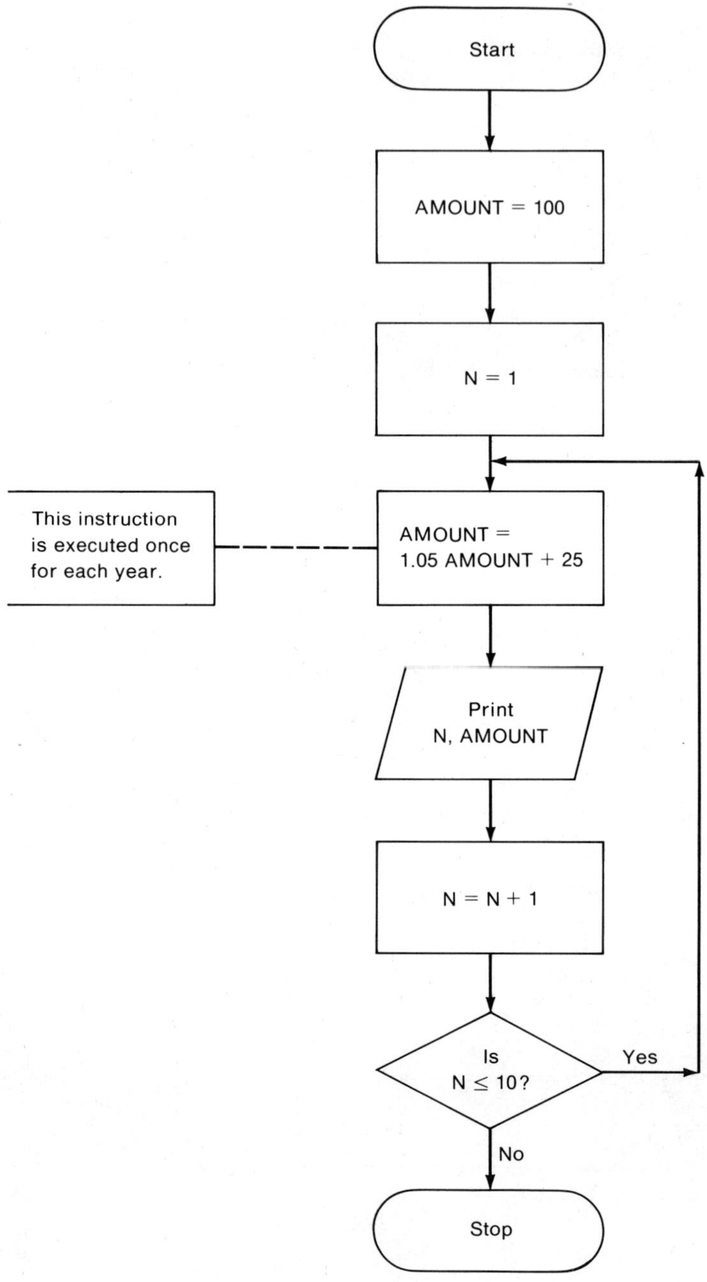

Figure 5.5 Procedure to compute compound interest for Example 3.

Exercises

Write FORTRAN statements to correspond to each of the following flowcharts, using IF and GO TO statements.

1.

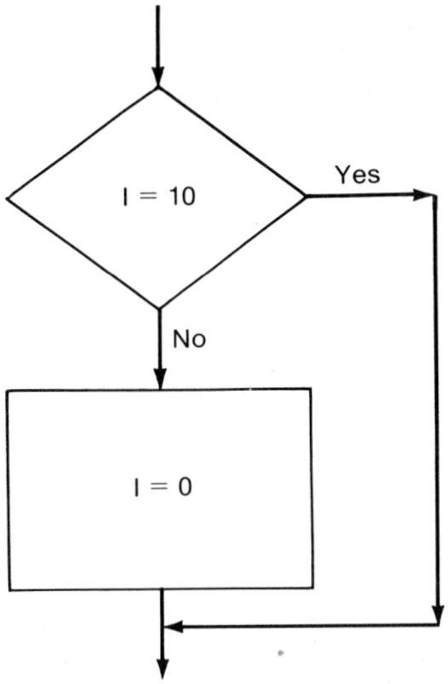

2.

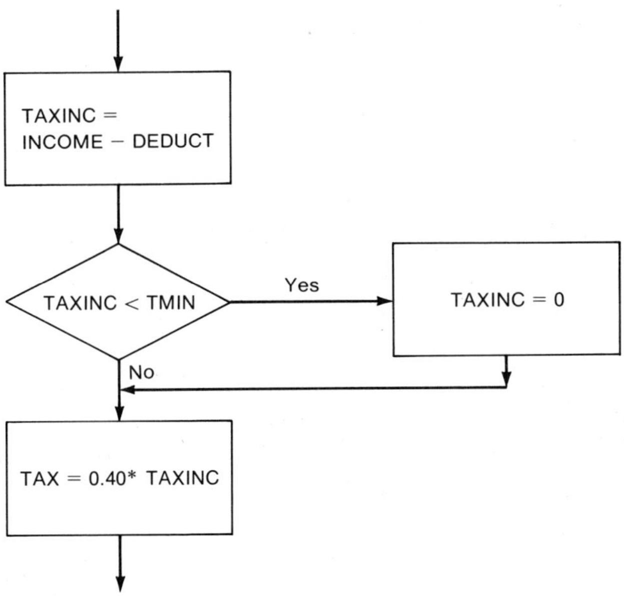

3.

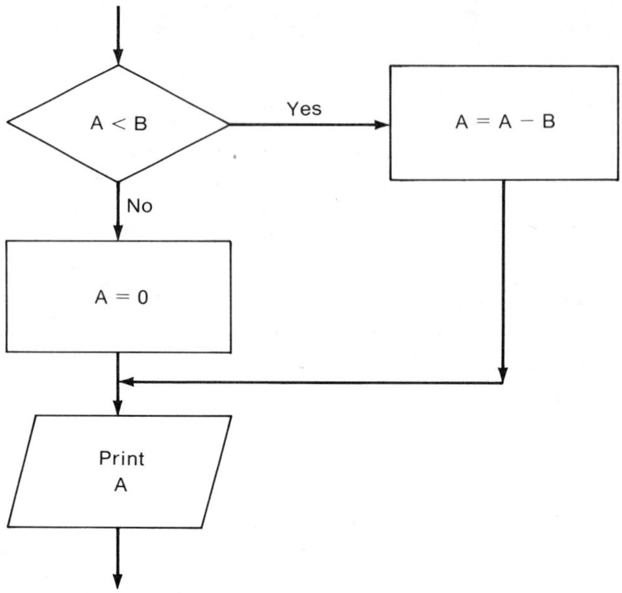

4.

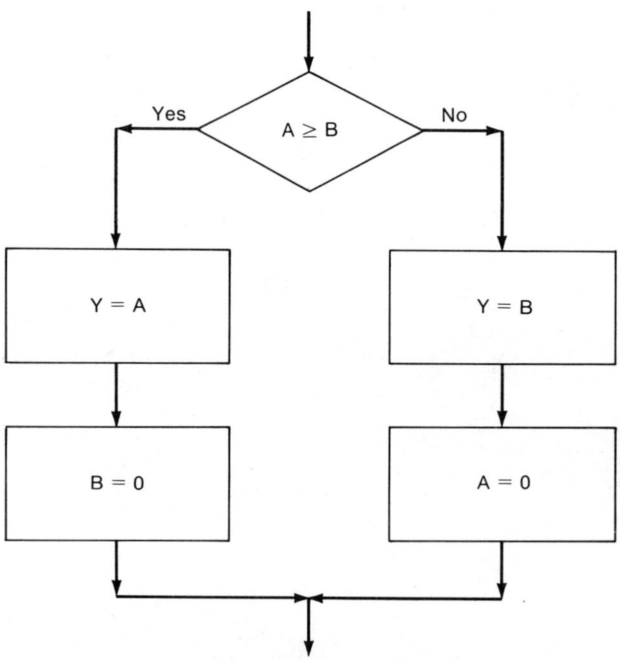

5.

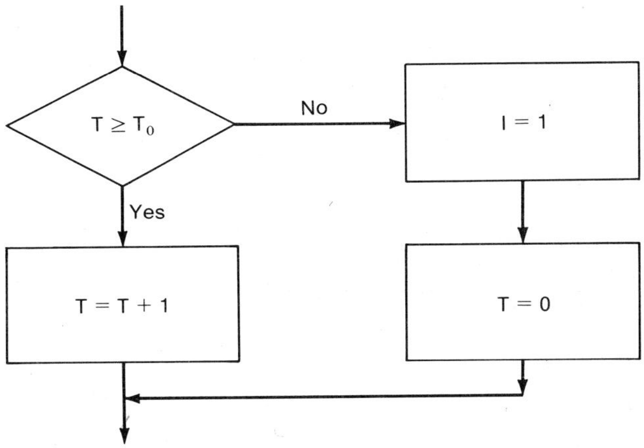

6.

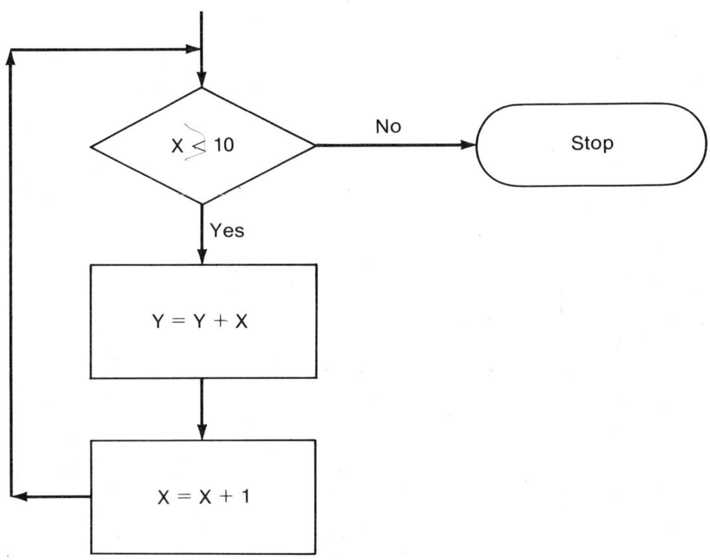

7.

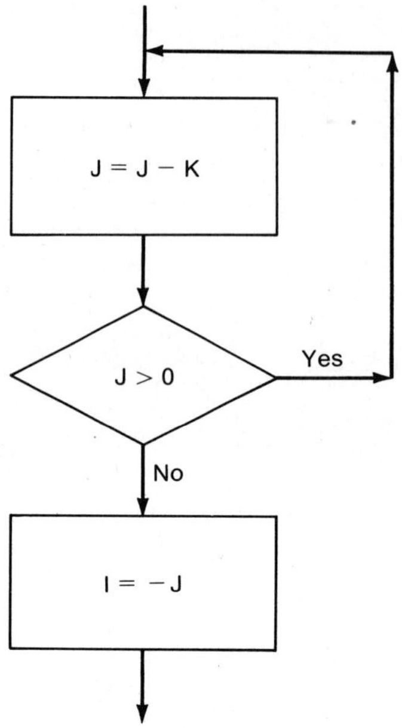

8.

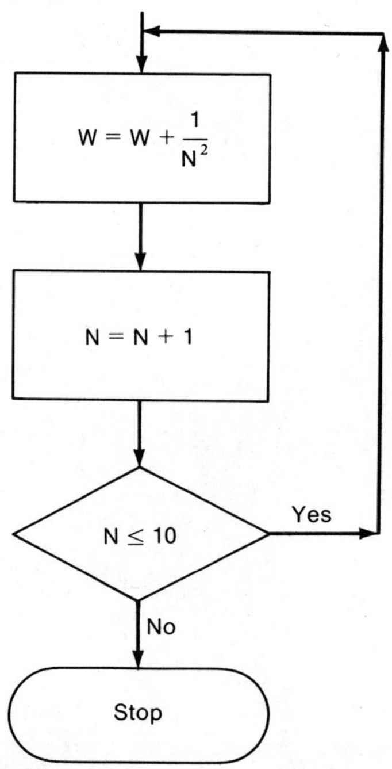

9.

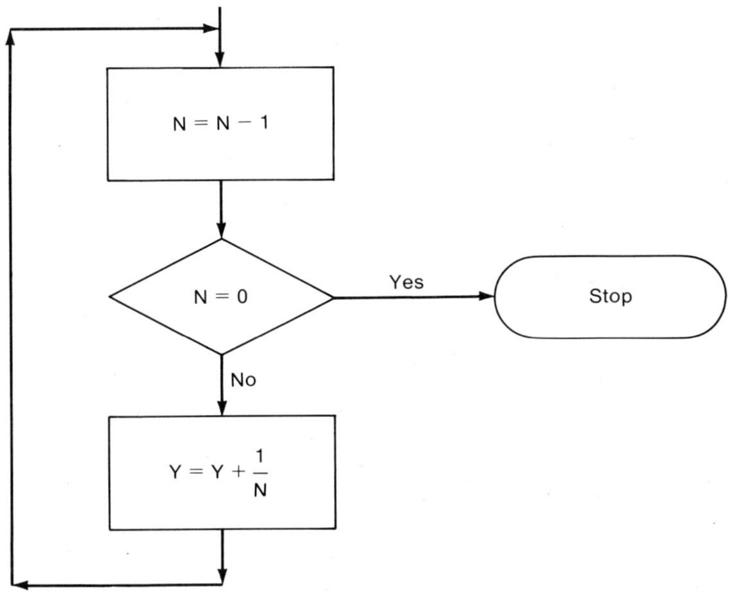

10.

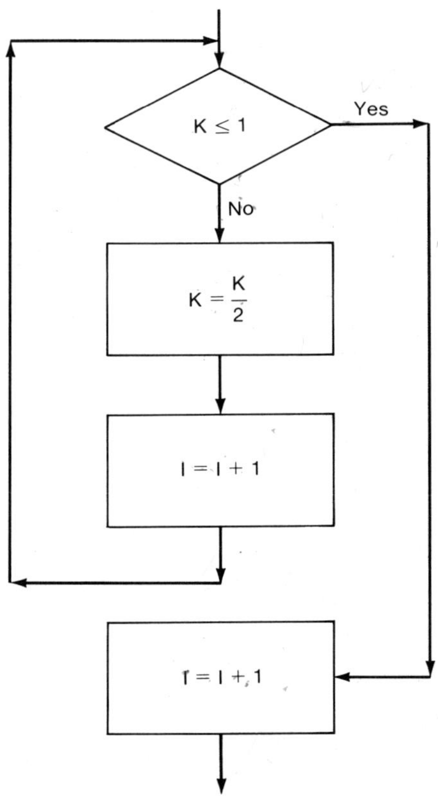

The following exercises call for a complete program. Write a program and run it on the computer.

11. Read a value for X. If X is less than 1000.0, let $Y = X^2 + 7.21X + 160.4$. Print X and Y. Repeat the entire process until a value of 1000 or more is read for X; then stop.

12. Read values for A, B, and C. On your input cards, separate the three numbers by one or more blank spaces. If $A = 0$ or if $B^2 - 4AC < 0$, stop. Otherwise, print the two solutions to the quadratic equation $AX^2 + BX + C = 0$. These solutions are given by the formulas.

$$X_1 = \frac{-B + \sqrt{B^2 - 4AC}}{2A} \text{ and } X_2 = \frac{-B - \sqrt{B^2 - 4AC}}{2A}$$

13. Read an integer N. Compute the value $M = 1^2 + 2^2 + \cdots + N^2$ using a program loop. Output this value.

14. Read a series of numbers, one from each card. Each number is a debit or a credit. If it is negative, add its absolute value to DEBIT. If it is positive, add it to CREDIT. Print the total credits and debits and their difference, which is the balance. Repeat this procedure until the number read is 0, in which case, stop.

MODULE I

Programming Style

Any program can generally be written in several different ways. As you gain more experience, you will develop your own programming style. This section examines the question of what constitutes good style in programming, and you will see some examples of various ways to use the control statements you learned in Chapter 5.

You have already explored several matters of style, such as choosing meaningful and organized names for variables, using comment cards, and indenting continuation lines. These considerations are important in writing a program that is easy to read. And if your program is easy to read, it will be easy to get it working right. This is the one of the most important principles of programming style.

---

1. Make your program easy to read and easy to understand.

If you can read a program and understand it completely, you can be confident that it will do what you intend it to.

One of the greatest difficulties faced by beginning programmers is how to express program logic clearly. Without care, even a simple program can become a confusing tangle of GO TO and IF statements. Consider, for example, the following statements.

```
5      IF (X .LE. XLIMIT) GO TO 15
       STOP
10     X = X + DX
       GO TO 5
15     Y = X**2
       PRINT, X, Y
       GO TO 10
```

These statements perform the desired procedure but are difficult to understand as written. See how much clearer this same procedure becomes when you rewrite it as follows.

```
10      IF (X .GT. XLIMIT) STOP
            Y = X**2
            PRINT, X, Y
            X = X + DX
            GO TO 10
```

The difference is that in the second version you can follow the program logic by reading the statements in the order they are written. As you consider different ways to write a procedure in FORTRAN, keep this principle in mind:

---

2. As much as possible, write your program so that control proceeds from top to bottom.

At first, this may seem difficult to do. Actually, though, all programs, no matter how complex, are built up of loops and decisions, and there are only a few basic forms you need to know.

Writing a Program Loop

A program loop consists of a series of statements to be repeated and a test to break out of the loop when some condition is true. As illustrated in Figure I.1, there are three cases to consider, depending on whether the test is made at the end, at the beginning, or in the middle of the loop.

CASE 1: A LOOP WITH THE TEST AT THE END. The general pattern here is this:

```
        statement 1
        statement 2
        . . .
    repeat the above statements if some condition is true
```

Figure I.2 shows the corresponding flowchart. You can program this in FORTRAN using an IF statement at the end of the loop, as follows.

```
100     statement 1
        statement 2
        . . .
    IF (condition) GO TO 100
```

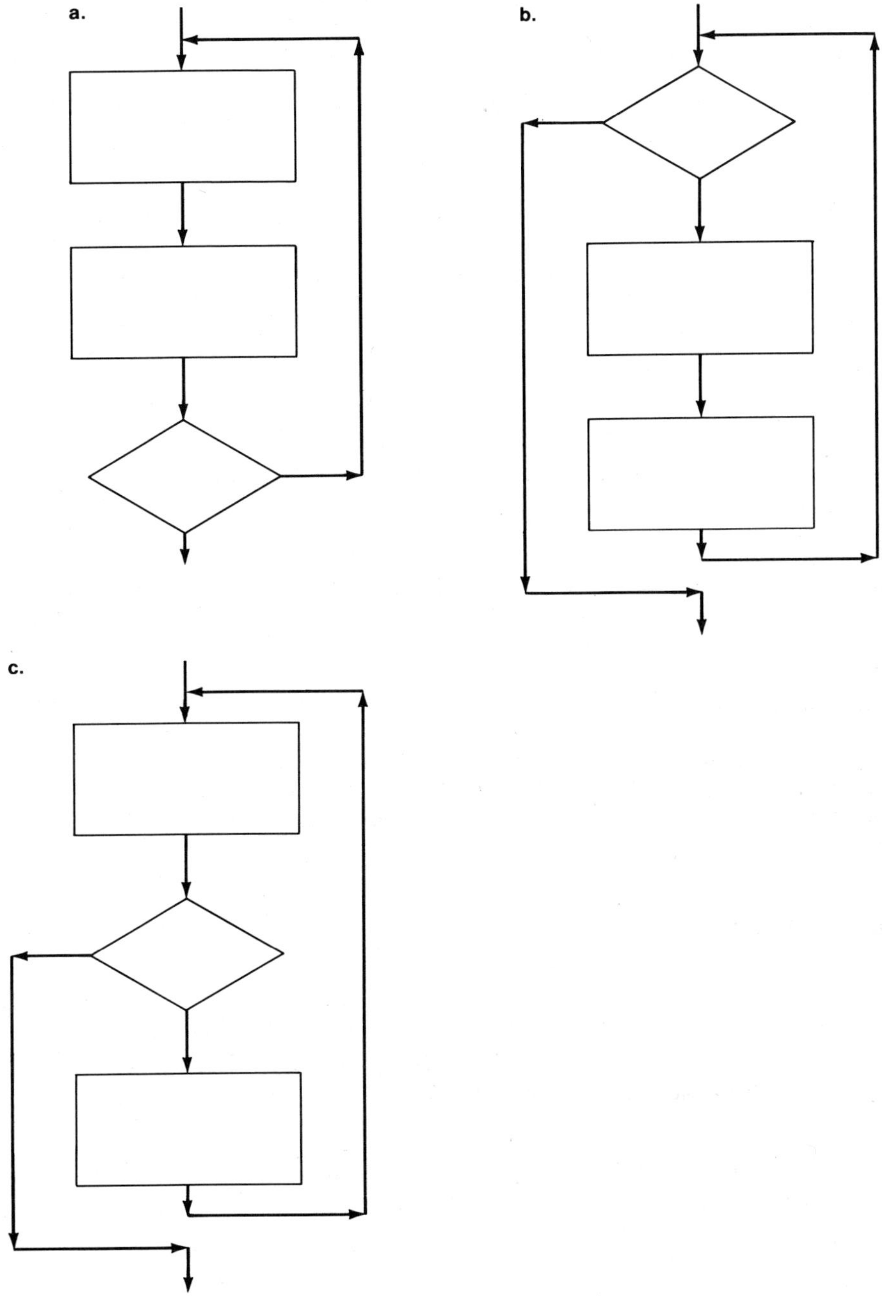

Figure I.1 Three types of loops: (a) a loop with the test at the end, (b) a loop with the test at the beginning, and (c) a loop with the test in the middle.

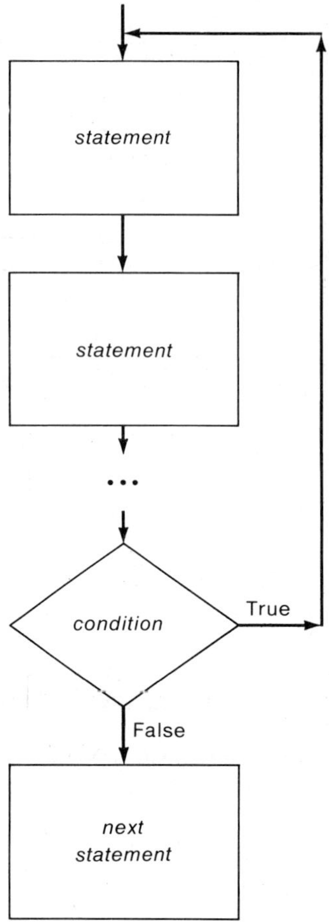


```
C
C   WHILE THE CONDITION IS TRUE,
C   REPEAT THE LOOP
C
100       Statement
          Statement
          . . .
      IF (condition) GO TO 100
      next statement
```

Figure I.2 General pattern for a loop with the test at the end.

CASE 2: A LOOP WITH THE TEST AT THE BEGINNING. The general pattern here is this:

until some condition is true, do the following:
 statement 1
 statement 2
 . . .

Figure I.3a shows the corresponding flowchart. You can write such a procedure in FORTRAN using an IF statement at the beginning of the loop, following the form:

```
100     IF (condition) GO TO 200
            statement 1
            statement 2
            . . .
            GO TO 100
200     next statement
```

Notice that the condition in the IF statement tells when to *exit* the loop: The statements are repeated *until* the condition is true.

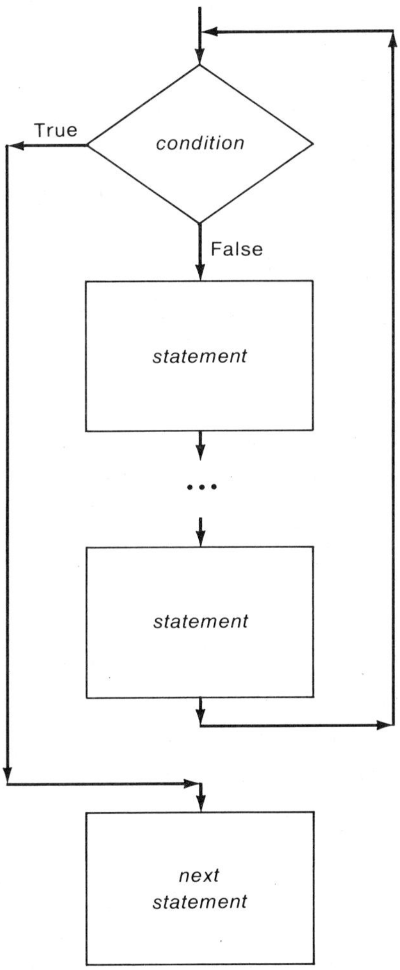


```
C    UNTIL THE CONDITION IS TRUE,
C    EXECUTE THE STATEMENTS IN
C    THE LOOP.
100       IF (condition) GO TO 200
              statement
              . . .
              statement
              GO TO 100
200       next statement
```

Figure I.3a A loop with the test at the beginning.

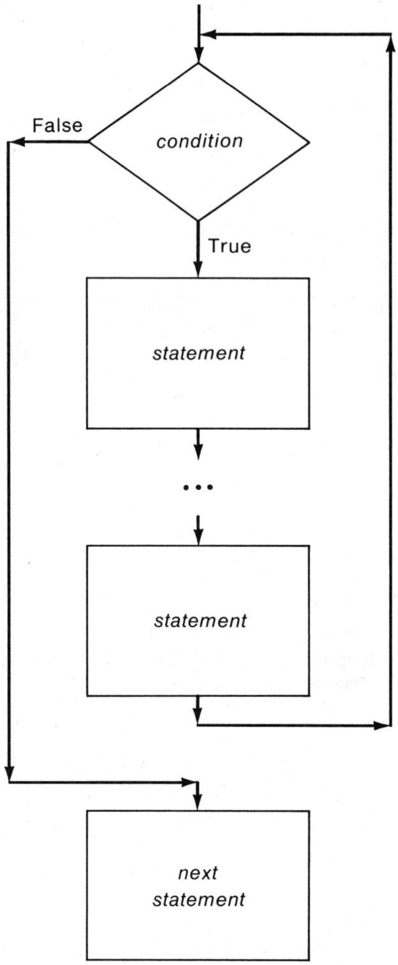


```
C   WHILE THE CONDITION IS TRUE,
C   EXECUTE THE STATEMENTS IN
C   THE LOOP.
100       IF ( .NOT. condition) GO TO 200
              statement
              . . .
              statement
              GO TO 100
200       next statement
```

Figure I.3b Another way of programming a loop with the test at the beginning.

You can regard this example in a slightly different way. If the "True" and "False" branches in the flowchart are reversed, as in Figure I.3b, the condition tells when to *continue* the loop: the statements are repeated *while* the condition is true. In this case, the general pattern is:

while some condition is true, do the following:
  statement 1
  statement 2
  . . .

which translates into FORTRAN statements of the form:

```
100     IF (.NOT. condition) GO TO 200
            statement 1
            statement 2
            . . .
            GO TO 100
200     next statement
```

CASE 3: A LOOP WITH THE TEST IN THE MIDDLE. In this case, the IF statement within the loop tells when to exit from the loop. This is illustrated in Figure I.4.

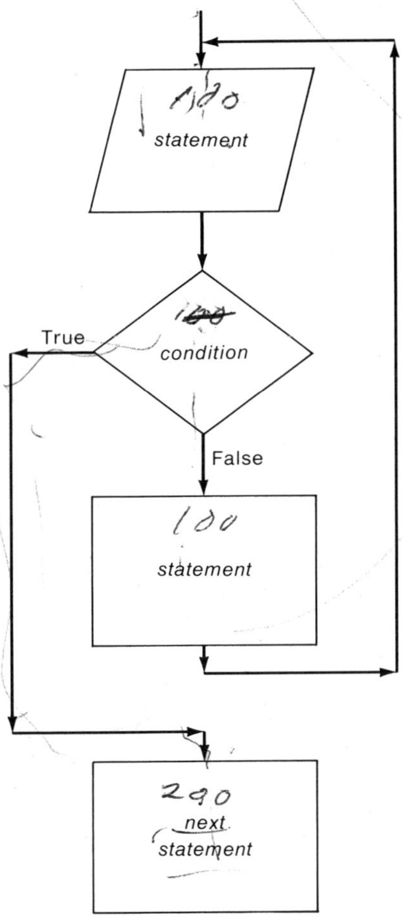


```
C
C    BREAK OUT OF THE LOOP
C    WHEN THE CONDITION IS TRUE
C
100         statement
            IF (condition) GO TO 200
            statement
            GO TO 100
200       next statement
```

Figure I.4 A loop with the test in the middle.

You will find that your programs will be easier to understand if you write loops following the form of Case 1 or Case 2. Sometimes it does not matter which of these methods you choose. There is one important difference to consider, though: In Case 1, the loop is always performed at least once (because the test is at the end); in Case 2, the loop might not be performed at all.

Loops with an exit in the middle, as in Case 3, tend to be more difficult to understand than those with the test at the beginning or the end. One common use for the Case 3 pattern is a loop containing an input statement followed by a test for the end of data, as illustrated in Figure I.4.

When writing a program loop, you should ask yourself two questions:

What, exactly, is the condition that determines when the loop is to be executed?

Should the test for this condition be made at the beginning or at the end of the loop (or possibly in the middle of it)?

We suggest the following:

---

3. If a program requires a loop to be executed one or more times, write the loop in the form shown in Figure I.2. If it is possible that in some cases the loop should not be executed at all, write it in the form shown in Figure I.3a or I.3b. Where possible, avoid using loops with an exit in the middle, as in Figure I.4.

There is a simple practice you can follow to improve the readability of program loops:

---

4. Indent all the statements that make up each program loop.

You can write the statements that make up the loop starting in column 11, for instance, instead of column 7. If your program has a loop within a loop, you can indent the statements in the outer loop by four spaces and indent the statements in the inner loop by eight spaces, and so on. This indentation does not affect the meaning of the statements, but it will make it easy to see at a glance just which statements are being repeated in each loop of your program.

Let us look now at some specific examples. We begin with a simple program that can be written four different ways.

EXAMPLE 1. Write a program to print the sum $1 + 2 + 3 + \cdots + 199 + 200$, using a program loop. The procedure is the same as you might use to perform this computation with paper and pencil. Start with the number 1; add 2; to the result, add 3; to that result, add 4; and so on. You use a variable NSUM to hold the total at each step. Another variable, N, is a counter that ranges from 1 to 200. On each iteration of the loop you add 1 to N, then add N to NSUM.

Figure I.5 shows a flowchart with the test at the end of the loop. When drawing a flowchart like this, it is easy to make a mistake in specifying how many times the loop is to be done. You should check that the loop is actually done 200 times. The value of N is initially 1, so on the first trip through the loop, NSUM = 0 + 1 = 1. Suppose N = 199. The program

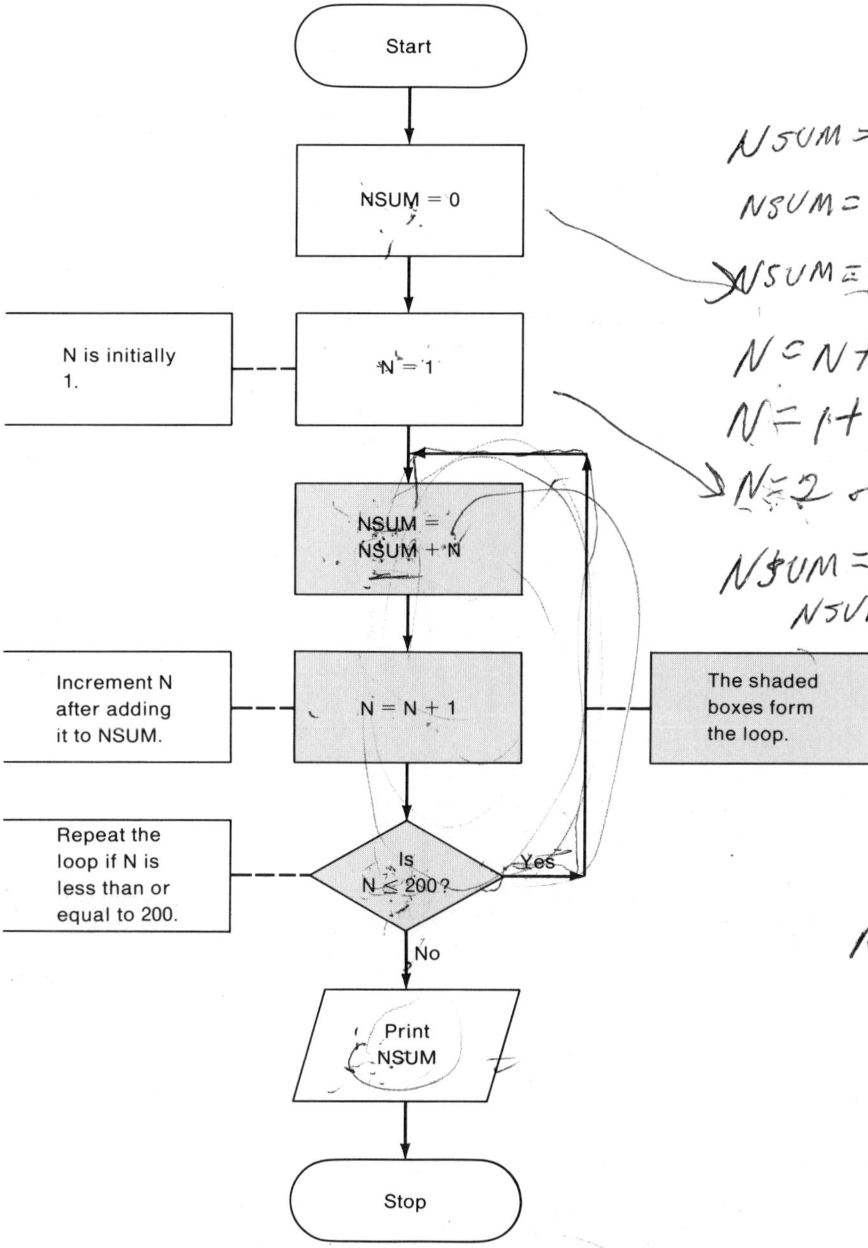

Figure I.5 Procedure to compute 1 + 2 + 3 + · · · + 199 + 200. In this method, the test is at the end of the loop, and the counter N is incremented *after* being added to NSUM.

adds 199 to NSUM in the first box of the loop, then add 1 to N, so N = 200. Notice that the condition in the diamond is still true, so the loop is repeated. Now the computer adds 200 to NSUM, and adds 1 to N, so N = 201. The condition in the diamond is now false, so you exit the loop. Thus, the first value added to NSUM is 1, and the last value added to NSUM is 200. Since N is incremented by 1 each time, the final value of NSUM must be $1 + 2 + 3 + \cdots + 199 + 200$. This is what you want. When making a flowchart or program loop, you should always ask yourself what happens on the first trip through the loop and on the last trip through the loop.

Following the pattern for loops with the test at the end, you can write the FORTRAN program from the flowchart as follows.

```
C    COMPUTE 1 + 2 + 3 + . . . + 199 + 200
C    METHOD 1
C
         NSUM = 0
         N = 1
10           NSUM = NSUM + N
             N = N + 1
         IF (N .LE. 200) GO TO 10
         PRINT, NSUM
         STOP
         END
```

The shaded statements form the loop corresponding to the shaded boxes in Figure I.5. Compare this with Figure I.2.

EXAMPLE 2. In Example 1, what if you were to increment the variable N *before* adding it to NSUM? In this case, the flowchart would look like Figure I.6. Besides switching the order of the rectangular boxes in the loop, there are two other important changes from the previous flowchart: The value of N is initially *zero* (not 1), and the loop is repeated if N is *less than* 200 (not less than or *equal to* 200). To understand why these changes are necessary, trace through the flowchart to see what happens the first and last times through the loop. The corresponding FORTRAN program follows the same basic pattern as before.

```
C    COMPUTE 1 + 2 + 3 + . . . + 199 + 200
C    METHOD 2—TEST AT THE END OF THE LOOP
C    INCREMENT THE COUNTER AT THE BEGINNING OF THE LOOP
C
         NSUM = 0
         N = 0
10           N = N + 1
             NSUM = NSUM + N
         IF (N .LT. 200) GO TO 10
         PRINT, NSUM
         STOP
         END
```

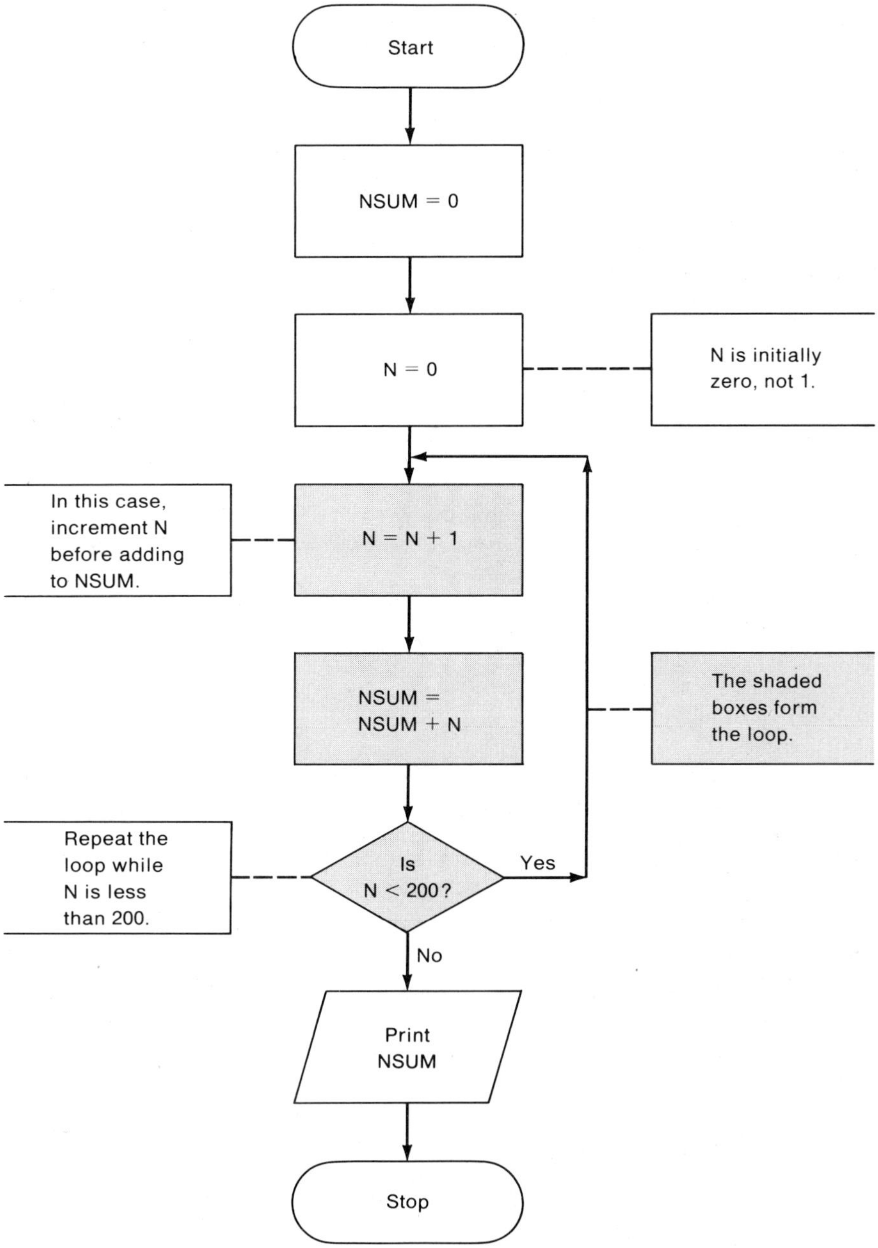

Figure I.6 Procedure to compute $1 + 2 + 3 + \cdots + 199 + 200$. In this method, the test is at the end of the loop, and the counter N is incremented *before* adding it to NSUM.

Method 2 gives the same result as Method 1, but it is a little harder to follow, and therefore it is more likely that you will make a mistake when using it. Our suggestion is:

---

5. When writing a loop controlled by a counter, increment the counter at the *end* of the loop.

EXAMPLE 3. Let us see how to write this same program with the test at the *beginning* of the loop. Figure I.7 shows a flowchart. N is initially equal to 1, the starting value. The test says to continue the loop while N is less than or equal to 200. In FORTRAN, you program this test with an IF statement of the form

```
IF (                    ) GO TO 20
```

Recall from our discussion of Case 2 that the condition in the IF statement tells when to *break out* of the loop. This is the opposite condition of when to *continue* the loop. Thus, you can write the IF statement as follows:

```
IF (.NOT. N .LE. 200) GO TO 20
```

Another way to write the IF statement is:

```
IF (N .GT. 200) GO TO 20
```

This means the same thing, since if N is not less than or equal to 200, N must be greater than 200. Use whichever form you find easier. Here is the complete program.

```
C     COMPUTE 1 + 2 + 3 + · · · + 199 + 200
C     METHOD 3—TEST AT THE BEGINNING OF THE LOOP
C
      NSUM = 0
      N = 1
10    IF (.NOT. N .LE. 200) GO TO 20
         NSUM = NSUM + N
         N = N + 1
         GO TO 10
20    PRINT, NSUM
      STOP
      END
```

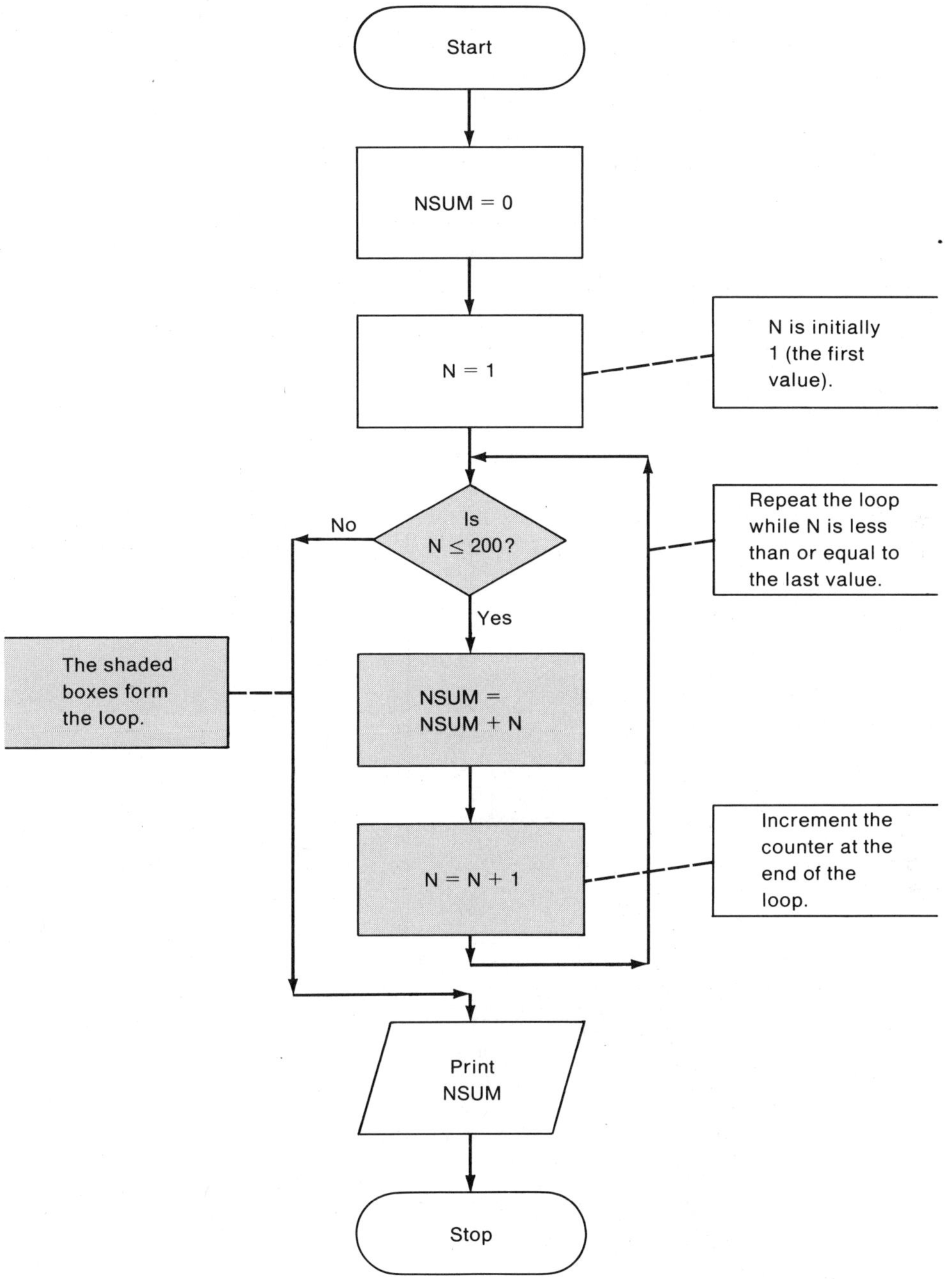

Figure I.7 Procedure to compute $1 + 2 + 3 + \cdots + 199 + 200$. In this method, the test is at the *beginning* of the loop.

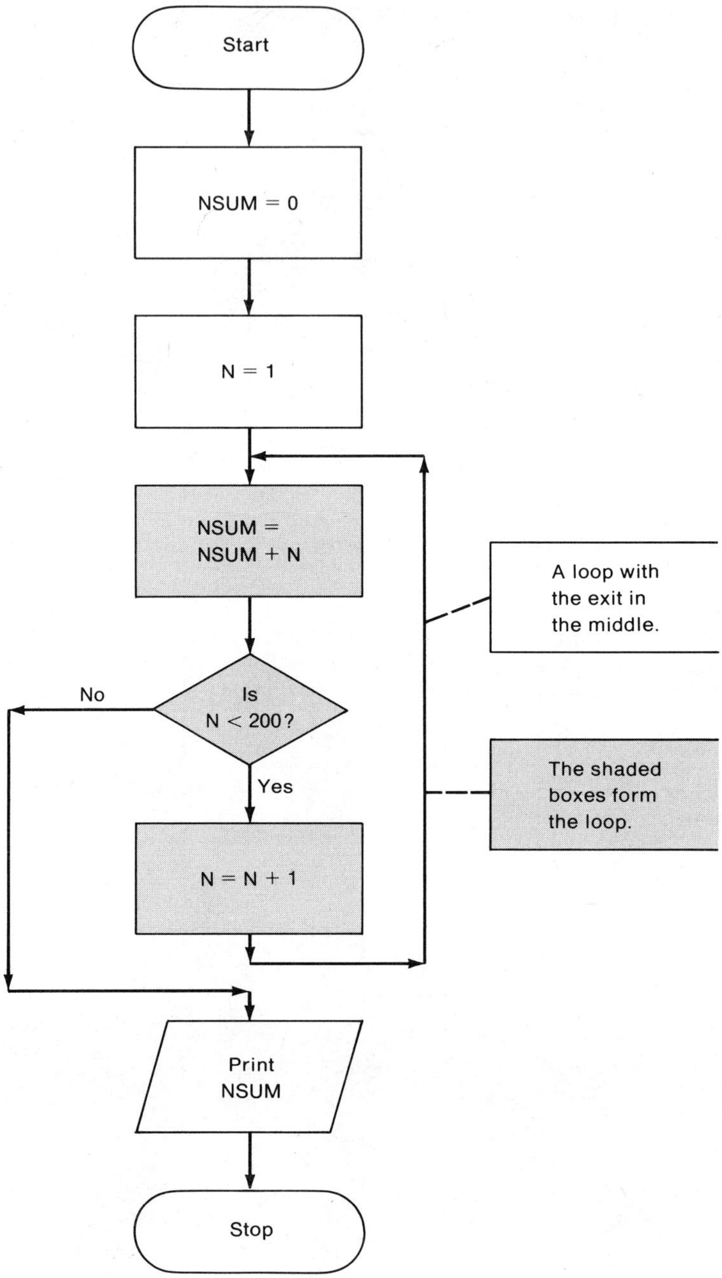

Figure I.8 Procedure to compute $1 + 2 + 3 + \cdots + 199 + 200$. Here, the test is in the *middle* of the loop. This method is not recommended.

EXAMPLE 4. Here is one more way to write this same program.

```
C    COMPUTE 1 + 2 + 3 + · · · + 199 + 200
C    METHOD 4
C
           NSUM = 0
           N = 1
10             NSUM = NSUM + N
               IF (.NOT. N .LT. 200) GO TO 20
               N = N + 1
               GO TO 10
20         PRINT, NSUM
           STOP
           END
```

Here, the test is in the middle of the loop, as shown in the flowchart in Figure I.8. This method is correct, but it is a little harder to follow and is not recommended. When possible, put the IF statement at the beginning of the loop or at the end of it.

Style in programming, as in writing or speaking, is a matter of choosing among alternative ways of saying the same thing. You have just seen four ways to solve a simple programming problem. There is no absolute "best" way to write any program; but there are different ways, and some are better than others. Our suggestion is simply this:

---

6. Consider the alternatives. If your program seems too complicated or difficult to understand, try rewriting it a different way.

In Chapter 5, you saw that the condition in an IF statement can compare integer expressions or real expressions. When comparing real expressions, watch out for a pitfall that is illustrated in the next two examples.

EXAMPLE 5. In Chapter 2 (page 47), you saw a program to convert a Fahrenheit temperature to the equivalent Celsius temperature. We used the formula

```
CELS = 5.0/9.0 * (FAREN − 32.0)
```

Suppose nurse wants a conversion table listing Fahrenheit temperatures and their Celsius equivalents for each tenth of a degree Fahrenheit in the range 95°F to 105°F. Write a program to print this table. The output will look like this:

```
95.0    35.00
95.1    35.06
```

95.2	35.11
95.3	35.22
(etc.)	(etc.)
104.8	40.44
104.9	40.50
105.0	40.56

You can start with a value 95.0 for FAREN. Within a program loop, you calculate CELS, print the values of FAREN and CELS, then add 0.1 to FAREN and repeat the loop while FAREN is less than or equal to 105.0. Figure I.9 shows this procedure. Here is the FORTRAN program.

```
C   PRINT A TEMPERATURE CONVERSION TABLE
          FAREN = 95.0
100           CELS = 5.0/9.0 * (FAREN - 32.0)
              PRINT, FAREN, CELS
              FAREN = FAREN + 0.1
          IF (FAREN .LT. 105.1) GO TO 100
          STOP
          END
```

EXAMPLE 6. Here is another program, very similar to the one in Example 5.

```
C   TEMPERATURE CONVERSION TABLE
C   (INCORRECT METHOD)
          FAREN = 95.0
100           CELS = 5.0/9.0 * (FAREN - 32.0)
              PRINT, FAREN, CELS
              FAREN = FAREN + 0.1
              IF (FAREN .EQ. 105.1) STOP
              GO TO 100
          END
```

This appears to be an equivalent program. The first time through the loop, FAREN = 95.0. The loop is repeated, adding 0.1 to FAREN each time, until finally FAREN = 105.1, and the program stops.

Unfortunately, the program would probably *not* work this way. The reason is that no computer can represent all real numbers exactly; there is (or may be) a slight error in arithmetic involving real numbers. Mathematically, on the 102nd trip through the loop, the value of FAREN should be exactly 105.1. In fact, it is only *approximately* 105.1: it will be a very close approximation—say, 105.099999, but it will probably not be exactly 105.1. Thus, the condition in the IF statement is false, the program will not stop, and the loop repeats

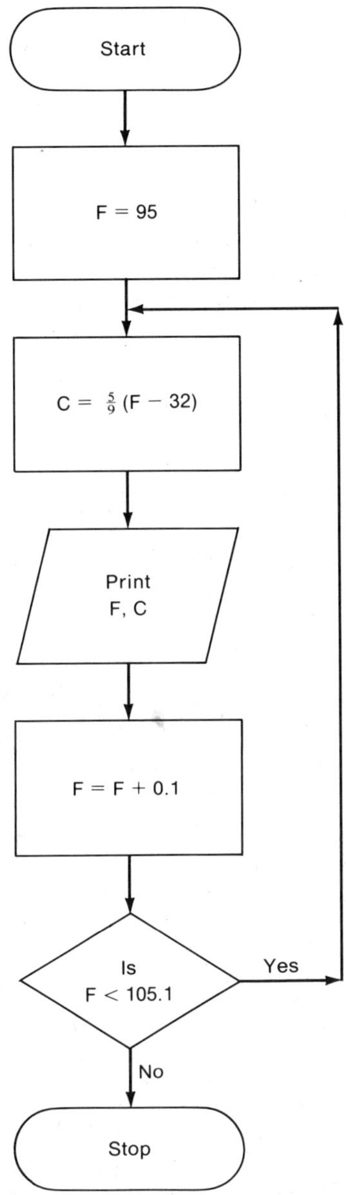

Figure I.9 Temperature conversion table.

again, with FAREN approximately equal to 105.2. The program is stuck in a loop. It will run forever unless the computer operator manually stops it by pressing a button. (Often, the computer operating system will be set up to stop student programs automatically if they run longer than a few seconds.)

To avoid this problem, you should observe the following practice:

---

7. Do not use the forms

IF (*A* .EQ. *B*) *statement*
IF (*A* .NE. *B*) *statement*

when *A* and *B* are real expressions. Rewrite the program to use one of the forms:

IF (*A* .LT. *B*) . . .

or

IF (*A* .LE. *B*) . . .

or

IF (*A* .GT. *B*) . . .

or

IF (*A* .GE. *B*) . . .

This rule is not a restriction of FORTRAN, and there are exceptions to it, but you must take care to avoid loops that never terminate.

An exception to this rule is illustrated by the following statements:

```
READ, T
IF (T .EQ. 0.0) STOP
```

The variable T is not computed by an assignment statement; it is defined by the READ statement, so there is no computational error involved. If a value 0 is read, the condition in the IF statement is true, and the program stops.

EXAMPLE 7. Another way to write the temperature conversion program is to use an integer variable to count the number of times the loop is done. Because integer values are exact, there is no round-off error.

In the following version of the program, we use the integer variable N to count the number of times the loop is done. Start with N = 0. On this first iteration, FAREN is 95.0. On the second iteration, N = 1 and FAREN = 95.1. On the last iteration, N = 100 and FAREN = 105.0. In fact, for any N, you can calculate FAREN from the formula

FAREN = 95.0 + FLOAT(N)/10.0

Recall that FLOAT is a built-in function that converts an integer value to real. This is the most precise way to compute FAREN, since it eliminates the cumulative round-off error that results from adding 0.1 to FAREN on each iteration. Using this method, you can write the program as follows.

```
C    PRINT A TEMPERATURE CONVERSION TABLE.
C    THIS METHOD USES AN INTEGER VARIABLE TO
C    COUNT THE ITERATIONS.
C
           N = 0
100           FAREN = 95.0 + FLOAT(N)/10.0
              CELS = 5.0/9.0 * (FAREN - 32.0)
              PRINT, FAREN, CELS
              N = N + 1
           IF (N .LE. 100) GO TO 100
           STOP
           END
```

Writing a Decision

A decision in a flowchart may control a loop, or it may just select among alternative paths. You have seen several ways to write a loop in FORTRAN. Similarly, for deciding among alternatives there are a few basic patterns you can follow.

Figure I.10 shows four types of decisions. In the flowchart in Figure I.10a, a single statement is conditionally executed. In Figure I.10b, the decision chooses between two statements. In Figure I.10c, a whole series of statements is either executed or skipped. Figure I.10d shows two paths, each consisting of a whole series of statements. The two paths converge to a common point. You can flowchart any decision in one of these forms. Let us see how to program each one in FORTRAN.

CASE 1: CONDITIONALLY EXECUTE A SINGLE STATEMENT. This is the easiest case to program in FORTRAN, because it is exactly what the IF statement does, as shown in Figure 5.1 (pages 94–95).

CASE 2: CONDITIONALLY EXECUTE ONE OF TWO STATEMENTS. You saw a decision of this type in Example 1 of Chapter 5 (page 97) where we programmed the procedure: "If A is

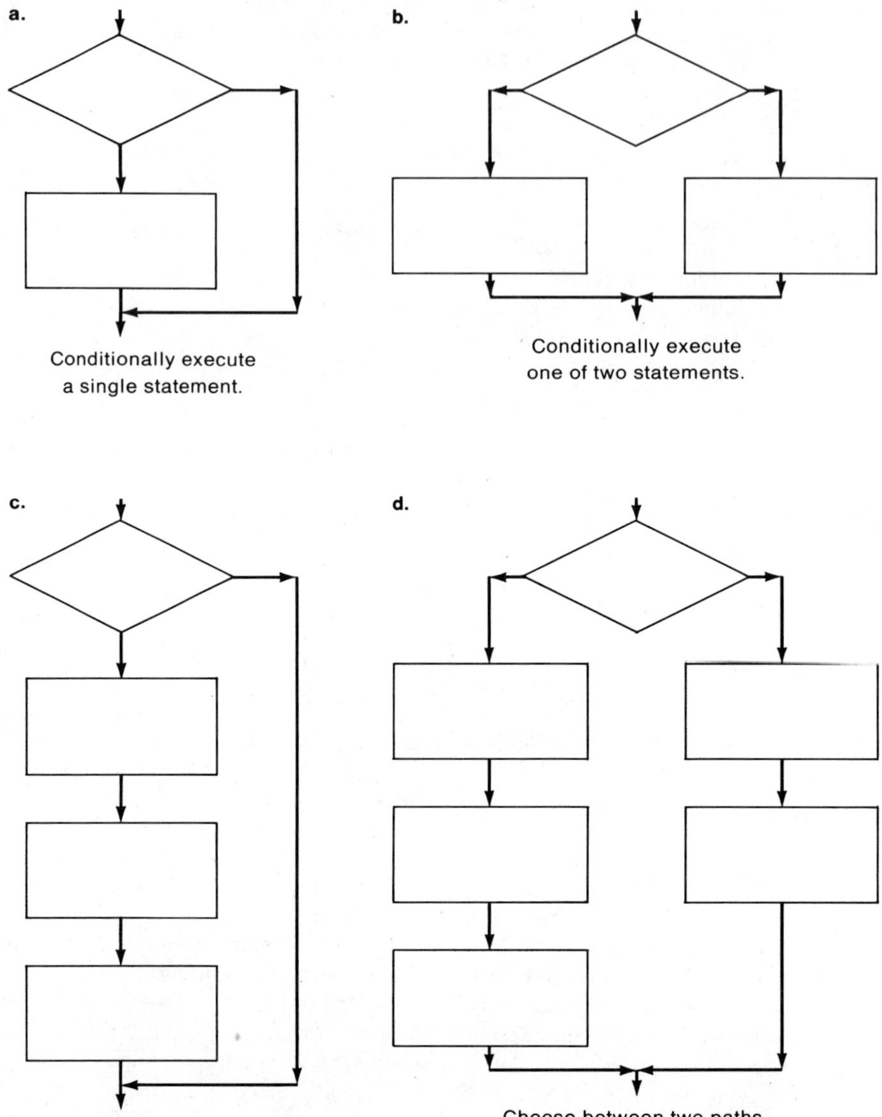

a. Conditionally execute a single statement.

b. Conditionally execute one of two statements.

c. Conditionally execute a series of statements.

d. Choose between two paths.

Figure I.10 Four types of decisions.

greater than B, print A; otherwise, print B." The general form is

if some condition is true,
    statement 1
else
    statement 2

as shown in Figure I.11. The easiest way to write this in FORTRAN is to use two IF statements in the form

IF (*condition*) *statement 1*
IF (.NOT. *condition*) *statement 2*

The condition in the second IF is the opposite of the condition in the first IF, so one condition or the other is always true. This method is not exactly the one indicated by the flowchart, since you use two decisions in FORTRAN where the flowchart uses one decision. But if you use a single IF statement, then you need to use two GO TO statements, as we saw in Example 1 of Chapter 5.

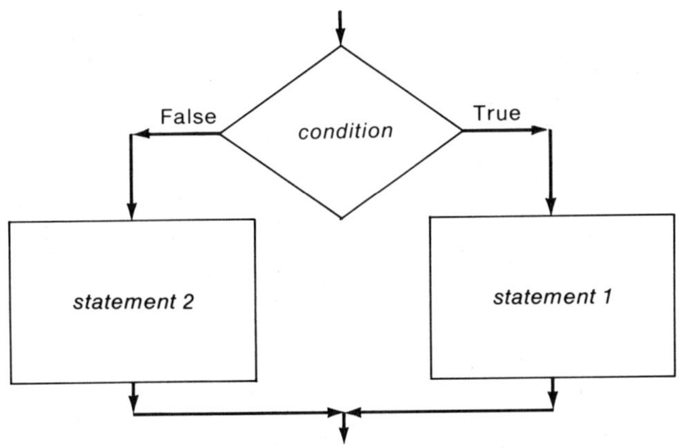

IF (*condition*) *statement 1*
IF (.NOT. *condition*) *statement 2*

Figure I.11 A two-branch decision can be programmed with two IF statements.

CASE 3: CONDITIONALLY EXECUTE A SERIES OF STATEMENTS. The general form here is

if some condition is true,
    statement 1
    statement 2
    . . .

That is, you want to execute several statements if the condition is true and bypass them otherwise, as shown in Figure I.12. To write this in FORTRAN, you can use the form

```
          IF (.NOT. condition) GO TO 100
             statement 1
             statement 2
             . . .
  100     next statement
```

As with program loops, you will find your programs more readable if you indent the statements that are conditionally executed.

CASE 4: CHOOSE BETWEEN TWO PATHS. The general form here is:

```
          if some condition is true,
             statement 1
             statement 2
             . . .
          else
             statement 3
             statement 4
             . . .
```

That is, there are two groups of statements, and you want to execute one group or the other depending on the condition, as shown in Figure I.13. To write this in FORTRAN, you can use the form

```
          IF (.NOT. condition) GO TO 200
             statement 1
             statement 2
             . . .
          GO TO 300
  200        statement 3
             statement 4
             . . .
  300     next statement
```

EXAMPLE 8. Dingle's Drugstore has compiled sales figures for each item in their inventory. For each item in stock, they have prepared a data card containing three numbers:

1. The inventory number of the item (an integer)
2. The dollar amount of sales of this item last year
3. The dollar amount of sales of this item this year

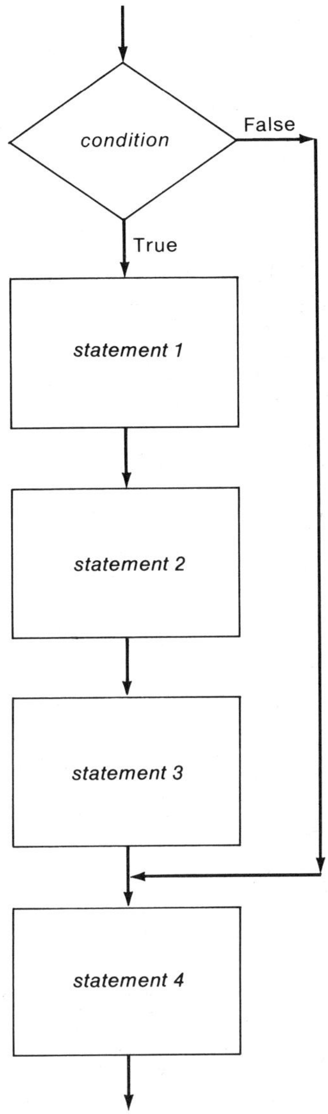


```
      IF (.NOT. condition) GO TO 100
         statement 1
         statement 2
         statement 3
100   statement 4
```

Figure I.12 A decision that conditionally executes more than one statement is programmed using a GO TO statement.

Last year's sales might be zero if it is a new item; this year's sales might be zero if it is a discontinued item. Write a program that will compute the percent increase in sales for each item.

You can read a data card with the statement

```
READ, INVEN, AOLD, ANEW
```

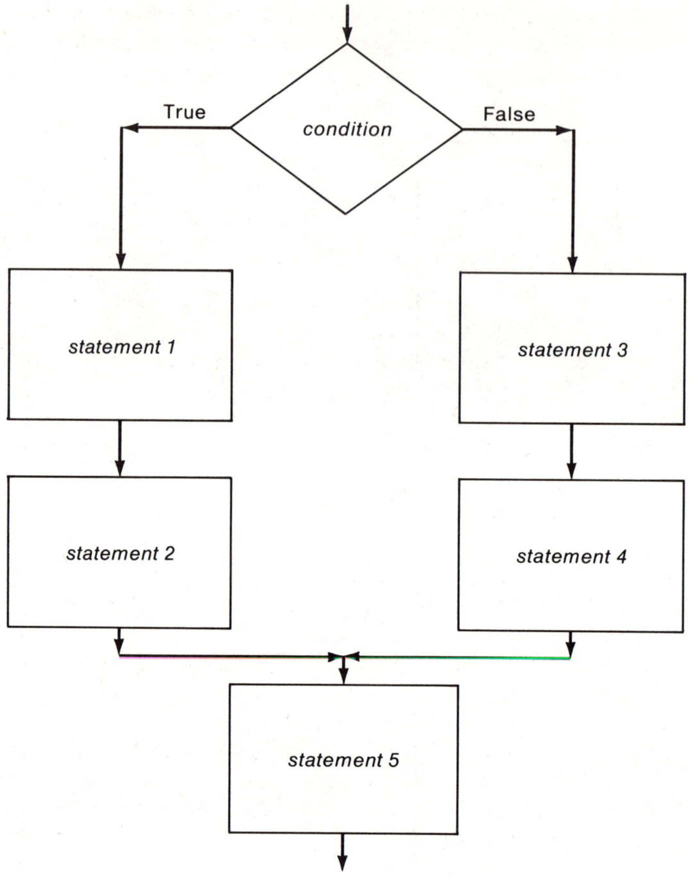


```
      IF (.NOT. condition) GO TO 200
         statement 1
         statement 2
      GO TO 300
200      statement 3
         statement 4
300   statement 5
```

Figure I.13 A choice between two paths is programmed with two GO TO statements.

storing last year's sales and this year's sales in AOLD and ANEW. Assume that AOLD and ANEW are not both zero. Include an extra data card at the end with three zero values, and stop the program when this card is read. You can use the statement

```
IF (AOLD .EQ. 0.0 .AND. ANEW .EQ. 0.0) STOP
```

The percent increase in sales is found by subtracting the old sales from the new sales and dividing the result by the old sales. To express it as a percentage, you multiply by 100. The FORTRAN statement for this is

```
PCTINC = 100.0*(ANEW - AOLD)/AOLD
```

If the new sales are less than the old sales, then PCTINC will be a negative number, representing the percent decrease in sales.

Here is a complete program to compute the percent increase.

```
10    READ, INVEN, AOLD, ANEW
      IF (AOLD .EQ. 0.0 .AND. ANEW .EQ. 0.0) STOP
      PCTINC = 100.0*(ANEW - AOLD)/AOLD
      PRINT, INVEN, AOLD, ANEW, PCTINC
      GO TO 10
      END
```

What would happen if this program read a card on which the amount of last year's sales were zero? AOLD would be zero when the assignment statement was executed. Mathematically, division by zero is undefined. On a computer, it will result in an error during program execution. On most systems, the program will print some error message, then stop running. This is a serious flaw in the program.

A better method is to test the value of AOLD before computing PCTINC. If AOLD is zero, print the values of INVEN, AOLD, and ANEW, then read the next card; otherwise, compute PCTINC and print all four values. Figure I.14 shows a flowchart for this procedure.

The FORTRAN program can be written following the pattern in Figure I.13.

```
C   INVENTORY PROGRAM
C   INVEN = INVENTORY NUMBER
C   AOLD = AMOUNT OF LAST YEAR'S SALES
C   ANEW = AMOUNT OF THIS YEAR'S SALES
C   READ SALES FIGURES
10    READ, INVEN, AOLD, ANEW
      IF (AOLD .EQ. 0.0 .AND. ANEW .EQ. 0.0) STOP
C   IF AOLD IS NOT ZERO, COMPUTE THE PERCENT INCREASE
      IF (AOLD .EQ. 0.0) GO TO 20
         PCTINC = 100.0*(ANEW - AOLD)/AOLD
         PRINT, INVEN, AOLD, ANEW, PCTINC
      GO TO 30
20       PRINT, INVEN, AOLD, ANEW
30    GO TO 10
      END
```

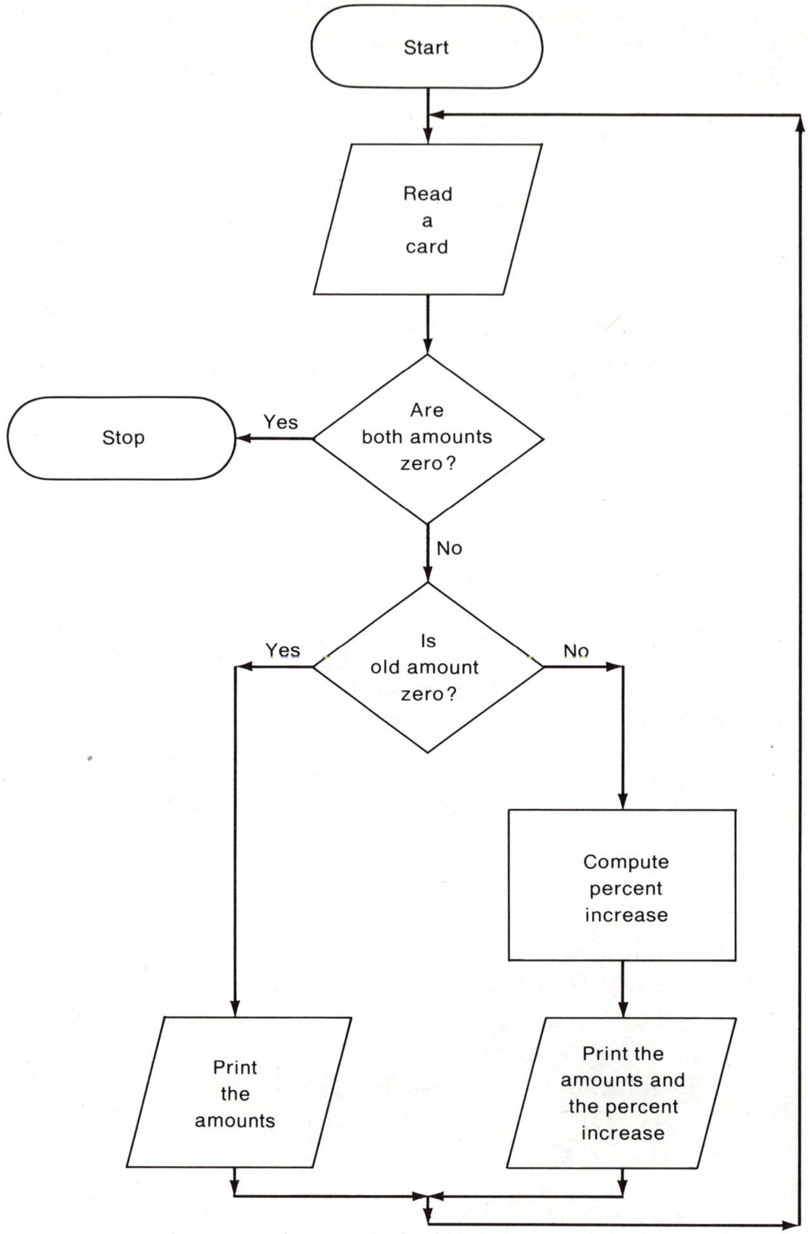

Figure I.14 Procedure to compute percent increases.

The program follows the form given in Case 4 for a decision to choose between paths. In this case, a simplification is possible. The statement

```
GO TO 30
```

branches to the end of the loop, which happens to be a GO TO statement that branches to the beginning of the loop. You could just as well replace the statement GO TO 30 with one that says GO TO 10.

Another good way to handle expressions like the formula for PCTINC is to decide on a value for the undefined case. You might decide that if AOLD is zero, you will assign the value zero to PCTINC and print it. Following this method, a simpler version of the program can be written using the pattern of Case 2.

```
C   INVENTORY PROGRAM
C   INVEN = INVENTORY NUMBER.
C   AOLD = AMOUNT OF LAST YEAR'S SALES.
C   ANEW = AMOUNT OF THIS YEAR'S SALES.
C   READ DATA AND COMPUTE THE PERCENT INCREASE IN SALES.
10      READ, INVEN, AOLD, ANEW
        IF (AOLD .EQ. 0.0 .AND. ANEW .EQ. 0.0) STOP
        IF (AOLD .EQ. 0.0) PCTINC = 0.0
        IF (AOLD .NE. 0.0) PCTINC = 100.0*(ANEW - AOLD)/AOLD
        PRINT, INVEN, AOLD, ANEW, PCTINC
        GO TO 10
        END
```

A final note about this program: The statements

```
IF (AOLD .EQ. 0.0) PCTINC = 0.0
IF (AOLD .NE. 0.0) PCTINC = 100.0*(ANEW - AOLD)/AOLD
```

mean, set PCTINC equal to zero if AOLD is zero, and compute PCTINC from the formula otherwise. An equivalent way of doing this computation is:

```
PCTINC = 0.0
IF (AOLD .NE. 0.0) PCTINC = 100.0*(ANEW - AOLD)/AOLD
```

We give PCTINC the "default" value of zero, then we redefine its value if AOLD is not zero. This is a common programming trick. It may seem redundant to set PCTINC equal to zero when we are usually going to redefine its value immediately afterward, but on most computers simple assignment statements can be executed faster than comparisons, so the second method is just as good as the first, if not better.

Writing a Chain of Decisions

Often you need to use a whole series of decisions in a procedure: for instance, in choosing among three or more alternative paths. The flowchart in Figure I.15 shows a procedure of the form

```
if condition 1 is true,
    statement 1
else, if condition 2 is true,
    statement 2
else, if condition 3 is true,
    statement 3
else,
    statement 4
```

In FORTRAN, a good way to write this is:

```
      IF (condition 1) GO TO 10
      IF (condition 2) GO TO 20
      IF (condition 3) GO TO 30
      GO TO 40
10        statement 1
      GO TO 100
20        statement 2
      GO TO 100
30        statement 3
      GO TO 100
40        statement 4
100   next statement
```

The same pattern can be used for any number of decision diamonds and any number of statements on each branch.

EXAMPLE 9. Table I.1 shows a hypothetical schedule for figuring income tax. Write a program to read values of income and compute the corresponding tax.

Table I.1 Hypothetical Schedule for Figuring Income Tax

If Income Is at Least	*But Less Than*	*Tax Is*
$0	$1000	5% of income
1000	2000	$ 50 + 15% of amount over $1000
2000	3000	200 + 20% of amount over 2000
3000	4500	400 + 30% of amount over 3000
greater than 4500		850 + 40% of amount over 4500

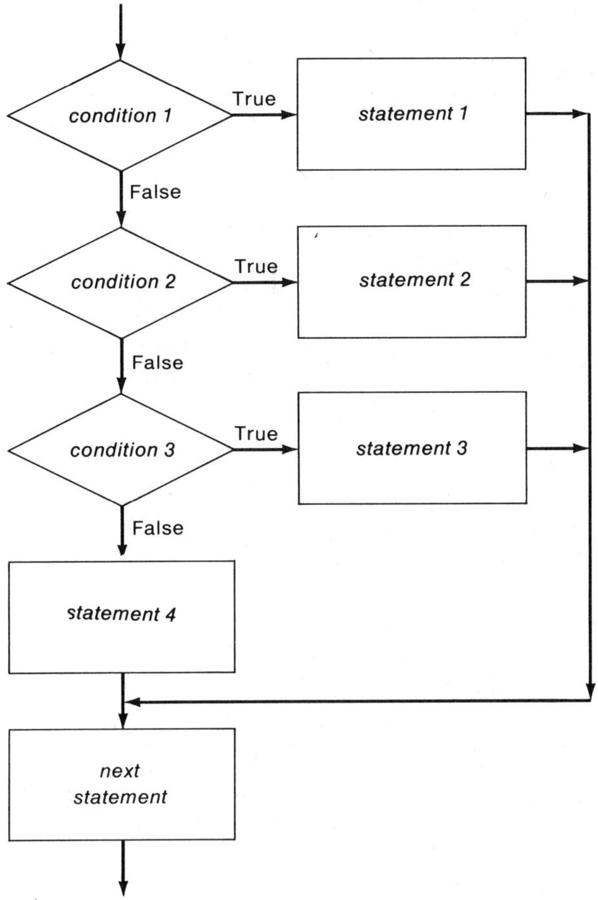


```
      IF (condition 1) GO TO 10
      IF (condition 2) GO TO 20
      IF (condition 3) GO TO 30
      GO TO 40
10       statement 1
      GO TO 100
20       statement 2
      GO TO 100
30       statement 3
      GO TO 100
40       statement 4
100   next statement
```

Figure I.15 A chain of decisions: If condition1 is true, do statement 1; otherwise, if condition 2 is true, do statement 2; otherwise, if condition 3 is true, do statement 3; otherwise, do statement 4.

Figure I.16 shows a flowchart for this procedure. Following the pattern outlined in Figure I.15, you can write the FORTRAN program as follows.

```
C    TAX CALCULATION.
          B1 = 0.0
          B2 = 1000.00
          B3 = 2000.00
          B4 = 3000.00
          B5 = 4500.00
C    READ EARNINGS. IF THEY ARE NEGATIVE, STOP.
C         OTHERWISE, COMPUTE THE TAX, PRINT IT, AND
C         REPEAT THE PROCEDURE.
100       READ, EARN
          IF (EARN .LT. 0.0) GO TO 300
          IF (B1 .LE. EARN .AND. EARN .LT. B2) GO TO 110
          IF (B2 .LE. EARN .AND. EARN .LT. B3) GO TO 120
          IF (B3 .LE. EARN .AND. EARN .LT. B4) GO TO 130
          IF (B4 .LE. EARN .AND. EARN .LT. B5) GO TO 140
          GO TO 150
C    --TAX BRACKET 1
110            TAX = 0.05 * EARN
               GO TO 200
C    --TAX BRACKET 2
120            TAX = 50.00 + 0.15 * (EARN - 1000.00)
               GO TO 200
C    --TAX BRACKET 3
130            TAX = 200.00 + 0.20 * (EARN - 2000.00)
               GO TO 200
C    --TAX BRACKET 4
140            TAX = 400.00 + 0.30 * (EARN - 3000.00)
               GO TO 200
C    --TAX BRACKET 5
150            TAX = 850.00 + 0.40 * (EARN - 4500.00)
C
200            PRINT, EARN, TAX
               GO TO 100
300       STOP
          END
```

As a matter of style, we used variables B1, B2, . . . to store the cut-off values for the various tax brackets. It is often more convenient to treat constants in a program as though

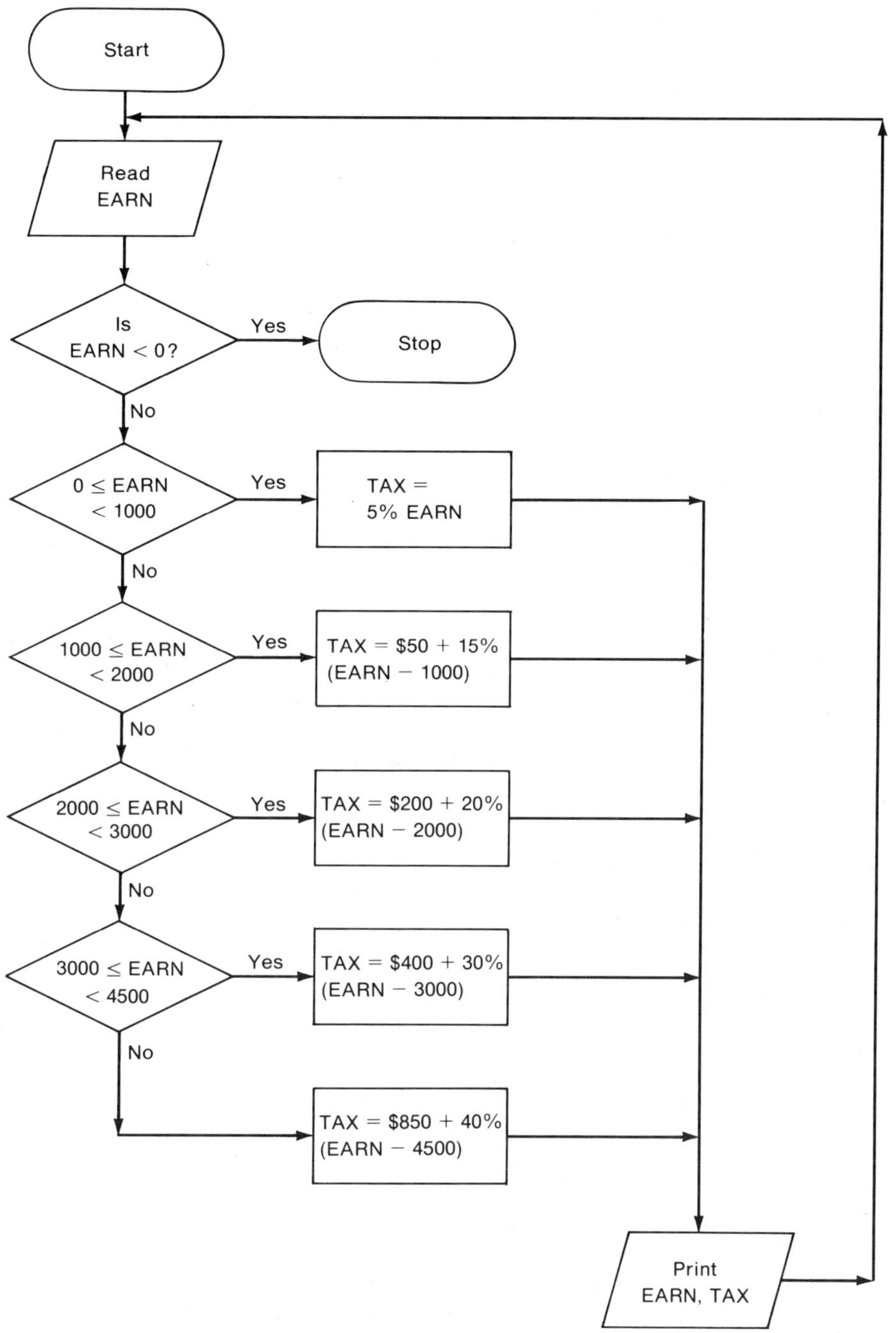

Figure I.16 Procedure for computing income tax.

they were variables. When names are given to the constants in this way, the program becomes more readable, reducing the chance of making an error through a typographical mistake. This practice also makes a program easier to modify.

Reliability

This unit has emphasized that a good program should be clearly written and easy to understand. An equally important criterion of good programming style is *reliability*. A program should work correctly not just some of the time, but all of the time.

Example 8 illustrated an important point about program reliability:

---

8. In any computation involving division, insure that your program will never divide by zero.

Even if you "know" that in a certain computation the denominator should never be zero, it is a good idea to include a test to make absolutely sure that it is not. You might have made a keypunch error when preparing your data, or you might have forgotten to initialize some variable in your program, or you might have made a mistake in reasoning in some part of your program. Any one of these mistakes could cause an unexpected division by zero. By including your own error-checking procedures, you can prevent such unexpected errors from halting your program and you can make it much easier to find the cause of the problem.

Division by zero is one common error that can cause a program to malfunction. In Chapter 8 we will discuss subscript range errors, one of the most insidious bugs for FORTRAN programmers to guard against. There are numerous other pitfalls to watch for, and we shall point them out as we proceed. The general principle to keep in mind is this:

---

9. Make your program foolproof. Anticipate error conditions that could cause it to malfunction, and include checking procedures to prevent such errors from occurring.

Be cautious: Do not make any unnecessary assumptions about the correctness of the program or the input data. Any potential source of error you overlook when writing the program will probably have to be dealt with when you are debugging it. A popular adage, known as Murphy's Law, should be familiar to every programmer: If anything *can* go wrong, it *will*.

Exercises

Write a flowchart for each of the following English sentences, then write the corresponding FORTRAN statements.

1. If X is negative, then add 1 to J.
2. If X is negative or zero, then add 1 to J and set X equal to 1.

3. If X is negative, then add 1 to J; otherwise, subtract 1 from J.
4. If I and J are equal, set C equal to 1; otherwise, set C equal to zero.
5. Unless X is zero, set Y equal to 1 divided by X.
6. While $K < 10$, add K to SUM and add 1 to K.
7. Until $A > 1$, multiply A by I; however, do not perform this procedure unless $A > 0$ and $I > 1$.
8. Read a value for A; and, if A is not equal to ENDATA, set X equal to X times B plus A, and repeat this procedure; otherwise, print X.
9. Set Y and K equal to 1; then, while Y is less than X, multiply Y by 2 and add 1 to K.
10. If D is less than zero, set X1 and X2 equal to A, set Y1 equal to B, and set Y2 equal to the negative of B; otherwise, set X1 equal to A plus B, set X2 equal to A minus B, and set Y1 and Y2 equal to zero.

Write a FORTRAN program for each of the following exercises.

11. Read a temperature T. If T is between 10° and 45°, then T represents a Celsius temperature; so convert it to Fahrenheit with the formula $TNEW = (9/5)T + 32$. If T is between 50° and 115°, then T represents a Fahrenheit temperature; so convert it to Celsius with the formula $TNEW = 5/9(T - 32)$. Output the values of T and TNEW with the statement

```
PRINT, T, TNEW
```

If the value of T does not fall in either of these ranges, the program should stop.

12. Example 9 showed one way to perform the tax calculation. Another way is to use four successive IF statements:

```
IF (EARN .GE. 1000.) TAX = . . .
IF (EARN .GE. 2000.) . . .
IF . . .
IF . . .
```

The dots indicate parts of the statements that you must supply. Rewrite the program on page 140 in this way. Now do the same thing using the following pattern for the IF statements.

```
      IF (EARN .GE. 1000.) GO TO 20
         TAX = 0.05 * EARN
         GO TO 100
20    IF (EARN .GE. 2000.) GO TO 30
         TAX = . . .
         GO TO . . .
30    IF( . . . ) . . .
         . . .
```

13. In computing the value of inventory in a retail store, it is common practice to list either the cost or the current market value, whichever is lower. In words, if the price paid per unit is less than the current price per unit, the value of the stock is the price paid per unit times the number of units; if the price paid is greater than the current price, then the value is the current price times the number of units. Write a program to read a set of data cards with four numbers on each card:
    a. The identification number for the item (an integer)
    b. The number of units of the item in stock
    c. The price paid per unit when the company bought the item
    d. The current market price of one unit of the item

    Compute and print the inventory value of each type of item. When a data card is read having a unit identification number zero, print the total value of the inventory, then stop.

14. At a certain bank, the monthly service charge on checking accounts is
    $0.10 per check for the first five checks
    $0.09 per check for the next five checks
    $0.07 per check on all checks thereafter

    Read a check amount, and print the check amount with the service charge, SC.
    To compute SC, you will have to count the checks as they are read. Continue this until reading a value of zero for a check. Then print the total amount of the checks and the total service charge.

15. Suppose you want to save some money each month in a savings account. Write a program that will print out the amount you will have on a given date in the future. Use the following procedure.
    a. Read A, the present amount of your savings.
    b. Read RANUL, the annual interest rate, expressed in percent (e.g., RANUL = 6.2 for an annual rate of 6.2%).
    c. Read N, the number of months, and DEP, the amount of deposit to be made at the beginning of each month.
    d. If N is negative or zero, stop the program
    e. Otherwise, compute the monthly interest rate R as
       R = RANUL/1200
    f. Compute the new amount of your savings with the statement
       A = A * (1 + R) ** N + DEP * ((1 + R) ** N − 1)/R * (1 + R)
       Print out this amount.
    g. Go back to step c.

16. Modify the program in Exercise 15 as follows. Instead of reading the number of months N in step c, read a date in the form MM, YYYY. For example, December 1999 would be read as 12,1999. Before step a, you will have to read in the current date, in the same form. The program will compute the amount of savings as of the end of the month specified.

17. Print all combinations of two different integers, I and J, both of which are between 1 and N (inclusive), where N is read as input. For example, if N = 3, the combinations are

```
1, 2
1, 3
2, 3
```

In counting combinations, the pair 1, 2 is counted as the same combination 2, 1, so you should not print the pair 2, 1 as a different combination. The following flowchart shows a procedure you can use.

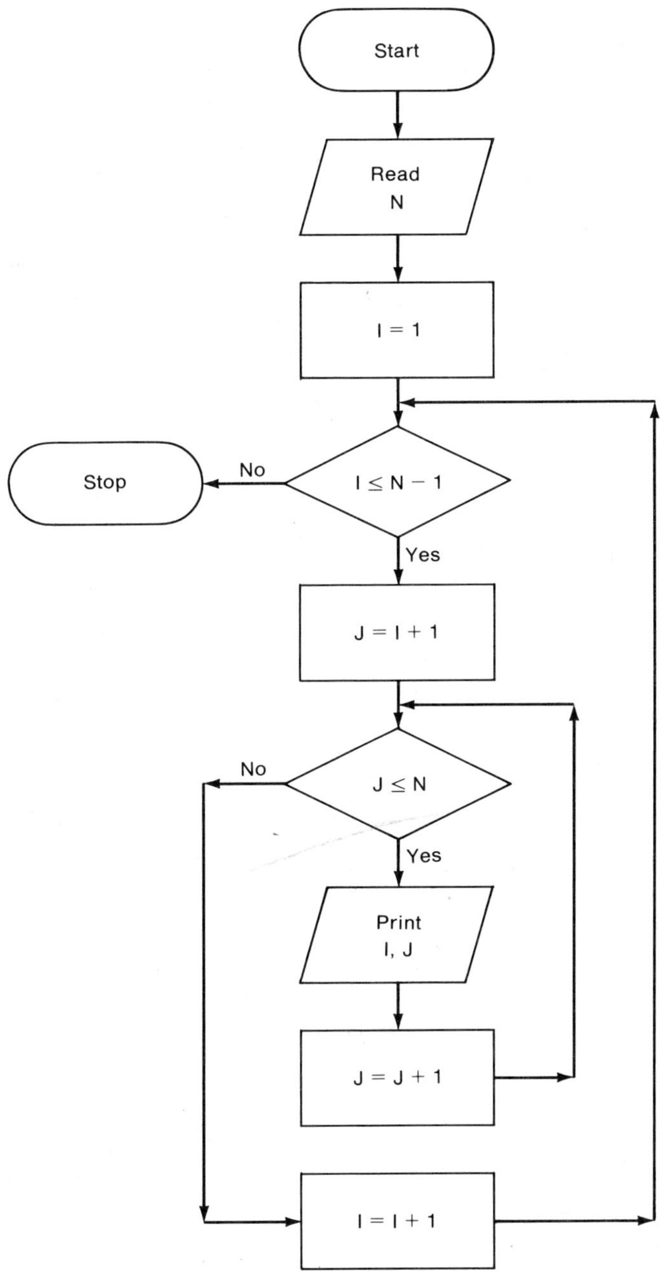

This procedure uses a loop within a loop. You can write an outline of the main part of the procedure in the following form.

```
I = 1
while I ≤ N − 1, do the following:
  J = I + 1
  while J ≤ N, do the following:
    print I and J
    J = J + 1
  I = I + 1
```

Write a complete FORTRAN program based on this procedure.

18. Write a program to print all combinations of three different integers, I, J, and K, all of which are between 1 and N (inclusive), where N is read as input. This is an extension of Exercise 17. Before writing the FORTRAN program, make an outline like the one in Exercise 17.

19. The *greatest common divisor* of two positive integers is the greatest number that divides both of them evenly. For example, the greatest common divisor of 35 and 21 is 7. **Euclid's algorithm** is a famous method invented by the Greek mathematician Euclid (circa 300 B.C.) for finding the greatest common divisor of two numbers. The flowchart on page 147 describes the algorithm.

    You can write an outline of this procedure in the following form.

```
read M and N
while N ≠ 0, do the following:
  KREM = MOD(M, N)
  M = N
  N = KREM
print M
```

    Write a FORTRAN program to perform this computation.

20. The **ideal gas law** is a formula from elementary science that gives the relation between the pressure, volume, and temperature of a quantity of gas. The formula is

$$PV = QRT$$

    where

P	is the pressure of the gas, in atmospheres
V	is the volume of the gas, in cubic centimeters
Q	is the quantity of the gas, in moles
R	is a constant, equal to 82.05
T	is the temperature of the gas, in degrees Kelvin

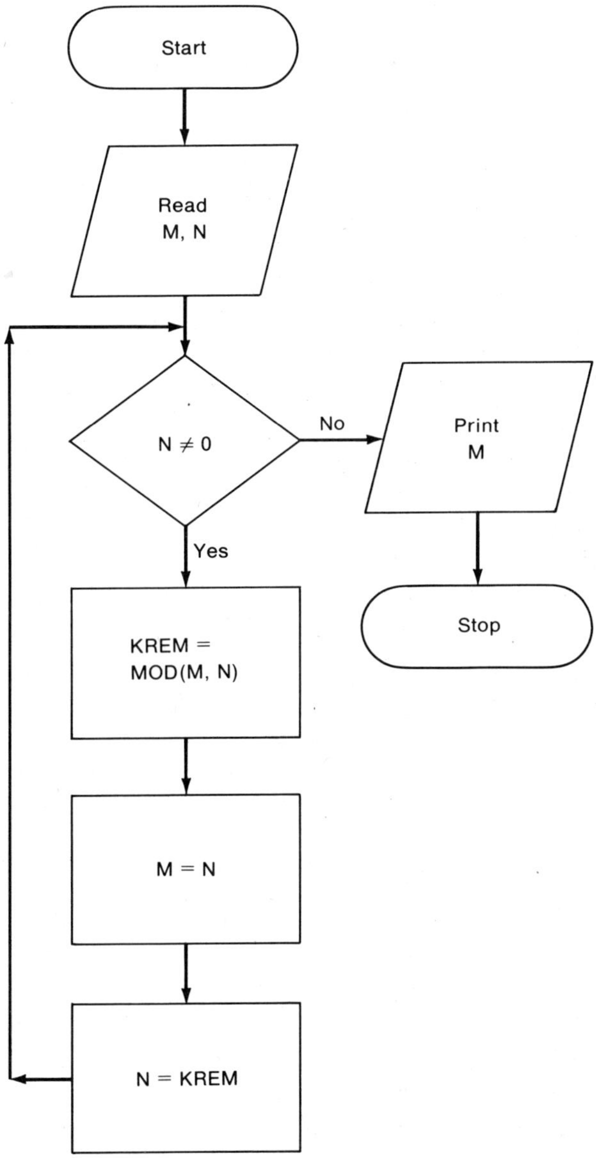

Flowchart for Exercise 19

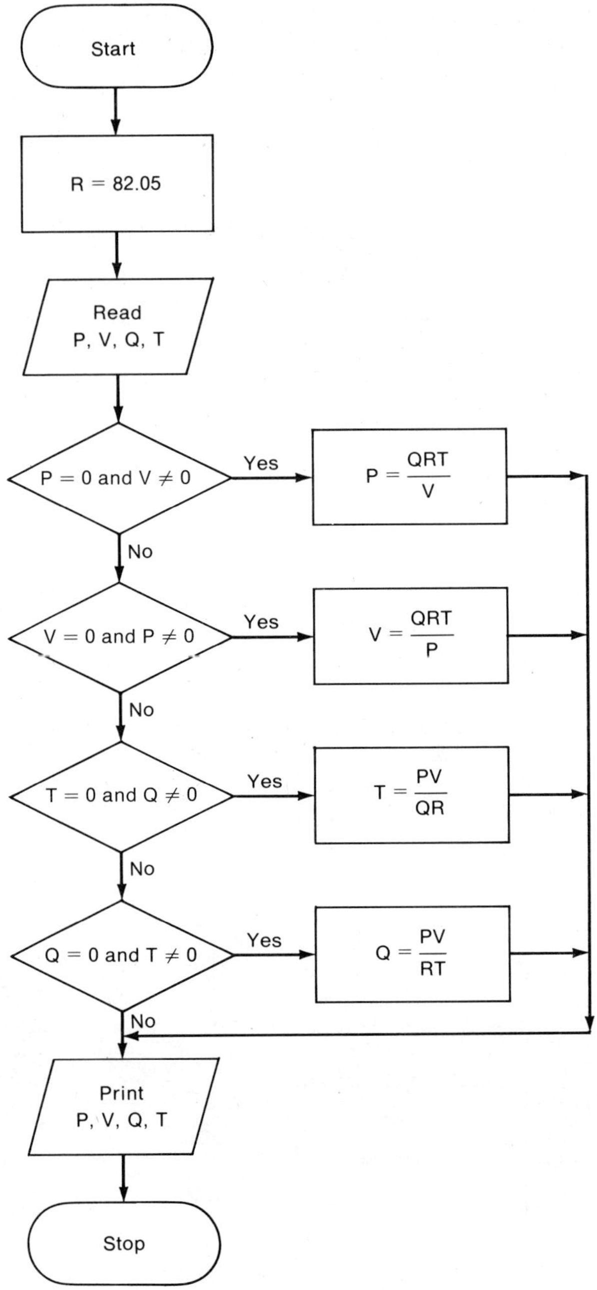

Flowchart for Exercise 20

If you know the values of any three of the variables P, V, Q, and T, you can use the formula to compute the value of the other variable. Write a program to read values for P, V, Q, and T, with a zero value as the input for the unknown variable, and print the values of all four variables. The flowchart on page 148 shows the procedure. Notice that the flowchart includes tests to prevent an accidental division by zero. You can write an outline of the program as follows.

```
R = 82.05
read P, V, Q, and T
if P = 0 and V ≠ 0, then
  P = Q * R * T/V
else, if V = 0 and P ≠ 0, then
  V = Q * R * T/P
else, if T = 0 and Q ≠ 0, then
  T = P * V/(Q * R)
else, if Q = 0 and T ≠ 0, then
  Q = P * V/(R * T)
print P, V, Q, and T
```

6

Formatted Input and Output

The Formatted PRINT Statement

The PRINT statement you have been using is easy to use, but it has a major shortcoming: There is little control over how the line actually looks. For example, how can you print a real variable so that it has exactly one decimal place? How can you make numbers line up into columns? To specify such details of output format, you use a different form of the PRINT statement, called the **formatted PRINT** statement. Here is an example.

```
        PRINT 75, N, A
   75   FORMAT(I4, F16.2)
```

After the word PRINT, there is a number rather than a comma. The number 75 is the statement label of a **FORMAT** statement, which describes in detail how the output variables N and A are to be written. (I4, F16.2) in the FORMAT statement is the **format specification** which tells the exact format to be used for printing the variables. I4 means that the variable N is to be printed as a four-digit integer. F16.2 means that the variable A is to be printed in 16 characters (counting blanks), with two digits to the right of the decimal point.

Each formatted PRINT statement tells two things: It tells which variables to print and which FORMAT statement to use. The **format identifier**, which comes after the word PRINT, is a statement label of some FORMAT statement. After the format identifier, you write a comma followed by the names of the variables to be printed, separated from each other by commas. The list of variables is called the **output list**. These parts of the PRINT statement are shown in Figure 6.1.

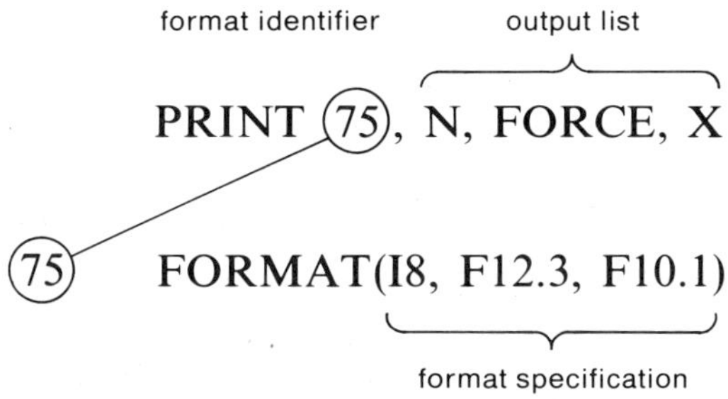

Figure 6.1 The variables in the output list will be printed according to the format specification. The statement number after the word PRINT tells which FORMAT statement to use.

As you will see later in this chapter, there is also a formatted READ statement which uses a format specification to tell exactly how to read numbers from a punch card.

The FORMAT Statement

The FORMAT statement is called a **nonexecutable** statement. This means that it does not actually *do* anything by itself; it is not *executed* by the computer. A nonexecutable statement gives information about the program but does not cause any machine action.

The READ and PRINT statements are executable statements which cause the actual reading or printing, and the FORMAT statement tells how the reading or printing is to be done.

Since FORMAT statements are nonexecutable, you can put them anywhere in your program. Some programmers put the FORMAT right after the READ or PRINT statement. Others prefer to put all the FORMAT statements at the end of the program, after the executable statements. It makes no difference.

You can think of each print line as being composed of a series of **output fields**. An output field is a group of columns on the print line. There is one field for each number printed. Figure 6.2 shows the number 37.0 printed in an output field of seven columns. We usually count a blank space as a character when talking about input and output fields. Thus, we say the output field in Figure 6.2 contains seven characters: three blank spaces, three digits, and a decimal point. Figure 6.3 shows a print line with three output fields.

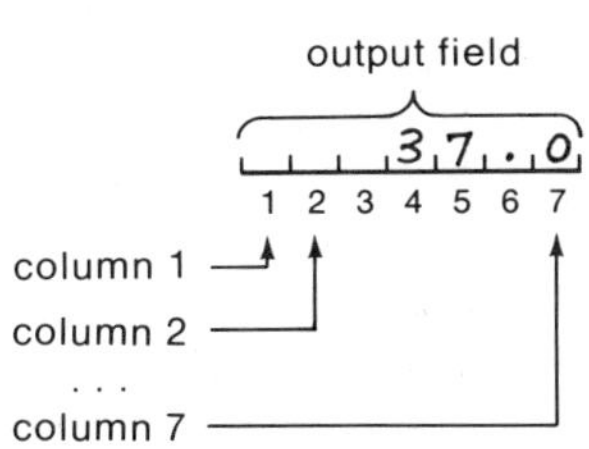

Figure 6.2 A *field* is a group of columns.

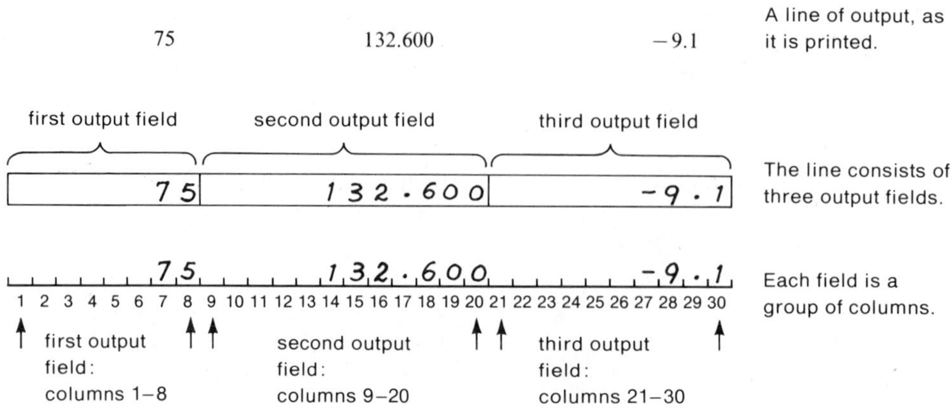

Figure 6.3 A print line with three output fields.

To specify the format of a print line, you tell the computer how to print each output field. This is exactly what the FORMAT statement is used for. The format specifier, which is written in parentheses in the FORMAT statement, is a series of **field descriptors**. These are codes that describe the format of each field. The first variable in the output list of the PRINT statement is printed according to the first field descriptor in the FORMAT statement; the second variable in the output list is printed according to the second field descriptor in the FORMAT statement, and so on. In Figure 6.4, the variable N is printed using the I8 field descriptor, the variable FORCE is printed using the F12.3 field descriptor, and the variable X is printed using the F10.1 field descriptor. We will cover four types of field descriptors in this chapter:

1. The I field descriptor, for integer numbers
2. The F field descriptor, for real numbers
3. The quote field, for printing titles
4. The X field descriptor, for skipping spaces

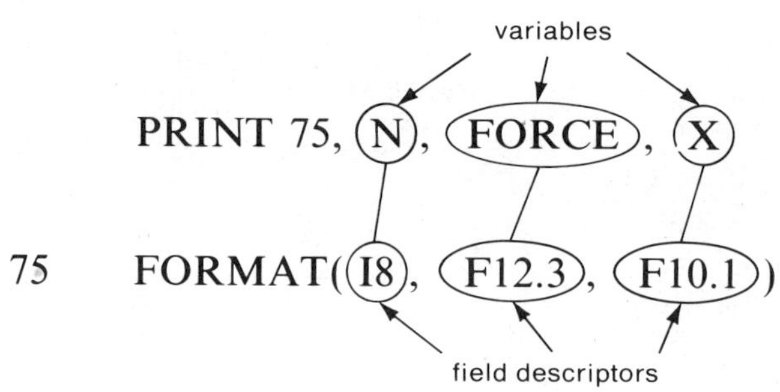

Figure 6.4 The first variable, N, will be printed according to the first field descriptor, 18; the second variable, FORCE, will be printed according to the second field descriptor, F12.3; and so on.

The I Field Descriptor (Output)

To describe an integer output field, you use an **I field descriptor**. The form is

```
In
```

where *n* is a number. The I tells that an integer is being printed, and the number *n* tells the size of the field: the number of characters to print, including blank spaces.

For example

```
I6
```

means a six-character integer field. To print a variable KAT in an I6 field, you can use the statements

```
      PRINT 75, KAT
75    FORMAT(I6)
```

Suppose that KAT = −12. Then the output will be three blank spaces, followed by a minus sign, followed by the digits 12, so that there are six characters in all. The number is always printed in the right part of the output field, with blank spaces to the left if necessary, as shown in Figure 6.5.

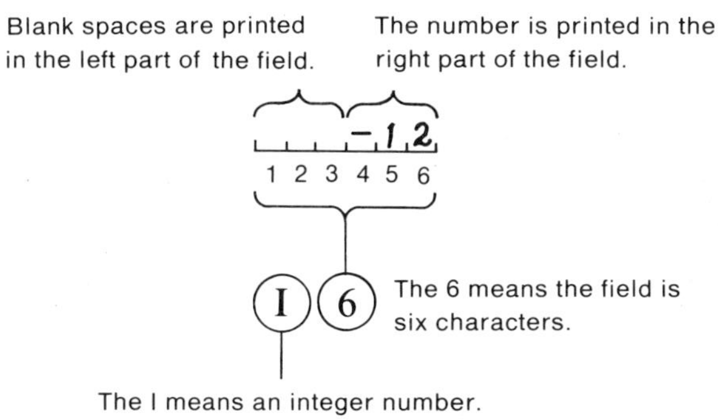

Figure 6.5 An I6 field descriptor means to print an integer number right justified in a field of six characters.

Table 6.1 shows the effect of these statements for different values of the variable KAT. Consider the statements

```
      J = 1234
      PRINT 7, J
7     FORMAT(I3)
```

Table 6.1 Sample Outputs Printed in an I6 Field*

```
        PRINT 75, KAT
75      FORMAT(I6)
```

Value of Variable	*Number Printed*						
	Column	*1*	*2*	*3*	*4*	*5*	*6*
123					1	2	3
−123				—	1	2	3
−12					—	1	2
0							0
23444			2	3	4	4	4
−7650			—	7	6	5	0
9							9

* An I6 field descriptor produces an output field of six characters, including blank spaces.

The I3 field descriptor means to print a three-digit number, which is impossible in this case, since the value of the variable J is a four-digit number. The actual output will be three asterisks:

```
***
```

to indicate that the number is too big for the output field.*

Here is another problem to watch out for:

```
        PRINT 100, X
100     FORMAT (I5)
```

The I field descriptor means to print an *integer*, but the variable X is a *real* variable. On many computer systems, the output would be zero—regardless of the value of X. According to standard FORTRAN, the result of these statements is undefined; at any rate, it is probably not what you intended. You should not use an I field descriptor for real numbers.

The F Field Descriptor (Output)

You use an **F field descriptor** for printing real numbers. (Think of the F as standing for "floating-point.") The F descriptor uses two numbers: one to tell how many characters

* Among FORTRAN compilers, there is some variation in the exact method of diagnosing this error.

in the field, and one to tell how many decimal places to print. The form is

F*n*. *m*

where *n* and *m* are numbers; *n* is the size of the field, and *m* is the number of decimal places.

For example,

F9.4

means a nine-character field with four digits to the right of the decimal point. The statements

```
      X = -273.160
      PRINT 100, X
100   FORMAT(F10.2)
```

will produce the output shown in Figure 6.6.

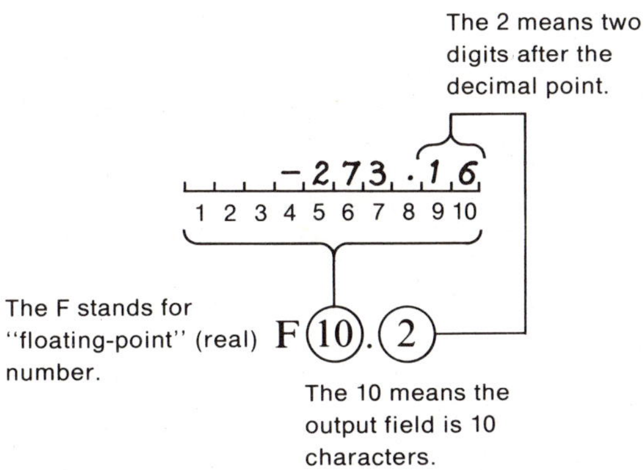

Figure 6.6 An F10.2 field descriptor means to print a real number right justified in a field of ten characters, with two decimal places.

In the computer memory, real numbers are stored as accurately as possible for the machine—typically with seven-place accuracy. When you print a real number, it is *rounded* to the correct number of digits. For instance, if you print the number 0.37 with an F6.1 field descriptor, the output is

bbb0.4

(where b stands for blank). Since the F6.1 says to print one digit to the right of the decimal point, the number 0.37 is rounded to 0.4. This is also illustrated by the following program, which prints the same number four ways.

```
11      FORMAT(F9.4)
        W = 0.3535
        PRINT 11, W
        PRINT 22, W
        PRINT 33, W
        PRINT 44, W
22      FORMAT(F8.3)
33      FORMAT(F7.2)
        STOP
44      FORMAT(F6.1)
        END
```

This produces the following output:

```
0.3535
0.354
0.35
0.4
```

which is the value 0.3535 rounded to 4, 3, 2, and 1 places. This program illustrates again the fact that FORMAT statements are nonexecutable. For example, FORMAT 11 is *not* the first statement executed in the program; the FORMAT is not executed at all. Likewise, after the statement

```
PRINT 44, W
```

the next statement to be executed is

```
STOP
```

The intervening FORMAT statements have no effect on the flow of control. Table 6.2 shows some examples of output printed in an F8.3 field.

As you saw before, you can print several values on one line. The statements in the following example print four values on a line.

```
        I = -10
        X = 2.0
        Y = 2.0/3.0
        PRINT 105, X, I, Y, I
105     FORMAT(F10.4, I10, F10.4, I10)
```

The output is shown in Figure 6.7.

Table 6.2 Sample Output Printed in an F8.3 Field*

```
      PRINT 30, DELTA
30    FORMAT (F8.3)
```

Value of DELTA	Number Printed							
	Column *1*	*2*	*3*	*4*	*5*	*6*	*7*	*8*
21.3			2	1	.	3	0	0
5.0				5	.	0	0	0
−2.34567			−	2	.	3	4	6
−0.01			−	0	.	0	1	0
−50.0		−	5	0	.	0	0	0
−1234.0	*	*	*	*	*	*	*	*
0.0005				0	.	0	0	1
0.00005				0	.	0	0	0
0.				0	.	0	0	0

* An F8.3 field descriptor produces an output field of eight characters, including blank space, with three digits to the right of the decimal point.

FORTRAN statements:

```
      PRINT 105, X, I, Y, I
105   FORMAT (F10.4, I10, F10.4, I10)
```

Output:

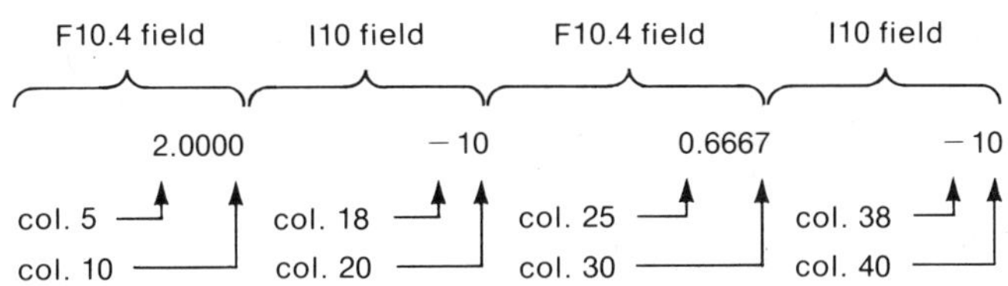

Figure 6.7 A line of output consisting of four fields.

EXAMPLE 1. Write a program to print a table of squares and square roots of numbers 1 through 100.

The first few lines of output will look like this:

```
 1     1   1.000000
 2     4   1.414214
 3     9   1.732051
 4    16   2.000000
```

The numbers in the first column are the numbers 1 through 100; the second column contains the squares: 1^2, 2^2, 3^2, ... The third column contains the square roots.

The numbers in the first two columns are all integers, so you can use integer variables: N for the number and NSQUAR for the square. The third column contains real numbers between 1.0 and 10.0. Use the real variable ROOT for these values. The FORTRAN function SQRT finds the square root of a number. To set ROOT equal to the square root of N, use the statement

```
ROOT = SQRT(FLOAT(N))
```

Remember that the SQRT function requires a real argument, so use the FLOAT function to convert N to a real value.

The last line of output will be

```
100      10000      10.000000
```

These are the largest numbers the program will print. Thus, the first output field must be at least three characters and the second output field at least five characters. If you want to print the square root with six decimal places, you must make the output field at least nine characters. To allow at least five blank spaces between the columns, use the format specification

```
(I8, I10, F14.6)
```

Here is the complete program:

```
C   PROGRAM TO PRINT A TABLE OF SQUARES AND SQUARE ROOTS
        N = 1
5           NSQUAR = N**2
            ROOT = SQRT(FLOAT(N))
            PRINT 100, N, NSQUAR, ROOT
            N = N + 1
        IF (N .LE. 100) GO TO 5
        STOP
100     FORMAT(I8, I10, F14.6)
        END
```

The Quote Field Descriptor

You use a **quote field descriptor** to print headings on your output. In the format specification, any text that is enclosed in single quotes (′) is printed on the output just as it appears in the FORMAT statement. Here is an example:

```
        X = 12.566
        PRINT 55, X
55      FORMAT(' THE ANSWER IS', F7.3)
```

The output from this is

```
THE ANSWER IS 12.566
```

Unlike the I and F field descriptors, the quote field descriptor does not correspond to any variable in the output list. The variable X in this example is printed according to the F7.3 field descriptor. The characters between the quote marks are simply copied to the print line.

You may want to use a quote field descriptor to put titles at the beginning of the output. If there are no variables to be printed, you can omit the output list of the PRINT statement and the comma following the format identifier, as illustrated by the following statements.

```
      PRINT 60
      PRINT 70
60    FORMAT(' ACME MFG. COMPANY')
70    FORMAT(' QUARTERLY SALES REPORT')
```

The X Field Descriptor (Output)

You can insert blank spaces in the print line with an **X field descriptor**. The form is

*n*X

where *n* is a number that tells how many spaces to insert. For example,

10X

means to leave 10 blank spaces. To print a five-character integer field in columns 61 through 65 of the print line, you can use the format specification (60X, I5) as in the statements

```
      PRINT 200, KILOGM
200   FORMAT(60X, I5)
```

Like the quote field descriptor, the X field descriptor does not correspond to any variable in the output list of the PRINT statement. Thus, the variable KILOGM in this example is printed according to the I5 field descriptor. The 60X means to print 60 blank spaces. So, the I5 field begins in column 61 of the print line.

EXAMPLE 2. A program for a customer billing application uses two variables: NORDER, the customer's order number, and AMOUNT, the dollar amount of the order. The output line is to look like the following sample:

```
ORDER NO. 1234      AMOUNT $304.75
```

Write the FORTRAN statements to print this line.

When designing an output format specification, you should begin with the field descriptors for the variables. You need to consider the size of the largest number the program might print. Suppose that the order number is always four or fewer digits, and is always a positive number (so you do not need to allow an extra column for a minus sign). You can use an I5 field descriptor for NORDER, and this will insure at least one blank space on the left of the field. If the amount of the order is always less than or equal to $9999.99, you can print it with an F7.2 field descriptor. Use quote fields for the titles (and for the dollar sign), and X field descriptors to provide a left margin of five spaces and to skip five spaces between the order number and the word AMOUNT. Thus, the PRINT and FORMAT statements can be written as follows.

```
      PRINT 200, NORDER, AMOUNT
200   FORMAT(5X, 'ORDER NO.', I5, 5X, 'AMOUNT $', F7.2)
```

Figure 6.8 shows the output fields produced by these statements.

FORTRAN statements:

```
      PRINT 200, NORDER, AMOUNT
200   FORMAT(5X, 'ORDER NO.', I5, 5X, 'AMOUNT $', F7.2)
```

Output:

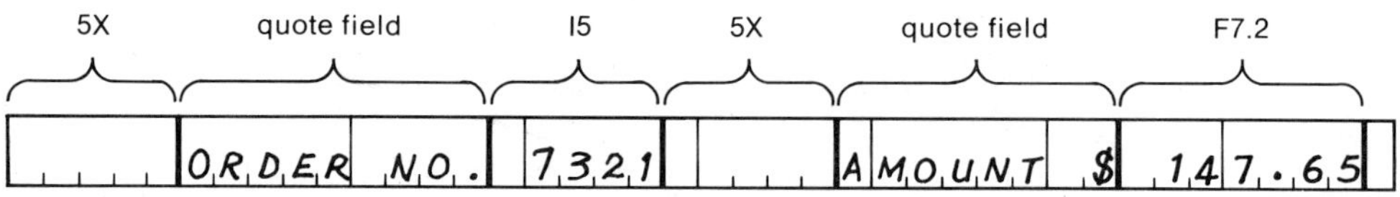

Figure 6.8 The output fields on the print line correspond to the field descriptors in the FORMAT statement.

■ Repeat Factors

Frequently, FORMAT statements include repeated groups of field descriptors. For example, the statement

```
100   FORMAT(I10, I10, I10, F12.6, F12.6)
```

involves three consecutive I10 field descriptors and two consecutive F12.6 field descriptors. This can be written more concisely as

```
100   FORMAT(3I10, 2F12.6)
```

Here 3I10 means the same as I10, I10, I10. In general, any field descriptor may be preceded by a number giving a repeat factor.

■ Carriage Control Characters

As you have seen, each PRINT statement begins printing on a new line. There is a feature of FORTRAN, however, which allows a little more control over the vertical spacing of output: The first character on any line of output is not actually printed but instead is used to control special printer functions. For example, consider the following:

```
        PRINT 110
110     FORMAT('123')
```

The first character printed, according to the FORMAT, is the number 1. But this character would *not* actually be printed; it is the **carriage control** character. The number 1 is the code for skipping to a new page. This PRINT statement will print the number 23 on the first line of the next page of output. Since the carriage control character does not occupy any space on the output line, the number 23 would be printed in the leftmost columns. Thus, column 1 is really a fictitious print column, used only for carriage control characters. The codes for carriage control characters are shown in Table 6.3.

Table 6.3 Codes for Carriage Control Characters in Column 1*

Character Printed in Column 1	*Result*
Blank	Single space before printing (normal spacing)
0 (zero)	Double space before printing
1 (one)	Skip to the beginning of next page before printing
+ (plus)	Do not space before printing
Other characters	Other special actions may be defined on particular systems

* The first character on a line of output is not printed; the character is a code that controls printer spacing.

When you use a list-directed PRINT statement, such as

```
        PRINT, N
```

the carriage control is taken care of automatically so that the output is single spaced. When you use a formatted PRINT statement, *you must always remember to allow for the carriage control character*. In many applications, you would want to leave column 1 blank so the output is single spaced. An easy way to do this is to begin each output FORMAT statement with a 1X field descriptor. For example,

```
      PRINT 500, N
500   FORMAT(1X, I2)
```

Another way to do this is to make the first output field wide enough so that a blank space is printed in the carriage control column. This method can lead to problems, however, as shown by the following example.

EXAMPLE 3. Consider the following program.

```
C  EXAMPLE OF A PROBLEM WITH CARRIAGE CONTROL
      N = 0
      NSUM = 0
10       NSUM = NSUM + N
         PRINT 20, N, NSUM
         N = N + 1
      IF (N .LT. 199) GO TO 10
      STOP
20    FORMAT(I3, I6)
      END
```

This program adds up the numbers from 1 to N and prints the result for each N from 1 to 199. The PRINT statement is executed 199 times. Assuming there are 66 lines of printing on a page, you might think this program would produce four pages of output. But what happens when N = 100? The I3 field descriptor causes the 1 to be printed in the carriage control column, so the line begins on a new page. In fact, lines 100 through 199 will each begin a new page, and the program actually produces 102 pages of output! Many a beginning student has learned about carriage control only after receiving an embarrassingly large pile of paper printed by programs like this one.

All of the examples you have seen so far in this chapter are vulnerable to this same problem. To simplify the discussion, the first output field has been made wide enough so a blank space would always be printed in the carriage control column. This practice is strongly discouraged, however, and from now on, the examples will adhere to the following suggestion:

Suggestion for Output Formats

If you want your output to be single spaced, begin the FORMAT statement with a 1X field descriptor to put a blank space in the carriage control column.

We think of a line of output as a sequence of columns, but in view of carriage control characters, the terminology is ambiguous. Some people call "column 1" the carriage control column; some people call "column 1" the first printable column, which is the column that follows the carriage control character. We will adopt the second definition: From now on, "column 1" will mean the first printable column on an output line. Thus, we would say that the statements

```
      PRINT 1000, NPAGE
1000  FORMAT('1', 'PAGE', I3)
```

write a "1" in the carriage control column, and write the word "PAGE" in columns 1 through 4 of the line.

The effects of output formats studied so far are summarized in the following rules.

Rules for Formatted Output Statements

Rule 1: The formatted PRINT statement has the form

PRINT *f*, *list*

where *f* is the statement label of the FORMAT statement to be used and *list* is the output list of variable names, separated by commas. If there is no output list, the comma after *f* is omitted. Each PRINT statement begins a new line of output.

Rule 2: The FORMAT statement has the form

FORMAT ($desc_1$, $desc_2$, . . . , $desc_n$)

where $desc_1$, $desc_2$, . . . are field descriptors. A series of identical field descriptors may be represented as a single field descriptor preceded by an integer number giving the repeat count.

Rule 3: The I field descriptor is used for printing integer values. The form is I*n*, where *n* is an integer number (with no sign). The number printed will be right justified in a field of *n* columns with blank spaces on the left if needed. If the number printed is negative, a minus sign is printed to the left of the leftmost digit.

Rule 4: The F field descriptor is used for printing real numbers. The form is F*n*.*m*, where *n* and *m* are integer numbers (with no sign). The number printed will occupy *n* columns, and *m* digits will be printed after the decimal point. As with the I field descriptor, a minus sign precedes the first digit of a negative number, and the number is right justified in the field with blank spaces on the left if needed.

Rule 5: The quote field descriptor is used to print character strings. Any characters included between single quote marks (′) are copied to the output line.

Rule 6: The X field descriptor is used to skip spaces. The form is *n*X, where *n* is an integer number (with no sign). This field skips *n* spaces on the output line.

Rule 7: The character printed in the first column of each output line does not actually appear in the output, but is used to control the vertical spacing. The codes for these carriage control characters are:

Blank	Single space before printing (normal spacing)
0 (zero)	Double space before printing
1 (one)	Skip to new page before printing
+ (plus)	Do not space before printing
Other characters	Other special actions may be defined on particular systems

---

The Formatted READ Statement

The **formatted READ** statement is similar to the PRINT statement, but it is used for input. Each READ statement uses a FORMAT statement to determine how to interpret the input line and assign values to the variables in the input list. For example, suppose that two values to be read from a card are keypunched like this:

```
111222
```

Are these two numbers 111 and 222? Or perhaps 11 and 1222? Or 11122 and 2? With the formatted READ, the FORMAT statement defines the input fields. If this card is read with the statements

```
      READ 7, M, K
    7 FORMAT(I2, I4)
```

then the first two columns are read into M and the next four columns are read into K. The result is M = 11 and K = 1222.

Think of each input card as a sequence of **input fields**. Each input field is a certain group of columns from which a number is to be read. The field descriptors in the FORMAT statement define which columns correspond to which input fields on a card. Usually, all the input cards for a program are prepared in the same way, so that each number to be read is always keypunched in the same columns. (See Figure 6.9.)

The form of the formatted READ statement is

READ *f*, *list*

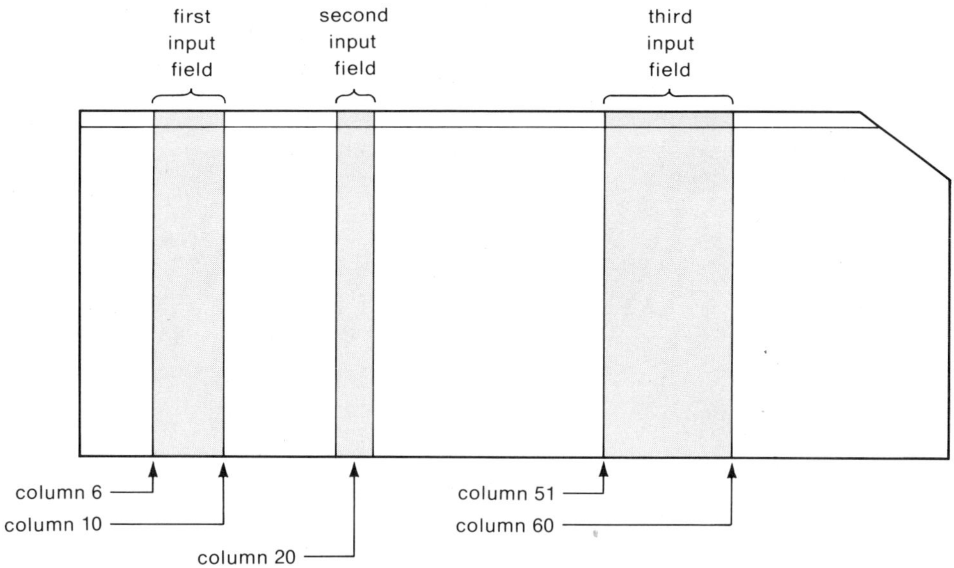

Figure 6.9 For formatted input, each input card is considered a sequence of input fields, each field being a certain group of columns from which a number is to be read. In this figure, the first field is columns 6–10; the second field is column 20; and the third field is columns 51–60.

where *f* is the format identifier and *list* is the input list, consisting of the variables to be read. The variables in the input list correspond to the field descriptors in the format specification, just as with the PRINT statement. For example, the statements

```
      READ 40, TIME, NUM
40    FORMAT(F6.2, I5)
```

mean to read the variable TIME according to the F6.2 field descriptor and NUM according to the I5 field descriptor. Used for input, these field descriptors have a slightly different interpretation than they do for describing output fields.

The I Field Descriptor (Input)

You specify an integer input field with an **I field descriptor** of the form

I*n*

where *n* is a number telling how many columns comprise the field.

The input field on the card should contain numeric digits. If you want to read a negative number, keypunch a minus sign in front of the number. Blank spaces in the field are treated as zeros. Table 6.4 shows the effect of reading a value from an I6 field.

Table 6.4 Effect of an I6 Field Descriptor*

Input Field							*Value Read*
Column	*1*	*2*	*3*	*4*	*5*	*6*	
				1	0	0	100
	0	0	0	1	0	0	100
	–	0	5	4	3	2	−5432
	–					8	−8
		+		1	0	0	100
							0

* An I6 field descriptor tells the computer to read an integer number from six columns.

The numbers in the table are right justified in the input field. This is the usual way data is prepared. *All* blanks in the input field are treated as zeros—even blanks to the right of a number. Table 6.5 shows the result, for various inputs, of the statements

```
      READ 95, J
95    FORMAT(I6)
```

Table 6.5 Blanks in Input*

Input Field							*Value Read*
Column	*1*	*2*	*3*	*4*	*5*	*6*	
				5			500
				5	0	0	500
	5						500000
			–	1	1		−110
		1		1		1	10101

* Blank spaces are treated as zeros everywhere in the input field—even to the right of the number.

If the input field contains a noninteger value (a decimal point, for example), an execution error will result when you read it with an I field descriptor.

The F Field Descriptor (Input)

As with output, you read a real number with an **F field descriptor** of the form

```
      Fn.m
```

The number *n* tells the size of the input field. The number *m* tells where to *assume* a decimal point if one is not present in the input field.

You can keypunch a real number as a sequence of digits with a decimal point, just as you would ordinarily write a real number in FORTRAN. In this case, the number *m* in the F*n.m* descriptor has no effect.

Frequently, it is convenient to omit decimal points from input data. For example, a billing program might read a five-digit number representing an amount in dollars and cents. Instead of writing a decimal point in each input line, you can omit the decimal point from the input data and have the program supply the decimal point automatically. You can do this by reading the number with an F5.2 field descriptor. In general, the field descriptor F*n.m* means to read *n* columns, and, if there is no decimal point in the input, place a decimal point in front of the *m*th digit from the right. Table 6.6 gives some examples of the effect of the statements

```
      READ 6, T
 6    FORMAT(F8.2)
```

Table 6.6 Effect of an F8.2 Field Descriptor*

Input Field									*Value Read*
Columns	*1*	*2*	*3*	*4*	*5*	*6*	*7*	*8*	
			4	4	.	6	0	0	44.6
				−	1	2	3	1	−12.31
	−					2	.	2	−2.2
	−					2	2	2	−2.22
						1			1.0
							1		0.1
				−	1	0	1		−10.1

* An F8.2 field descriptor means to read eight columns and assume a decimal point before the second-to-last digit if no decimal point is present in the input.

As Table 6.6 indicates, the same rules apply for leading and trailing blank spaces with the F field descriptor as with the I field descriptor: Blanks are treated as zeros. If the decimal point is written in the data to be read, trailing blanks do not make any difference since, for example, 3.2 = 3.20000. If no decimal point is written in the data, trailing blanks *will* make a difference since they are counted in determining where the assumed decimal points is to be placed.

The assumed decimal point may go anywhere in the input field. Reading under an F3.0 field descriptor will cause the decimal point to be placed to the right of the last digit, if a decimal point is not already present in the input. An F3.3 field descriptor assumes a decimal point at the very left of the field.

The X Field Descriptor (Input)

The **X field descriptor** skips spaces on input. For instance, if an integer number is written in columns 1 through 5 of an input line and a real number in columns 11 through 15, the following READ statement can be used:

```
      READ 10, JOE, SAM
10    FORMAT(I5, 5X, F5.0)
```

The 5X means to skip five columns, so that the F5.0 field begins in column 11. In general, *n*X means to skip *n* columns. Here *n* must be an integer number. Another way to read the input line just described is with the statements

```
      READ 11, JOE, SAM
11    FORMAT(I5, F10.0)
```

If columns 6 through 10 are blank or zeros, this is equivalent. The X field descriptor, however, will skip over columns 6 through 10 of the input line even if they contain nonblank characters.

The effects of the input formats studied so far can be summarized as follows.

Rules for Formatted Input Statements

Rule 1: The formatted READ statement has the form

READ *f*, *list*

where *f* is the statement label of the FORMAT statement to be used and *list* is the list of variable names to be read. Each READ begins a new input line.

Rule 2: The general form of the FORMAT statement is the same for input as for output.

Rule 3: The I field descriptor is used for reading integer values. The form is I*n*, where *n* is an integer number (with no sign). The number is read from the next *n* columns. Blanks are considered to be zeros. Thus, the number must be right justified in the input field. A negative number must have a minus sign before it.

Rule 4: Real numbers are read with an F field descriptor. The form is F*n*.*m*, where *n* and *m* are integer numbers (with no sign). The number is read from the next *n* columns. Blanks are considered to be zeros. If the input is written with a decimal point, the *m* in the F*n*.*m* field descriptor has no effect. If the number read has no decimal point, one will be inserted to the left of the *m*th digit from the right. A negative number must have a minus sign before it.

Rule 5: The X field descriptor is used to skip spaces. The form is *n*X, where *n* is an integer number (with no sign). This field descriptor skips *n* columns of the input line. If the skipped columns contain any characters, they are ignored.

EXAMPLE 4. The Acme Company is taking an inventory of the floor space in their building. They have measured the dimensions of each room (all of which are conveniently rectangular). They need a program to compute the total area.

A simple way to prepare the data for this program is to use one input card for each room. Each card will contain the length and width of the room, along with the room number. The input for each room might be prepared as shown in Table 6.7.

Table 6.7 Acme Company Floor Space Data Input

Columns	*Data*
1–5	Room number (five-digit integer, right justified)
6–10	Length (in centimeters, five-digit integer, right justified)
11–15	Width (in centimeters, five-digit integer, right justified)

The length and width are expressed as integers on the input card. The program could read them as integers and multiply them to obtain the area, in square centimeters. Square centimeters, however, is an inappropriate dimension for measuring floor space; square meters would be much better. Instead of computing square centimeters and dividing by 10,000, you can just read the length and width in meters to begin with. This is done by using an F5.2 format, which will place a decimal before the last two digits, effectively dividing the number by 100. The real variables A and B are used for the length and width. An integer variable NROOM is used for the room number. Since there is no room zero in the building, you can put a blank card after the last room card. The program will test for a room number zero; when it is read, the program will print the total area and then stop. The flowchart for this program is shown in Figure 6.10. The program is as follows.

```
C     ACME COMPANY FLOOR SPACE INVENTORY
      PRINT 100
      TOTAL = 0.0
10       READ 105, NROOM, A, B
         IF (NROOM .EQ. 0) GO TO 50
         AREA = A * B
         TOTAL = TOTAL + AREA
         PRINT 110, NROOM, A, B, AREA
         GO TO 10
50    PRINT 115, TOTAL
      STOP
100   FORMAT('1', 5X, 'ROOM', 4X, 'LENGTH', 5X, 'WIDTH',
     $   6X, 'AREA')
105   FORMAT(I5, 2F5.2)
110   FORMAT(5X, I5, 3F10.2)
115   FORMAT('0', 14X, 'TOTAL AREA = ', F12.2,
     $   'SQ. METERS')
      END
```

Notice that the first field in FORMAT statement 100 prints a 1 in the carriage control column, causing a new page of output to be started. Likewise, the first field in FORMAT statement 115 prints a 0 in the carriage control column, double-spacing the output.

EXAMPLE 5. Each student in a class has taken three tests during the semester. On each test, the student received a grade of 4, 3, 2, 1, or 0. Each student has a five-digit matriculation number. Write a program that reads each student's grades and prints the average grade. A possible way to prepare the input is shown in Table 6.8.

Table 6.8 Input for Average Grade Program

Column	*Item*
1–5	Matric number
6	First grade
7	Second grade
8	Third grade

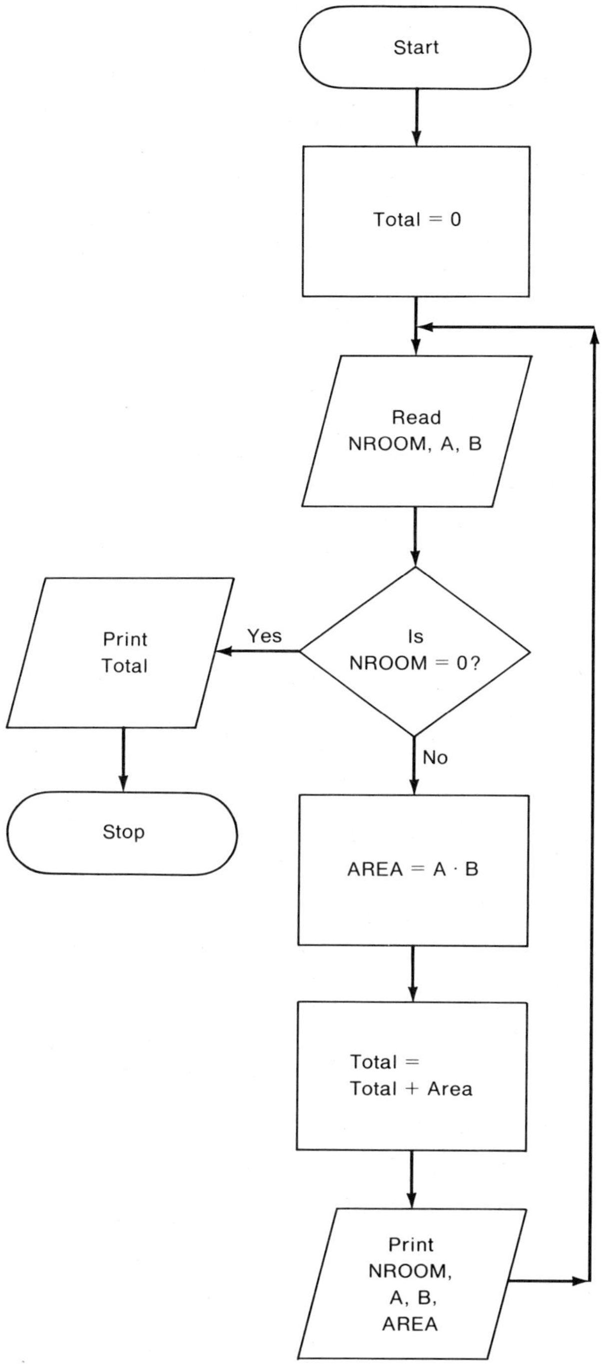

Figure 6.10 Flowchart for Acme program.

A card punched in this format would be easy to read in FORTRAN, but it would be difficult for a person to read, since there are no blank spaces. A more readable format is shown in Table 6.9. This data layout allows for additional information to be written in columns 12 through 80. Since no more information is required for this problem, the program can skip these columns.

Table 6.9 Input for Average Grade Program with Blanks

Column	*Item*
1–5	Matric number
6	Blank
7	First grade
8	Blank
9	Second grade
10	Blank
11	Third grade
12–15	Blank
15–20	Number of classes missed
21–25	Number of homework assignments turned in
26–80	Not used

Each grade is an integer, but since an average is to be computed, the grade can be read as a real number. An F2.0 field descriptor will be used for input. An F10.0 field descriptor will be used to output each grade, which will provide some space between the numbers. An X field could be used to skip over the additional information in columns 12 through 80, but it is not necessary. Since each READ begins a new line, the characters in columns 12 through 80 are automatically skipped simply by not reading them into variables. The grade average will be given with three decimal places. An F18.3 field descriptor is used to provide extra spaces.

Titles are provided at the top of the output by a FORMAT statement with quote fields, which was written after the output format was decided upon. The spacing was chosen by counting characters, so the titles would appear over the appropriate columns. Here is the complete program.

```
C   PROGRAM TO AVERAGE STUDENT GRADES.
C   THE LAST CARD MUST HAVE A ZERO VALUE FOR THE
C   MATRIC NUMBER.
C
        PRINT 100
10          READ 200, MATRIC, GRADE1, GRADE2, GRADE3
            IF (MATRIC .EQ. 0) STOP
```

```
            GRADE = (GRADE1 + GRADE2 + GRADE3)/3.0
            PRINT 300, MATRIC, GRADE1, GRADE2, GRADE3, GRADE
            GO TO 10
100     FORMAT('1', 'MATRIC', 5X, 'TEST1', 5X,
     $      'TEST2', 5X, 'TEST3', 10X, 'AVERAGE')
200     FORMAT(I5, 3F2.0)
300     FORMAT(1X, I5, 3F10.0, F18.3)
        END
```

The Slash in the FORMAT Statement

As you have seen, each READ statement begins a new line of input, and each PRINT statement begins a new line of output. It is possible to use a single READ statement to read more than one line of input. Likewise, a single PRINT statement can produce more than one line of output. This can be done with a **slash character** (/) in the FORMAT statement. For example,

```
        X = 1.0
        N = 2
        PRINT 5, X, N
5       FORMAT(F10.0/I10)
```

will produce the output

```
        1.
         2
```

The variable X is printed with the F10.0 field descriptor. The slash in the FORMAT means to begin a new line. The variable N is printed with the I10 field beginning on the new line.

In general, whenever a slash is encountered in the FORMAT statement, a new line of input or output begins. It is not necessary to use commas in addition to the slash to separate field descriptors.

On input, a slash will cause the remainder of the input line to be ignored; the following field descriptor applies to the beginning of the following line of input. For example,

```
        READ 10, A, B
10      FORMAT (F5.4/F5.4)
```

would read the input

```
        1.   2.   3.
        4.   5.   6.
```

and assign the values A = 1 and B = 4. The numbers 2 and 3 on the first input line are ignored because of the slash in the FORMAT. The numbers 5 and 6 on the second input line are ignored because only two variables were read.

It is important to allow for carriage control when a slash is used to begin a new line of output. Consider the statements

```
         I = 9
         J = 10
         PRINT 11, I, J
11       FORMAT(1X, I2/I2)
```

This will print a 9 on the next line of output and then skip to the top of a new page and print a 0. The reason is that when the slash begins a new line, column 1 of the new line is a carriage control character and the 1 from the number 10 causes a page eject. To avoid this problem, the FORMAT statement just given could be changed to

```
11       FORMAT(1X, I2/1X, I2)
```

The slash can also be used at the beginning or end of the FORMAT specification. The statements

```
         A = 1.0
         PRINT 55, A
         PRINT 66, A
55       FORMAT (10X, F10.2)
66       FORMAT(/// 10X, F10.2)
```

produce the output

```
1.00
         (three blank lines)
1.00
```

The three slashes at the beginning of statement 66 produce the three blank lines.

In general, the function of the slash in a FORMAT is given by the following rules:

Rules for the Slash (/) in a FORMAT

Rule 1: One or more slashes (/) may appear at the beginning or end of a series of field descriptors or between any two field descriptors in a FORMAT statement.

Commas are not required to separate the slash from adjacent field descriptors in the FORMAT statement.

Rule 2: On input, the slash means to skip to the beginning of the next input record. Any remaining data on the current input record is ignored.

Rule 3: On output, the slash means to skip to the next line. The first character of the next line is a carriage control character, which must be allowed for in the FORMAT statement.

The T Field Descriptor

The **T field descriptor** is used in a FORMAT statement to indicate tabbing. It is not a standard FORTRAN feature and may not be available on some systems; but it is available in WATFIV and in many other versions of FORTRAN, and can be very convenient.

Like the X field descriptor, the T field descriptor does not correspond to a variable in the input or output list; it only controls spacing. Instead of specifying how many spaces to skip, as the X field descriptor does, the T field descriptor is used to tab to a certain column. The form is

T*n*

where *n* is an unsigned integer number. This means to "tab to column *n*." In other words, it causes the next field descriptor to begin in column *n* of the input or output line.

For example, consider the statements

```
      PRINT 100, A, B
100   FORMAT(T20, F10.4, T50, F10.4)
```

The T20 field descriptor causes the F10.4 field for the variable A to begin in column 20. The T50 field descriptor causes the F10.4 field for the variable B to begin in column 50. An equivalent FORMAT statement is

```
10    FORMAT(19X, F10.4, 20X, F10.4)
```

Note that the 19X field is in columns 1–19, and the first F10.4 is in columns 20–29; the 20X spaces over 30–49; then the last F10.4 field is in columns 50–59.

Used for input, this field descriptor has a similar effect. The FORMAT statement that follows reads A, B, and C from the beginning of a card and then tabs to column 80 to read the variable K.

```
      READ 10, A, B, C, K
10    FORMAT(3F6.0, T80, I1)
```

The T field can be very useful in aligning headings on output fields. Suppose a program needs to print the headings

```
QUANTITY    AMOUNT
SOLD        RECEIVED
```

where the first heading starts in column 20 and the second heading starts in column 40. This can be easily done as follows:

```
       PRINT 505
505    FORMAT('1', T20, 'QUANTITY', T40, 'AMOUNT'/
     $     T20, 'SOLD', T40, 'RECEIVED')
```

The basic function of the T format may be stated as follows:

Rule for T Field Descriptor

Rule: The T*n* field descriptor specifies that the next field to be read (or printed) will be read (or printed) beginning in column *n* of the input (or output) line.

Other Input and Output Statements

The forms of the READ and PRINT statements you have been using are not available on some systems. However, there is an equivalent form of input and output statement that is available on all systems. For input, the form is

READ(*unit*, *format*) *list*

where

unit	is the unit number of the device used for input
format	is the statement number of the FORMAT statement to be used for input
list	is the list of variables to be read

The **unit number** is an integer number or an integer variable. The value of the unit number determines what device is to be used for input. For example, unit 1 might be a teletype, unit 2 might be a card reader, and so on. The actual values vary, depending on the particular computer system you are using.

As an example,

```
READ(5, 101) A, B, C
```

means to read the variables A, B, and C from unit 5 using FORMAT statement 101.

The corresponding output statement is the WRITE statement, which has the form

WRITE(*unit*, *format*) *list*

For example,

WRITE(6, 17) I, J

means to write the values of I and J on unit 6 according to FORMAT statement 17.

Some versions of FORTRAN, including WATFIV, permit a special form of the READ statement which gives the number of a statement to be executed at the end of the input data. The form is

READ(*unit*, *format*, END = *stmt*) *list*

where

unit, format, and *list* are as given previously

stmt is the statement number of the statement to branch to if there is no input data on the unit when the READ statements is executed

For example,

READ(5, 101, END = 900) A, B, C

means to read the variables A, B, and C from unit 5 using FORMAT statement 101, and, if there is no more input data, to go to statement 900.

Exercises

1. Using I and X field descriptors, print the design

```
    1
   111
  11111
 1111111
111111111
```

2. Let PI = 3.14159265. Print the value of PI with 8, 7, 6, 5, 4, 3, 2, 1, and 0 decimal places. As fewer digits are printed, is the number rounded or truncated?
3. A ball is dropped from a building 200 feet high and bounces off the pavement to 75% of its previous height. In theory, it would continue to bounce indefinitely. Print the height after each bounce until the ball bounces less than one inch. How many times has the ball bounced? What is the total distance traveled by the ball? Label all the output.

4. A deck of cards is punched, with each card in the following format:

Column	(Size)	Item
1–5	(5)	Student identification number
6–10	(5)	Blank
11	(1)	Class 1 if freshman 2 if sophomore 3 if junior 4 if senior 5 if other (grad or unclassified)
12	(1)	Blank
13	(1)	1 if student enrolled in tennis
14	(1)	1 if student enrolled in swimming
15–80		Other information

Lockers must be assigned to all students enrolled in either swimming or tennis. Read all the cards and print a list of students enrolled in either swimming or tennis. For each student, print the identification number and (unless the class code is 5) print the word FRESHMAN, SOPHOMORE, JUNIOR, or SENIOR. Put a title and heading at the top of each page.

5. Salesmen for the Foobar Company have two data cards punched for them at the end of each quarter. The first for each salesman has the salesman number and his sales for each month of last quarter. The second card has the salesman number and the total sales for each month of the current quarter. These cards have the following format.

Column	(Size)	Item
1–3	(3)	Salesman number (an integer)
4	(1)	Quarter number (1, 2, 3, or 4)
5–10	(6)	Blank
11–18	(8)	First month's sales (dollars and cents, with an assumed decimal point before the cents)
19–20	(2)	Blank
21–28	(8)	Second month's sales
29–30	(2)	Blank
31–38	(8)	Third month's sales

Read both cards and check to see that the salesman number is the same on both of them; if it is not, print an error message and stop. Print the salesman number and the sales for each month of the current quarter. Compute and print the total sales for the current quarter and the percent increase or decrease in total sales from the previous quarter. Terminate the input with a zero value for the salesman number.

6. A card contains two numbers. The first is a code, and the second is a measurement. The code determines the units of the measurement as follows:

Code	*Units*
1	Centimeters
2	Inches
3	Grams
4	Ounces

The code is punched in column 1 and the measurement is punched in columns 3–10 with a decimal point. For each card, print a line giving the measurement in both metric and U.S. units, with each line labeled. For example, if the code is 2 and the measurement is 12.0, the program should print

30.48 CM 12.0 INCHES

Stop the program when a card is read having a code number other than 1 through 4. (*Note:* There are 2.54 centimeters in an inch, and approximately 0.352739 grams in an ounce.)

7. A prospective football player must be a male, must be of height greater than 60 inches and weight greater than 180 pounds, must not be a freshman, and must have a score of 85 or higher on the test of athletic ability. Write a program to print out all the information for prospective football players. A deck of cards is punched in the following format:

Column	*(Size)*	*Item*
1–5	(5)	Student identification number
6	(1)	Sex (1 if male, 2 if female)
7–8	(2)	Height in inches
9–11	(3)	Weight in pounds
12	(1)	Class: 1, 2, 3, or 4 for freshman, sophomore, junior, or senior
13–14	(2)	Percentile rank on a test of athletic ability

Terminate the input with a card having a zero for the identification number. Print 55 lines per page, maximum, double-space the output, and provide column headings at the top of each page.

8. The Boondoggle Company just inventoried office furniture. For each piece, a card has been punched in the format:

Column	*(Size)*	*Item*
1–3	(3)	Type of item 100 for chair 200 for desk (small) 210 for desk (large) 230 for table 300 for filing cabinet (other codes are not used by this program)
4–5	(2)	Blank
6–8	(3)	Room number where located

Read all the data cards and print out the total number of chairs, desks, tables, and filing cabinets in the company.

9. Acme Company payroll records are very simple: The card gives the employee number in columns 1–5 and the pay rate in columns 8–14 (with an assumed decimal point before column 13). The pay rate is either an hourly wage, a monthly salary, or an annual salary (depending on the type of employee). If the rate is less than $20.00, it represents an hourly wage. If the rate is greater than or equal to $20.00 but less than $4000.00, it is a monthly salary. If the rate is greater than or equal to $4000.00, it is an annual salary. Write a program to read each employee record and print the equivalent annual salary, assuming 12 months or 2080 hours per year. Also print the total annual payroll for the company.

10. A shopper is comparing prices on various brands and sizes of laundry detergent. For each item surveyed, a data card is prepared in the following format:

Column	*(Size)*	*Item*
1–3	(3)	Product code
4–9	(6)	Date purchased (MMDDYY)
10–13	(4)	Store number where purchased
14–18	(5)	Price
19	(1)	0 if this is the regular price; 1 if this is a sale price
20–24	(5)	Net weight (pounds)
25–29	(5)	Net weight (ounces)

Some brands have the weight given in pounds, some in ounces, and some in both pounds and ounces. The total weight is the sum of the numbers in columns 20–24 and 25–29 (converted to the same units, of course). For each input card, print the product code, date purchased, store number where purchased, weight in pounds, and price per pound. Also print (SALE) if the product was on sale.

7

The DO Statement

A group of statements that is performed over and over is called a *loop*. You have seen many examples of loops. For instance, here is part of a program you saw in Chapter 5.

```
      NSUM = 0
      N = 1
10       NSUM = NSUM + N
         N = N + 1
         IF (N .LE. 200) GO TO 10
      PRINT, NSUM
```

This program sets NSUM = 1 + 2 + 3 + · · · + 199 + 200. The three indented lines form a loop that is performed for N = 1, 2, 3, . . . , 200. This kind of loop is common in programming. The **DO** statement in FORTRAN provides an easy way to write such loops.

Here is how the same procedure is programmed using a DO statement.

```
      NSUM = 0
      DO 10 N = 1, 200
         NSUM = NSUM + N
10       CONTINUE
      PRINT, NSUM
```

The statement

```
      DO 10 N = 1, 200
```

means to execute all the statements up to and including statement 10, first for N = 1, then for N = 2, then for N = 3, and so on until N = 200. After executing the loop with N = 200, the DO loop is finished, and the PRINT statement is executed. The **CONTINUE** statement here is a do-nothing statement that is used to terminate the DO loop.

There are several parts in the DO statement. After the word DO is a statement number, which is the number of the last statement in the loop. Following the statement number is an integer variable, called the **DO variable**. This variable is used as a counter in the loop. The DO variable is followed by an equal sign, which is followed by the **initial parameter**. The initial parameter can be an integer number or an integer variable. It will be the value of the DO variable on the first trip through the loop. After the initial parameter comes a comma, followed by the **terminal parameter**: an integer number or variable that specifies the maximum allowable value of the DO variable. The parts of the DO statement are shown in Figure 7.1.

Figure 7.2 shows that the DO statement means to carry out a procedure consisting

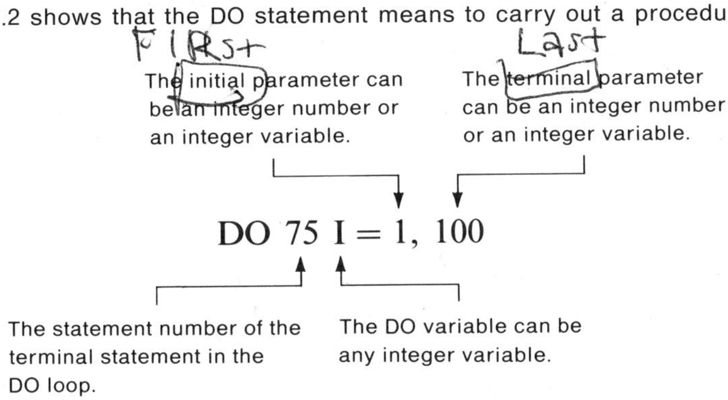

Figure 7.1 Parts of the DO statement.

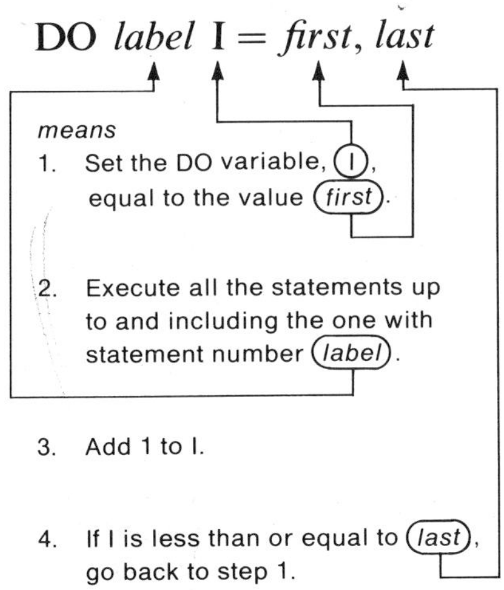

Figure 7.2 The DO statement means to carry out a procedure that uses the DO variable to count the times a loop is done.

of four steps: Initialize the DO variable, execute the statements in the loop, increment the DO variable, and repeat the loop if the DO variable is less than or equal to the terminal parameter. Figure 7.3 shows this same procedure written as a flowchart.

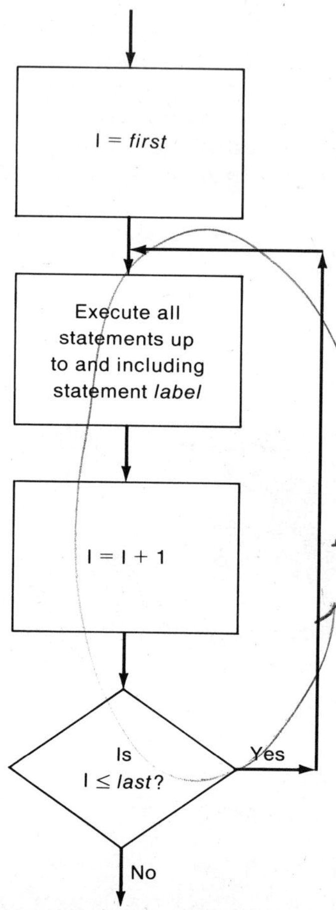

DO *label* I = *first*, *last*

Figure 7.3 A flowchart of the DO statement.

In Figures 7.2 and 7.3, the variable I has been used as a DO variable, but you can use any integer variable instead. The initial parameter and the terminal parameter can be either integer numbers or integer variables. Table 7.1 gives some examples of DO statements.

Table 7.1 Examples of DO Statements

DO 75 KOUNT = N1, N2
DO 100 J = 1, N
DO 50 LOAD = 2, LIMIT
DO 1 I = 10, 1000
DO 70 MAX = L, 10

The CONTINUE Statement

The **CONTINUE** statement has a very simple form:

```
CONTINUE
```

This statement also has a very simple purpose: It does nothing. You can write a CONTINUE statement anywhere in your program, and it has no effect. As a matter of style, you generally use a CONTINUE statement at the end of a DO loop. The CONTINUE statement merely emphasizes that this is the last statement in the loop. You will see later that there are a few cases where a CONTINUE statement is actually required, but in most cases you use it just to make the program easier to read.

Also as a matter of programming style, you should indent the statements in the DO loop. This does not affect the meaning of the program, but it will let you see at a glance just which statements are being repeated by the DO statement.

EXAMPLE 1. Write a program to print out the value

$$1 + \tfrac{1}{2} + \tfrac{1}{3} + \tfrac{1}{4} + \cdots + \tfrac{1}{9} + \tfrac{1}{10}$$

You can use a variable H for the sum of the fractions, and a variable N as a counter. N will take on the values 1, 2, 3, . . . , 10. In a program loop, you find the value of 1/N and add it to H. When the loop has been done for all values of N, you print H. A flowchart for this is shown in Figure 7.4.

A FORTRAN statement that executes a loop for N = 1, N = 2 and so on up to N = 10 is

```
DO 5 N = 1, 10
```

where 5 is the statement number of the last statement in the loop, which is a CONTINUE statement. Remember that 1/N is an integer expression whose value will be truncated to 0

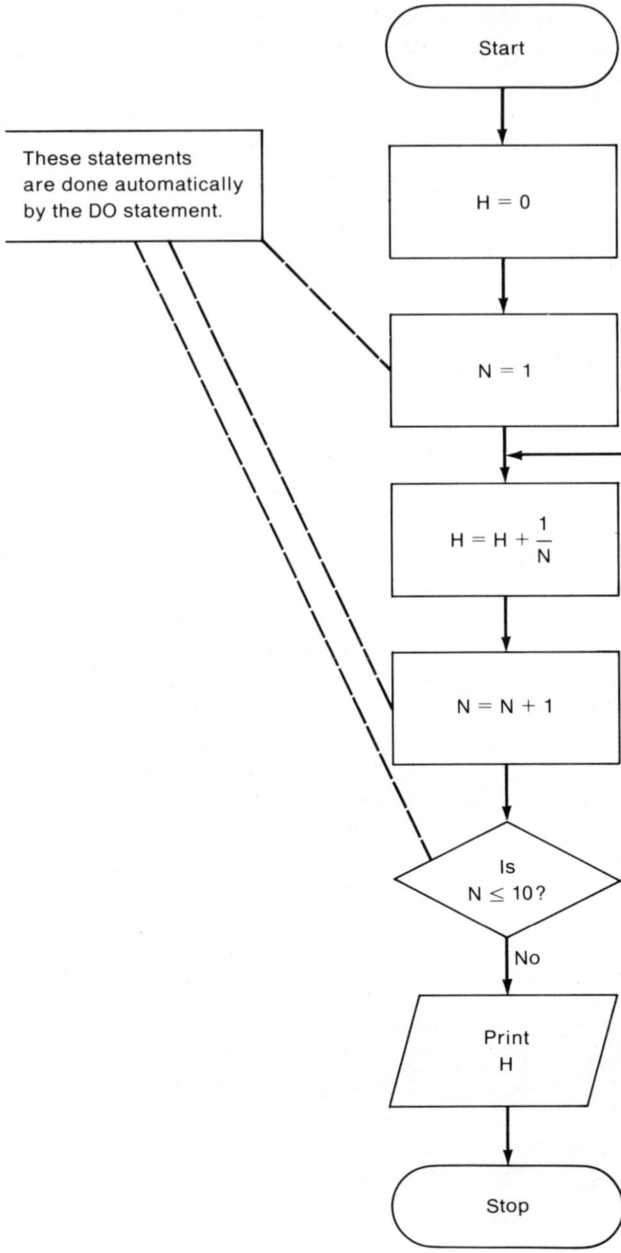

Figure 7.4 A procedure to compute $1 + \frac{1}{2} + \frac{1}{3} + \cdots + \frac{1}{9} + \frac{1}{10}$.

if N is greater than 1. To avoid this problem, let F = N, then use the real expression 1.0/F to compute the value of the fraction. Here is a complete program.

```
      H = 0.0
      DO 5 N = 1, 10
         F = N
         H = H + 1.0/F
5        CONTINUE
      PRINT 10, H
10    FORMAT(1X, F10.4)
      STOP
      END
```

We recommend using a CONTINUE statement at the end of a DO loop, but it is optional, and you could write the same program as follows with exactly the same effect.

```
      H = 0.0
      DO 5 N = 1, 10
         F = N
5        H = H + 1.0/F
      PRINT 10, H
10    FORMAT(1X, F10.4)
      STOP
      END
```

In each case, the statements indented are performed over and over by the DO statement. The PRINT statement is not executed until the DO loop has been done 10 times.

EXAMPLE 2. Modify the program in Example 1 to read an integer number from a card, then print out the number

$$1 + \frac{1}{2} + \frac{1}{3} + \cdots + \frac{1}{L}$$

where L is the number read.

As you saw, the terminal parameter in a DO statement can be a variable or a number. A statement that performs a loop L times is

```
      DO 5 N = 1, L
```

To modify Example 1, you need only read in a value for L, then execute this DO statement to perform the loop. Here is the program.

```
      READ 10, L
      H = 0.0
      DO 5 N = 1, L
         F = N
         H = H + 1.0/F
5        CONTINUE
      PRINT 15, H
      STOP
10    FORMAT(I3)
15    FORMAT(1X, F10.4)
      END
```

EXAMPLE 3. The Great Depression Bank offers daily interest on savings accounts. Suppose the interest rate is R percent per year. If a sum of money is deposited at the beginning of the year, find the amount on deposit each day for one year.

You can program this easily using a DO statement to execute a loop once for each day of the year. The daily interest on the account is 1/365th the annual interest. This means that if the sum AMOUNT is on deposit at the end of a day, then at the end of the following day, the amount on deposit is

```
AMOUNT = (1.0 + 0.01 * R/365.0) * AMOUNT
```

This becomes the new value of the variable AMOUNT, and the loop is repeated for each day. The program reads the values of R and AMOUNT as input. Here is a complete program.

```
C     PROGRAM TO PRINT THE AMOUNT OF SAVINGS EACH DAY.
C     R = THE ANNUAL INTEREST RATE (PERCENT)
C     AMOUNT = THE AMOUNT ON DEPOSIT
C
      READ 10, AMOUNT, R
      PRINT 20, AMOUNT
      PRINT 30, R
      DO 5 I = 1,365
         AMOUNT = (1.0 + 0.01 * R/365.0) * AMOUNT
         PRINT 40, I, AMOUNT
5        CONTINUE
      STOP
10    FORMAT(2F10.2)
20    FORMAT(1X, 'INITIAL AMOUNT', F10.2)
30    FORMAT(1X, 'INTEREST RATE', F10.3, ' PERCENT')
40    FORMAT(1X, 'DAY NUMBER', I4, 3X, '$', F10.2)
      END
```

This DO loop contains a PRINT statement as well as an assignment statement. You can have any number of statements, of any type, in a DO loop. Notice that the DO variable, I, is printed with the amount. Within a DO loop, you can use the DO variable just as you would any other variable as long as you do not change its value.

A More General Form of the DO Statement

There is a form of the DO statement that is more general than the one you have used so far. After the terminal parameter in the DO statement, you can write a comma followed by a **step**, an incrementation parameter, which is an integer number or an integer variable. This form is shown in Figure 7.5.

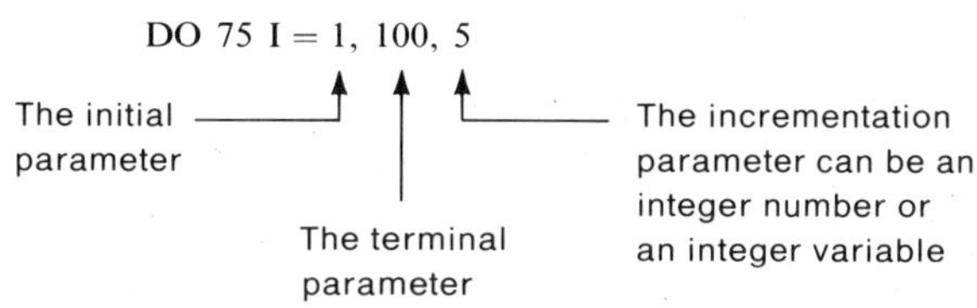

Figure 7.5 The incrementation parameter is added to the DO variable on each trip through the loop. In this case, the loop is performed for I = 1, then for I = 6, I = 11, . . . , up to I = 96.

This DO statement works just like the ones you have been using, with one difference: Instead of adding 1 to the DO variable at the end of the loop, the program adds the incrementation parameter to the DO variable at the end of the loop. If the value of the DO variable is less than or equal to the terminal parameter, the loop continues; otherwise, the loop is finished and the next statement is executed. Figure 7.6 gives the flowchart for this procedure.

Rules for DO Loops

There are several restrictions on the use of the DO statement. Some versions of FORTRAN relax these restrictions; you can consult the reference manual for the particular system you are using. In standard FORTRAN, your programs should follow the six rules in this section.

Rule 1: The initial parameter, the terminal parameter, and the incrementation parameter must be integer numbers or integer variables. They cannot be expressions.

This means that the following statement is not allowed.

```
DO 10 I = 1, N + 1
```

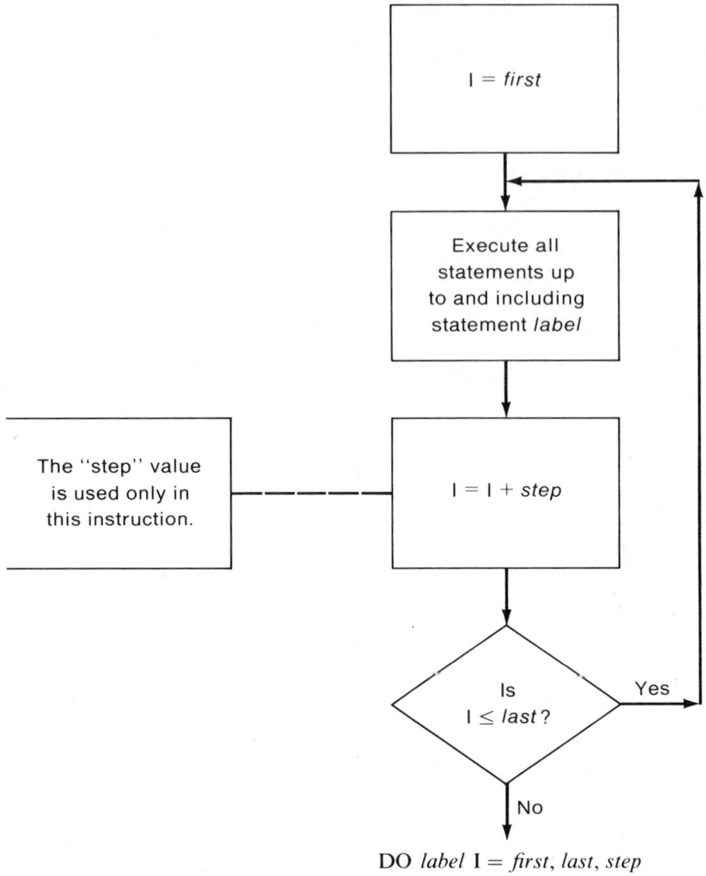

Figure 7.6 The parameter "step" is used in the incrementation instruction of the DO procedure. The value of "step" is added to the DO variable on each iteration of the loop.

You can obtain the same effect with two statements:

```
NPLUS1 = N + 1
DO 10 I = 1, NPLUS1
```

and this is legal, because NPLUS1 is a variable.

Rule 2: The three parameters must all be positive when the DO statement is executed, and the terminal parameter must not be less than the initial parameter.

This rule implies that all of the following DO statements are illegal.

```
DO 10 I = 2, 1
DO 10 I = 10, 1, -1
DO 10 I = 0, 10
```

Furthermore, the following DO statement *might* be illegal.

```
DO 10 I = 1, N
```

The form of this statement is correct, but it is illegal if the value of N is less than 1. If N is greater than or equal to 1, there is no problem. (Notice that if N is equal to 1, the DO loop is executed once.)

Rule 3: The DO variable cannot be redefined within the loop; neither can the initial, terminal, or incrementation parameters.

Here is an example of a loop that violates Rule 3.

```
      DO 70 J = 20, 30
         J = 1
         Y = Y + Y/X
70       CONTINUE
```

The statement J = 1 redefines the DO variable J.

Rule 4: The program cannot branch into a DO loop from outside the loop.

This rule implies that the following program is illegal.

```
      DO 100 KNTR = 1, LIMIT
50       PRINT 200, KNTR
100      CONTINUE
      GO TO 50
```

The statement GO TO 50 is *outside* the DO loop, but it branches to a statement *inside* the loop.

It is all right to branch *out of* a DO loop. Branching from one point to another *within* a DO loop is also allowed. For example, you may sometimes want to skip over the remaining statements in a DO loop and continue with the next value of the DO variable. The following statements illustrate this case.

```
      DO 5 I = 1, N
         READ 100, X
         IF (X .LT. 0.0) GO TO 5
            Y = SQRT(X)
            PRINT 200, X, Y
5        CONTINUE
```

These statements read a sequence of values and print the square roots of those values that are nonnegative. If X is negative, the IF statement causes a branch to statement 5, the CONTINUE statement. The DO variable is incremented, and the loop repeats if I is less than or equal to N. This example illustrates the rule:

Rule 5: To skip over the remaining statements in a DO loop and continue iteration, branch to the *last* statement in the loop.

It would be incorrect to branch back to the DO statement from within the loop.

When a program branches out of a DO loop, the value of the DO variable is still defined. This is illustrated by the following statements.

```
      DO 5 K = 1, 10
         IF (K .GT. MAX) GO TO 10
5        CONTINUE
10    PRINT 20, K
```

If MAX = 3, then the program will branch to statement 10 on the fourth trip through the DO loop. The value of K is defined, and the program will print the number 4. However, if MAX = 100 in this example, the GO TO statement is never executed. The loop is executed 10 times and then the DO loop is finished, so the PRINT statement is executed. In this case, the value of K is *undefined*, so you do not know what value would be printed. This illustrates the following rule:

Rule 6: When the DO loop is executed the last time, the program then executes the statement following the last statement in the DO loop. In this case, the value of the DO variable is undefined.

When we say that the value of the DO variable is "undefined," we mean that according to the rules of standard FORTRAN, you should not use the DO variable in a computation or an output statement unless you first redefine its value. You may find that on your particular computer system the DO variable *is* defined in this case. For instance, if MAX = 100 in the example just given, you may find that the value 11 is printed for K. This is an **implementation-dependent** feature: it might work differently in a different implementation of FORTRAN. As a general rule, *never rely on any special knowledge of implementation-dependent features of FORTRAN*. A good program should be written so that it will work correctly on *any* computer system.

The last statement in a DO loop cannot be a GO TO statement, and it cannot be a logical IF that contains a GO TO statement. Thus, the following DO loop is illegal.

```
          DO 10 I = 1, N
   10     IF (M .EQ. I**2) GO TO 30
```

This restriction, however, is easily circumvented using a CONTINUE statement, as follows,

```
          DO 10 I = 1, N
              IF (M .EQ. I**2) GO TO 30
   10         CONTINUE
```

There are some other statements, some of which we have not covered yet, which are not allowed as the last statement in a DO loop. This brings us to the last rule:

Rule 7: The terminal statement of a DO loop cannot be a GO TO, STOP, DO, PAUSE, RETURN, or an arithmetic IF statement, and it cannot be a logical IF statement containing any of these statements.

Exercises

1. Modify Example 3 to compute the principal plus interest, assuming the interest is compounded N times a year, where N is read in. Run the program for several values of N to see what difference it makes on the amount saved at the end of one year.

2. Some of the following sequences of statements are valid and some are not. If a sequence is invalid, state why.

a.
```
          DO 100 J = 1, 10, 2
          X = N - J
   100    GO TO 50
          CONTINUE
```

b.
```
          DO 10 I = 1, 10
          DO 9 J = 1, 5
          X = I*J
          PRINT, X
    9     CONTINUE
   10     CONTINUE
```

c.
```
          DO 20 K39 = 3, 9
   20     W39 = K39 + W39
          PRINT, W39
          GO TO 20
```

3. The **factorial** of a number is the product of all the positive numbers less than or equal to it. For example, 5! (read "five factorial") is 1*2*3*4*5 = 120. Write a program to print the factorials of the numbers 1 through 10.

4. Mark-On Department Store had total sales of $241, 901.98 during a six-month period. Monthly inventories for the period showed that the value of stock on hand was as follows:

Jul $70,785.50	Oct $85,297.57
Aug $80,462.12	Nov $90,059.05
Sep $90,138.49	Dec $55,268.74

The average inventory is the sum of these numbers divided by 6 (the number of months). The average rate of turnover is the total sales divided by the average inventory. Write a program to read total sales and monthly inventory, one number from each card, and compute the average inventory and average rate of turnover.

5. A popular example of elementary probability theory is to compute the probability that two people out of a randomly chosen group of *n* people have the same birthday. Ignoring leap years, the probability of any two prople not having the same birthday is 364/365. The probability that a third person's birthday will differ from the first two is (364/365) × (363/365), and so forth. For 10 people, we have 10 such fractions to be multiplied together to give the probability that all have different birthdays. This result subtracted from 1 is the probability that at least two have the same birthday. Write a program to find the probability that at least two out of *n* people have the same birthday, when *n* ranges from 2 to 50.

6. A company records sales for each branch office by punching a card for each month in the following format:

Columns	*(Size)*	*Item*
1–3	(3)	Branch office number
4–5	(2)	Blank
6–7	(2)	Month
8–9	(2)	Year
10	(1)	Blank
11–20	(10)	Total sales for month

Additionally, each branch office has a card giving the branch office number in columns 1–3 and the previous year's sales in columns 11–20. Assume that this card comes first and that the monthly sales cards for the office come next, in order by the month. Read and print all this data, with labels. Have the program stop if the input cards are out of order or if some months are missing. At the bottom of each page, print the percent increase in sales over the previous year.

7. The distance from an observer at sea to the apparent horizon depends on the observer's height above the surface of the sea. If the height H is expressed in feet, then the distance to the horizon in miles is given by the formula

$$D = \sqrt{\tfrac{3}{2}H}$$

Write a program to compute this distance for all integer values of H from 1 to 100.

8. Compute the values of the fractions

$$\frac{2}{1}, \frac{3}{2}, \frac{5}{3}, \frac{8}{5}, \frac{13}{8}, \frac{21}{13}, \ldots$$

where the numerator is the sum of the denominator and numerator of the previous fraction. Print the value of the first 50 terms in this sequence.

9. The atmospheric pressure P, in inches of mercury, is given approximately by

$$P = 29.9(10)^{-0.093H}$$

where H is the altitude in feet above sea level. Give the pressures at intervals of 400 feet from 0 to 20,000 feet.

10. The number of combinations of N things taken K at a time is given by

$$C = \frac{N!}{K!(N-K)!}$$

where N! is N factorial (see Exercise 3). The values of N and K must be nonnegative integers with $0 \leq K \leq N$. (*Note:* 0! is defined to be 1.) Read N and K, and compute C.

11. An experiment was conducted with several groups of plants. There were the same number of plants in each group. One card has been prepared for each plant, giving the following data: plant number, group number, date planted (MMDD), height (in centimeters). Print the date planted and height for each plant. At the end of the output for each group, print the average height. Provide column headings. Assume the first data card gives the number of groups and the number of plants in each group. (*Hint:* Use one DO loop inside another.)

12. Print all pairs of integers so that both numbers are between 1 and 7, inclusive, and the first number is less than the second number.

13. Assume that the population of the United States is 210,000,000 and the population of Canada is 25,000,000. If the annual growth rates of the United States and Canada remain constant at 1.10% and 4.75% per year, what will be the population of each country over the next 50 years? Will the population of Canada ever exceed that of the United States? If so, in what year? (This data is hypothetical, of course.)

14. An outdoor movie screen is 15 feet above eye level and is itself 40 feet high. (see figure.) The best spot to park your car is at the point where the angle that your eye

makes with the screen is maximum. Let X be the distance from the screen. It can be shown that the angle will be maximum when T is maximum, where T is given by the formula

$$T = \frac{40X}{X^2 + 825}$$

Compute the value of T for X = 1, 2, 3, . . . , 1000, and print out the value of X that gives the largest value of T.

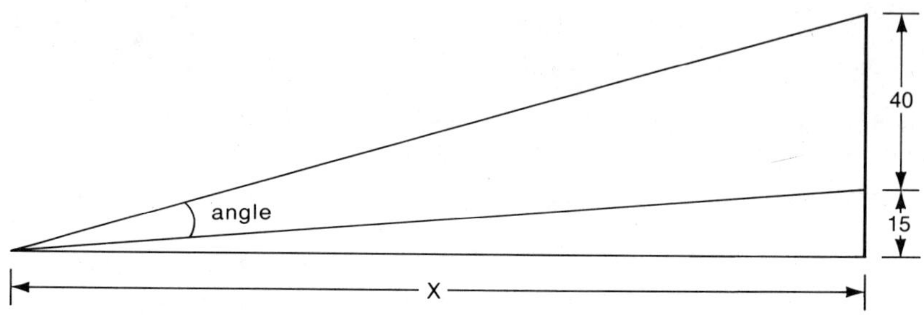

15. One mile is equal to 1.609344 kilometers. Print a conversion table that tells how many kilometers correspond to 1 mile, 2 miles, 3 miles, . . . , up to 50 miles.

8

Arrays

In mathematics, a variable is often written with a **subscript**.* For instance,

$$X_2$$

(read "X sub 2") is a subscripted variable, with the subscript 2. Subscripts are useful in programming, especially in cases where there are many related variables. Suppose a program uses one hundred different variables. It would be tedious just to give each one a distinct name such as A, B, . . . , SUM, and so on. But suppose we write one hundred values in a list:

1.3, 2.0, 6.1, 9.4, . . . , 5.9

When we speak of "the third number in the list," we mean the number 6.1. This is the basic idea of subscripted variables. Instead of giving a different name to each number in the list, you give a name, say X, to the whole list. Then you can write the list as

$$X_1, X_2, X_3, X_4, \ldots, X_{100}$$

The **array** X is the whole collection of 100 variables. X_1, X_2, and so on, are **elements** of the array X. So an array is a collection of variables, and each element of an array is a variable. You use the subscript to distinguish the different elements of the array.

* Variables in mathematical equations are usually shown as lowercase italic letters, as seen here. Computers, however, can print only uppercase (capital) roman letters. Therefore, the computer programs and flowcharts in this book are shown with uppercase roman variables corresponding to the italic variables in the equations.

Procedures That Use Arrays

Using an array provides a systematic way to name a collection of variables. More importantly, you can use the subscript systematically to describe an operation to be performed on the whole array, as you'll see in the following example.

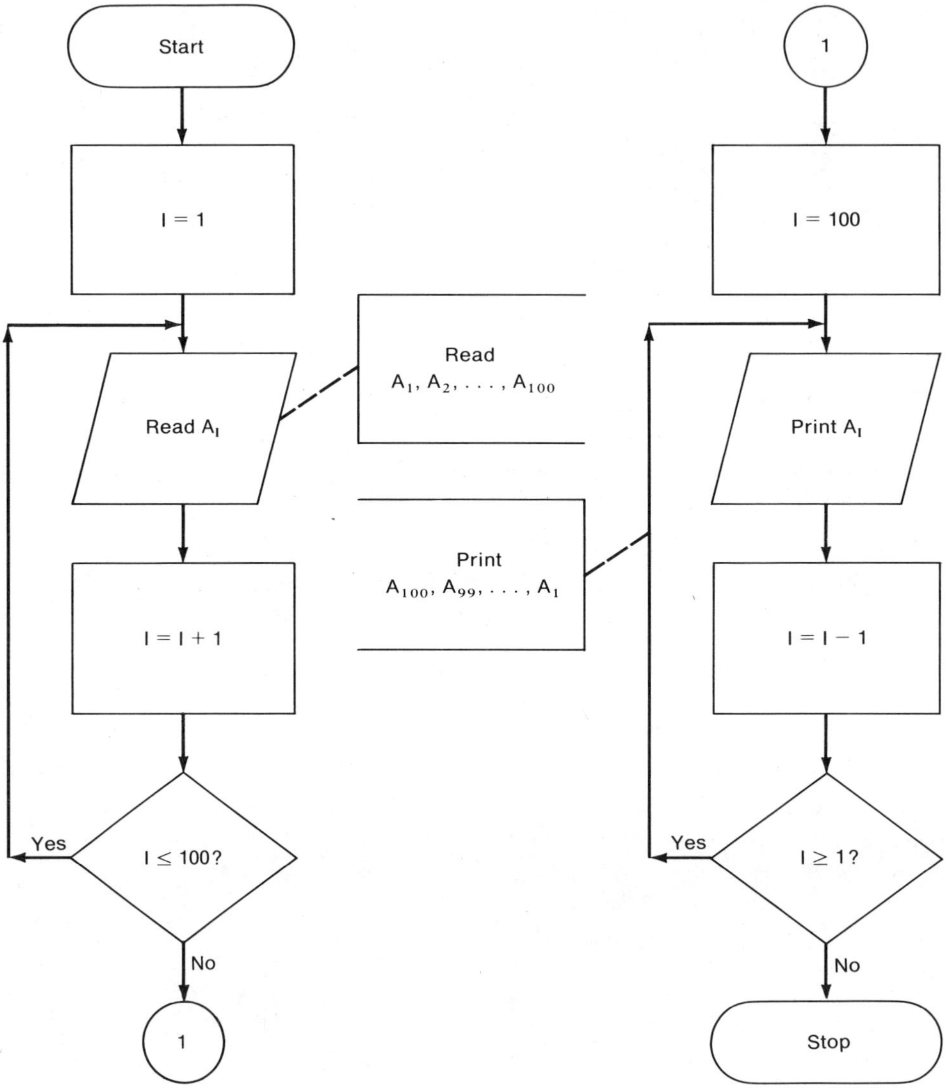

Figure 8.1 A procedure to read 100 numbers and print them in reverse order.

EXAMPLE 1. Suppose you want to read three numbers and print them in reverse order. A procedure for this is simple: Read *X*, read *Y*, read *Z*, print *Z*, print Y, print *X*. Now write a procedure that will read 100 numbers and print them in reverse order.

If you were patient enough, you could make up 100 variable names and write 200 instructions to read them and print them—but it is much easier to use an array. Call the array *A*. To read a number into the variable A_1, you could use the instruction: read A_1. But instead of using a different input instruction to read each number, use the instruction: Read A_i, in which the subscript *i* is a variable. First, you set $i = 1$. The instruction, Read A_i, reads the first number into the first element of the array. Next, set $i = i + 1$, then go back to the instruction, Read A_i. This time, the instruction reads the second number into the variable A_2. You can use a program loop that repeats the process for $i = 3$, $i = 4$, and so on until $i = 100$.

The last number read was stored in A_{100}. This is the number you want to print out first, so let $i = 100$, and perform the instruction: Print A_i. Then let $i = i - 1$, and go back to the instruction, Print A_i, which prints A_{99}, the second-to-last number that was read. You use a program loop that repeats the process for $i = 98$, $i = 97$, and so on until $i = 1$, then the program stops. Figure 8.1 shows the complete flowchart.

Arrays in FORTRAN

In FORTRAN, you represent a subscript by enclosing it in parentheses. Thus, instead of A_i, you write A(I), which is read "A sub I." A is the name of the array, and A(I) is the Ith element of the array.

An array can be either an integer array or a real array. An array called NUMBER will be an integer array, because NUMBER is an integer variable name (since it begins with "N"). This means that each of the variables NUMBER(1), NUMBER(2), . . . is an integer variable. An array called ADAM is a real array, which means that the variables ADAM(1), ADAM(2), . . . are real variables.

The subscript must always be an integer. It can be an integer number, as in A(47); or an integer variable, as in A(LOUIS); or an integer expression, as in A(I + 1). Table 8.1 gives some examples of subscripted variables.

Table 8.1 Examples of Subscripts*

Algebra	*FORTRAN*
x_1	X(1)
y_j	Y(J)
y_{j+1}	Y(J + 1)
a_{2k}	A(2 * K)
h_{3i-2}	H(3 * I − 2)

* A subscript can be an integer number, an integer variable, or an integer expression.

Specifically, we have the following rules:

Rules for Arrays

Rule 1: If the array name is an integer variable name, then the array is an integer array, meaning that each array element is an integer variable. If the array name is a real variable name, then the array is a real array, meaning that each array element is a real variable.

Rule 2: The subscript, which is enclosed in parentheses, must be an integer expression. (In some versions of FORTRAN, only certain simple types of expressions are allowed.)

The DIMENSION Statement

Suppose you want to use an array X in a program. How does FORTRAN know that X is an array and not a real variable? The answer is, you *tell* it, using a DIMENSION statement. An example is

```
DIMENSION X(10)
```

This is a **nonexecutable** statement (like the FORMAT statement) which goes at the beginning of the program. It means that within the program, X will be an array of 10 elements. The number 10 is called the **size** of the array X (sometimes it is referred to as the **dimension** of the array).

In general, a DIMENSION statement gives an array name followed by the size of the array, enclosed in parentheses. If you use several arrays in a program, you can use separate DIMENSION statements for each of them, or you can write the array declarations, separated by commas, in a single DIMENSION statement such as

```
DIMENSION X(100), Y(100), NUMBER (10)
```

which sets up the three arrays X, Y, and NUMBER, having 100, 100, and 10 elements.

This brings us to the following important rules:

More Rules for Arrays

Rule 3: Each array must be declared in a DIMENSION statement which comes before the first executable statement in the program.

Rule 4: The value of every subscript must be greater than or equal to 1 and less than or equal to the size of the array, as defined by the DIMENSION statement.

To understand the reason for these rules, you need to remember that a variable is a name for a location in computer memory. An array is a *set* of variables which is stored in a

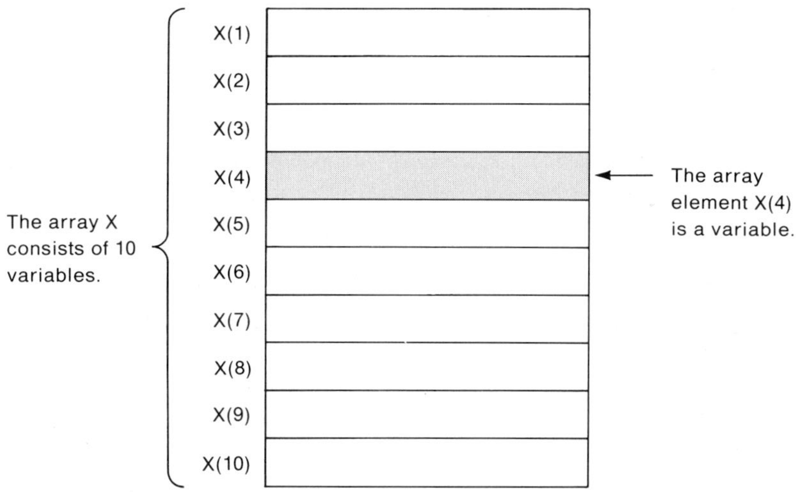

Figure 8.2 An array is a set of variables which is stored in a sequence of memory locations. Each array element is one variable.

sequence of memory locations. The boxes in Figure 8.2 represent locations in computer memory. The array element X(4) is a particular memory location, just like any other variable. The array X consists of the 10 memory locations X(1), X(2), . . . , X(10).

The DIMENSION statement

```
DIMENSION A(11), B(5)
```

tells that A and B are arrays. It also sets aside the memory locations for these arrays: 11 locations for A and 5 for B, as illustrated in Figure 8.3.

Rule 4 means that the subscript for A in this example must always be between 1 and 11, and the subscript for B must always be between 1 and 5. From the figure, you can see why. If the program contains the statement

```
A(12) = 0.0
```

this means to store a value in the twelfth element of A; but only 11 memory locations were reserved for the array, so there is no way to carry out the instruction correctly.

EXAMPLE 2. Write a FORTRAN program that reads 100 real numbers and prints them out in reverse order.

A flowchart for this was provided in Example 1. (See Figure 8.1.) You will need a DIMENSION statement at the beginning of the program to declare the array A with 100 elements. There are two loops in the program, and you can use a DO statement for each of them. In the first loop, use the DO variable, I, as a subscript for the array A. You cannot do this in the second loop, because the DO variable cannot go backwards from 100 to 1.

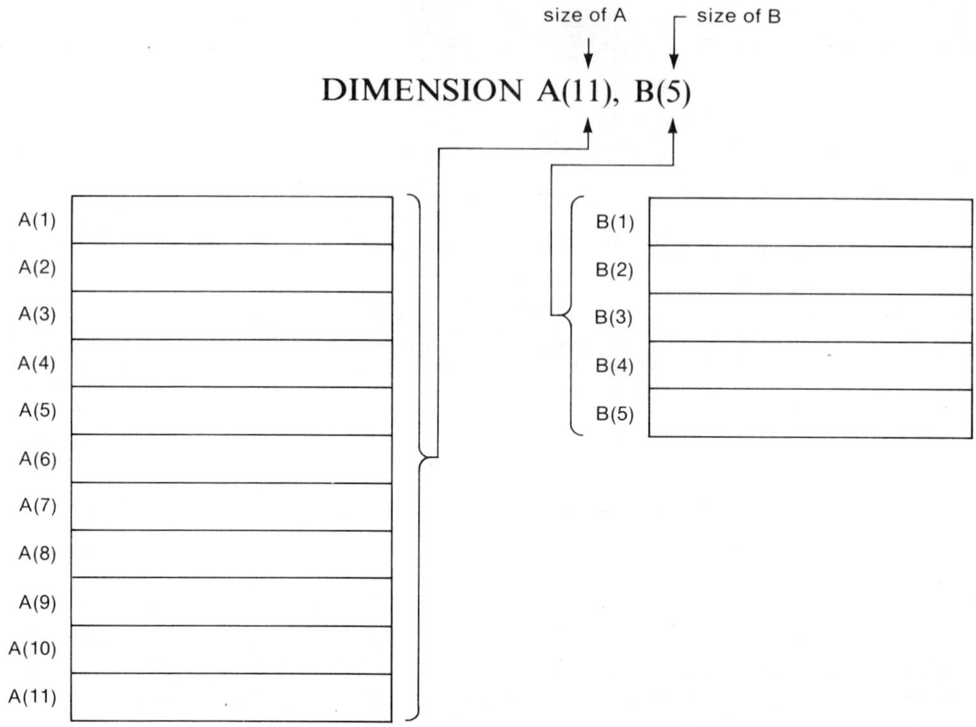

Figure 8.3 The DIMENSION statement is a declaration statement that specifies the sizes of arrays. The statement shown here tells that A and B are arrays of sizes 11 and 5. FORTRAN reserves 11 memory locations for A and 5 memory locations for B.

Instead, use a variable N which starts with the value 100, and subtract 1 from N each trip through the loop. Here is the complete program.

```
C   READ 100 NUMBERS AND PRINT THEM IN REVERSE ORDER.
C
        DIMENSION A(100)
C......... READ THE NUMBERS INTO THE ARRAY A
        DO 10 I = 1, 100
            READ 500, A(I)
10          CONTINUE
C......... PRINT THE ARRAY IN REVERSE ORDER
        N = 100
        DO 20 I = 1, 100
```

```
              PRINT 500, A(N)
              N = N - 1
20            CONTINUE
          STOP
500       FORMAT(F10.0)
          END
```

EXAMPLE 3. The program in Example 2 always requires 100 input cards. Let us generalize it to work for any number of input cards. Suppose that you have a set of data cards, each card containing a nonnegative number. You can put an extra card at the end containing a negative number to signal the end of data. Write a program to read these cards and print them in reverse order.

You can write the program in much the same way as Example 2. Within the DO loop, you add a statement

```
          IF (A(I) .LT. 0.0) GO TO 15
```

which branches out of the loop when a negative number is read.

When the program branches out of the first DO loop, the value of I is the number of cards that were read, including the last card with the negative number. You don't want to print this last value, so you subtract 1 from I and store the value in a variable N, which tells how many times to perform the second DO loop. Here is the complete program.

```
C    READ A LIST OF NUMBERS, TERMINATED BY A NEGATIVE
C    NUMBER, AND PRINT THEM IN REVERSE ORDER.
C    VERSION 1
C
          DIMENSION A(100)
C
C.........READ THE NUMBERS INTO THE ARRAY A
C
          DO 10 I = 1, 100
              READ 500, A(I)
              IF (A(I) .LT. 0.0) GO TO 15
10            CONTINUE
C
C.........N NUMBERS WERE READ (NOT COUNTING
C             THE LAST CARD)
C
15        N = I - 1
C
C.........PRINT THE ARRAY IN REVERSE ORDER
```

```
C
        J = N
        DO 20 I = 1, N
            PRINT 500, A(J)
            J = J − 1
20          CONTINUE
        STOP
500     FORMAT(F10.0)
        END
```

If you test this program with 20 data cards, it will work correctly. What will happen, however, if you run the program with 200 data cards? Remember, Rule 4 says that a subscript cannot exceed the size of an array. You have used a DO statement that executes the first loop a maximum of 100 times, so this does not seem to be a problem. But remember from Chapter 7 that when a DO loop runs to completion, the value of the DO variable is undefined. This implies that you have no way of knowing, for sure, what value is assigned to N in statement 15; it might be 0, or it might be greater than 100, in which case the program could malfunction. To avoid this possibility, you should add instructions after statement 10 to print an error message and set I = 101 (which will make N at most 100).

You should also consider what happens if the first data card contains a negative number. In this case, N is zero when the second DO statement is executed. This is illegal, and the results are undefined. Rather than having the program terminate with an execution error, you can include an IF statement before the second DO which will stop the program if N is zero.

In the second version of this program, these changes have been made. One other change is that you use a variable MAX as the upper limit of the first DO loop, rather than the number 100. MAX is set to 100 at the start of the program. By using variables for program parameters such as array size, you can make a program much easier to modify.

In this simple example, such considerations may seem unimportant. But the same problems arise in complicated applications, where they are usually harder to discover if something goes wrong. To be on the safe side, you should keep in mind the following suggestions.

Suggestions

1. Write your program in such a way that you cannot possibly have a subscript that is less than 1 or greater than the size of the array. It is far easier to include an extra IF statement when writing the program than it is to spend hours debugging a program that produces wrong answers for no apparent reason.
2. Write your program in such a way that it will work regardless of how much data you give it.
3. Whenever possible, use variables, rather than numbers, for program parameters such as array sizes. Then if you modify the program, you can simply redefine the variables instead of rewriting the entire program.

Here is the revised version of this program.

```
C     READ A LIST OF NUMBERS, TERMINATED BY A NEGATIVE
C     NUMBER, AND PRINT THEM IN REVERSE ORDER.
C     VERSION 2
C
         DIMENSION A(100)
C     MAX = SIZE OF THE ARRAY A
         MAX = 100
C
C.........READ THE NUMBERS INTO THE ARRAY A
C
         DO 10 I = 1, MAX
            READ 500, A(I)
            IF (A(I) .LT. 0.0) GO TO 15
10          CONTINUE
         I = MAX + 1
         READ 500, X
         IF (X .GE. 0.0) PRINT 600
C
C.........N NUMBERS WERE READ (NOT COUNTING
C           THE LAST CARD)
15       N = I - 1
C
C.........PRINT THE ARRAY IN REVERSE ORDER
C
         IF (N .EQ. 0) GO TO 30
         J = N
         DO 20 I = 1, N
            PRINT 500, A(J)
            J = J - 1
20          CONTINUE
30       STOP
C
500      FORMAT(F10.0)
600      FORMAT(1X, 'TOO MANY DATA CARDS')
         END
```

EXAMPLE 4. Write a program to read a set of numbers and print out the average, the minimum value and the maximum value. Terminate the input by a number 9999.

You can begin by reading the numbers into an array X, using the same technique as in Example 3. The average of a set of numbers $X_1, X_2, \ldots, X_n$ is given by

$$\text{average} = (X_1 + X_2 + \cdots + X_n)/n$$

We can use a program loop to compute the sum, then divide by n.

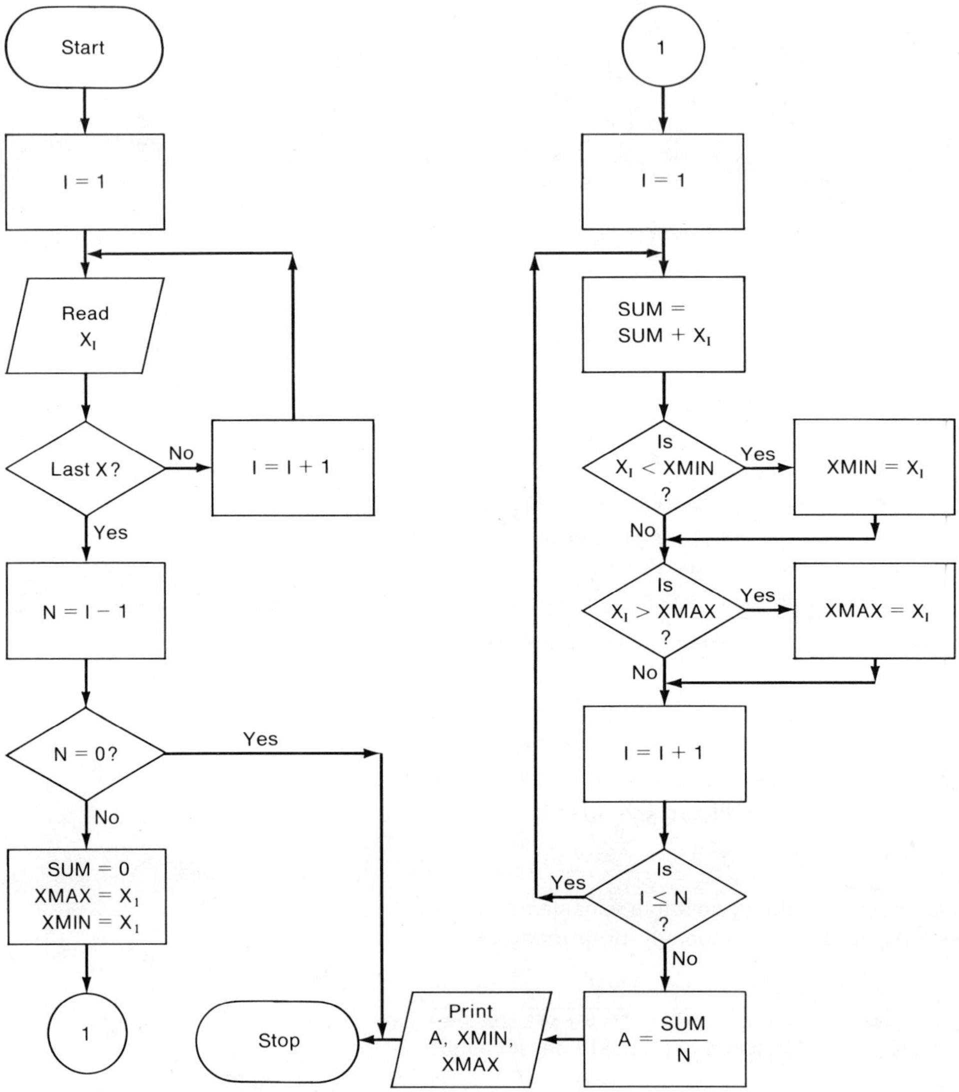

Figure 8.4 Procedure to find the average, minimum, and maximum of a set of numbers, using an array.

To find the minimum of a set of numbers, begin by setting XMIN = X_1. Then compare XMIN with each number X_i. If X_i is less than XMIN, then X_i becomes the new value of XMIN. When all numbers have been compared, XMIN is the minimum of all the numbers. A similar procedure holds for finding the maximum.

The complete procedure is shown in the flowchart in Figure 8.4. Here is the corresponding FORTRAN program.

```
C   FIND THE AVERAGE, THE MINIMUM, AND THE MAXIMUM
C   OF A SET OF NUMBERS.
C   VERSION 1
C
C   THE END OF DATA IS MARKED BY A CARD WITH THE
C   VALUE XSTOP.
C
C.........READ THE DATA
        DIMENSION X (100)
        LIMIT = 100
        XSTOP = 9999.0
        DO 10 I = 1, LIMIT
            READ 500, X(I)
            IF (X(I) .EQ. XSTOP) GO TO 15
10          CONTINUE
        PRINT 505
        STOP
15      N = I - 1
        IF (N .EQ. 0) STOP
C
C.........COMPUTE THE SUM, MIN AND MAX
C
        SUM = 0
        XMIN = X(1)
        XMAX = X(1)
        DO 20 I = 1, N
            SUM = SUM + X(I)
            IF (X(I) .LT. XMIN) XMIN = X(I)
            IF (X(I) .GT. XMAX) XMAX = X(I)
20          CONTINUE
C
C.........PRINT THE RESULTS
C
        AVERAG = SUM/FLOAT(N)
```

```
      PRINT 510, N, AVERAG, XMIN, XMAX
      STOP
500   FORMAT(F10.0)
505   FORMAT(1X, 'TOO MUCH DATA')
510   FORMAT(1X, 'N = ', I5, 5X, 'AVERAGE = ', F13.4,
     $     5X, 'MIN = ', F13.4, 5X, 'MAX = ', F13.4)
      END
```

This program works fine for up to 100 numbers. How could it be modified to find the average, minimum, and maximum of 10,000 numbers? The simplest way is to increase the size of the array X. But an array of 10,000 numbers might be beyond the range of the computer. (Even if that much memory were available, student jobs would probably not be allowed to use it.)

There is an easy way around the problem: Don't use an array at all. It is not necessary to store all the numbers in an array to compute the sum; you simply add each number to the variable SUM as the number is read. Similarly, you can count each number as it is read, and compare each number to XMIN and XMAX as it is read. All the work can be done in a single program loop. A flowchart for this method is shown in Figure 8.5.

This example illustrates an important point: Frequently, subscripts are used in a mathematical formula (such as the one for the average) to indicate a procedure that can be computed without the use of subscripts by a loop. Avoiding the use of subscripts, where possible, is usually more efficient, since it simplifies the computation and reduces the amount of memory used by the program.

Here is the revised version of the program.

```
C     FIND THE AVERAGE, THE MINIMUM, AND THE MAXIMUM
C     OF A SET OF NUMBERS.
C     VERSION 2
C
C     THE END OF DATA IS MARKED BY A CARD WITH THE
C     VALUE XSTOP.
C
      XSTOP = 9999.0
C
C.........READ THE FIRST VALUE AND INITIALIZE
C         THE VARIABLES
C
      READ 500, X
      IF (X .EQ. XSTOP) STOP
      N = 1
      SUM = X
      XMIN = X
      XMAX = X
```

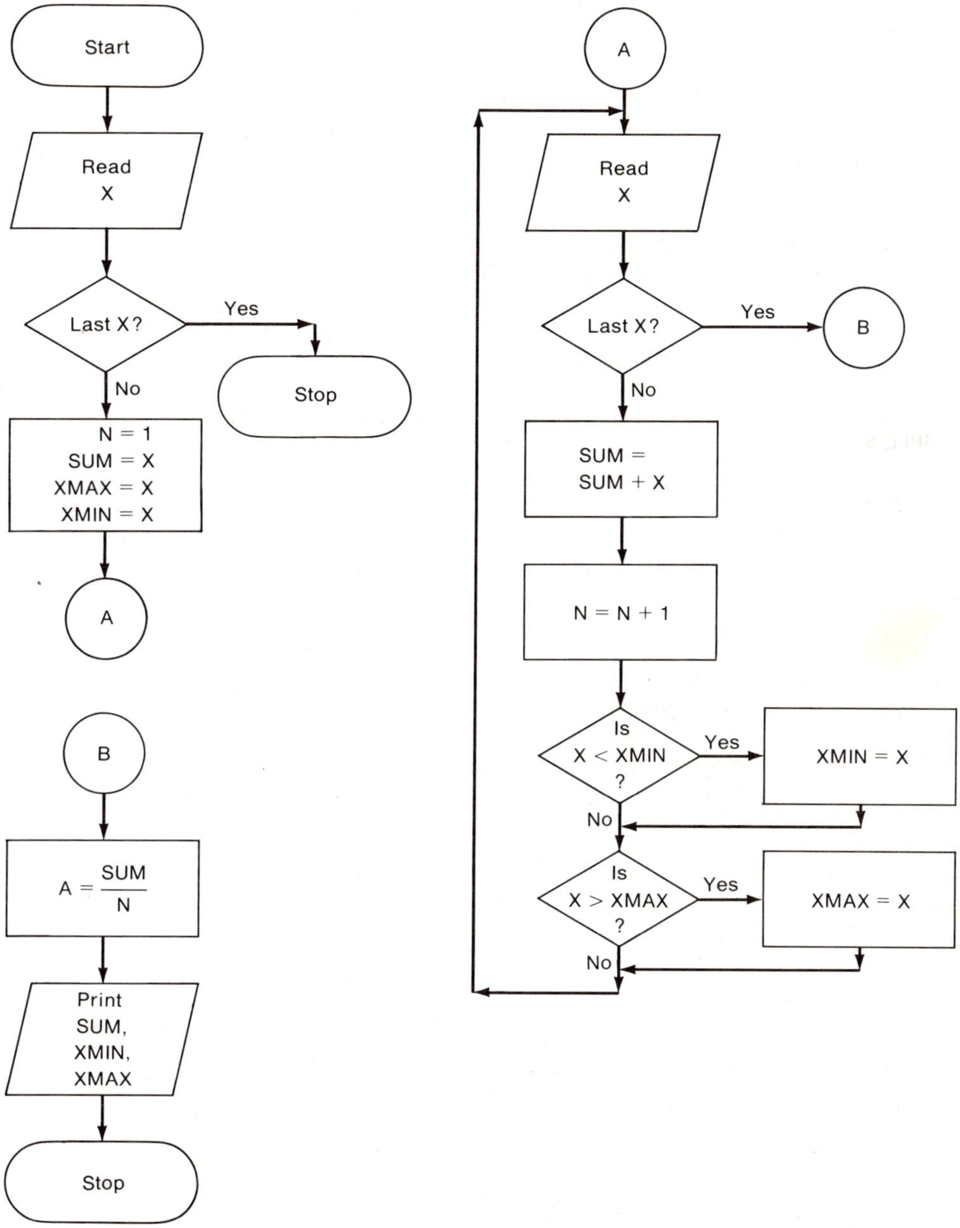

Figure 8.5 Procedure to find the average, minimum, and maximum of a set of numbers without using an array. This method is preferable to the one shown in Figure 8.4.

```
C.........LOOP UNTIL READING THE VALUE XSTOP
C
100         READ 500, X
            IF (X .EQ. XSTOP) GO TO 200
            SUM = SUM + X
            N = N + 1
            IF (X .LT. XMIN) XMIN = X
            IF (X .GT. XMAX) XMAX = X
        GO TO 100
C
C.........PRINT THE RESULTS
C
200     AVERAG = SUM/FLOAT(N)
        PRINT 510, N, AVERAGE, XMIN, XMAX
        STOP
500     FORMAT(F10.0)
510     FORMAT(1X, 'N = ', I5, 5X, 'AVERAGE = ', F13.4,
     $      5X, 'MIN = ', F13.4, 5X, 'MAX = ', F13.4)
        END
```

EXAMPLE 5. An artist is preparaing to make a "pie chart" showing a breakdown of expenditures for a corporation (see Figure 8.6). There are six categories, and the artist has a list of the total amounts spent in each category. Write a program which will tell, for each category, what percentage of the whole it is, and how many degrees wide to make the corresponding slice of the pie in the chart.

The program can read one number per line of input. There will be one line of output for each input card. Each line of output gives the expenditure, as read from the input, the percentage of the total, and the corresponding size of the slice in degrees. Since all the input must be read before the percentages can be computed, an array EXPEND is used to

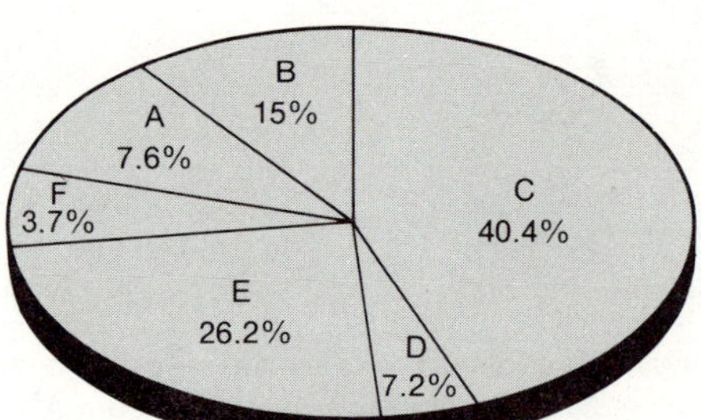

Category	Amount
A	1011
B	2000
C	5400
D	965
E	3500
F	500

Figure 8.6 A pie chart.

store the input data. You can set up two other arrays, PCT and SLICE, whose elements are defined as

```
PCT(I) = (EXPEND(I)/TOTAL)*100.0
SLICE(I) = (EXPEND(I)/TOTAL)*360.0
```

where TOTAL is the sum of all the expenditures. A flowchart is shown in Figure 8.7. Here is the program.

```
C   PIE CHART CALCULATIONS
C   READ UP TO 20 NUMBERS, TERMINATED BY A ZERO.
C   FOR EACH NUMBER, PRINT THE PERCENTAGE OF THE TOTAL,
C   AND THE NUMBER OF DEGREES IN THE CHART.
C   VERSION 1
C
        DIMENSION EXPEND(20), PCT(20), SLICE(20)
C           MAX = SIZE OF ARRAYS
        MAX = 20
C.........READ THE NUMBERS AND STORE IN ARRAY EXPEND.
C           ALSO, COMPUTE THE TOTAL.
C
        DO 10 N = 1, MAX
            READ 500, EXPEND(N)
            IF (EXPEND(N) .EQ. 0.0) GO TO 15
10          CONTINUE
        N = MAX + 1
15      N = N - 1
        IF (N .EQ. 0) STOP
C
C...................COMPUTE THE TOTAL
C
        TOTAL = 0.0
        DO 30 I = 1, N
            TOTAL = TOTAL + EXPEND(I)
30            CONTINUE
C
C...................COMPUTE THE PERCENT AND SLICE SIZE.
C
        DO 40 I = 1, N
            PCT(I) = 100.0 * EXPEND(I)/TOTAL
            SLICE(I) = 360.0 * EXPEND(I)/TOTAL
```

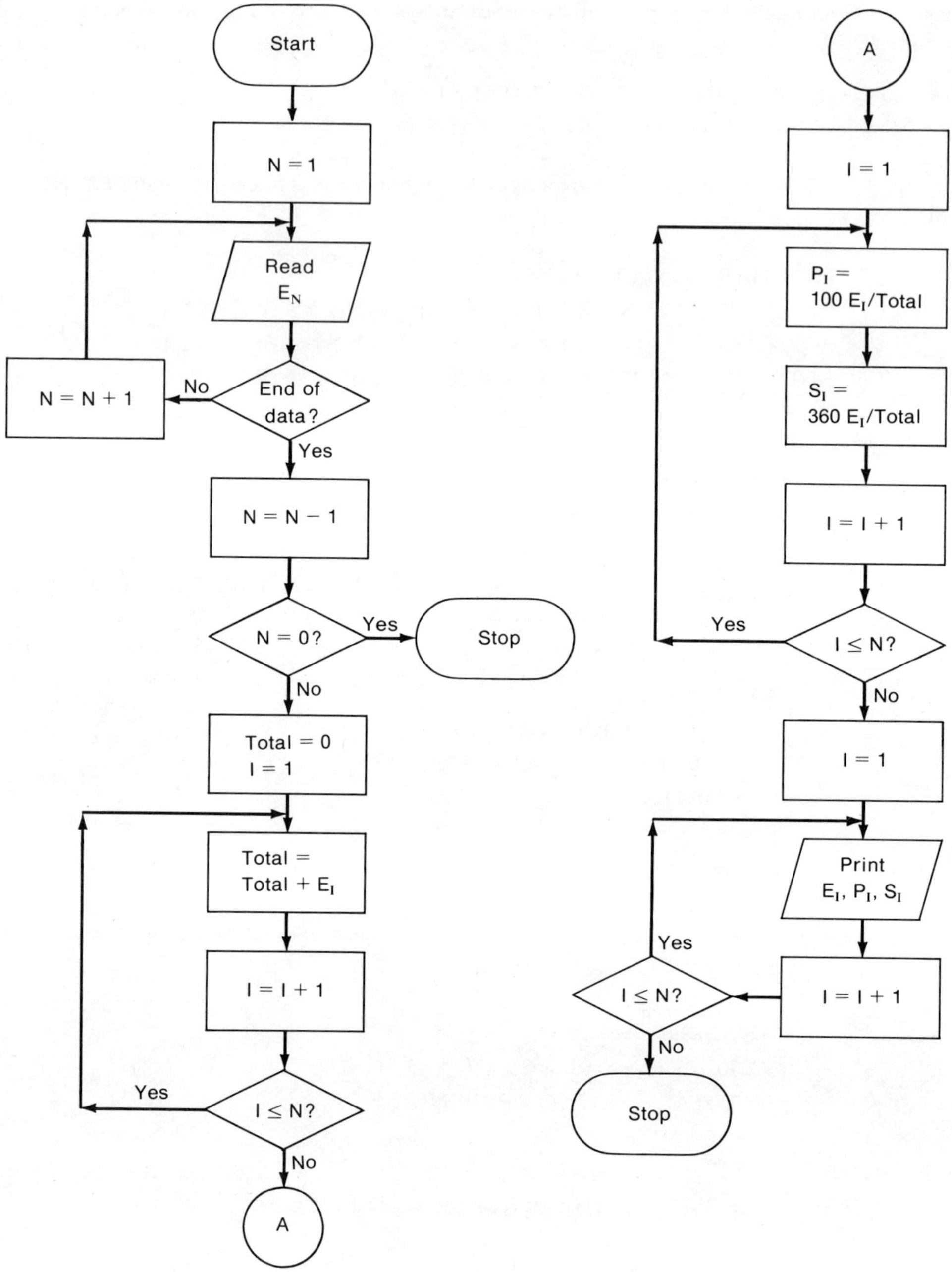

Figure 8.7 Pie chart calculations, first version. This method uses three arrays and four loops.

```
40          CONTINUE
C
C...................PRINT THE HEADING, THEN PRINT
C           EACH LINE OF OUTPUT.
C
        PRINT 510
        DO 50 I = 1, N
            PRINT 520, I, EXPEND(I), PCT(I), SLICE(I)
50          CONTINUE
        STOP
500     FORMAT(F10.0)
510     FORMAT(10X, 'CATEGORY', 2X, 'EXPEND.', 3X,
      $      'PCT.', 4X, 'DEG.')
520     FORMAT (10X, I5, F12.2, F8.1, F7.0)
        END
```

Unlike Example 4, you do need to use subscripts for this program, because the value of TOTAL must be known before you can compute the percentage for each category. You can make some improvements in the loop structure, however. The value of TOTAL can be computed in the same loop that reads the values. Also, the values of PCT and SLICE can be computed in the same loop that prints them. In fact, there is really no need to save the values of PCT and SLICE in an array since each value is just computed then printed. Many problems that are naturally formulated in terms of arrays can be just as easily solved without the use of arrays, often resulting in a simpler, more efficient program. Figure 8.8 shows a flowchart for this improved procedure. Here is the program.

```
C   PIE CHART CALCULATIONS
C   READ UP TO 20 NUMBERS, TERMINATED BY A ZERO.
C   FOR EACH NUMBER, PRINT THE PERCENT OF THE TOTAL,
C   AND THE NUMBER OF DEGREES IN THE CHART.
C
        DIMENSION EXPEND(20)
C           MAX = SIZE OF ARRAY EXPEND
        MAX = 20
C
C.........READ THE NUMBERS AND STORE IN ARRAY EXPEND.
C           ALSO, COMPUTE THE TOTAL.
C
        TOTAL = 0.0
        DO 10 N = 1, MAX
            READ 500, EXPEND(N)
```

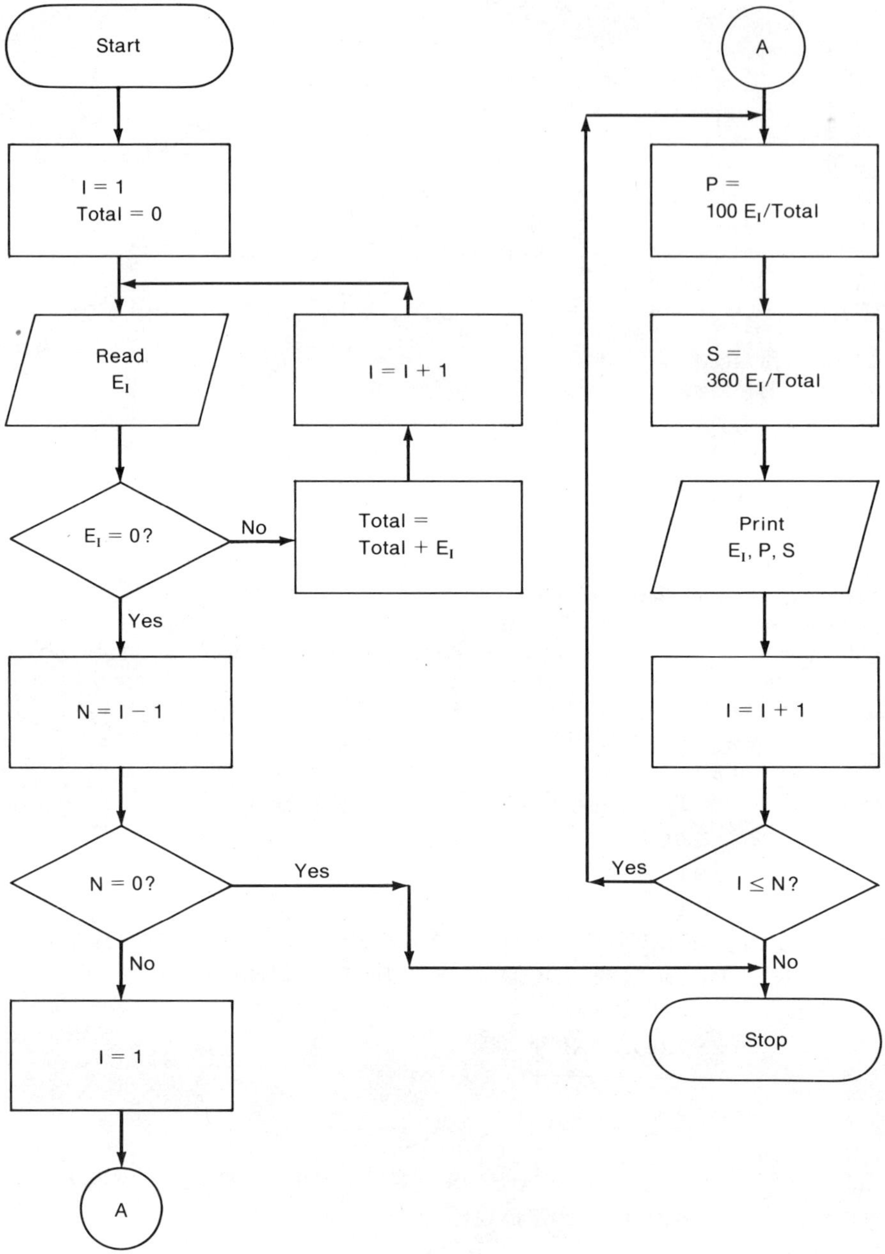

Figure 8.8 Pie chart calculations, second version. This method uses one array and two loops.

```
               IF (EXPEND(N) .EQ. 0.0) GO TO 15
               TOTAL = TOTAL + EXPEND(N)
10             CONTINUE
           N = MAX + 1
15         N = N - 1
C
C..........PRINT HEADING, THEN COMPUTE AND PRINT THE
C              PERCENTAGE AND NUMBER OF DEGREES.
C
           PRINT 510
           IF (N .EQ. 0) STOP
           DO 20 I = 1, N
               PCT = 100.0 * EXPEND(I)/TOTAL
               SLICE = 360.0 * EXPEND(I)/TOTAL
               PRINT 520, I, EXPEND(I), PCT, SLICE
20             CONTINUE
           STOP
500        FORMAT(F10.0)
510        FORMAT(10X, 'CATEGORY', 2X, 'EXPEND.', 3X,
         $     'PCT.', 4X, 'DEG.')
520        FORMAT(10X, I5, F12.2, F8.1, F7.0)
           END
```

EXAMPLE 6. The Acme Warehouse stores ten different types of machine parts. Each type has a number from 1 to 10. An inventory has been taken, and a set of data has been prepared in the format shown in Table 8.2. For each part number, there may be many input cards (the inventory was done on a shelf-by-shelf basis). Write a program which reports the total quantity on hand for each type of part.

The basic idea of the solution is to have an array, which we will call NQUAN, so that NQUAN(I) is the quantity on hand of part number I. For each input line, the part number, NPART, is used as a subscript of the array NQUAN. Then the quantity read is added to the appropriate element of the array NQUAN.

Table 8.2 Acme Warehouse Machine Part Data

Columns	*Item*
1–2	Part number (1 to 10)
3–4	Blank
5–9	Quantity on hand

The program should check for valid part numbers (i.e., between 1 and 10) to avoid a subscript out of range (as well as insuring a meaningful final answer from the program). One possible course of action is to have the program stop upon reading any invalid data. While easy to program, such a method makes the program difficult to use. A better method is to report invalid data and then ignore it. A part number of zero is used to terminate the input.

```
C   ACME WAREHOUSE PARTS INVENTORY.
C
        DIMENSION NQUAN(10)
C           NSIZE = SIZE OF ARRAY NQUAN
        NSIZE = 10
C
C......... INITIALIZE THE ARRAY NQUAN
C
        DO 10 I = 1, NSIZE
        NQUAN(I) = 0
10      CONTINUE
C
C ......... READ PART NUMBER AND QUANTITY
C           ADD QUANTITY TO THE APPROPRIATE
C           ELEMENT OF THE ARRAY.
C
20      READ 500, NPART, NUMBER
           IF (NPART .EQ. 0) GO TO 30
           IF (NPART .LT. 1 .OR. NPART .GT. NSIZE)
     $        PRINT 505, NPART, NUMBER
           IF (NPART .GE. 1 .AND. NPART .LE. NSIZE)
     $        NQUAN(NPART) = NQUAN(NPART) + NUMBER
           GO TO 20
C
C.......... AT END OF INPUT, PRINT THE ARRAY
C
30      DO 40 I = 1, NSIZE
           PRINT 510, I, NQUAN(I)
40         CONTINUE
        STOP
C
500     FORMAT (2I10)
505     FORMAT (10X, 'INVALID CODE', 2I10)
510     FORMAT (10X, 'PART', I5, 5X, 'QUANTITY', I10)
        END
```

EXAMPLE 7. A set of data cards has been prepared with one card for each student in a large history class. Each card contains a six-digit matriculation number followed by grades and other data not used in this example. The professor wants to make sure there is no more than one card per student. Write a program that will print a list of any matriculation numbers occurring more than once in the input data.

One approach to this problem would be to use the matriculation number as a subscript to an array, as in Example 6. In Example 6, however, there were only 10 possible values for the subscript. Here, there are a million possible matriculation numbers. An array with a million elements is totally impractical and, on most computer systems, impossible, since there is not that much memory available.

Instead of using the matriculation number as a subscript, you can set up an array NUMBER whose elements store the values of the matriculation numbers read so far. Thus, NUMBER(1) is the first matriculation number read, NUMBER(2) is the second matriculation number read, if it is different from NUMBER(1), and so on. A variable LENGTH tells how many distinct matriculation numbers have been read. You use a second array, KOUNT, to tell how many times each matriculation number has been read. KOUNT(1) is the number of times that NUMBER(1) has been read, and so on.

Figure 8.9 shows a specific example. Suppose that the program reads the numbers

117694, 220000, 390100, 220000

There are four numbers, but only three *distinct* numbers, which are stored in the first three elements of NUMBER. KOUNT(1) = 1, indicating that the first matriculation number has occurred only once; but KOUNT(2) = 2, indicating that the second matriculation number has occurred twice (see Figure 8.9).

The basic idea of the program is to read a matriculation number and compare it with each of the numbers NUMBER(1), . . . , NUMBER(LENGTH). If the number read is equal to

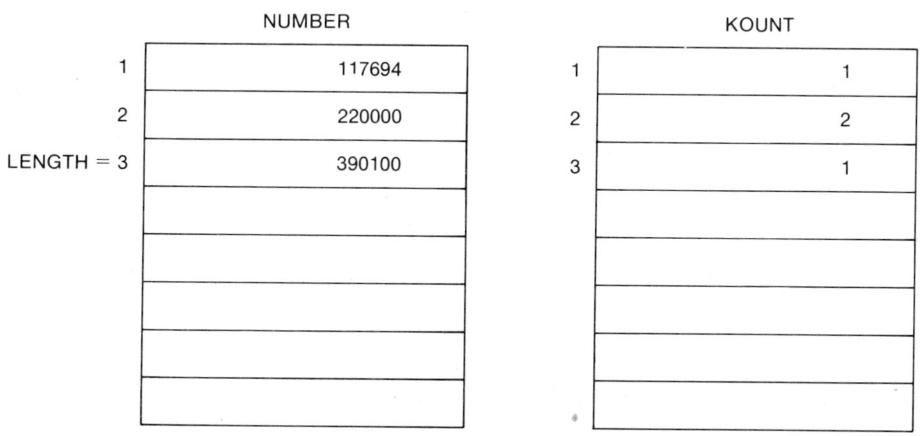

Figure 8.9 The problem of printing duplicates can be solved using two arrays: NUMBER stores the numbers themselves, and KOUNT tells how many times each number has been read.

one of these numbers, you add 1 to the corresponding element of KOUNT; if the number read is equal to none of the numbers, you add 1 to LENGTH, store the number read in NUMBER(LENGTH), and set KOUNT(LENGTH) = 1.

When this procedure has been carried out for all the input data, print all the values NUMBER(I) for which KOUNT(I) is greater than 1, since these are the matriculation numbers that occurred more than once. Here is the program.

```
C   PROGRAM TO READ A LIST OF NUMBERS AND PRINT ALL
C   THE NUMBERS THAT OCCUR MORE THAN ONCE.
C
        DIMENSION NUMBER (300), KOUNT(300)
C
C   MAX = SIZE OF THE ARRAYS
C
        MAX = 300
C   LENGTH = THE NUMBER OF VALUES ACTUALLY STORED IN
C   THE ARRAY NUMBER
C
        LENGTH = 0
C
C.........READ THE NEXT NUMBER, N.
C       (A ZERO INDICATES END OF DATA)
C
10      READ 500, N
        IF (N .EQ. 0) GO TO 100
C
C.........SEE IF N IS IN THE ARRAY.
C
        IF (LENGTH .EQ. 0) GO TO 25
        DO 20 I = 1, LENGTH
           IF (NUMBER(I) .EQ. N) GO TO 40
20         CONTINUE
C
C.........NOT FOUND IN ARRAY
C
25      LENGTH = LENGTH + 1
        IF (LENGTH .LE. MAX) GO TO 30
           PRINT 600
           STOP
30      NUMBER(LENGTH) = N
```

```
          KOUNT(LENGTH) = 1
          GO TO 10
C
C.........FOUND IN ARRAY
C
40        KOUNT(I) = KOUNT(I) + 1
          GO TO 10
C
C.........AT END OF DATA, PRINT ALL NUMBERS FOR
C            WHICH KOUNT IS GREATER THAN 1.
C
100       IF (LENGTH .EQ. 0) STOP
          DO 110 I = 1, LENGTH
             IF (KOUNT(I) .GT. 1) PRINT 510, NUMBER(I)
110          CONTINUE
          STOP
500       FORMAT(I6)
510       FORMAT(10X, I6)
600       FORMAT(1X, 'SIZE OF ARRAY EXCEEDED')
          END
```

The process of searching through all the elements of an array to find some particular number is called a **linear search**. Exercise 20 suggests a different way to program the linear search used in this example.

Two-Dimensional and Three-Dimensional Arrays

All the arrays you have been using have had a single subscript. You can also set up a **two-dimensional array**, which has two subscripts. You can think of a two-dimensional array as a rectangular grid of array elements, as shown in Figure 8.10. The first subscript gives the row, and the second subscript gives the column. In mathematics, such an array is called a **matrix**. (An array with one subscript is called a **one-dimensional array**, or a **vector**.)

To set up a two-dimensional array, you use a DIMENSION statement such as

```
DIMENSION A(3, 4)
```

This sets up an array of twelve elements:

```
A(1, 1)    A(1, 2)    A(1, 3)    A(1, 4)
A(2, 1)    A(2, 2)    A(2, 3)    A(2, 4)
A(3, 1)    A(3, 2)    A(3, 3)    A(3, 4)
```

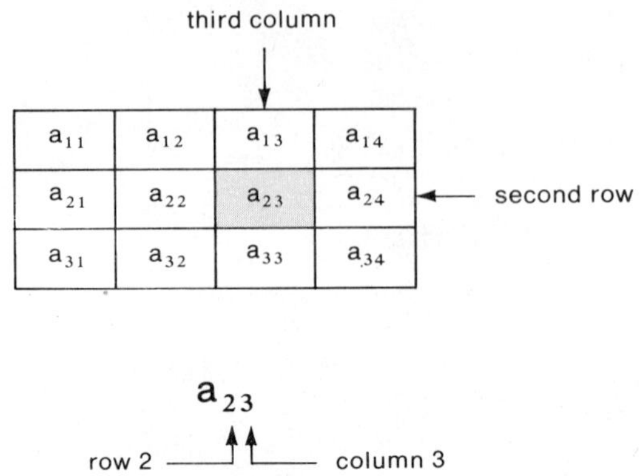

Figure 8.10 A two-dimensional array can be thought of as a rectangular grid with the subscripts giving the row and column.

We say that A is a "3 by 4" array, meaning that it has three rows and four columns. In general, the size of an array in a DIMENSION statement can be defined by a pair of numbers, separated by a comma. The first number is the number of rows in the array, and the second number is the number of columns in the array (see Figure 8.11).

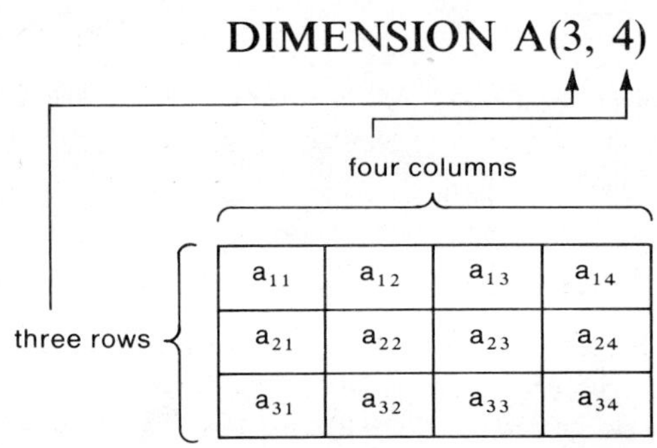

Figure 8.11 A 3 by 4 array has three rows and four columns.

You can think of a two-dimensional array as having rows and columns, but actually it is stored in the computer memory just like a one-dimensional array: as a sequence of consecutive memory locations (see Figure 8.12).

Standard FORTRAN also allows three-dimensional arrays, which are defined in a similar manner. For instance,

```
DIMENSION T(2, 2, 2)
```

declares T to be an array consisting of eight elements. The rules we gave earlier for one-dimensional arrays apply also to higher-dimensional arrays.

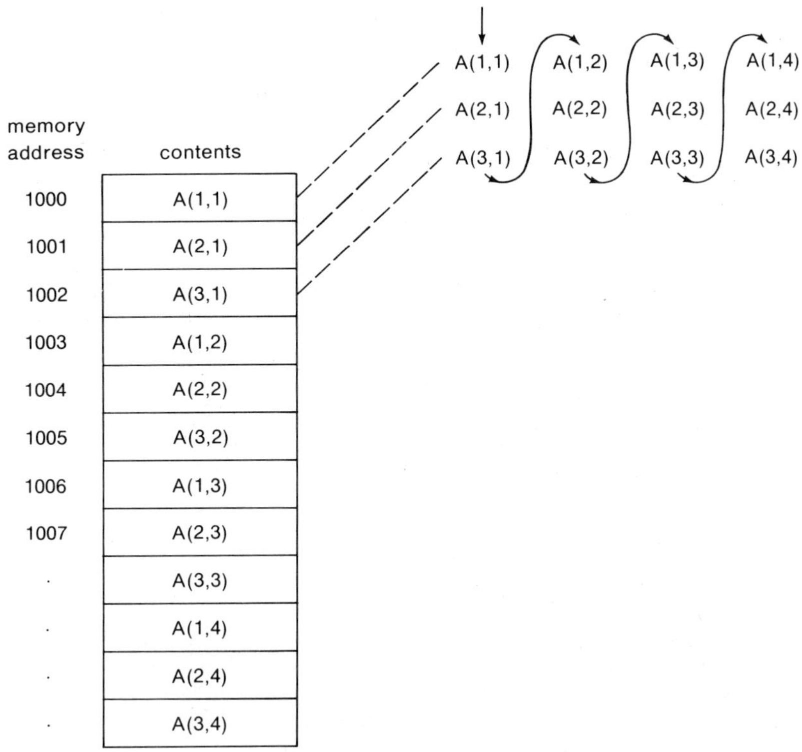

Figure 8.12 In computer memory, a two-dimensional array is stored in consecutive locations (like a one-dimensional array). The array is stored "by columns": the first column before the second column, and so on.

Rules for Higher-Dimensional Arrays

Rule 1: A two-dimensional array can be set up by a DIMENSION declaration of the form

DIMENSION *name*(*size1*, *size2*)

where *name* is an integer or real array name, and *size1* and *size2* are numbers that define the size of the array. Similarly, a three-dimensional array can be set up by a declaration of the form

DIMENSION *name*(*size1*, *size2*, *size3*)

(Some versions of FORTRAN allow arrays with up to seven subscripts.)

Rule 2: Each subscript of the array must be greater than or equal to 1 and less than or equal to the corresponding size, as defined by the DIMENSION statement.

The second rule means that if X is a 3 by 4 array, then whenever the program refers to to X(I, J), I must be between 1 and 3, and J must be between 1 and 4.

Implied DO Loops in Input and Output Lists

Consider the statements

```
        READ 5, X(1), X(2), X(3), X(4), X(5),
     $     X(6), X(7), X(8)
   5    FORMAT(8F10.0)
```

which read values into the first eight elements of the array X. Obviously, it is tedious having to write each array element in the input list; it would be even more so if the array had 100 elements. You might put the READ statement in a DO loop:

```
        DO 10 I = 1, 8
  10       READ 15, X(I)
  15    FORMAT(F10.0)
```

This is not quite the same thing, however. Each execution of a READ statement begins a new line of input. So, while the first example reads a single card, the DO loop in the second example reads eight cards. To specify a sequence of array elements in an input or output list, you can use an **implied DO loop**, which is something like a DO loop, but which is part of the READ or PRINT statement itself. An example is

```
        READ 5, (X(K), K = 1, 8)
```

This means exactly the same thing as

```
        READ 5, X(1), X(2), X(3), X(4), X(5),
     $     X(6), X(7), X(8)
```

It reads in the first eight elements of the array X. As in the DO statement, the expression K = 1, 8 means K = 1 through 8. The implied DO loop is enclosed in parentheses. It may contain more than one variable. For example,

```
        PRINT 7, (A(I), B(I), I = 1, 3)
```

means the same thing as

```
        PRINT 7, A(1), B(1), A(2), B(2), A(3), B(3)
```

The entire list of variables in the parentheses is repeated for each value of the control variable.

The variables in the implied DO loop do not have to be subscripted variables. For example, the statements

```
        PRINT 1, (J, J = 1, 10)
1       FORMAT(10I3)
```

produce the output

```
1  2  3  4  5  6  7  8  9  10
```

Like a DO statement, the implied DO loop may have a *step* parameter, as in

```
        PRINT 95, (NUM(I), I = 1, 7, 2)
```

This means the same as

```
        PRINT 95, NUM(1), NUM(3), NUM(5), NUM(7)
```

In general, the use of the implied DO loop is governed by the following rules:

Rules for Implied DO Loops

Rule 1: An implied DO loop may be used in an input or output list anywhere a variable name would be used.

Rule 2: The general form is

(*List*, *INDEX* = *first*, *last*)

or

(*List*, *INDEX* = *first*, *last*, *step*)

where *List* is any list of variable names or implied DO loops separated by commas, *INDEX* is any integer variable, and *first*, *last*, and *step* are integer constants or integer variables. If *step* is not specified, it is assumed to be 1

Rule 3: The values of *first*, *last*, and *step* must be positive when the implied DO loop is executed; and *first* must be less than or equal to *last*.

Rule 4: The variables in the list are read or written in the order specified, from left to right, first for *INDEX* = *first*, then for *INDEX* = *first* + *step*, and so on while *INDEX* ≤ *last*.

Rule 3 means, for example, that the following is not a legal way to print out an array in reverse order:

```
        PRINT 10, (A(I), I = N, 1, -1)
```

Some versions of FORTRAN relax this restriction and allow this statement.

Implied DO loops can be nested. For example, the following statement reads the elements A(1, 1), A(1, 2), A(1, 3), A(2, 1), A(2, 2), and A(2, 3), in that order:

```
      READ 101, (A(I, J), J = 1, 3), I = 1, 2)
```

The inner loop varies J from 1 to 3 for each value of I in the outer loop.

The values of *first*, *last*, and *step* must be defined in accordance with Rule 3 when the implied DO loop is executed. On an input statement, they may be defined by reading a value in the same statement. For example,

```
      READ 7, LOW, NHIGH, (F(J), J = LOW, NHIGH)
  7   FORMAT(2I2, 10F5.0)
```

This feature should be used with caution. If the limits read cause an illegal subscript reference, an error results. For example, if a keypunch error caused a value of −9 to be read for LOW, the result of the implied DO loop is undefined.

EXAMPLE 8. Five data cards are punched with four numbers on each card. Read them in and print them out so that there are four columns of output: the numbers in the first column of output are the numbers from the first card, the numbers in the second column are the numbers from the second card, and so on. Thus, if the input data is

```
  1   2   3   4
  5   6   7   8
  9  10  11  12
 13  14  15  16
 17  18  19  20
```

then the output should be

```
  1   5   9  13  17
  2   6  10  14  18
  3   7  11  15  19
  4   8  12  16  20
```

The program to do this will use an array A of size 5 by 4. The first task is to read the cards into the array. This is done by the following statements:

```
      DO 10 I = 1, 5
         READ 500, (A(I, J), J = 1, 4)
 10      CONTINUE
```

Each READ stores four values (one card) in a row of A. The DO loop repeats the READ so that the first card goes into the first row of the array, the second card goes into the second row, and so on.

The second task is to print out the values of the array by columns. On the first print line, you want A(1, 1), A(2, 1), A(3, 1), A(4, 1), and A(5, 1). These values can be written with the implied DO loop:

```
(A(I, J), I = 1, 5)
```

Notice that it is I, rather than J, that varies this time. The complete program is

```
C   READ AN ARRAY AND PRINT IT WITH THE ROWS
C   AND COLUMNS TRANSPOSED.
        DIMENSION A(5, 4)
        DO 10 I = 1, 5
            READ 500, (A(I, J), J = 1, 4)
10          CONTINUE
        DO 20 J = 1, 4
           PRINT 510, (A(I, J), I = 1, 5)
20         CONTINUE
        STOP
500     FORMAT(5F10.0)
510     FORMAT(1X, F15.3)
        END
```

Exercises

1. The program in Example 2 (page 202) uses two DO statements. Some special precautions had to be taken because of the restrictions on the DO statements (for instance, the DO variable cannot count down from 100 to 1). Write this program without using any DO statements.

2. Read a number N, and then read a sequence of values $X_1, X_2, \ldots . X_N$, one number per card. Replace each X_I with the number

$$\frac{X_I - A}{B - A}$$

where B is the maximum of all the X's and A is the minimum. Print these new numbers, one number per line.

3. In statistics, one frequently needs to compute the *variance* of a set of measurements. If the measurements are $X_1, X_2, \ldots, X_n$, define S (the sum of the measurements) and Q (the sum of the squares) by the formulas

$$S = X_1 + X_2 + X_3 + \cdots + X_n$$
$$Q = X_1^2 + X_2^2 + X_3^2 + \cdots + X_n^2$$

Then the variance V is given by the formula

$$V = (Q - S/N)/(N - 1)$$

(where N must be greater than 1).

Write a program to read a number *N*, then read a sequence of *N* numbers (one number per card) and store them in an array *X*. Print out the *X* values along with the average value and the variance.

4. Work Exercise 3 without storing the numbers in an array.

5. The **standard deviation** of a set of measurements is defined to be the square root of the variance (see Exercise 3). The standard deviation gives an indication of how much the measurements differ from their average value. Modify the program in Exercise 4 to print the standard deviation, the minimum value, and the maximum value as well as the average and the variance.

6. Measurements have been made of the heights of a group of first-grade students. The data is prepared with one measurement per card, as shown in the following table. To help assure the correctness of the data, a researcher decides to verify the original handwritten sheets. There are about 1000 students, total, so instead of checking all the measurements, he decides to check only those that differ from the mean by more than one standard deviation. (This should be about 32%, or 317 students.)

Column	*Item*
1–4	Student code number
5	Blank
6–8	Height (centimeters)

Print a list of student code numbers for all such students. This method is especially useful for finding gross errors such as keypunching 220 instead of 110.

7. The standings of teams in a baseball league might be listed as follows:

Team	*Wins*	*Losses*	*Percent*	*Games Behind*
6	10	2	0.833	0
2	9	3	0.750	1
1	8	3	0.667	1.5
3	6	6	0.500	4
5	4	8	0.333	6
4	0	11	0.000	9.5

Let NWIN(I) be the number of wins for team I and LOSS(I) be the number of losses. Then the number of games behind for team J is given by

$$\frac{(\text{NWIN(I)} - \text{LOSS(I)}) - (\text{NWIN(J)} - \text{LOSS(J)})}{2}$$

where I is the number of the leading team (the team with the highest percentage of wins). Read the team number, wins, and losses for each of up to 10 teams and print a table similar to the one above. You may assume that the input is sorted with the best team first.

8. Employees at Shlepco, Inc., punch a time clock each day. Hours and minutes are recorded on a 24-hour clock system. Thus, 1 P.M. is 1300. Time cards are prepared weekly in the following format:

Column	*Item*
1–4	Employee number
5	Blank
6–9	Time in Monday
10	Blank
11–14	Time out Monday
15	Blank
16–19	Time in Tuesday
20	Blank
21–24	Time out Tuesday
25	Blank
26–29	Time in Wednesday
30	Blank
31–34	Time out Wednesday
35	Blank
36–39	Time in Thursday
40	Blank
41–44	Time out Thursday
45	Blank
46–49	Time in Friday
50	Blank
51–54	Time out Friday

Read each day's times in and out. Each time is punched as four digits: the first two digits give hours, and the second two digits give minutes. Your should read these as two separate numbers, then convert to hours by dividing the minutes by 60 and adding that to the hours. Now let H(I) be the number of hours worked each day, for I from 1 to 5. If either the time in or the time out for a day is zero, then the employee did not punch the time clock; so set the corresponding H(I) to zero. For each employee, print the hours worked each day and the total hours worked all week.

9. The Acme Warehouse (see Example 6, page 215) is under new management. They still stock 10 types of parts, as before, but the part numbers have all been changed. The following is a list of possible part numbers:

13	40	43	60	89
21	42	50	70	99

Modify the program of Example 6 so that it will work with this new system.

10. Let NF be an integer array of 20 elements. Let NF(1) = 0, NF(2) = 1. For I = 3, 4, 5, . . . , 20, let NF(I) = NF(I − 1) + NF(I − 2). Print the array NF. This sequence of numbers is called the **Fibonacci sequence**. Each number in the sequence is the sum of the preceding two numbers.

11. In Example 8 of Chapter 1, we drew a flowchart to compute the annual premium for a client of the Bellemorte Insurance Company. Write a FORTRAN program for this procedure. Instead of using different decision boxes for each age category, set up an array and use a program loop to determine the correct age bracket of the client.

12. Professor Moriarty uses the following grading system for his class:

Final Exam Score	*Course Grade*
91–100	4
81–89	3
71–79	2
61–69	1
59 and below	0

For the borderline cases with scores of 90, 80 70, or 60, he decides the grade on the basis of homework assignments turned in. A borderline student gets the higher grade if and only if he has turned in at least three homework assignments. Student data is prepared on cards, with one card per student. Each card contains the student number, followed by the final exam score, followed by the number of homework assignments submitted. The last data card is a dummy card with the student number 0. Write a program that reads each card and computes and prints the course grade.

13. An array A contains N measurements. A researcher wants to consider only those measurements that are greater than ALOW and less than AHIGH. Let B be an array of all such As, and let M be the number of all such measurements. Write FORTRAN statements to compute B and M.

14. Work Exercise 13 without using a separate array B. That is, given an array A with N measurements, modify A and N so that the new A contains only those elements between ALOW and AHIGH.

15. Let NUMBER be an array of size 100, initially all zeros. Set every second element equal to 1. Now look at every third element. If it is 1, set it to 0; if it is 0, set it to 1. Now look at every fourth element. Again, if it is 0, set it to 1; if it is 1; set it to 0. Now look at every fifth element, every sixth element, and so forth. (On the last step, you look at every 100th element.) Print out all numbers I so that NUMBER(I) = 0.

16. Read two numbers: The first represents the amount of a purchase, and the second represents the amount you give the clerk. Print out the exact change you should receive. For example,

```
PURCHASE              $11.23
AMOUNT GIVEN          $20.00
CHANGE                $ 8.77
NUMBER        DENOMINATION
    1              $5.00
    3              $1.00
    1              $0.50
    1              $0.25
    2              $0.01
```

You may assume that the change is less than $20.00. (*Hint:* Use an array to store the possible denominations for change. To avoid round-off errors, store the amounts in pennies and use integer arithmetic.)

17. Example 8 showed how to read in rows of data and print them out by columns. Suppose that A is a 5 by 4 matrix. Construct a 4 by 5 matrix B so that the first *row* of *B* is the first *column* of A, the second *row* of B is the second *column* of A, and so forth. (B is called the **transpose** of the matrix A.)

18. Consider the 3 by 3 matrix

```
8   1   6
3   5   7
4   9   2
```

Read this into an array M. M is a **magic square**, that is, the sum of each row, column, and diagonal is the same. Subtract each number in M from 10 and print out the result. Is this also a magic square? (Have the program decide.)

19. An array NA, of integers, has NSIZEA elements. Some of these elements may be the same. For example,

1, 3, 5, 3, 3, 7, 5, 8

Construct an array NB which has all the elements of NA, with duplicates removed.

Set NSIZEB equal to the number of elements in NB. Thus, in the case, just given, NSIZEB = 5 and NB contains

1, 3, 5, 7, 8

20. Example 7 showed one way to program a linear search. Here is another method. To see if the number N is in the array NUMBER(1), NUMBER(2), NUMBER(3), . . . , NUMBER(LENGTH), let NUMBER(LENGTH + 1) = N. Then, starting with I = 1, write a loop that finds the first value of I for which NUMBER(I) = N. If I is less than or equal to LENGTH, then the number N was already in the array; if I is greater than LENGTH, add 1 to LENGTH to indicate that the new number is in the array. Rewrite Example 7 to use this search method.

9

Subprograms

In Chapter 4 you encountered the FORTRAN-supplied functions such as ABS, SQRT, and so on. Any time you want the square root of a number in a program, you can write a statement such as

$$Y = SQRT(X)$$

This statement causes a **function subprogram** to be executed. The subprogram that does the actual computation of the square root may be quite complicated, but you can use it easily because it is predefined by the FORTRAN system. You can write subprograms of your own in FORTRAN. For example, a certain program may require computing the factorial of several numbers. There is no FORTRAN-supplied function to do this, but you can write such a function, then use it as needed in this program or in any other program where you want to compute factorials.

Subprograms in a Flowchart

In general, a subprogram is any procedure that is defined separately. For example, Figure 9.1 shows a procedure for reading an integer N and printing N!, the factorial of N. We can consider the procedure for computing the factorial as a distinct subprogram. The main procedure for reading N, computing the factorial, and printing it can be represented as a flowchart without giving the detailed definition of the factorial computation. This is done in the left half of Figure 9.2. The box in Figure 9.2 means to perform the factorial subprogram. The right half of Figure 9.2 defines the factorial subprogram. The left half of Figure 9.2 is the main procedure (or main program). We say that this main procedure **calls** the subprogram, meaning that the main procedure includes an instruction that causes the entire subprogram to be performed.

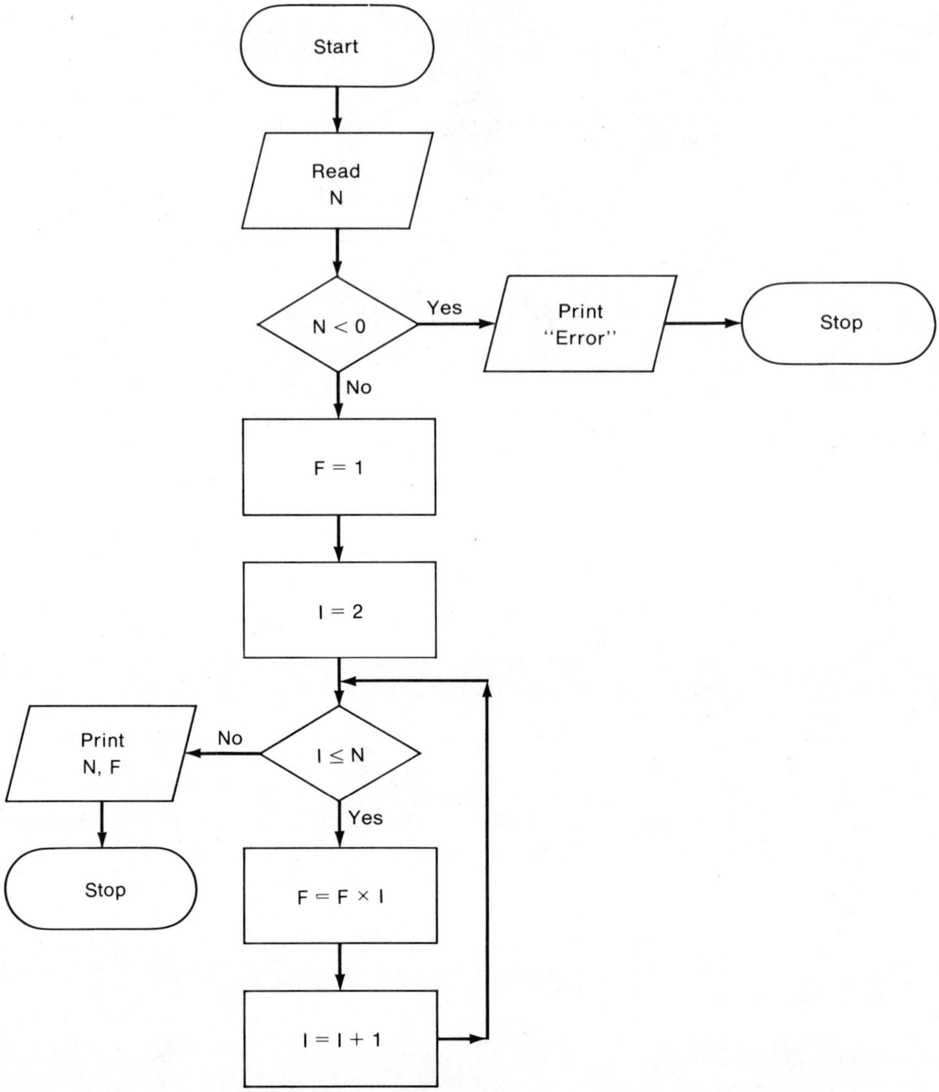

Figure 9.1 A procedure to read a number N and print N!, the factorial of N. The procedure consists of three main steps: Read N, compute F, and print N and F. The procedure to compute F can be considered a subprogram and written in a separate flowchart, as shown in Figure 9.2.

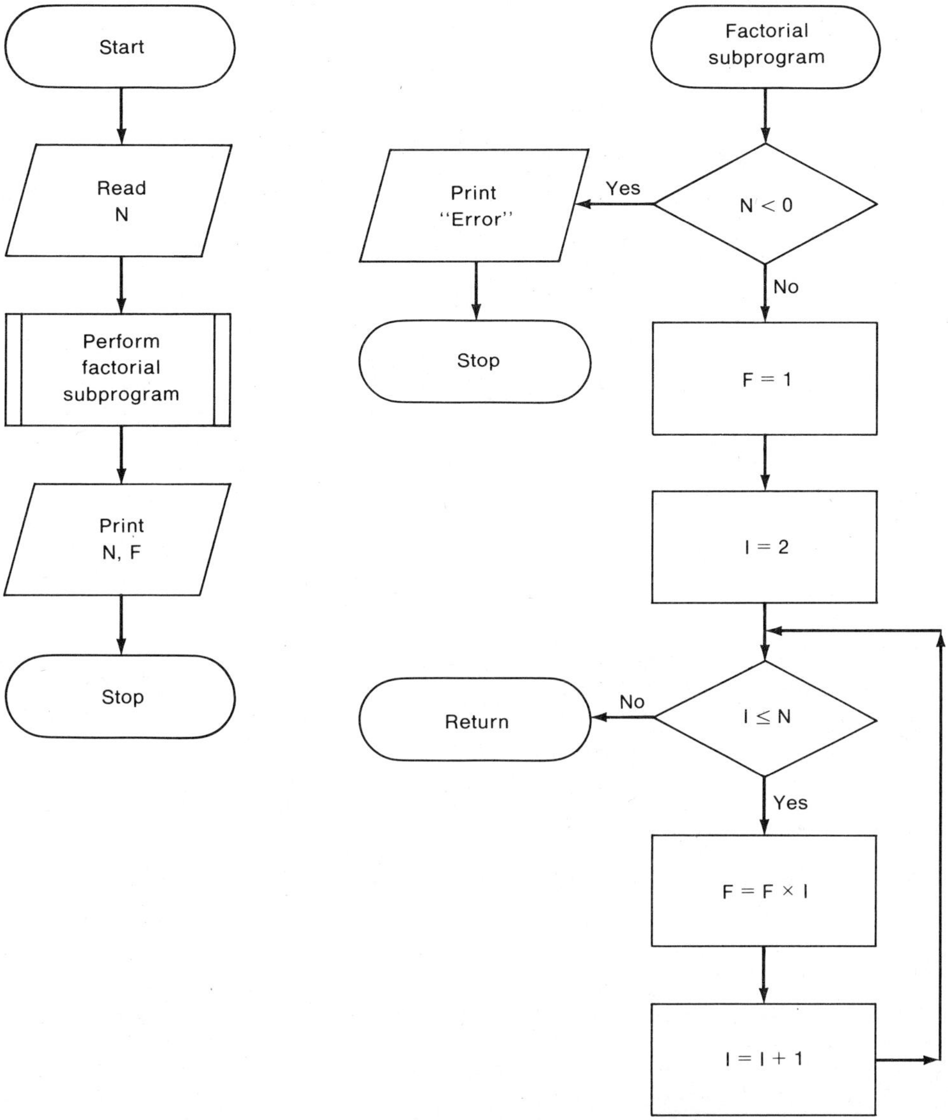

Figure 9.2 This flowchart is equivalent to Figure 9.1. The difference is that the procedure to compute the factorial is written as a separate subprogram. The rectangular box in the left half of the flowchart means to perform the entire procedure in the right half of the flowchart. The "Return" instruction in the subprogram means to go back to the main procedure from which the subprogram was called.

To indicate in a flowchart that a subprogram is to be performed, you use a rectangular box with two vertical lines:

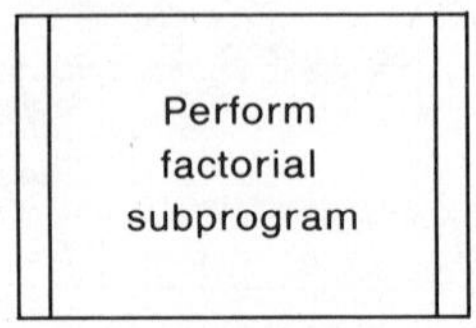

The beginning of a subprogram is indicated by a terminal containing the name of the subprogram:

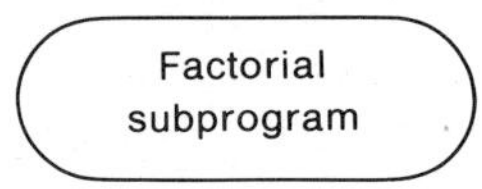

The flowchart symbol

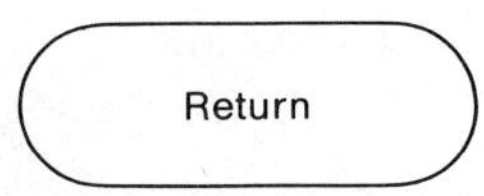

means to **return** from the subprogram to the procedure that called the subprogram.

Subroutines

There are two types of subprograms in FORTRAN: subroutines and functions. They are very similar. We begin with subroutines.

A **subroutine** is a self-contained program. It may be referenced in a program or in another subroutine, but the subroutine is separate from the program that calls it.

The first statement in a subroutine defines the name of the subroutine and the parameters it uses. An example is

```
SUBROUTINE DISPLA(X)
```

This **SUBROUTINE** statement says that the name of the subroutine is DISPLA. All the statements that follow, up to the next END statement, are part of the DISPLA subroutine. This group of statements is an independent program unit. Statement numbers and variable names in the subroutine are distinct from statement numbers and variable names used in the main program or in any other subprogram.

A subroutine communicates with the main program through its **parameters** (also called **dummy arguments**), which are defined in the SUBROUTINE statement. The statement

```
SUBROUTINE DISPLA(X)
```

says that the DISPLA subroutine has one parameter: X. Within the subroutine, X is used like any other variable.

To call the subroutine DISPLA from the main program (or from another subroutine), you use a **CALL** statement such as

```
CALL DISPLA(3.0)
```

This means to perform the DISPLA subroutine, using the value 3.0 in place of the variable X wherever X occurs in the subroutine. The expression in parentheses in the CALL statement is the **actual argument** of the subroutine. When the subroutine is executed, the value of the actual argument takes the place of the dummy argument.

In most cases, when a subroutine is finished, you will want it to go back to the program that called it. The **RETURN** statement is an instruction that does just that: It returns control to the statement following the CALL statement that executed the subroutine. The form of the **RETURN** statement is simply.

```
RETURN
```

A subroutine can do anything a main program can do. It can perform input and output, it can stop, it can declare and use arrays, and it can call other subroutines. In fact, wherever we have used the word "program" in this book, we could have said "program or subroutine." An even better term is **program unit**, which means a main program, a subroutine, or a function subprogram.

EXAMPLE 1. Here is a subroutine DISPLA(X) that simply prints the value of X and then returns.

```
      SUBROUTINE DISPLA(X)
      PRINT 10, X
      RETURN
10    FORMAT(1X, F10.3)
      END
```

X is the dummy argument of this subroutine. A main program can use this subroutine by including a statement such as

```
CALL DISPLA(Z)
```

which prints the value of the variable Z. A statement such as

```
CALL DISPLA(3.2)
```

will print the number 3.2. The actual argument in this case is a number. But it may also be an expression, as in

```
CALL DISPLA(SQRT(X**2 + 1.0))
```

which evaluates the expression SQRT(X**2 + 1.0) and then passes this value to the subroutine, where it is printed.

In a job that uses subprograms, there will always be one main program and an arbitrary number of subprograms. These are run just like jobs consisting of a main program only. The main program usually comes first (on many systems, it can come anywhere); its last statement, of course, is the END statement. If a subroutine is used, the SUBROUTINE line comes next, followed by the definition of the subroutine, followed by the END line of the subroutine. More subroutines may follow that.

A main program that makes several calls to the subroutine DISPLA is shown as follows.

```
      X = 1.0
      CALL DISPLA(X)
      VALUE = 2.0
      CALL DISPLA(VALUE)
      CALL DISPLA(3.0)
      CALL DISPLA(1.0 + X + VALUE)
      STOP
      END

      SUBROUTINE DISPLA(X)
      PRINT 10, X
      RETURN
10    FORMAT(1X, F10.3)
      END
```

This illustrates how the argument of the subroutine can be used to pass a value from the main program to the subroutine. The argument can also be used to pass values from the subroutines to the main program, as shown in Example 2.

EXAMPLE 2. The subroutine GET(X) reads values from a card until a nonzero value is encountered; then it returns this value in the variable X. In the main program which follows, the subroutine GET is used to read one number from a card and print the next five nonzero values on a line.

```
C-- MAIN PROGRAM
C-- PRINT THE NEXT FIVE NONZERO VALUES ON ONE LINE
      DIMENSION A(5)
      DO 10 I = 1, 5
         CALL GET(A(I))
10       CONTINUE
      PRINT 500, (A(I), I = 1, 5)
      STOP
500   FORMAT(10X, 5F10.3)
      END

      SUBROUTINE GET(X)
C-- READ THE NEXT NONZERO VALUE INTO THE VARIABLE X
10    READ 500, X
      IF (X .EQ. 0.0) GO TO 10
      RETURN
500   FORMAT(F5.0)
      END
```

The first call to the subroutine stores a value in A(1); successive calls store values in A(2) through A(5). The array A is defined by the main program, but values are stored in it by the subroutine.

Note there is a statement 10 and a statement 500 in both the main program and the subroutine. This causes no conflict; the main program and the subroutine are compiled separately. Statement numbers apply only to the program unit in which they are used. The same is true of variable names, except for dummy arguments (and, as you will see later, names in a COMMON statement).

Subroutines can call other subroutines. The only restriction is that a subroutine cannot call itself, either directly or indirectly. In the following example, the subroutine DISPLA is called both from the main program and from the subroutine GET.

```
C-- MAIN PROGRAM (CALLS SUBROUTINES GET AND DISPLA)
      S = 0.0
      DO 10 I = 1, 5
         CALL GET(X)
         S = S + X
10       CONTINUE
      CALL DISPLA(S)
      STOP
      END
```

```
C-- READ THE NEXT NONZERO VALUE INTO THE VARIABLE X
          SUBROUTINE GET(X)
C   CALLS SUBROUTINE DISPLAY
10        READ 500, X
          IF (X .EQ. 0.0) GO TO 10
          CALL DISPLA(X)
          RETURN
500       FORMAT(F5.0)
          END

C-- PRINT THE VALUE OF A
          SUBROUTINE DISPLA(A)
          PRINT 10, A
          RETURN
10        FORMAT(1X, F10.3)
          END
```

The flowchart for this is shown in Figure 9.3.

EXAMPLE 3. As you have seen, a constant or an expression may be used as an actual argument to a subroutine call. When the subroutine stores a value in a dummy argument, however, the actual argument in the call *must* be a variable. Consider the following subroutine and program:

```
          DIMENSION A(25)
          DO 10 I = 1, 25
             CALL ZERO(A(I))
10           CONTINUE
          STOP
          END

          SUBROUTINE ZERO(V)
          V = 0.0
          RETURN
          END
```

The subroutine ZERO simply sets its argument to zero. The calling program shows how this can be used to initialize an array. This is a legitimate use of the subroutine. Now consider the statement

```
          CALL ZERO(1.0)
```

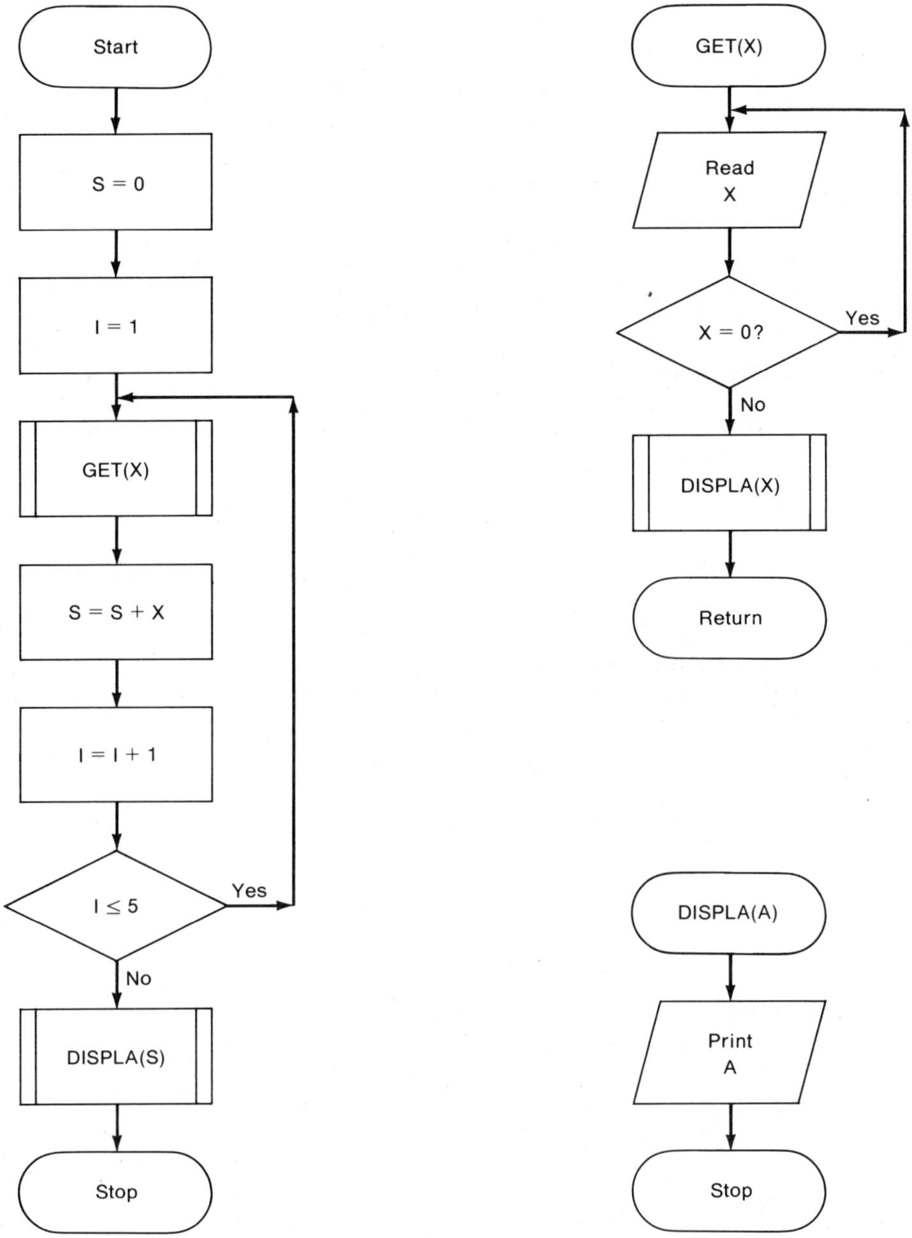

Figure 9.3 The main program (on the left) calls GET and DISPLA. The subroutine GET also calls DISPLA.

The effect of this call is to set the constant value 1.0 to zero! This is like having a statement in the program saying

$$1.0 = 0.0$$

In fact, it is worse. This statement is incorrect FORTRAN and would be detected by the compiler and diagnosed. The subroutine call would probably execute without any diagnostics, very likely causing wrong answers in the program.

EXAMPLE 4. Subroutines provide a good way of handling error checking. For instance, you have seen examples of programs which read values into successive array elements. The subroutine CHECK(N, NMAX), defined as follows, will simply return if N $\leq$ NMAX. But otherwise, it will print an error message and stop the program. As this illustrates, a subroutine may contain a STOP statement. The subroutine and a simple calling program are:

```
C--MAIN PROGRAM
      DIMENSION MVECT(25)
      LENGTH = 0
C---------------------------------------------
C  READ NUMBERS INTO MVECT(1), MVECT(2), . . . , MVECT(LENGTH)
C---------------------------------------------
100   READ 105, M
105      FORMAT(15)
         IF (M .EQ. 0) GO TO 200
C        ---------------
C        ADD 1 TO LENGTH AND MAKE SURE THAT
C        LENGTH IS NOT GREATER THAN 25.
C        ---------------
         LENGTH = LENGTH + 1
         CALL CHECK(LENGTH, 25)
         MVECT(LENGTH) = M
         GO TO 100
C---------------------------------------------
C  ADD ALL THE ARRAY ELEMENTS, AND PRINT THE SUM
C---------------------------------------------
200   NSUM = 0
      DO 210 I = 1, LENGTH
         NSUM - NSUM + MVECT(I)
210      CONTINUE
      PRINT 215, NSUM
215   FORMAT(10X, I10)
      STOP
      END
```

```
      SUBROUTINE CHECK(N, NMAX)
C-------------------------------------------
C  CHECK THAT N IS GREATER THAN OR EQUAL TO 1
C  AND LESS THAN OR EQUAL TO NMAX.
C-------------------------------------------
      IF (N .GE. 1 .AND. N .LE. NMAX) RETURN
      PRINT 100, N, NMAX
100   FORMAT(1X, '***ERROR - N = ', I9, 5X, 'MAXIMUM = ', I9)
      STOP
      END
```

A subroutine can have any number of dummy arguments. For example, a subroutine named PROC with five arguments could begin with the statement

```
      SUBROUTINE PROC(I, J, K, X, Y)
```

To call this subroutine, the CALL statement would also need five arguments: for example,

```
      CALL PROC(100, 2*L, 3*L + 1, 0.0, T)
```

Each of the expressions in the CALL statement is evaluated, and the value is substituted for the corresponding variable in the subroutine when it is executed (see Figure 9.4).

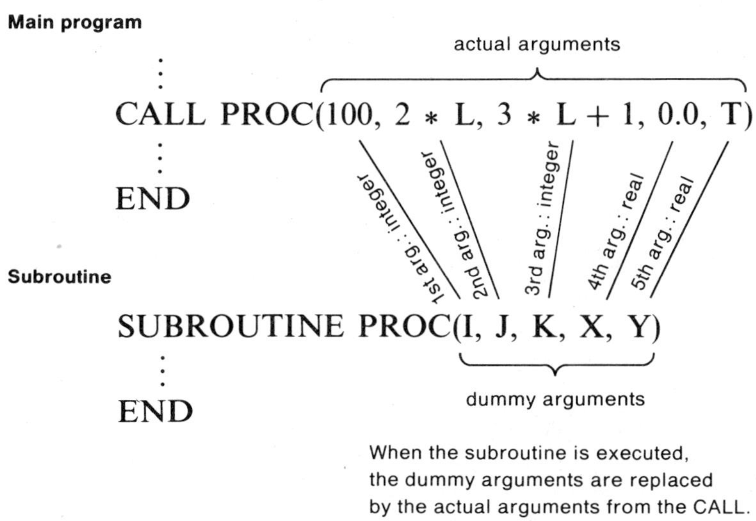

Figure 9.4 There must be the same number of arguments in the CALL statement as in the SUBROUTINE statement, and they must be of the same type.

Occasionally you may want a subroutine with *no* dummy arguments. In this case, the list of arguments and the enclosing parentheses are omitted from the SUBROUTINE and CALL statements. For instance, a subroutine ERROR might simply print an error message and stop. It could begin with the statement

```
      SUBROUTINE ERROR
```

and it could be called with the statement

```
      CALL ERROR
```

There are two important restrictions regarding the arguments in a CALL statement: The CALL statement must have the same number of arguments as the SUBROUTINE statement, and each argument in the CALL must be of the same type (integer or real) as the corresponding argument in the SUBROUTINE statement.

EXAMPLE 5. Write a subroutine ORDER(A, B) that will interchange the values of A and B, if necessary, so that A is less than or equal to B. The procedure for this is simple. If A is less than or equal to B, the subroutine does not have to do anything, so you just execute a RETURN statement. Otherwise, you interchange the values of A and B, then return. The FORTRAN statements are as follows.

```
      SUBROUTINE ORDER(A, B)
C---------------------------------------------
C  INTERCHANGE THE VALUES OF A AND B,
C  IF NECESSARY, SO THAT A IS LESS THAN
C  OR EQUAL TO B.
C---------------------------------------------
      IF (A .LE. B) RETURN
      TEMP = A
      A = B
      B = TEMP
      RETURN
      END
```

What would happen if a main program contained the statement

```
      CALL ORDER(X, Y, Z)
```

The answer is, the result is "undefined"; on some systems it would cause an execution error, and on some systems it might cause the subroutine to produce the wrong answers. The subroutine was defined with two dummy arguments, and every call to the subroutine should supply two arguments.

Now consider the statements

```
I = 2
J = 1
CALL ORDER(I, J)
PRINT 500, I, J
```

What values would be printed? Again, the result is undefined; most likely, it would not work right. The reason in this case is that the subroutine was defined for *real* arguments (since the dummy arguments A and B were real variables), but the actual arguments in the call are *integer* variables. This will not work; each actual argument must be of the same type as the corresponding dummy argument.

It is interesting to note that if you look only at the main program that calls the subroutine, you cannot tell that it is incorrect. The CALL statement *looks* all right, and FORTRAN has no way of knowing that the subroutine is being called with the wrong kind of arguments. It is up to the programmer to make sure that subroutines are called with the right number and the right type of arguments. This is a common source of error, and one that you should watch out for.

Rules for Subroutines

At this point, let us summarize the facts of FORTRAN subroutines.

Rules for Subroutines

Rule 1: A subroutine begins with a statement of the form

SUBROUTINE *name*(arg_1, arg_2, . . .)

or

SUBROUTINE *name*

where *name* is the name of the subroutine, and arg_1, arg_2, . . . are the dummy arguments. The subroutine consists of all the statements through the next END statement. The dummy arguments in the declaration are variable names or array names.

Rule 2: Each subroutine is an independent program unit. Statement numbers in the subroutine have no relation to statement numbers in the main program or any other subroutine. Except for the dummy arguments (and variables in COMMON statements), variables in the subroutine have no relation to variables in any other program unit.

Rule 3: A subroutine is executed by a statement

CALL *name*(arg_1, arg_2, . . .)

or

CALL *name*

Each actual argument may be a number, a variable, an array element, an array name, or an expression. The value of the actual argument is used in the subroutine in place of the dummy argument.

Rule 4: There must be the same number of actual arguments in the CALL statement as there are dummy arguments in the SUBROUTINE statement.

Rule 5: Each actual argument must be of the same type as the corresponding dummy argument.

Rule 6: If a dummy argument is assigned a value in the subroutine, the corresponding actual argument must be a variable or an array name.

Rule 7: A subroutine may not call itself, either directly or indirectly.

Function Subprograms

A **function** subprogram is very much like a subroutine. The main differences are that a function returns a value, and a function can be referenced without using a CALL statement. Like a subroutine, a function is a self-contained program unit which is compiled separately. It begins with a **FUNCTION** statement such as

```
FUNCTION F(X)
```

The name of this function is F, and it has one argument: X. The statements that follow, up to the next END statement, constitute the definition of the function subprogram.

A function can do anything a subroutine can do. It can perform input and output, it can stop, it can reference the value of the dummy arguments, and it can assign a value to a dummy argument. The function returns to the calling program by executing a RETURN statement.

One difference between a function and a subroutine is that at some point within the function, a **value** must be assigned to the function name. This is done with an assignment statement such as

```
F = 2.0 * X
```

Here F is the name of the function, as defined by the FUNCTION statement. Within the subprogram, F is a variable, used just like any other variable. Assigning a value to the function name stores a value in the variable. But it does one other thing, too: When a RETURN statement is executed, the value assigned to the variable becomes the value of the function, which is returned to the calling program.

Instead of using a CALL statement, you invoke a function subprogram by writing the function and its actual arguments as part of an expression. For example, a main program might call the function F with the statement

```
Y = 1.0 + F(10.0)
```

This statement means to perform the function subprogram F, substituting the actual argument 10.0 for the dummy argument X, then add 1.0 to the value of the function (which is defined in the subprogram) and store the result in Y.

In general, a function subprogram begins with a statement of the form

FUNCTION *name*(arg_1, arg_2, . . .)

and the function is called from the main program or from another subprogram whenever

name(arg_1, arg_2, . . .)

is evaluated as part of an expression. The actual arguments are evaluated, and their values replace the corresponding dummy arguments in the function subprogram.

Notice that a function reference looks exactly like a reference to a subscripted variable. But in FORTRAN, there is one important difference: A subscripted variable name *must* appear in a DIMENSION statement; a function name does *not* appear in a DIMENSION statement, and thus cannot be a subscripted variable.

A common mistake (which you may already have made at some time) is illustrated by the following program.

```
      DIMENSION XXX(10)
      DO 10 I = 1, 10
         READ 50, XXX(I)
10       CONTINUE
      Y = 0.0
      DO 20 I = 1, 10
         Y = Y + XX(I)
20       CONTINUE
      PRINT 60, Y
      STOP
50    FORMAT(F10.5)
60    FORMAT(1X, F15.5)
      END
```

This program compiles without any errors, but an execution error results when the program runs. The reason is that the programmer wrote

```
Y = 1.0 + XX(I)
```

instead of

```
      Y = 1.0 + XXX(I)
```

This was a simple keypunching error. Since XX does not appear in a DIMENSION statement, however, FORTRAN assumes that XX(I) is a function reference. If the programmer had supplied a function subprogram for the function XX, all would have been well. Since program units are compiled independently of each other, FORTRAN has no way of knowing that XX(I) was not intended to be a function reference.

EXAMPLE 6. A **geometric series** is an expression of the form

$$1 + R + R^2 + R^3 + \cdots + R^n$$

This sum is given by the formula

$$\frac{1 - R^{n+1}}{1 - R}$$

Write a function subprogram to compute this value.

We can call the function GEOM(R, N). It consists of the FUNCTION declaration, an assignment statement to define the value of GEOM according to the formula, and the RETURN and END statements. Here is the function, and a simple main program to test it. (See also Exercise 11.)

```
C     TEST PROGRAM
      R = 0.5
      DO 10 I = 1, 10
          X = GEOM(R, I)
          PRINT 20, I, X
10        CONTINUE
      STOP
20    FORMAT(F20.3)
      END

      FUNCTION GEOM(R, N)
C---------------------------------------------
C     GEOMETRIC SERIES
C     GEOM = 1 + R + R**2 + R**3 + . . . + R**N
C---------------------------------------------
      GEOM = (1.0 - R**(N + 1))/(1.0 - R)
      RETURN
      END
```

In this test program, the value of GEOM is used in a simple assignment statement. It could, however, be used as part of a more complicated expression, such as

```
X = 2.0 * GEOM(0.5, I) – GEOM(2.0, 2)
```

As with subroutines, the actual arguments to the functions can be expressions, as in the statement

```
X = GEOM(R + 1, 2 * N)
```

EXAMPLE 7. Like a subroutine, a function can alter the value of its arguments. Consider the following function:

```
      FUNCTION NPLUS1 (N)
      N = N + 1
      NPLUS1 = N
      RETURN
      END
```

This function returns a value of N + 1, where N is the argument. It also sets the argument itself to the value N + 1. As with subroutines, it would be incorrect to call this function with an actual argument that is a constant or an expression, because the function would attempt to change the value of the argument. Although this technique of altering the arguments is less frequently used with functions, it can occasionally be useful.

EXAMPLE 8. Functions do not always have to be defined in terms of formulas. In a program we may wish to check whether a variable X lies in a certain interval. This can be done with a function INTRVL(A, X, B). If $A \leq X \leq B$, then INTRVL = 1; otherwise, INTRVL = 0. This function and a sample main program are programmed as follows:

```
C     TEST PROGRAM
      DO 10 I = 1, 10
         READ 500, A, B, X
         PRINT 510, A, B, X
         IF (INTRVL(A, X, B) .EQ. 1) PRINT 520
         IF (INTRVL(A, X, B) .EQ. 0) PRINT 530
10       CONTINUE
      STOP
500   FORMAT(3F10.0)
510   FORMAT(10X, 3F10.3)
520   FORMAT(10X, 'YES')
530   FORMAT(10X, 'NO')
      END
```

```
      FUNCTION INTRVL(A, X, B)
C--------------------------------------------
C   IF X IS BETWEEN A AND B, INTRVL = 1,
C   OTHERWISE, INTRVL = 0.
C--------------------------------------------
      INTRVL = 0
      IF (A .LE. X .AND. X .LE. B) INTRVL = 1
      RETURN
      END
```

Rules for Functions

We can summarize the facts about function subprograms in a few rules, which are similar to the rules given earlier for subroutines.

Rules for Functions

Rule 1: A function subprogram begins with a statement of the form

FUNCTION *name* (arg_1, arg_2, . . .)

where *name* is the name of the function, and arg_1, arg_2, . . . are the dummy arguments. The function consists of all the statements through the next END statement. The dummy arguments in the declaration are variable names or array names.

Rule 2: Each function subprogram is an independent program unit. Statement numbers in the function have no relation to statement numbers in the main program or any other subprogram. Except for the dummy arguments (and variables in COMMON statements), variables in the function have no relation to variables in any other program unit.

Rule 3: A function is executed by putting the expression

name(arg_1, arg_2 . . .)

as part of an expression in the calling program. Each actual argument may be a number, a variable, an array element, an array name, or an expression. The value of the actual argument is used in the function in place of the dummy argument.

Rule 4: There must be the same number of actual arguments in the function reference as there are dummy arguments in the FUNCTION statement.

Rule 5: Each actual argument must be of the same type as the corresponding dummy argument.

Rule 6: If a dummy argument is assigned a value in the function, the corresponding actual argument must be a variable or an array name.

Rule 7: The name of the function may be used as a variable within the function subprogram. If it is a real variable name, it is used as a real variable; if it is an integer variable name, it is used as an integer variable. Before returning to the calling program, a value must be assigned to the name. This value becomes the value of the function in the calling program.

Rule 8: A function may not reference itself, either directly or indirectly.

Adjustable Dimensions

As you have seen, an actual argument to a subroutine or function can be an array element. For example,

```
CALL SUB(A(I))
```

In fact, an actual argument or a dummy argument can be an array name, without any subscript. When a dummy argument is an array name, the argument should appear in a DIMENSION statement within the subprogram. For example,

```
SUBROUTINE ABC(V)
DIMENSION V(10)
. . .
```

This says the dummy argument is an array of 10 elements. The calling program can call this subroutine with a statement such as

```
CALL ABC(VECT3)
```

where VECT3 is the name of an array which is defined in the calling program and has ten elements.

Rather than having a fixed number of array elements, a subprogram can be written to handle a variable number of array elements. In a subprogram, a DIMENSION statement such as

```
DIMENSION X(N)
```

may be used; X can be any array name and N can be any integer variable name. Both the array name and the variable name must be dummy arguments of the subprogram. This is called an **adjustable dimension** for the array. There are some important rules which must be observed when adjustable dimensions are used.

Rules for Adjustable Dimensions

Rule 1: In the DIMENSION statement of a subprogram, an integer variable may be used for one or more of the dimensions of an array, provided that both the array name and the variable name are dummy arguments of the subprogram.

Rule 2: When a one-dimensional array is declared with an adjustable dimension, the value of the adjustable dimension when the subprogram is called must be less than or equal to the actual size of the array as declared in the calling program.

Rule 3: When a higher-dimensional array is declared with an adjustable dimension, the size of the array (the total number of elements) when the subprogram is called must be less than or equal to the actual size of the array as declared in the calling program. Furthermore, the value of each adjustable dimension, except possibly the last, must be exactly equal to the corresponding actual dimension if the normal association of array elements is to be maintained.

Rule 4: The values of the adjustable dimensions may not be changed in the subprogram.

EXAMPLE 9. Write a function KOUNT that counts the number of zeros in a real array of 100 elements.

Let X be the dummy argument for the real array. The function subprogram could begin:

```
      FUNCTION KOUNT(X)
      DIMENSION X(100)
      . . . .
```

Since the problem is stated in terms of an array of 100 elements, this would suffice. It is no more trouble, however, to make a general function which finds the number of zeros in an array of N elements for a variable N. This is done as follows:

```
      FUNCTION KOUNT(X, N)
      DIMENSION X(N)
      KOUNT = 0
      DO 10 I = 1, N
         IF (X(I) .EQ. 0.0) KOUNT = KOUNT + 1
10       CONTINUE
      RETURN
      END
```

Note that the variable N is used in the subprogram. This is perfectly all right; Rule 4 just says the value cannot be changed.

Rule 2 means that if the main program declares an array called GEM with a statement

```
DIMENSION GEM(62)
```

then in the call to the function KOUNT, the second parameter must be less than or equal to 62.

EXAMPLE 10. A three-by-three **identity matrix** looks like this:

$$\begin{matrix} 1 & 0 & 0 \\ 0 & 1 & 0 \\ 0 & 0 & 1 \end{matrix}$$

The diagonal entries are 1 and the other entries are 0. In general, an identity matrix is a square matrix A where $A_{ij} = 1$ if $i = j$, and $A_{ij} = 0$ otherwise. Write a subroutine IDEN which will set up a real N-by-N identity matrix.

This is a case where two adjustable dimensions will be useful. The DIMENSION statement will be

```
DIMENSION A(N, N)
```

Both dimensions are the same in this subroutine but in general they could be different. One of the dimensions could be a constant while the other was a variable. Similarly, three-dimensional arrays can have any combination of adjustable dimensions as long as the four rules are followed.

The subroutine and a program to test it are as follows:

```
C   TEST PROGRAM.
C   PRINT AN IDENTITY MATRIX.
C
          DIMENSION A(5, 5)
          M = 5
          CALL IDEN(A, M)
          DO 10 I = 1, M
              PRINT 20, (A(I, J), J = 1, M)
10            CONTINUE
20        FORMAT(1X, 5F5.0)
          STOP
          END
```

```
      SUBROUTINE IDEN(X, N)
C--------------------------------------------
C  DEFINE THE N BY N MATRIX X TO BE AN
C  IDENTITY MATRIX.
C--------------------------------------------
         DIMENSION X(N, N)
C  SET ALL THE ELEMENTS EQUAL TO ZERO.
      DO 20 I = 1, N
         DO 10 J = 1, N
            X(I, J) = 0.0
10          CONTINUE
20       CONTINUE
C
C  NOW SET ALL THE DIAGONAL ELEMENTS TO 1.
      DO 30 I = 1, N
         X(I, I) = 1.0
30       CONTINUE
      RETURN
      END
```

EXAMPLE 11. Write a program that will read in 100 real numbers and print them out in ascending order.

The problem of sorting numbers arises frequently in programming. There are a number of different ways it can be done. We will use a simple technique called a **linear selection with exchange**. Although it is not the fastest possible method, it is quite good and easy to understand.

The solution consists of three steps: Read the numbers into an array, sort the array, and print the array. The sorting process is written as a subroutine. This allows it to be written as a general-purpose procedure which could be used in other programs as well. The main program reads numbers, one from each input line. Input is terminated by a value 999. A check is made to insure that no more than 100 values are read so that the array dimension is not exceeded. A variable MAX is used for the number of values read. Although the problem is stated for 100 numbers, the program will work for 100 or fewer numbers. The DO loop which reads the numbers is written so that if it falls through without finding the 999 line, the program sorts the first 100 numbers only. The main program is follows:

```
C  READ A LIST OF NUMBERS, TERMINATED BY THE
C  NUMBER 999, AND PRINT THEM IN SORTED ORDER.
C
      DIMENSION A(100)
C  MAX = SIZE OF ARRAY (MAXIMUM NUMBER OF INPUT CARDS)
      MAX = 100
      DO 10 N = 1, MAX
```

```
          READ 500, A(N)
          IF (A(N) .EQ. 999.0) GO TO 20
10        CONTINUE
      N = MAX + 1
20    N = N - 1
C
C  N NUMBERS WERE READ. CALL THE SORT ROUTINE
C  TO PUT THEM IN ORDER, THEN PRINT THEM.
C
      CALL SORT(A, N)
      DO 30 I = 1, N
          PRINT 510, A(I)
30        CONTINUE
      STOP
500   FORMAT(F10.0)
510   FORMAT(10X, F10.3)
      END
```

The main program is done, and you need only write the subroutine SORT. This subroutine has two arguments. The first is the name of the array to be sorted. The second is the adjustable dimension of the array. In accordance with Rule 2, the value of the adjustable dimension must be less than or equal to the actual size of the array. The subroutine cannot check this, however, so it is up to the main program to insure that this is the case.

The method used for sorting the array is first to go through the entire array to find the smallest value. The element with the smallest value is interchanged with the first element of the array. The next step is to look at all values *except* the value of the first element, and interchange the smallest of these with the second element of the array. The array now has the smallest and next smallest values in the first two elements. On the third step, the third smallest value is placed in the third element, and so on. This process may be understood by considering the example shown in Figure 9.5. The specific process is given in the flowchart in Figure 9.6. This flowchart can be translated into FORTRAN without difficulty. One addition has been made to the program. The first IF statement checks the number of elements in the array. If there are one or fewer elements, the subroutine returns. Since a DO

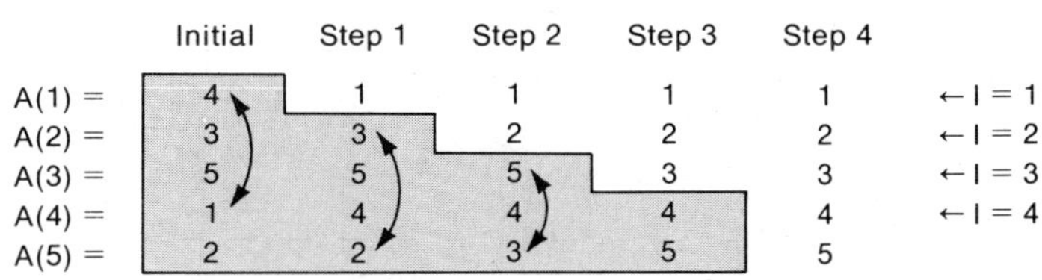

Figure 9.5 Shaded area shows which elements are being compared on each step. Arrows show which elements are interchanged on each step.

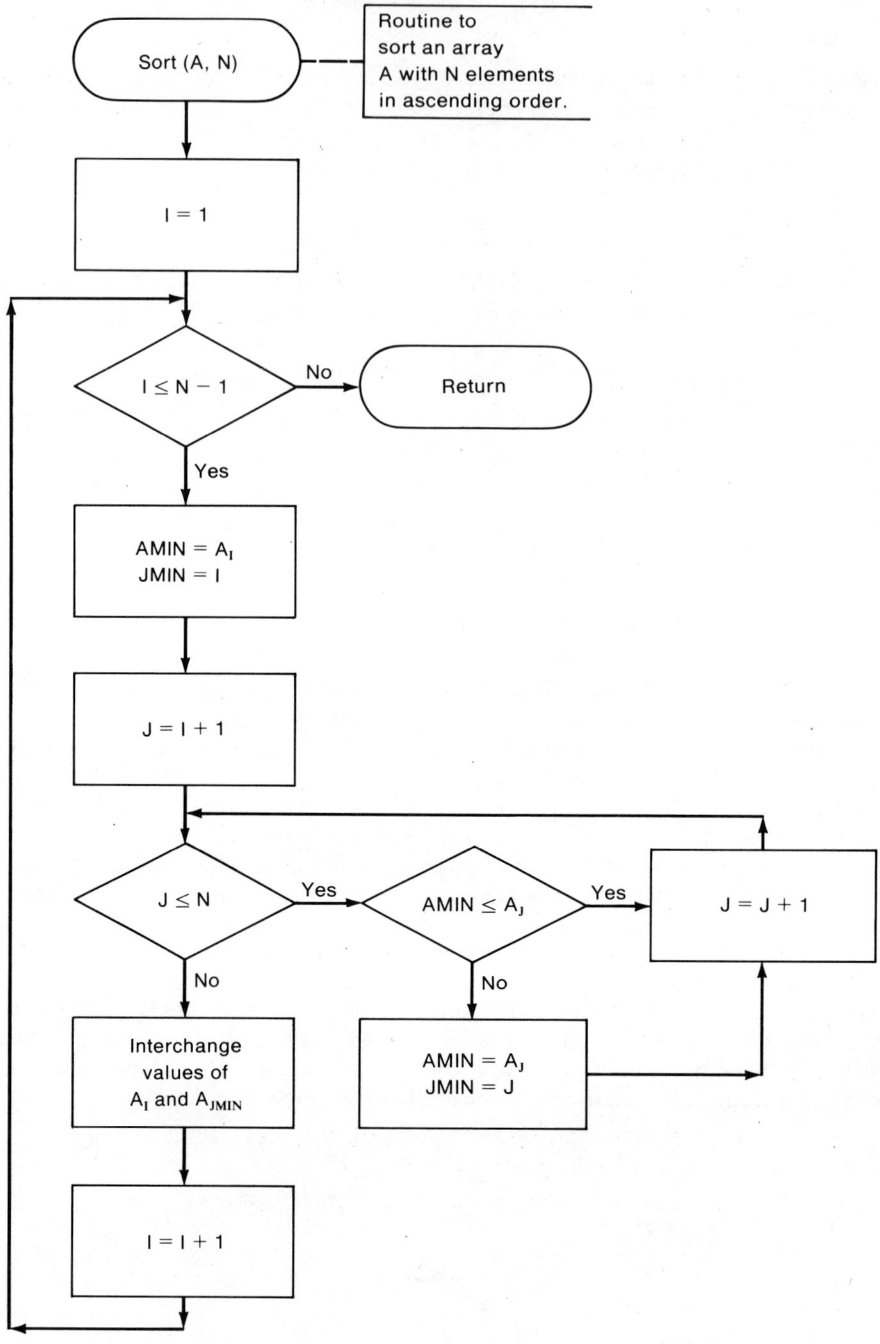

Figure 9.6 The procedure to sort an array works by finding the smallest value of the array and putting it in the first element, then finding the next smallest value and putting it in the second element, and so on.

loop is always executed once, this check is needed to handle correctly arrays with zero or one element.

```
      SUBROUTINE SORT(A, N)
C
C------------------------------------------------------------------
C  SORT THE ARRAY A IN ASCENDING ORDER.
C------------------------------------------------------------------
C
      DIMENSION A(N)
      IF (N .LE. 1) RETURN
      LAST = N - 1
      DO 20 I = 1, LAST
C
C------------------------------------------------------------------
C              LET AMIN BE THE MINIMUM OF
C              A(I) . . . A(N)
C              AND LET JMIN BE THE
C              CORRESPONDING SUBSCRIPT.
C------------------------------------------------------------------
C
         AMIN = A(I)
         JMIN = I
         JFIRST = I + 1
         DO 10 J = JFIRST, N
            IF (AMIN .LE. A(J)) GO TO 10
               AMIN = A(J)
               JMIN = J
10          CONTINUE
C
C------------------------------------------------------------------
C              NOW INTERCHANGE THE VALUES OF
C              A(I) AND A(JMIN)
C------------------------------------------------------------------
C
         A(JMIN) = A(I)
         A(I) = AMIN
20       CONTINUE
      RETURN
      END
```

To understand this subroutine, compare it with Figure 9.5. Each trip through the outer DO loop corresponds to one "step" in the figure. The variable AMIN is set to A(I) in the outer loop. The inner DO loop compares the value of AMIN with each A(J). The value of AMIN is changed to the value of A(J) if and only if the value of A(J) is less than the current value of AMIN. This means that when the inner DO loop terminates, AMIN is the minimum value of A(I), A(I + 1), . . . , A(N). The variable JMIN is the smallest value of J so that J ≥ I and A(J) = AMIN. The statements after statement 10 interchange the values of A(I) and A(JMIN).

Common Storage

As you have seen, subroutines and function subprograms are independent program units, compiled separately from the main program. This means, for instance, that a variable named K may be used in a main program for one purpose and in a subroutine for an entirely different purpose. Until now, the arguments of the subroutine or function have provided the only method of passing values between program units. There is another way by which program units can communicate with each other: This is **common storage**, which is used by means of the **COMMON** statement.

Common storage may be thought of as a sequence of memory locations in the computer. The COMMON statement lets you specify that particular variables be kept in a certain area of common storage. For example, normally when a variable named XXX is used in a program, the programmer has no control over where in the computer memory the variable is located. With the COMMON statement, the programmer can specify that XXX is to be in the first location of common storage. Now suppose a subroutine says a variable named ABC is to be in the first word of common storage. Then ABC and XXX are in the same place; that is, they are really the same variable. If the main program sets XXX = 1.0, then when the subroutine is called, ABC will have the value 1.0, since ABC is the same memory location as XXX. This is how common storage is used to pass values among program units. The following program gives an example.

```
      COMMON XXX
      XXX = 3.1416
      PRINT 10, XXX
      CALL SUB
      STOP
10    FORMAT(F20.5)
      END

      SUBROUTINE SUB
      COMMON ABC
      PRINT 10, ABC
C-- THE VALUE PRINTED IS THE VALUE STORED
C-- IN THE FIRST WORD OF THE COMMON STORAGE
C-- AREA. THIS VALUE IS 3.1416, WHICH WAS
C-- STORED BY THE MAIN PROGRAM
```

```
10      FORMAT(F20.5)
        RETURN
        END
```

This program will print:

```
3.14160
3.14160
```

In general, the COMMON statement has the form

COMMON $name_1$, $name_2$, . . . , $name_n$

where $name_1$, $name_2$, and so on are variable names or array names. Like the DIMENSION statement, the COMMON statement is a nonexecutable declaration which must come at the beginning of the program unit, before the first executable statement. This statement means that the variables or arrays named are to be stored in common storage in the order in which they are listed. If the names are real or integer variable names (not arrays), then each name occupies one memory location in common storage. For example,

```
COMMON I, V, M
```

means to store I in the first location of common, V in the second location, and M in the third.

The names in the COMMON statement may also be array names. When this is done, the COMMON statement may give dimension information. For example,

```
DIMENSION W(10)
COMMON I, W, X
```

is the same as the shorter form

```
COMMON I, W(10), X
```

This statement means that the first location of common storage is occupied by I, the second through eleventh locations are occupied by the array W, and the twelfth location by X.

The list of variable names in a COMMON statement can be different in different program units. The main program might include the statement

```
COMMON X(3), Y, Z(2)
```

and a subroutine might contain the statement

```
COMMON A, B, C, D, E, F
```

Then the variable A and X(1) are both stored in the same location, X(2) and B are stored in the same location, and so on. This is illustrated in Figure 9.7. Each variable should be the same type (integer or real) as the corresponding variable. You would not want to use

In main program:
COMMON X(3), Y, Z(2)

In subroutine:
COMMON A, B, C, D, E, F

		Common storage		
X(1)	=	Location 1	=	A
X(2)	=	Location 2	=	B
X(3)	=	Location 3	=	C
Y	=	Location 4	=	D
Z(1)	=	Location 5	=	E
Z(2)	=	Location 6	=	F

Figure 9.7 Example of COMMON statement.

a statement

```
COMMON I
```

in one program unit while using

```
COMMON X
```

in another, since problems could arise from treating the same storage location as both a real and an integer variable.

Although the COMMON statements can be different in different program units, in practice they are frequently identical. This has the effect of making the variables in common **globally** defined. That is, the variables in common can be used by any program unit. This is an efficient way to pass information among subprograms, especially when much information has to be shared.

Exercises

1. Cards have been prepared with six real numbers in each, followed by an integer code number. Write a subroutine NEXT which does the following: CALL NEXT(X, N) will find the next card having a code number N. If there is such a card, the six-element array X will contain the values. If there is no such card, the subroutine will execute a STOP statement. Assume that the input data is terminated by a card with code number 1000.
2. Write a function NGOOD(X, A, B) which returns the value 1 if X is between A and B (inclusive). If X is not in this range, it prints the value of X and returns the value 0.
3. NVALID is an array of NSIZE items. NCODE is a code number. Write a subroutine CHK(NCODE, NVALID, NSIZE) which will print a message and then stop if NCODE is not one of the numbers in the array NVALID. Otherwise, the subroutine does nothing.

4. Write a subroutine REVERS(B, A, N) which takes an array A of N elements and sets B equal to an array of N elements, with B being the reverse of A. That is, the first element of B is the last element of A, and so on.

5. Suppose you want to reverse the array A without using a separate array B. That is, you want to store the reverse of A in A itself. Can this be done using the subroutine of Exercise 4 by writing

```
      CALL REVERS (A, A, N)
```

   If not, write a new subroutine REVERS(A, N) which reverses A.

6. Run the following program. What happens? Did you predict this correctly?

```
      A = 0.0
      B = -1.0
      CALL CUT(A, 1.2345)
      CALL CUT(B, 6.7890)
      C = 1.2345
      D = 6.7890
      PRINT 10, A, B, C, D
10    FORMAT(1X, 4F12.4)
      STOP
      END

      SUBROUTINE CUT(X, Y)
C     SET BOTH X AND Y TO THE MINIMUM OF X AND Y.
      IF (X .GT. Y) X = Y
      IF (Y .GT. X) Y = X
      RETURN
      END
```

7. Run the following program. What happens? Did you predict this correctly?

```
      DO 20 I = 1, 10
         CALL OUT(I)
20       CONTINUE
      STOP
      END

      SUBROUTINE OUT(X)
      PRINT 10, X
10    FORMAT(1X, F10.3)
      RETURN
      END
```

8. Write a function PARITY(N) that returns (−1)** N, without using exponentiation (*Hint:* The value depends only on whether N is even or odd.)

9. Write a function P(X, A) to compute:

$$P(X, A) = \begin{cases} X^{**}A & \text{if } X > 0 \\ 0 & \text{if } X = 0 \\ -(-X)^{**}A & \text{if } X < 0 \end{cases}$$

10. Write a function K(I) which computes K from I as in the following table:

I . . .	−5	−4	−3	−2	−1	0	1	2	3	4	5	6	7	8 . . .
K(I) . . .	4	1	2	3	4	1	2	3	4	1	2	3	4	1 . . .

11. The function GEOM in Example 6 does not work correctly if R = 1. What should the function do in this case? How would you change the function subprogram?

12. Run the following program and analyze the results.

```
      A = 5.0
      B = 4.0
      C = 3.0
      D = 2.0
      I = LEAST(A, B)
      J = LEAST(A, B, C)
      K = LEAST(A, B, C, D)
      PRINT 10, I, J, K
10    FORMAT(1X, 3I10)
      END

      FUNCTION LEAST(A, B)
      IF (A .LT. B) LEAST = A
      IF (B .LT. A) LEAST = B
      RETURN
      END
```

13. The **greatest common divisor** of two positive numbers *m* and *n* is the largest number that divides both of them. For example, the greatest common divisor of 15 and 25 is 5, because 5 goes into both 15 and 25 evenly, but no greater number does. The greatest common divisor of 15 and 30 is 15, because 15 goes into 15 and 30 evenly. The flowchart on page 261 shows a procedure for finding the greatest common divisor *r* of the numbers *m* and *n*. Write a function subprogram NGCD(M, N) that returns the greatest common divisor of M and N. (*Note:* Use the built-in FORTRAN function MOD(M, N).)

14. Suppose that $Y_1, Y_2, \ldots, Y_n$ are tabulated values of a function corresponding to the X values $X_1, X_2, \ldots, X_n$. Assume that $X_1 < X_2 < \cdots < X_n$. We want to find the value Y of the function at some point Z where $X_1 \leq Z \leq X_n$. An approximate value of Y is given by the following formula for *linear interpolation:*

$$Y = Y_I + (Y_{I+1} - Y_I)\left(\frac{Z - X_I}{X_{I+1} - X_I}\right)$$

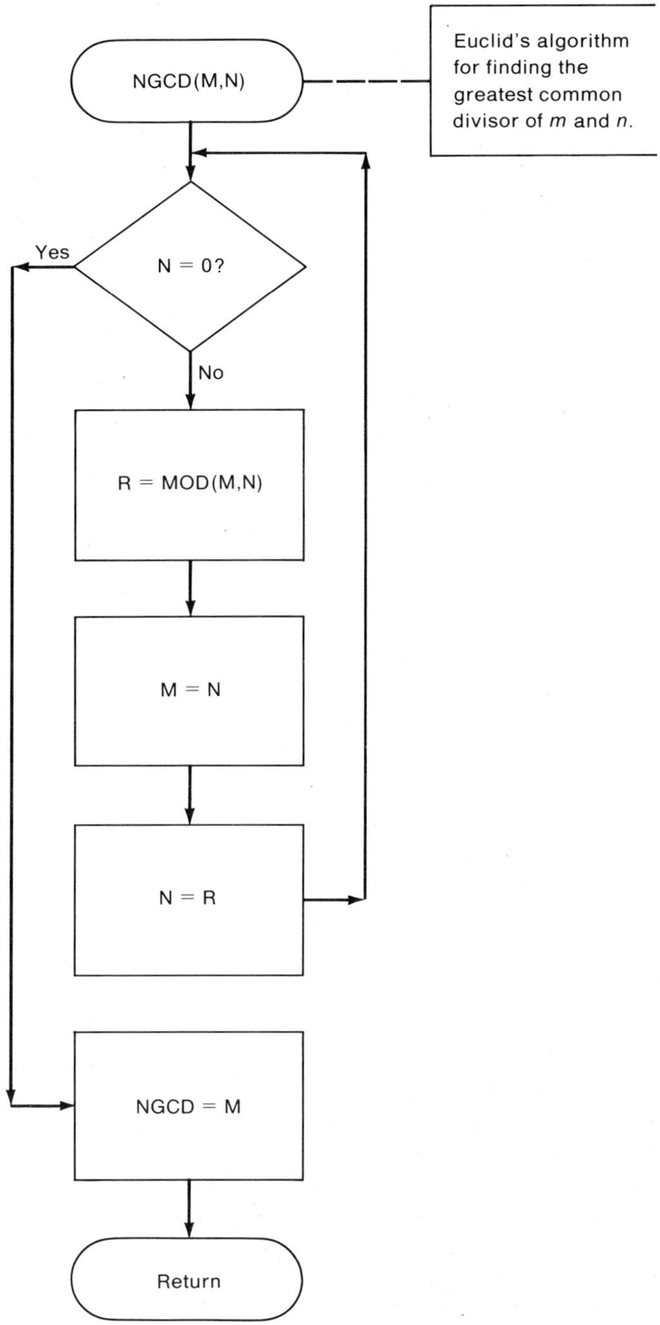

Flowchart for Exercise 13

where I is the index so that $X_I \leq Z \leq X_{I+1}$. (see the figure below). Write a function subprogram F(Z, X, Y, N) to compute this value of Y. Write a main program to test it.

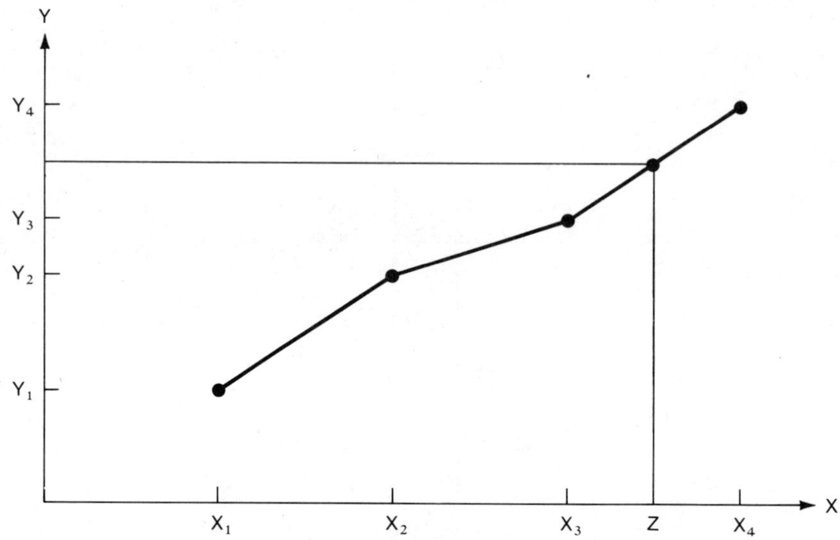

Linear interpolation

Figure for Exercise 14

15. The number of ways to choose *K* things from a group of *N* things is given by

$$\frac{N!}{K!(N-K)!}$$

Write a function subprogram NC(N, K) to compute this. Write a main program to test it. (*Hint:* Try computing this formula with pencil and paper for $N = 8$, $K = 5$. Notice that you can cancel out parts of the factorial in the top and bottom of the fraction.

16. Consider the function subprogram:

```
FUNCTION F(N, A)
F = 1.0
IF (N .LE. 0) RETURN
F = -1.0
A = A * N
N = N - 1
RETURN
END
```

How do the values of the arguments change with the function call? Suppose that a main program contains the statements.

```
        N = 5
        A = 1.0
10      IF (F(N, A) .LT. 0.0) GO TO 10
        PRINT, A
```

Note that the IF statement branches to itself. Is this an infinite loop? What value (if any) will be printed?

17. In Example 11, we wrote a subroutine SORT(A, N) to sort an array of N elements. A related problem that is often useful in applications, is the following: Write a subroutine SORT(A, N, NPTR) that will take an array A of N elements and will set up an array NPTR of N elements so that NPTR(1) is the subscript of the smallest element of A, NPTR(2) is the subscript of the next smallest element of A, NPTR(3) is the subscript of the third smallest element of A, and so on. The original array A is unchanged. The array NPTR is an array of *pointers*; that is, each element of NPTR points to an element of A. Test your subroutine with the following program, which will print the elements of an array in increasing order.

```
        DIMENSION A(100), NPTR(100)
        READ 10, N
10      FORMAT(I5)
        IF (N .GT. 100) STOP
        DO 20 I = 1, N
           READ 15, A(I)
15         FORMAT(F10.0)
20         CONTINUE
        CALL SORT(A, N, NPTR)
        DO 30 I = 1, N
           J = NPTR(I)
           PRINT 15, A(J)
30         CONTINUE
        STOP
        END
```

18. The binary number system is a way of counting that uses only the digits 0 and 1. For example, the numbers 1 through 10 in binary notation are as follows:

1 = 1 (binary)

2 = 10 (binary)

3 = 11 (binary)

4 = 100 (binary)

5 = 101 (binary)

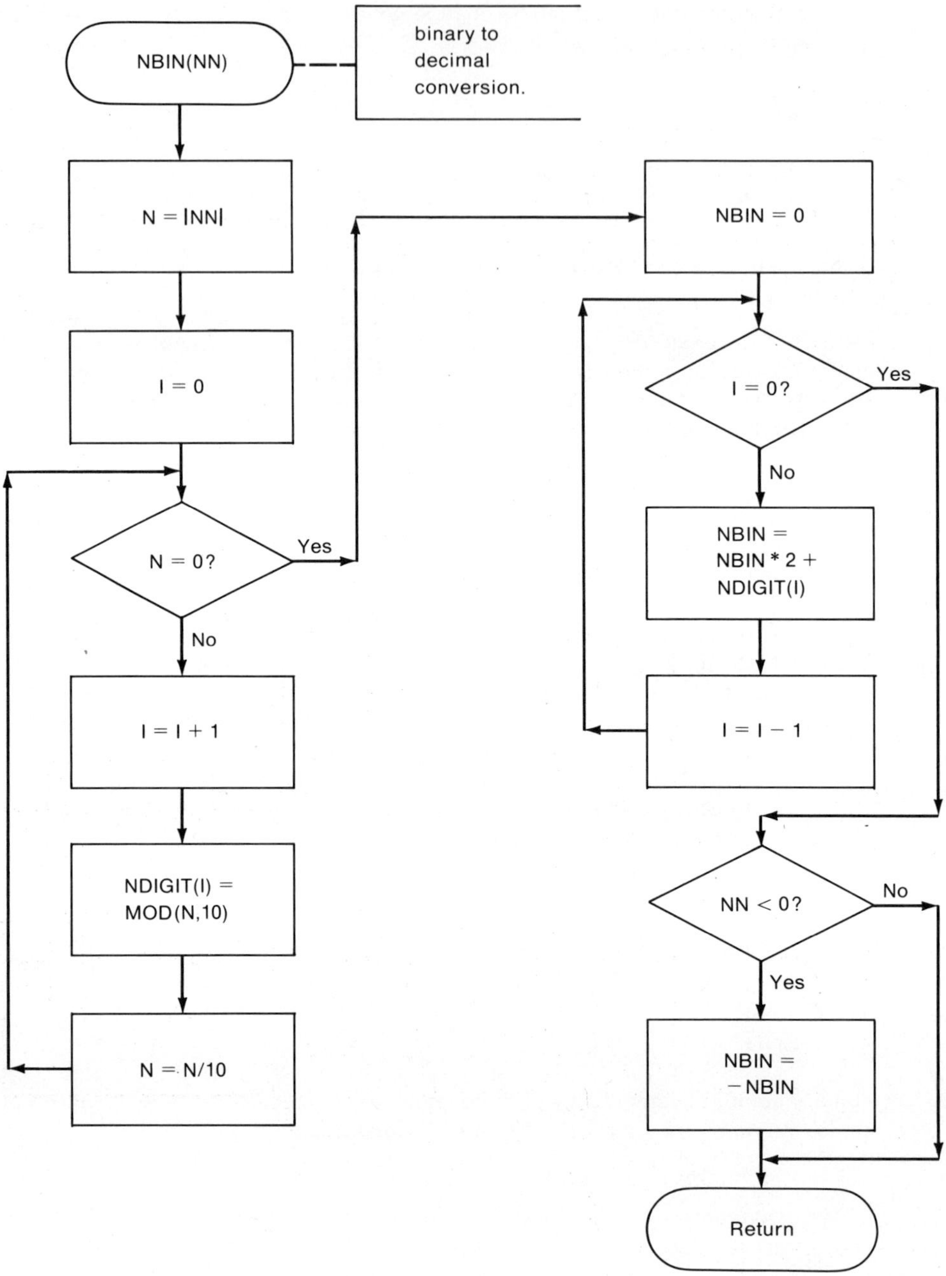

Flowchart for Exercise 18

6 = 110 (binary)

7 = 111 (binary)

8 = 1000 (binary)

9 = 1001 (binary)

10 = 1010 (binary)

Write a function NBIN(N) that will take a binary number N and return the decimal value. For example, NBIN(1010) is 10, NBIN(1001) is 9, and so on. The flowchart on page 264 shows how to do this.

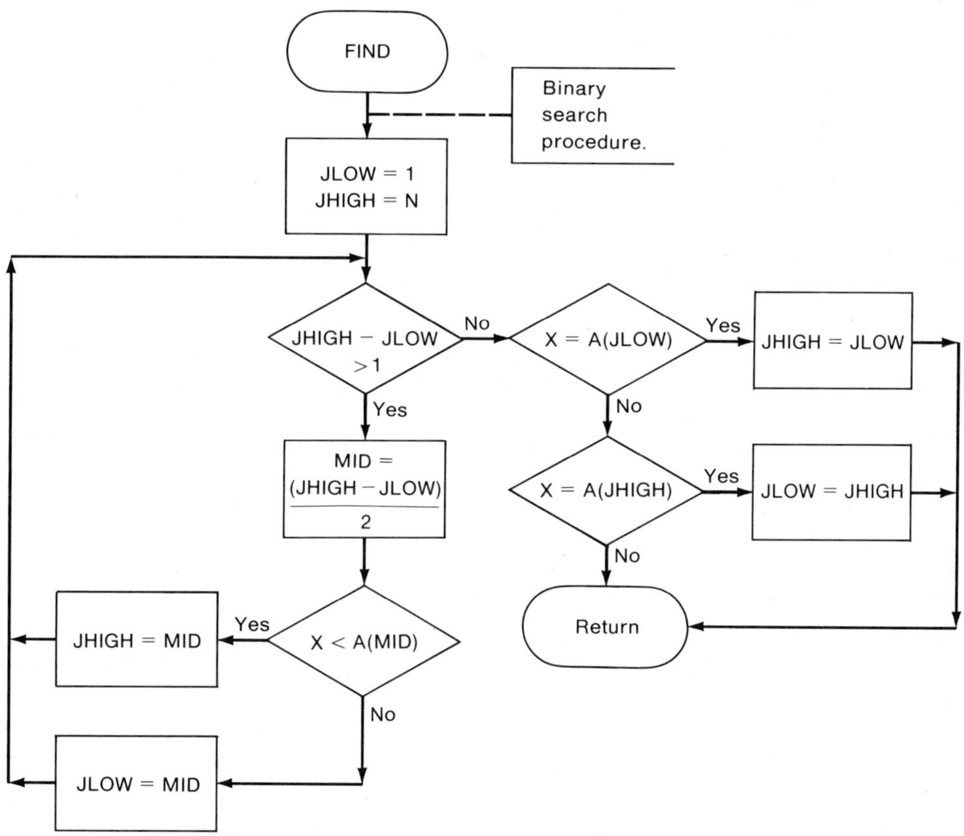

Flowchart for Exercise 20

19. Let A be an array of N elements, and let X be a variable. Suppose that

$$A(1) < A(2) < A(3) < \cdots < A(N-1) < A(N)$$

Write a subroutine FIND(A, N, X, JLOW, JHIGH) which will set JLOW = JHIGH = J if X = A(J) for some J, (that is, if X is one of the elements of the array A). If X is between A(J) and A(J + 1), for some J, let JLOW = J and JHIGH = J + 1. If X < A(1), let JLOW = 1 and JHIGH = 2. If X > A(N), let JLOW = N − 1 and JHIGH = N.

20. Solve Exercise 19 using the procedure shown in the flowchart on p. 265. This procedure is called a *binary search*.

MODULE II

Structured Programming

Now that you know the FORTRAN language, let us reconsider a basic question: How do you write a program? Most of the programs you have written have been short and fairly simple. If you are undertaking a large project, one that will require perhaps thousands of FORTRAN statements, where do you begin? How do you proceed? In this section we offer some guidelines for a methodology commonly called **structured programming**. To "structure" something means to arrange it into a definite pattern of organization. What you are attempting to structure, in this case, is not just the program itself, but the whole process of developing the program.

Our first suggestion is this:

1. Write your whole program in general, abstract terms before trying to write it in FORTRAN.

If you are working on a very easy program, such as one to find the average of a set of numbers, you may be able to write the complete program on your first try. When you are confronted with a more difficult problem, however, it is usually neither possible nor desirable to attempt a complete program without some prior planning. For instance, if you want the computer to play a game of chess with you, obviously you cannot just start right in with a DO loop and write a chess program. Begin by solving the problem in abstract terms, perhaps breaking it into several subproblems in the process.

Top-down design is a method of writing a program so that the structure of the final program reflects the abstract concepts of the problem's solution. It is not an infallible way of making a difficult programming task simple; it is a way of regarding the programming process. Basically, the method is as follows.

The first step is to solve the problem completely in terms of concepts and language which are appropriate to the problem. A solution can be written in English, or in a combination of English, FORTRAN, and mathematical notation.

It is not necessary to go into too much detail at this stage. In fact, decisions about details of the program should be postponed if possible. For example, a statement in the first draft might say "read a card." This is enough detail for the first draft. Later, after a complete solution has been reached, you can decide on the detailed format of the card.

The next step is to refine the solution, elaborating each step to obtain a more detailed algorithm. In this manner, the program is developed in various **levels**. The top level is a general solution. Each successive level is obtained from the previous level not by changing it but by making it more specific.

Decisions about the program are made at the appropriate level in the development. In the top-down method, general decisions are made first. Decisions on specific details are deferred to succeeding levels.

As an example, if you were writing a program to play chess, you might formulate a tentative solution as follows.

Program to Play Chess: Version 1

1. Read player's move.
2. Make player's move.
3. If player wins, stop.
4. Decide on computer's move.
5. Make computer's move.
6. If computer wins, stop.
7. Go to step 1.

This program is still abstract, but it is, in a sense, a complete solution to the problem. If you could program each one of the steps, you would be finished.

In this case, we have really not made much progress toward a finished program, since most of the steps in this version are enormously difficult problems in their own right. But it is a useful start. In fact, without going any further, we can find a bug: It fails to account for the possibility of a draw. Needless to say, it is easier to correct the bug at this level than to rewrite a whole FORTRAN program.

Writing a program in this way is like making an outline. The first version gives the general outline: It shows the overall plan without giving the details. The next version uses the same basic outline, but it adds more details. For example, a second version of the chess program might begin:

Program to Play Chess: Version 2

1. Read player's move.
   a. Tell player to enter his move.
   b. Read the move.
   c. See if it is a legal chess move; if not, tell him so and go back to Step 1a.
2. Make player's move.
   a. If the new square is occupied by a piece, capture the piece and remove it from the board.
   b. Move player's piece to the new square.
   . . .

Through further refinement, you outline eventually becomes detailed enough that you can translate it into a FORTRAN program.

---

2. Use simple control structures. Keep the program logic as clear and simple as possible.

In Module I, you saw several examples of how to write a decision and how to write a program loop. The basic forms covered there are really all you need to write any program. Don't make things more complicated than necessary by writing GO TO statements that branch around the program in a seemingly random fashion. Your program will be much easier to read and understand if the flow of control proceeds from top to bottom.

Write down the program logic in a form that is easy to understand, then translate this into FORTRAN in a straightforward manner.

---

3. Decide in advance how data will be represented in the program.

It is important to have a clear understanding of what your data represents. You might find it useful to write down a dictionary, listing the variables and arrays to be used by the program with a precise definition of each item. Include the dictionary as comments at the beginning of the program so you can refer to it later.

If a program uses nine variables that are unrelated to each other, it might be best to give each one a distinct name. If the variables are closely related, it might be better to store them as an array of nine elements. Another possibility is to store them as a 3 by 3 two-dimensional array. Choosing among such alternatives is an important decision in writing a program.

In general, a **data structure** is a systematic method of representing information in a program. You must choose among alternative ways of doing this based on consideration of the properties and interrelations of the variables involved in a particular problem. The careful design and specification of the data structure goes hand in hand with the design and specification of the algorithm to manipulate the data.

For example, the chess program mentioned before had a statement "make your move." In the first draft of the program, this is a meaningful instruction. Much of the chess program could (and should) be written without even deciding exactly what a "move" is. When the problem has been solved using this general concept of a "move," it will be time to define the concept in terms of something you can use in FORTRAN, such as an array. Maybe the chessboard will be represented as an 8 by 8 matrix, where each element has a value denoting the piece which occupies the square. Then "making a move" means assigning a new value to some element of the matrix. Maybe some other representation of the chessboard is easier to use. This is an important decision in writing the program, but it is a decision which does not have to be made until fairly late in the development of the program, after you have marked out the general solution.

At an appropriate point in the program development, you rewrite the general algorithm in terms of the specific data structure. For example, where the first version of the chess program said "make your move," this version of the program will define a procedure for making moves, using the matrix representation of the chessboard.

---

4. Write the program as a collection of short subprograms that can be written and tested independently.

The larger a program is, the harder it is to work with and debug. It is usually much easier to write 10 subroutines, of 20 lines each, than to write a single 200-line program to do the same thing. Perhaps your main program will consist almost entirely of CALL statements to invoke a series of subroutines. This is an excellent way to organize your program, because it lets you break it down into manageable parts.

In deciding what should be a subprogram, there are several things you should keep in mind. Does a procedure seem to involve many repetitive tasks? Perhaps several related tasks are special cases of a more general procedure which could be written as a separate subprogram.

Make sure each subprogram has a clearly defined purpose. If you can test each subprogram separately, as you go along, debugging your program will be fairly easy. Put another way, if you have a 2000-line program that doesn't work, you will have to search out the bugs among 2000 lines of code; but if you can isolate the problem to a 20-line subroutine, your debugging task will be greatly simplified.

Keep the subprograms short. You can always break up a long subprogram into a series of CALL statements to invoke several short subprograms. Some people advocate limiting a subprogram to a maximum of one page.

Many decisions have to be made when writing a program. Try to anticipate possible changes to your program and isolate things that might change to separate program units. For example, suppose data is being read from cards. If you later decide that the program should read data from magnetic tape, how hard will it be to modify the program? If all the reading is done by a single subprogram, the change might be very easy; if READ statements are spread throughout the program, it might be difficult. A good programming practice: Don't commit yourself any more than you have to.

One final point about subprograms: Build on the work of others. Most computer centers have libraries of subprograms available for general use. Don't overlook the possibility that they may have just the subroutine you're looking for. Furthermore, you can build on your own work. If you write a program in terms of general-purpose subprograms, you won't have to rewrite them the next time you have a similar task.

---

5. Pay attention to your programming style.

In Module I, we gave several suggestions for developing good programming style. There are no rigid rules you can follow to insure good style, but there is a guiding principle you should always keep in mind: Make your program easy to read and easy to understand.

You have only two ways of insuring that your program is working correctly. The first way is to run it and test it. But a complex program may be difficult or impossible to test completely; it may have so many possible cases that they cannot all be tried. You must then resort to the second way of insuring program correctness: Read your program and analyze it. This is where readability and style become important.

---

6. Make your program foolproof.

In Module I, we discussed the need to be cautious in programming, to anticipate possible error conditions, and to write programs that work reliably for all possible input data. An ounce of prevention is worth a pound of cure, so the old adage goes. We can paraphrase this by saying that in programming, a few minutes spent devising good error-checking procedures when writing a program can save hours of laborious and frustrating debugging later on.

Our final suggestion is this:

---

7. Revise and rewrite.

Conscientious programming requires time and thought. You may find that you have not fully understood a problem until you have worked out a tentative solution. Don't be afraid to start over if necessary. In the long run, it may be easier to rewrite a program completely that to slave away trying to debug your first draft. When you are satisfied with your own program, have someone else read and critique it—he or she may see something you've overlooked.

EXAMPLE 1. LOAN PAYMENT PROGRAM. Suppose an amount of money A is borrowed at interest rate R, to be paid back in N years. Let P be the annual payment. These quantities are related by the formula

$$A = P\left(\frac{1 - (1 + R)^{-N}}{R}\right)$$

which gives A if P, R, and N are known. If A, R, and N are known, we can find P. If A, P, and R are known, we can solve for N. Write a program which reads in any three of these quantities and computes the value of the unknown fourth quantity.

The first version of the program will be written entirely in English. It is really just a specific description of what the program is to do.

Loan Payment Program: Version 1

The input consists of four numbers: amount of loan, annual payment, interest rate, and number of years. The interest rate must be positive. Exactly one of the other inputs must be zero, and the remaining inputs must be positive. If these conditions are not met, the program prints an error message and stops. Otherwise, the program computes the value of the zero quantity from the values of the other three, using the appropriate formula for compound interest, and prints the values of all four quantities.

At this point, observe that the program consists of several steps which are logically independent: input and verification of data, computation of the missing value, and output of values. Each of these functions can be written as a separate module. The only information which needs to be shared among the modules is the value of each of the four numbers. You can write the second version of the program as follows.

Loan Payment Program: Version 2

data = { amount of loan
annual payment
interest rate
number of years }

Input and verify data.

Compute missing value from other values of data.

Output data.

This is actually a final version of the program. It will be translated directly into FORTRAN in a later refinement. The three modules here can be written independently, as follows.

Loan Payment Program: Version 3

Procedure to Input and Verify Data: Version 1

Input interest rate and verify it is positive.

Input years and verify it is a nonnegative integer.

Input amount and verify it is nonnegative.

Input payment and verify it is nonnegative.

If exactly one of the values (years, amount, payment) equals zero, data is good; otherwise, data is bad, so print error message and start this procedure over.

Procedure to Compute Missing Value from Other Values

$$\text{Let}\begin{cases} R = \text{interest rate} \\ N = \text{number of years (an integer)} \\ A = \text{amount of loan} \\ P = \text{annual payment} \end{cases}$$

if A = 0, then let

$$A = P\left(\frac{1-(1+R)^{-N}}{R}\right)$$

else, if P = 0, then let

$$P = A\left(\frac{R}{1-(1+R)^{-N}}\right)$$

else, if N = 0, then let N = the smallest integer greater than

$$\frac{\log\left(\frac{P}{P-AR}\right)}{\log(1+R)}$$

Procedure to Output Values

Print "Interest Rate": interest rate.

Print "Years of loan": years.

Print "Amount of Loan": amount.

Print "Annual payment": payment.

The procedure to compute the missing values from the other values required a little mathematical analysis to write since the formulas for P and N had to be derived from the formula for A given in the original statement of the problem. It is not necessarily the programmer's job to do this. An outside consultant (a banker, say) might be engaged for this task.

The procedures for computing the missing value and for printing the values are both well defined. These can easily be translated into FORTRAN as they stand. The procedure for input and verification of the data is not quite explicit enough. Assume that the program is to run on a timesharing system, so that if the input data is not valid, the program should output a message and ask the user to recenter the data. The instruction "If exactly one of the values (years, amount, payment) equals zero, data is good" needs to be clarified. One way of implementing this is with a variable named NZERO which counts the number of variables (among years, amount, and payment) that are equal to zero. With this method, the procedure can be written as follows.

Procedure to Input and Verify Data: Version 2

a. Print "Enter interest rate."
   Read interest rate. If it is not positive, print "Interest rate must be positive" and repeat this step.

b. Print "Enter a zero for the item you want to find." NZERO = 0

c. Print "Enter years."
   Read YEARS. If it is negative, print "Must be nonnegative" and repeat this step.
   If YEARS is zero, add 1 to NZERO.

d. Print "Enter amount."
   Read AMOUNT. If it is negative, print "Must be nonnegative" and repeat this step.
   If AMOUNT is zero, add 1 to NZERO.

e. Print "Enter payment."
   Read PAYMENT. If it is negative, print "Must be nonnegative" and repeat this step.
   If PAYMENT is zero, add 1 to NZERO.

f. If NZERO is not 1, print "Exactly one item must be zero"; then go to step b.

You are almost done now, although not one line of executable code has been written. The analysis is done, and the procedures have been specified in such a way that it is a simple matter to translate them to FORTRAN. To do this, you must first decide on legal FORTRAN names for the variables and subroutines. You also must decide on the input format to be used to read the variables: in this case, freeform input. You must decide on exactly how the output is to look. The final program can then be written as follows:

```
C   RATE = ANNUAL INTEREST RATE (E.G., 0.20 FOR 20 PERCENT)
C   NYEARS = NUMBER OF YEARS OVER WHICH LOAN IS TO BE REPAID
C   AMOUNT = AMOUNT OF LOAN
C   PAYMT = ANNUAL PAYMENT, BEGINNING ONE YEAR HENCE
        CALL INPUT (RATE, NYEARS, AMOUNT, PAYMT)
        CALL COMPUT (RATE, NYEARS, AMOUNT, PAYMT)
        CALL OUTPUT (RATE, NYEARS, AMOUNT, PAYMT)
        STOP
        END
```

```
      SUBROUTINE INPUT (RATE, NYEARS, AMOUNT, PAYMT)
C   INPUTS THE FOUR PARAMETERS IN FREE-FORMAT
C   CHECKS VALIDITY AS FOLLOWS
C       RATE   MUST BE POSITIVE
C       NYEARS,
C       AMOUNT, AND
C       PAYMT   MUST BE NONNEGATIVE
C   EXACTLY ONE OF NYEARS, AMOUNT, AND PAYMT
C   MUST BE ZERO.
C--------------------------------------------------------------------------RATE
10      PRINT 15
15      FORMAT(1X, 'ENTER INTEREST RATE (PERCENT)')
        READ, RATE
        RATE = RATE/100.0
        IF (RATE .GT. 0.) GO TO 20
            PRINT 19
19          FORMAT(1X, 'MUST BE POSITIVE')
            GO TO 10
C
20      PRINT 25
25      FORMAT(1X, 'ENTER A ZERO FOR THE ITEM'/
     $      1X, 'YOU WANT TO FIND')
        NZERO = 0
C--------------------------------------------------------------------------NYEARS
30      PRINT 35
35      FORMAT(1X, 'ENTER NUMBER OF YEARS')
        READ, NYEARS
        IF (NYEARS .GE. 0) GO TO 40
            PRINT 39
39          FORMAT(1X, 'CANNOT BE NEGATIVE')
            GO TO 30
40      IF (NYEARS .EQ. 0) NZERO = NZERO + 1
C--------------------------------------------------------------------------AMOUNT
50      PRINT 55
55      FORMAT(1X, 'ENTER AMOUNT')
        READ, AMOUNT
        IF (AMOUNT .GE. 0.) GO TO 60
            PRINT 39
            GO TO 50
60      IF (AMOUNT .EQ. 0.) NZERO = NZERO + 1
C--------------------------------------------------------------------------PAYMT
70      PRINT 75
75      FORMAT(1X, 'ENTER PAYMENT')
```

```
      READ, PAYMT
      IF (PAYMT .GE. 0.) GO TO 80
         PRINT 39
         GO TO 70
80    IF (PAYMT .EQ. 0.) NZERO = NZERO + 1
C--------------------------------------------------------------ENSURE ONE IS ZERO
      IF (NZERO .EQ. 1) RETURN
      PRINT 90
90    FORMAT(1X, 'EXACTLY ONE ITEM MUST BE ZERO')
      GO TO 20
      END

      SUBROUTINE COMPUT(R, N, A, P)
C   ONE OF THE PARAMETERS N, A, OR P IS ZERO.
C   USING THE FORMULAS FOR COMPOUND INTEREST,
C   COMPUTE THE ZERO VALUE FROM THE OTHER THREE.
      IF (A .NE. 0.) GO TO 20
         A = P*(1. - (1. + R)**(-N))/R
         RETURN
20    IF (P .NE. 0.) GO TO 30
         P = A*R/(1. - (1. + R)**(-N))
         RETURN
30    IF (N .NE. 0) GO TO 40
         RN = ALOG(P/(P - A*R))/ALOG(1. + R)
         N = 1. + RN
         RETURN
40    PRINT 50
50    FORMAT(1X, 'ERROR IN COMPUT')
      STOP
      END

      SUBROUTINE OUTPUT(RATE, NYEARS, AMOUNT, PAYMT)
      PERCNT = 100.*RATE
      PRINT 100, PERCNT, NYEARS, AMOUNT, PAYMT
      RETURN
100   FORMAT('1', 10X, 'AT', F6.2, 'PERCENT'/
     $            '0', 10X, 'OVER', I3, 'YEARS'/
     $            '0', 10X, 'A LOAN OF', F10.2/
     $            '0', 10X, 'HAS AN ANNUAL PAYMENT OF', F10.2)
      END
```

Exercises

1. Select one of the projects suggested in Appendix C and write a proposal for a program to solve the problem. Your proposal should specify *what* the program will do but not

how it will do it. Include a description of how to set up the input data and what the output will look like.

2. Write an outline, less than one page long, describing how the program you proposed in Exercise 1 will work. Include all the necessary steps, but keep the description general. This outline should be understandable to a nonprogrammer.
3. Describe the data structures that will be used in the program you outlined in Exercise 2. Write a precise definition of what information needs to be stored and how it will be represented in the program.
4. Write a description of a set of FORTRAN subprograms that could be used to build the program you outlined in the previous exercises. The description of each subprogram should specify how it is called and what it does but not the details of how it works.
5. Write a main program, modeled on your outline from Exercise 2, that calls some or all of the subprograms you defined in Exercise 4.
6. Complete your program and check it out on the computer. Revise your design documents, if necessary, and prepare them in final form.

10

Character Data

So far, all the data used in your programs has been numeric data. You have used quote fields to provide labels for output fields; but you have not been able to read in alphabetic data, or to manipulate it within a program. This type of data is called **alphanumeric** (meaning alphabetic or numeric), or **character** data. In this chapter you will see how character data is used in FORTRAN.

You can use an ordinary real or integer variable to contain alphabetic or numeric characters. One way to do this is to read characters into the variable by using an A field descriptor in a FORMAT. Another way is to assign a value to the variable with an assignment statement. These will be explained shortly. One concept fundamental to the use of variables for character data is this: Each variable can store only a certain number of characters. The number of characters per variable varies among different computer systems.

The A Field Descriptor

Character data can be read or printed using the **A field descriptor** in a FORMAT statement. The form of this field descriptor is

$$\mathrm{A}n$$

where n is an integer number telling how many characters comprise the field. Usually, $n \leq 4$ when using IBM computers. For example,

```
      READ 7, K
7     FORMAT(A3)
```

will read the first three characters from the input line and store them in the variable K. The variable K is just an ordinary integer variable. However, after a value has been read into K with the A3 format, K does not have an integer value. That is, the value of K is not particularly meaningful when considered as an integer. The statements

```
        READ 7, K
        PRINT 8, K
7       FORMAT(A3)
8       FORMAT(1X, I10)
```

would likely produce meaningless output. The A3 field descriptor stores a value in K which is meaningful only as a string of characters. K might contain three alphabetic characters such as ABC. It might contain numeric characters such as 123. This is *not* the same as the integer value assigned to K by the statement

```
        K = 123
```

K might also contain special characters such as +, −, *, and so on. If the input line is blank, K would contain three blank spaces. In character data, a blank space is a character, just like a letter or a number.

One very important fact is that a variable can hold only a certain number of characters. The actual limit depends on the particular computer used, but a typical limit is four characters. This means that a variable such as K could contain the character string ABCD, but it could not contain the five-character string ABCDE. To store five characters, two variables might be used. The following statements read and print the first five characters from the input line:

```
        READ 10, A, B
        PRINT 11, A, B
10      FORMAT(A4, A1)
11      FORMAT(1X, A4, A1)
```

The first four characters will be stored in the variable A and the fifth character will be stored in B. We have used real variables A and B in this example. Either real or integer variables can be used to contain character data.

Suppose that the computer can store four characters per variable. Then each variable used for character data will contain exactly four characters. If a variable is read with an A field descriptor specifying a field width of less than four, then the remaining characters will be stored as blanks. For example, consider

```
        READ 5, N, K
5       FORMAT(A1, A2)
        PRINT 10, N, K
10      FORMAT(1X, 2A4)
```

The READ statement reads three characters. The first character is stored in the leftmost character position of the variable N. Blank spaces are stored in the rightmost three character positions of N. Similarly, the second and third input characters are stored in the leftmost two character positions of the variable K, while the rightmost character positions are filled with blank spaces. On output, the A4 fields mean to print all four characters of each variable, including the blank spaces. This is illustrated in Figure 10.1.

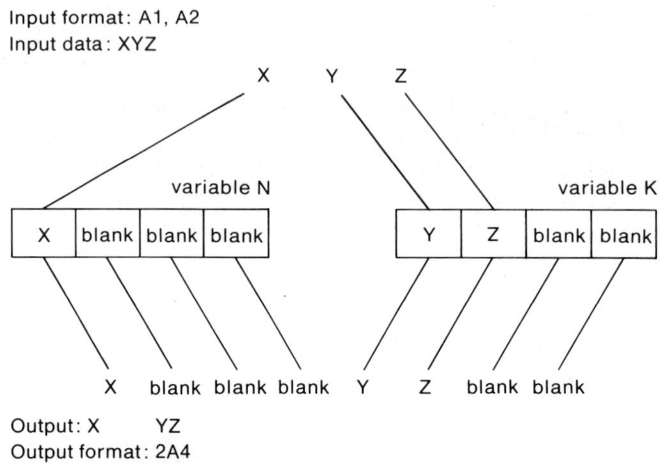


```
        READ 10, N, K
10      FORMAT(A1, A2)
        PRINT 20, N, K
20      FORMAT(2A4)
```

Figure 10.1 Storage of character data in variables.

Again supposing the computer stores four characters per variable, consider the statements

```
        READ 75, X
        PRINT 75, X
75      FORMAT(A10)
```

if the input line is

ABCDEFGHIJKLMNOPQRSTUVWXYZ

what will the output be? The input field consists of the first ten characters, A through J. Only four of these can be stored in the variable X. The rightmost four, GHIJ, are stored (the rest are lost). The output field will be ten characters long, but since X contains only four characters, the leftmost six characters will be blanks.

The effect of the A field descriptor is summarized by the following rules.

Rules for the A*n* Field Descriptor

Rule 1: The A*n* field descriptor, where n is an integer number, transmits character data to or from a variable. The variable may contain any character capable of representation in the computer. Let k be the number of characters that can be stored in a single variable. The specific effect of the A*n* field descriptor depends on whether it is used for input or output and on whether $n < k$.

Rule 2: If $n < k$, the A*n* input field descriptor reads n characters from the input line and stores them in the leftmost n character positions of the variable. The remaining character positions are filled with blank spaces.

Rule 3: If $n \geq k$, the A*n* input field descriptor reads n characters from the input line and stores the rightmost k characters in the variable.

Rule 4: If $n < k$, the A*n* output field descriptor writes the leftmost n characters of the variable.

Rule 5: If $n \geq k$, the A*n* output field descriptor writes the contents of the variable preceded by $n - k$ blank spaces.

EXAMPLE 1. Write a program which will read and print a deck of input cards. The data on the cards can be alphabetic or numeric. The data cards are terminated by a card with a dollar sign in column 1 and blanks on the rest of the card.

Suppose the computer used can store six characters in a variable. To store 80 characters will require 13 variables with six characters per variable plus one more variable with two characters. The easiest thing to do is to use an array, say DATA, with 14 elements. The entire array is read using the format 13A6, A2. It is then printed using a similar format. A program to accomplish this is:

```
C    PROGRAM TO READ AND PRINT A DECK OF CARDS.
C    THE CARDS ARE TERMINATED BY A CARD WITH
C    A DOLLAR SIGN IN COLUMN 1.
C
          DIMENSION DATA (14)
10        READ 100, (DATA(I), I = 1, 14)
          IF (DATA(1) .EQ. '$') STOP
          PRINT 110, (DATA(I), I = 1, 14)
          GO TO 10
C
100       FORMAT(13A6, A2)
110       FORMAT(15X, 13A6, A2)
          END
```

The IF statement that stops the program compares the first array element with the character '$'. We will discuss this topic in the next section.

One drawback of this program is that it will not run correctly on a computer system on which a variable cannot contain six characters (because of Rule 3). The fact that different computer systems can store different numbers of characters per word is a major impediment to the FORTRAN programmer concerned with writing efficient programs that are reasonably independent of the machine used. The only solution is to store no more than four characters per variable, which is within the capability of almost all machines. Many programmers make it a practice to store only one character per variable. This is inefficient in the sense that it uses more variables than necessary, but it will work on any machine. Using this method, the program can be rewritten as:

```
C     PROGRAM TO READ AND PRINT A DECK OF CARDS.
C     THE CARDS ARE TERMINATED BY A CARD WITH
C     A DOLLAR SIGN IN COLUMN 1.
C     IN THIS VERSION, ONE CHARACTER IS STORED IN
C     EACH ELEMENT OF THE ARRAY DATA.
C
          DIMENSION DATA (80)
10        READ 100, (DATA(I), I = 1, 80)
          IF (DATA(1) .EQ. '$') STOP
          PRINT 110, (DATA(I), I = 1, 80)
          GO TO 10
C
100       FORMAT(80A1)
110       FORMAT(15X, 80A1)
          END
```

Character Constants

A character string may be specified as a constant using the form

nH

where *n* is an unsigned integer number. The H is followed by any *n* characters, which are the value of the constant. A blank space is counted as a character within a character constant. Some examples are

```
2H+-
4H****
26HABCDEFGHIJKLMNOPQRSTUVWXYZ
```

The H form of character constant is the only form permitted in standard FORTRAN. Many versions of FORTRAN, including WATFIV, permit an alternative, which is to enclose the character string in quotes.

```
'+-'
'****'
'ABCDEFGHIJKLMNOPQRSTUVWXYZ'
'DON''T'
```

A quote mark may be represented by two consecutive quotes within a character constant.

Standard FORTRAN is quite restrictive in the allowable uses for character constants: They can be used only in the argument list of a function or subroutine call (and in the DATA initialization statement, which we cover in the appendix). Many compilers, including WATFIV, allow more general use of character constants. For example, a character constant can be used in a list-directed PRINT statement or in an assignment statement.

Assignment and Comparison

We shall assume that the system being used permits a general use of quoted character constants (as does WATFIV).

Character constants may be assigned to variables of any type (real or integer). This is shown by the following statements.

```
      L = 'LIKE'
      M = 'M'
      A = 'AG'
      I = 'I'
      C = 'C'
      PRINT 10, L, M, A, I, C
10    FORMAT(10X, A4, 1X, A1, A2, 2A1)
```

This prints the words LIKE MAGIC. When a character constant is assigned to a variable like this, the length of the character string must not be greater than the maximum number of characters that can be stored in a variable. Thus, you could *not* rewrite the foregoing as

```
      X = 'LIKE MAGIC'
      PRINT 10, X
10    FORMAT(10X, A10)
```

This would work on a computer that can store ten characters per variable; but on a computer that cannot store that many characters per variable, it would not have the desired effect.

Two character items can be compared for equality. A relational expression such as

```
X .EQ. 'A'
```

will be true if and only if X contains the character A, followed by all blanks. Suppose the first column of an input line contains the character A and the rest of the input line is blank. Then the statements

```
      READ 5, X
5     FORMAT(A4)
      IF (X .EQ. 'A') PRINT 6
6     FORMAT(1X, 'IT''S AN A')
      STOP
```

will print IT'S AN A. The A4 field descriptor reads the character A followed by three blanks. The reason the comparison for equality succeeds is that the constant A is actually stored as an A followed by three blanks (assuming the computer stores four characters per variable). The entire contents of the memory location for X is compared with the entire contents of the memory location for the constant A. Since both are padded with blanks on the right, they are equal. They would also be equal if X were read with an A3, A2, or A1 field (because of Rule 2).

A slight modification of this example is the following:

```
      READ 5, X
5     FORMAT(A4)
      W = 'A'
      IF (X .EQ. W) PRINT 6, W
6     FORMAT(10X, 'IT''S AN', 1X, A1)
      STOP
```

The difference is that here two variables are being compared, rather than a variable and a constant. If the input data is the letter A followed by three blanks, the comparison will again succeed. The constant A is stored as the character A followed by three blanks. The assignment statement W = A assigns this same value to the variable W. The relational expression X .EQ. W compares the entire contents of both variables. Since both are padded on the right with blanks, they are equal.

The results are less intuitive when two character items are compared to determine which is greater. One might assume that the relational expression

```
'A' .LT. 'B'
```

is true. But what about the expression

```
'A' .LT. '9'
```

or, worse yet,

```
'+' .LT. '*'
```

Each of these expressions is either true or false. The actual result depends on how the particular computer represents character data internally. One common system is the American Standard Code for Information Interchange (ASCII). In this code, the FORTRAN characters are ordered as follows:

space $ ′ ( )* + , − . / 0 1 2 3 4 5 6 7 8 9 = A B C D E F G . . . Z

This defines the **collating sequence** for the FORTRAN character set. This is only one possible sequence, however. Some computers might use a collating sequence in which the numbers come after the letters. For example, this is the case on IBM computers, which use the Extended Binary Coded Decimal Interchange Code (EBCDIC) to represent characters.

Type conversion can be a problem when using character data. Consider the statements

```
      N = 'ABC'
      X = N
      PRINT 11, X
1     FORMAT(1X, A3)
```

The first assignment statement works correctly, assigning the value ABC to the variable N. The second assignment statement, however, will not assign this value to X. The reason is that X is a real variable while N is an integer variable. As always, FORTRAN converts the integer contents of N to a real number. In this case, N does not really contain an integer, it contains the codes for the letters ABC. The result is undefined. It certainly will not print out the letters ABC.

A more subtle example is this:

```
      READ 10, H
      READ 10, I
10    FORMAT(A1)
      IF (H .EQ. I) PRINT 20
      IF (H .NE. I) PRINT 25
20    FORMAT(1X, 'SAME')
25    FORMAT(1X, 'DIFFERENT')
      STOP
```

Two characters are read from consecutive input lines and are compared for equality. The problem is that H is a real variable while I is an integer variable. The A1 format reads both correctly. The relational expression H .EQ. I, however, implies mixed-mode arithmetic, and I will be converted to real form before the variables are compared. This program would almost certainly print DIFFERENT even when the input lines are the same. These problems can be avoided by observing the following:

Rule for Comparison of Character Data

Rule: Do not use variables of different types in an assignment statement or in a comparison when the variables contain character data.

EXAMPLE 2. Student grade cards are prepared in the format shown in Table 10.1. There is one card for each student. Each grade is a letter A, B, C, D, or F (if it is not one of these, it is a mistake). An A corresponds to a number grade of 4, B to 3, and so on. Write a program which will read and print the grades of each student along with numerical average of the grades. Also, print the corresponding letter grade. A blank name will terminate the input data.

Table 10.1 Student Grade Card

Columns	*Item*
1–20	Name
21	Blank
22	Grade in English
23	Blank
24	Grade in math
25	Blank
26	Grade in social studies

The name is read into an array NAME using a 5A4 format. (This assumes the computer can store at least four characters per variable.) The letter grades A through F are stored in an array LETTER so that LETTER(I) is the letter grade corresponding to the numeric grade I − 1. It is convenient to use I − 1 rather than I so that we can set up a DO loop to convert the letter grade to the appropriate number grade. I is used as the index of the DO loop. The number grade is added to the variable SUM so that the average may be computed. The program follows:

```
C   PROGRAM TO AVERAGE STUDENT GRADES
C   NG IS THE NUMBER OF GRADES PER CARD.
C   LETTER IS AN ARRAY WHICH CONTAINS THE LETTER GRADES
```

```
C  IN ORDER SO THAT LETTER (I) CORRESPONDS TO THE
C  NUMBER GRADE I − 1.
C  INPUT DATA IS TERMINATED BY A BLANK NAME FIELD.

      DIMENSION NGRADE(3), LETTER(5), NAME(5)
      NG = 3
      NBLANK = ' '
      LETTER(5) = 'A'
      LETTER(4) = 'B'
      LETTER(3) = 'C'
      LETTER(2) = 'D'
      LETTER(1) = 'F'
C
10    READ 20, NAME, NGRADE
20    FORMAT(5A4, 3(1X, A1))
      DO 30 I = 1, 5
         IF (NAME(I) .NE. NBLANK) GO TO 40
30       CONTINUE
      STOP
C
40    SUM = 0.0
      DO 60 I = 1, NG
         DO 50 J = 1, 5
            IF (NGRADE(I) .NE. LETTER(J)) GO TO 50
              SUM = SUM + FLOAT(J − 1)
              GO TO 60
50          CONTINUE
         PRINT 55, NAME, NGRADE
55       FORMAT(1X, '***ERROR***', 5A4, 1X, 3A2)
         GO TO 10
60       CONTINUE
      AVER = SUM/FLOAT(NG)
C  ROUND AVERAGE TO NEAREST INTEGER
C  LET LAVER BE CORRESPONDING LETTER GRADE
      I = AVER + 0.5
      LAVER = LETTER(I + 1)
      PRINT 65, NAME, NGRADE, AVER, LAVER
65    FORMAT(1X, 5A4, 1X, 3A2, F6.3, 1X, A4)
      GO TO 10
      END
```

Character Data Type

Some versions of FORTRAN, including WATFIV, permit a **CHARACTER** statement which declares certain variables to be character variables. This is a declarative statement (like DIMENSION) which must come at the beginning of the program, before any executable statements. The form is

CHARACTER *name* * *n* :

where

name is a FORTRAN variable name

n is an integer number giving the number of characters which can be stored in the variable *name*

You can make several character declarations in a single CHARACTER statement. For example,

```
CHARACTER X*4, NAME*20, A*1
```

means that X is a character variable comprised of four characters, NAME is a character variable comprised of twenty characters, and A is a character variable comprised of a single character.

The character count can be given at the beginning of the CHARACTER statement. The form of this declaration is

CHARACTER * n $\text{name}_1, \text{name}_2, \ldots, \text{name}_k$

For example,

```
CHARACTER*1 A, B, C
CHARACTER*20 NAME
CHARACTER I*1, J*2, K*3
```

An entire array can be declared to be type character. For instance,

```
CHARACTER*1 X(20)
```

means that X(I) is a one-character variable for each I = 1, 2, . . . , 20. This can also be written as

```
CHARACTER X*1(20)
```

Similarly, the declaration

```
CHARACTER G*5(3, 3), X*10(3)
```

sets up a 3 by 3 matrix G, each element of which is a character variable of five characters, and sets up an array X of three elements, each of which is a character variable of ten characters. If the size is omitted from a CHARACTER declaration, a size of one is assumed. Thus,

```
CHARACTER X(20)
```

is the same as

```
CHARACTER * 1 X(20)
```

Character variables can be used just like the noncharacter variables you have used for character data. Character variables have some advantages, however. For one thing, the number of characters per variable is explicitly declared, so there is no question about the effect of a certain A format, for instance. If NAME is a CHARACTER*25 variable, then it can be read with an A25 format. An assignment statement can assign the entire contents of one character variable to another. If the receiving variable is longer, it will be padded on the right with spaces. In a comparison between two character variables, the entire contents are compared, whatever the length. If one is longer than the other, they are treated as though they were the same length with the shorter one padded on the right with blanks.

EXAMPLE 3. A *palindrome* is a number, word, or sentence that reads the same backward or forward (e.g., 1881, dad, Able was I ere I saw Elba). Write a program which determines if the input line is a palindrome.

Since you want to consider individual characters in this problem, you read the input line into a character array defined by

```
CHARACTER X(80)
```

This program would work as well if X were a real array of size 80, but making it a character array is more efficient.

The first step in the solution is to find the length of the input line. That is, you want to find the subscript of the last nonblank character. You could start with X(1) and search for a blank, but if the input contained more than one word, you would not know if you had found the last blank. Instead, you can start at the end of the array, X(80), and search backward until coming to a nonblank. Let LENGTH be the subscript of the last nonblank. Assuming there are no leading blanks in the input, then the string of characters to be considered is in X(1) through X(LENGTH). It is a palindrome if and only if

$$X(1) = X(LENGTH)$$
$$X(2) = X(LENGTH - 1)$$
$$X(3) = X(LENGTH - 2)$$

This is programmed by comparing X(I) with X(J), adding 1 to I and subtracting 1 from J until $I \geq J$.

The program has been written so that it takes an arbitrary number of input lines. It stops upon encountering an input line with a blank in column 1. The program follows:

```
C-- PROGRAM TO TEST FOR A PALINDROME
C-- INPUT IS TERMINATED BY A LINE WITH COLUMN 1 BLANK
      CHARACTER X(80), BLANK
      BLANK = ' '
5     READ 10, (X(I), I = 1, 80)
      PRINT 11, (X(I), I = 1, 80)
10    FORMAT(80A1)
11    FORMAT(10X, 80A1)
      IF (X(1) .EQ. BLANK) STOP
C
C-- FIND LENGTH OF INPUT
C
      LENGTH = 80
15    IF (X(LENGTH) .NE. BLANK) GO TO 20
         LENGTH = LENGTH - 1
         GO TO 15
C
C-- TEST FOR PALINDROME
C
20    I = 1
      J = LENGTH
25    IF (I .GE. J) GO TO 30
         IF (X(I) .NE. X(J)) GO TO 40
         I = I + 1
         J = J - 1
         GO TO 25
C-- YES
30    PRINT 35
35    FORMAT(11X, 'IS A PALINDROME')
      GO TO 5
C
C-- NO
40    PRINT 45
45    FORMAT(11X, 'IS NOT A PALINDROME')
      GO TO 5
      END
```

EXAMPLE 4. Write a program to read an input line and count the number of words on it.

The difficulty of this problem depends on the definition of *word*. If it is taken to mean a string of letters found as a main entry in an English dictionary, then this problem would be extremely difficult to program. We shall adopt the following simple definition: A word is a consecutive sequence of letters (A through Z) followed by a nonletter or by the end of the input line.

The general procedure is indicated in Figure 10.2. Starting with the leftmost character, you look at each character on the line. As long as the character is a letter, you go on to the next character. When the character is not a letter you have reached the end of a word, so you add 1 to a variable that counts the number of words. Then you keep scanning from left to right until you reach another letter, and the process repeats.

The procedure continues until you reach the end of the line. You have to be careful here, though, and consider what happens if the last word goes to the very end of the line. To make sure the word is counted, you can add an extra blank space at the end of the line

Step 1:

THE QUICK BROWN FOX JUMPS.

↑ This character is a letter, so examine the next character to the right.

Step 2:

THE QUICK BROWN FOX JUMPS.

↑ This character is a letter, so examine the next character to the right.

Step 3:

THE QUICK BROWN FOX JUMPS.

↑ This character is a letter, so examine the next character to the right.

Step 4:

THE QUICK BROWN FOX JUMPS.

↑ This character is *not* a letter, so you are at the end of a word. Add 1 to the number of words.

Step 5:

THE QUICK BROWN FOX JUMPS.

↑ Examine the next character to the right until you come to a letter, then repeat the procedure, as in step 1.

Figure 10.2 A procedure to count the number of words in an input line.

so that the procedure will have already counted the last word when the end of the line is reached.

To be specific, you read the input line into an array, with one character per array element. The first character goes in A(1) and the last character goes in A(80). You store a blank space in A(81), then begin examining each character. The complete procedure is shown in the flowchart of Figure 10.3.

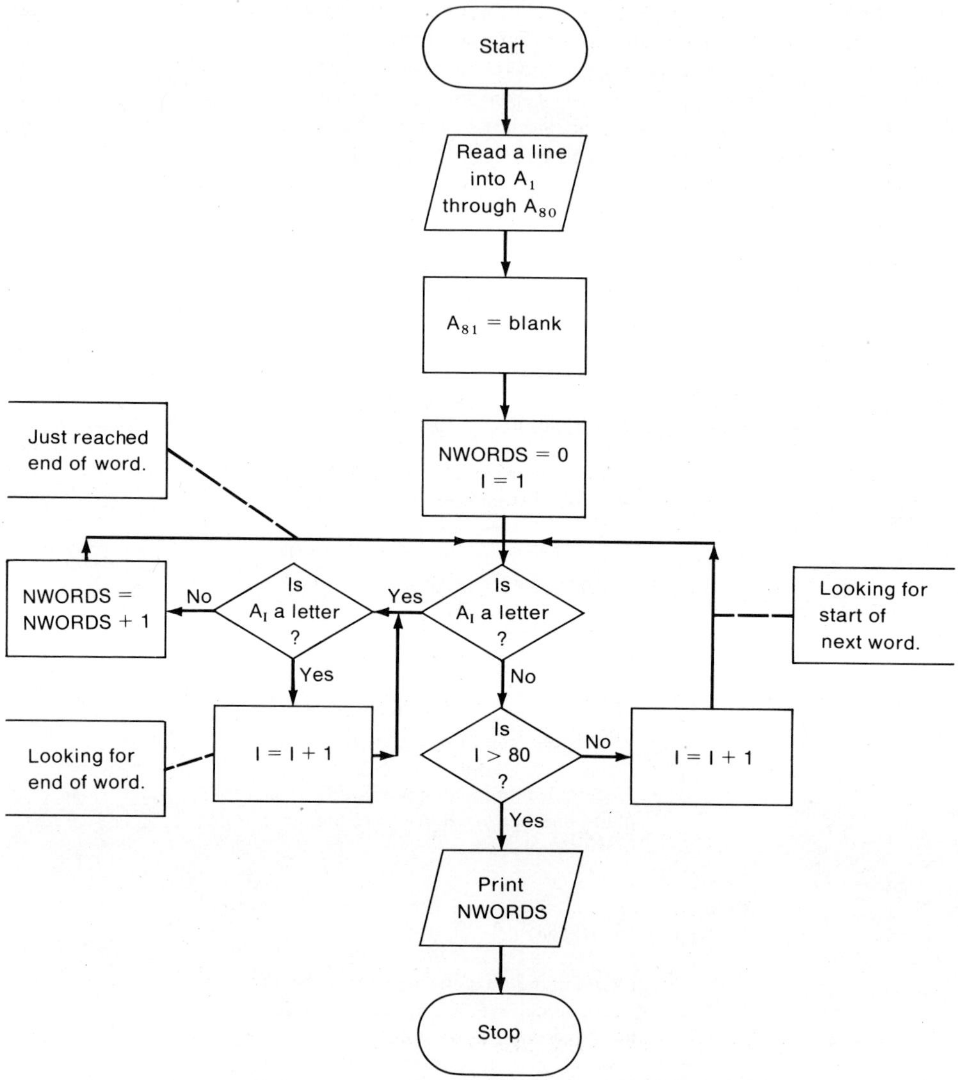

Figure 10.3 Flowchart for the procedure to count the number of words on a line.

To carry out this procedure in FORTRAN, you can use a function LETTER(X) that has the value 1 if X is a letter and 0 if X is not a letter. This function uses a DO loop to compare X with each letter of the alphabet. You can use separate subroutine SETLET that reads the letters of the alphabet from a data card and stores them in an array XLET, which is in common storage (so that it can be accessible to both the SETLET and LETTER subprograms). Here is the complete program.

```
C-- THIS PROGRAM READS AN INPUT CARD AND COUNTS
C-- THE NUMBER OF WORDS ON IT.
        CHARACTER A(81)
        A(81) = ' '
        NWORDS = 0
C
C-- SETLET INITIALIZES THE LETTER SUBROUTINE.
C
        CALL SETLET
C
C-- READ THE LINE AND PRINT IT.
C
        READ 5, (A(I), I = 1, 80)
5       FORMAT(80A1)
        PRINT 10, (A(I), I = 1, 80)
10      FORMAT(10X, 80A1)
C
C-- FIND THE NEXT LETTER.
C
        I = 1
100     IF(LETTER(A(I)) .EQ. 1) GO TO 200
            IF (I .LE. 80) GO TO 110
                PRINT 105, NWORDS
                STOP
105             FORMAT(10X, I5, 1X, 'WORDS.')
110         I = I + 1
            GO TO 100
C
C-- FIND THE NEXT NONLETTER AND ADD 1 TO NWORDS.
C
200     IF (LETTER(A(I)) .EQ. 0) GO TO 300
            I = I + 1
            GO TO 200
```

```
300       NWORDS = NWORDS + 1
          GO TO 100
          END

          SUBROUTINE SETLET
C--  READS THE LETTERS OF THE ALPHABET.
          CHARACTER XLET
          COMMON XLET(26)
          READ 10, (XLET(I), I = 1, 26)
10        FORMAT(26A1)
          RETURN
          END

          FUNCTION LETTER(X)
C
C--  LETTER(X) = 1 IF X IS A LETTER
C              = 0 IF X IS NOT A LETTER
          CHARACTER X, XLET
          COMMON XLET(26)
          LETTER = 1
          DO 10 I = 1, 26
             IF (X .EQ. XLET(I)) RETURN
10           CONTINUE
          LETTER = 0
          RETURN
          END
```

EXAMPLE 5. A **histogram** is a graph that shows the relative frequency of occurrence of a set of measurements. For example, Table 10.2 shows the results of a hypothetical survey.

Table 10.2 Hypothetical Survey Results

Brand of Laundry Soap	*Percentage of People Surveyed Who Use Brand*
Brand A	10
Brand B	15
Brand C	5
Brand D	31
Brand E	2
Brand X (all others)	37

For each of five major brands of laundry soap, the percentage of people using the brand is computed.

The histogram in Figure 10.4 displays these results as a bar graph, where the length of each bar is proportional to the percentage of people who use the corresponding brand of laundry soap.

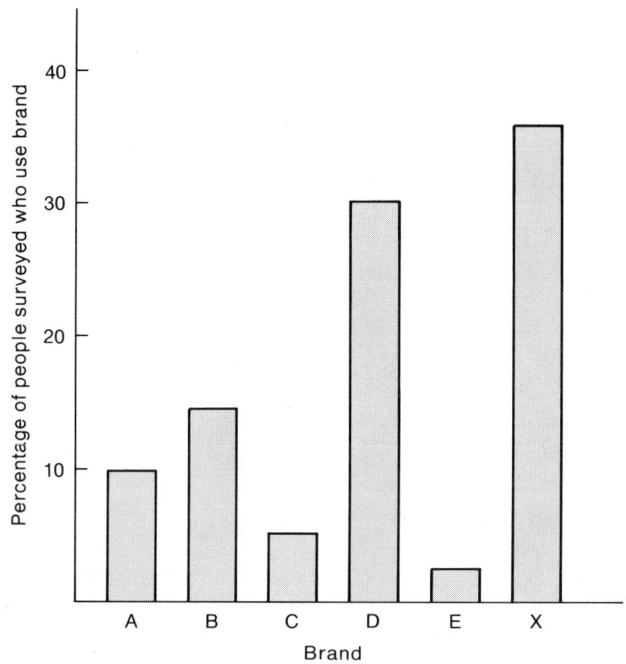

Figure 10.4 A histogram.

You can write a subroutine HISTO to print a simple histogram, using asterisks to mark the bars on the graph. The parameters to the subroutine are an integer variable N and a real array PCT of N elements. The value of PCT(I) is the relative frequency of measurements in category I, expressed as a number between 0 and 1. For instance, for the data of Figure 10.4, PCT(1) = 0.10, PCT(2) = 0.15, etc.

Each print line corresponds to one bar on the histogram. The number of asterisks to print is 100 times PCT(I). One way to do this is to set up an array of 100 elements, initialize it to all blank spaces, set the first 100* PCT(I) elements to the character '*', and then print the entire array. An easier way uses an implied DO loop to print the single character '*' the appropriate number of times. This can be done with the statements

```
L = 100. * PCT(I)
PRINT 100, (STAR, J = 1, L)
```

This is an example of an implied DO loop where the output list does not include any subscripted variables.

The subroutine HISTO, with a simple test program, is given as follows. Sample output from the test program is shown in Figure 10.5.

```
PERCENTAGE OF PEOPLE WHO USE BRAND
0.05 *****
0.16 ***************
0.26 **************************
0.37 *************************************
0.11 **********
0.05 *****
```

Figure 10.5 Sample output from Example 5.

```
      SUBROUTINE HISTO(PCT, N)
C     PRINTS A HISTOGRAM CORRESPONDING TO ARRAY PCT.
C     PCT(I) IS THE RELATIVE FREQUENCY.
      CHARACTER STAR
      DIMENSION PCT(N)
      STAR = '*'
      DO 10 I = 1, N
         L = 100. * PCT(I)
         PRINT 5, PCT(I), (STAR, J = 1, L)
5        FORMAT('0', F5.2, 2X, 100A1)
10       CONTINUE
      RETURN
      END

C     TEST PROGRAM
      DIMENSION KOUNT(6), FREQ(6)
      READ, (KOUNT(I), I = 1, 6)
      N = 0
      DO 10 I = 1, 6
10       N = N + KOUNT(I)
      DO 20 I = 1, 6
20       FREQ(I) = FLOAT(KOUNT(I))/FLOAT(N)
      PRINT 30
30    FORMAT('1 PERCENTAGE OF PEOPLE WHO USE BRAND')
      CALL HISTO(FREQ, 6)
      STOP
      END
```

Exercises

1. Data cards are prepared with names and addresses. Only the first 30 columns of each card are used. The first card contains the name; the second card contains the first line of the address; and so forth. There may be up to six cards per person, total. The last card for each person has some nonblank characters in columns 31–34. We want to print mailing labels, one for each person. The forms they are to be printed on require that there be exactly five labels per page and that each label consist of exactly eight lines, six or fewer lines of name and address, followed by two or more blank lines. Write a program to read the data and produce the required output.
2. Here is a small, solid square, made up of Xs:

```
XXXX
XXXX
XXXX
```

   Write a program to print a large square, 8 inches by 8 inches. Assume that the printer prints six lines per inch of vertical spacing and ten characters per inch on each line.
3. Instead of a square, as in Exercise 2, print a large circle, 10 inches in diameter, filled with Xs.
4. Print a checkerboard pattern large enough to be used for playing checkers.
5. Write a program to read a FORTRAN program and print only the comment lines. Have the program stop when it reads a card with a '*' in column 1.
6. Write a program to read a sequence of cards containing a paragraph of English prose. Count the total number of occurrences of each letter of the alphabet, and print this.
7. Expand the program of Exercise 6 so that it not only prints out how many times each letter appeared, but also prints this information in order, with the most frequently used letter first, and so on. For example,

```
THE LETTER E OCCURRED 72 TIMES
THE LETTER A OCCURRED 40 TIMES
THE LETTER T OCCURRED 39 TIMES
. . .
```

8. Let NA and NB be two words of alphabetic data. Assume that NA is lexically less than NB (i.e., comes before it in alphabetical order) if NA . LT. NB. (This will be true on many machines, but not necessarily on all machines.) Suppose the machine can store four characters per word. Let NA(5) and NB(5) each be an array of five four-character words. Write a function of LGT(NA, NB) that returns 1 if NA is lexically greater than NB and returns 0 otherwise.
9. Read a sequence of up to 25 cards, terminated by a blank card, reading the first 25 characters of each card. Using the function in Exercise 8, put them in alphabetical order and print them.

10. Let A and B be character arrays of M and N characters, respectively, one character per word. Assume M ≤ N. Write a function IOTA(A, M, B, N) to do the following. If A appears anywhere in B as a substring, let IOTA be the index where A begins in B. For example, if A = 'LIGHT' and B = 'DELIGHT', then IOTA = 3. If A does not appear as a substring in B, let IOTA = 0.

11. Write a program to print your initials in 2-inch high letters made up of individual characters. For example,

```
XXXXXXXX        XXXXXX
   XX             XX
   XX             XX
   XX             XX
   XX       XX    XX
   XX       XX    XX
   XX       XXXXXXXX
```

12. In Roman numerals,

    M stands for 1000

    D stands for 500

    C stands for 100

    L stands for 50

    X stands for 10

    V stands for 5

    I stands for 1

    The numeral XXVII stands for 27. However, XXIV is 24; since the I comes before the V, it reduces its value by 1. Write a program that reads a Roman numeral and prints the equivalent number.

APPENDIX A

FORTRAN-Supplied Functions

The general rules for using functions may be summarized as follows.

Rules for Using FORTRAN-Supplied Functions

Rule 1: A function may be used in an expression by writing the function name followed by a pair of parentheses which enclose the argument (or arguments). If there is more than one argument, they are separated by commas.

Rule 2: Each argument can be any arithmetic expression, including one which involves another function reference. The arguments must be of the correct type (integer or real), depending on the function. Also, the correct number of arguements must be supplied.

Rule 3: The function returns either an integer value or a real value, depending on whether the name of the function follows the rules for integer variables or for real variables.

In the following table, functions that require integer arguments are written with integer variable names, such as IABS(N). N is an integer name, so the function requires an integer argument. Likewise, functions that require real arguments are written with real variable names, such as ABS(X). The value of the function is integer or real, depending on whether the name of the function is an integer or real variable name.

Conversion from real to integer (truncation)

INT(X)	Sign of X times the largest integer less than or equal to ABS(X). This converts the real expression X to integer form. Examples: INT(3.2) = 3; INT(−3.2) = −3
AINT(X)	Sign of X times the largest integer less than or equal to ABS(X). Same as INT, but returns a real number. Examples: AINT(3.7) = 3.0; AINT(−3.7) = −3.0

Conversion from integer to real

FLOAT(N)	The real (floating-point) form of the integer N. Example: FLOAT(2) = 2.0

Absolute value

IABS(N)	Absolute value of N. That is, IABS(N) = N if N $\geq$ 0; IABS(N) = −N if N $<$ 0. Example: IABS(−3) = 3
ABS(X)	Absolute value of X. ABS(X) = X if X $\geq$ 0; ABS(X) = −X if X $<$ 0. Example: ABS(−3.2) = 3.2

Remaindering

MOD(N, K)	The remainder when N is divided by K (i.e., N modulo K). The definition of this function is N − INT(N/K)*K. Examples: MOD(17, 5) = 2; MOD(8, 2) = 0; MOD(−5, 3) = −2
AMOD(X, A)	The remainder when X is divided by A (similar to MOD, but for real numbers). The definition is X − AINT(X/A)*A. Examples: AMOD(3.123, 1.0) = 0.123; AMOD(8.0, 2.0) = 0.0; AMOD(−7.5, 2.0) = −1.5

Maximum and minimum

MAX0(L, M, N, . . .)	Maximum of two or more integer arguments. MAX0(2, 5) = 5; MAX0(2, −5) = 2; MAX0(2, 3, 4) = 4
MAX1(A, B, C, . . .)	Maximum of two or more real arguments. Result is converted to integer. Examples: MAX1(2.1, 5.2) = 5; MAX1(−2.1, −5.2) = −2; MAX1(2.0, 3.0, 4.1) = 4

Maximum and minimum (continued)

AMAX0(L, M, N, . . .)	Maximum of two or more integer arguments. Result is converted to real. Example: AMAX0(2, 3) = 3.0
AMAX1(A, B, C, . . .)	Maximum of two or more real arguments. Example: AMAX1(2.0, 3.1) = 3.1
MIN0(L, M, N, . . .)	Minimum of two or more integer arguments. Examples: MIN0(2, 5) = 2 MIN0(2, −5) = −5 MIN0(2, 3, 4) = 2
MIN1(A, B, C, . . .)	Minimum of two or more real arguments. Result is converted to integer. Example: MIN1(2.1, 5.2) = 2
AMIN0(L, M, N, . . .)	Minimum of two or more integer arguments. Result is converted to real. Example: AMIN0(2, 3) = 2.0
AMIN1(A, B, C, . . .)	Minimum of two or more real arguments. Example: AMIN1(2.0, 3.1) = 2.0

Transfer of sign

ISIGN(N, K)	Sign of K with the absolute value of N. Examples: ISIGN(3, −1) = −3 ISIGN(−4, 2) = 4
SIGN(X,A)	Sign of A with the absolute value of X. Examples: SIGN(2.1, −3.0) = −2.1 SIGN(−2.1, 3.0) = 2.1

Positive difference

IDIM(N, K)	Equal to N − K if N $\geq$ K. Otherwise, equal to zero. Examples: IDIM(5, 4) = 1 IDIM(4, 5) = 0
DIM(X, A)	Equal to X − A if X $\geq$ A. Otherwise, equal to zero. Examples: DIM(4.0, 0.0) = 4.0 DIM(−4.0, 0.0) = 0.0

Square root

SQRT(X)	Square root of X, where X $\geq$ 0. Example: SQRT(9.0) = 3.0

Exponential and logarithmic

EXP(X)	Exponential function e^x. Example: EXP(1.0) = 2.718282
ALOG(X)	Natural logarithm $\log_e x$, where $x > 0$. Example: ALOG(2.718282) = 1.0
ALOG10(X)	Common logarithm $\log_{10} x$, where $x > 0$. Example: ALOG10(100.0) = 2.0

Trigonometric

SIN(X)	Trigonometric sine of X, where X is in radians Example: SIN(3.14159) = 0.0
COS(X)	Trigonometric cosine of X, where X is in radians. Example: COS(3.14159) = −1.0
TAN(X)	Trigonometric tangent of X, where X is in radians. (This function is not available on all systems.) Example: TAN(3.14159/4.0) = 1.0

Inverse trigonometric

ASIN(X)	Arcsine of X, in radians, where $-1 \leq X \leq 1$. The value will lie in the range $-\pi/2 \leq$ ASIN(X) $\leq \pi/2$. (This function is not available on all systems.) Example: ASIN(0.0) = 0.0
ACOS(X)	Arccosine of X, in radians, where $-1 \leq X \leq 1$. The value will lie in the range $0 \leq$ ACOS(X) $\leq \pi$. (This function is not available on all systems.) Example: ACOS(0.0) = 1.570796
ATAN(X)	Arctangent of X, in radians. The value will lie in the range $-\pi/2 <$ ATAN(X) $\leq \pi/2$. Example: ATAN(1.0) = 0.785398
ATAN2(Y, X)	Arctangent of Y/X, in radians. The value will lie in the range $-\pi \leq$ ATAN2(Y, X) $\leq \pi$. This will correctly handle the case where X is zero. Examples: ATAN2(1.0, 1.0) = 0.785398 ATAN2(1.0, 0.0) = 1.570796 ATAN2(−1.0, −1.0) = −2.356194 ATAN2(1.0, −1.0) = 2.356194

Hyperbolic

SINH(X)	Hyperbolic sine $(e^x - e^{-x})/2$. (This function is not available on all systems.) Example: SINH(0.0) = 0.0
COSH(X)	Hyperbolic cosine $(e^x + e^{-x})/2$. (This function is not available on all systems.) Example: COSH(0.0) = 1.0
TANH(X)	Hyperbolic tangent $(e^x - e^{-x})/(e^x + e^{-x})$. Example: TANH(1.0) = 0.761594

APPENDIX B

Additional FORTRAN Features

There are a few features in the FORTRAN language which we have not covered. Beginning students will probably not find much occasion to use these features, but they are quite useful in certain circumstances.

The Arithmetic IF Statement

The type of IF statement studied so far is called the **logical IF** statement because it tests a relational expression (e.g., N. EQ. 10), which is a type of logical expression. There is another type of IF statement in FORTRAN, called the **arithmetic IF** statement because it tests the value of an arithmetic expression.

The general form of the arithmetic IF is

IF (*E*) *n*, *z*, *p*

where *E* is any arithmetic expression, and *n*, *z*, and *p* are statement labels. This statement means to evaluate the expression *E* and, if it is negative, go to statement *n*; if it is zero, go to statement *z*; if it is positive, go to statement *p*. Thus, it corresponds to the flowchart box in Figure B.1. In terms of the logical IF, the arithmetic IF is equivalent to the three statements:

```
IF (E .LT. 0) GO TO n
IF (E .EQ. 0) GO TO z
GO TO p
```

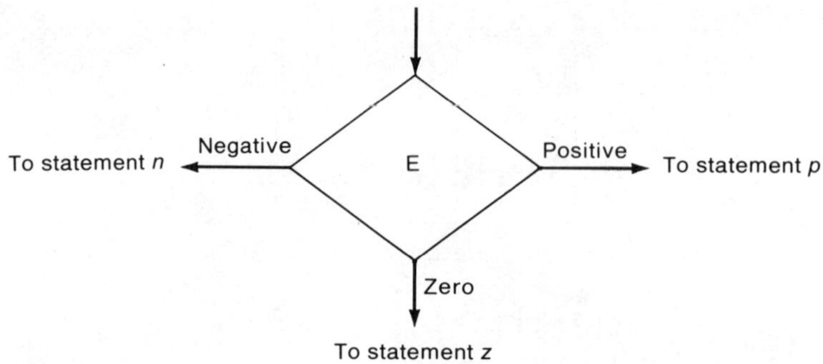

Figure B.1

For example,

IF (X − 5.0) 10, 10, 20

means if X − 5.0 is negative or zero, go to statement 10; otherwise, go to statement 20. This is equivalent to

IF (X .LE. 5.0) GO TO 10
GO TO 20

The statement

IF ((5.0 * X * Y + 14.0) * Z)20, 10, 10

means if the expression (5.0* X* Y + 14.0)* Z is negative, go to statement 20; otherwise, go to statement 10.

The Computed GO TO

The **computed GO TO** is a form of GO TO statement which selects one of a number of statements to be executed, depending on the value of an integer variable. The form is

GO TO($s_1, s_2, \ldots, s_n$), I

where

$s_1, s_2, \ldots, s_n$ is a list of statement numbers. They must be integer constants.

I is a simple integer variable.

This statement means,

if $I = 1$, GO TO s_1

if $I = 2$, GO TO s_2

. . .

if $I = n$, GO TO s_n

If $I < 1$ or $I > n$, the result is undefined. On some systems, an error results in this case. For example,

```
GO TO(10, 10, 20, 99), NVAR
```

means to GO TO statement 10 if NVAR = 1 or 2, GO TO statement 20 if NVAR = 3, and GO TO 99 if NVAR = 4.

The Assigned GO TO

The **assigned GO TO** is a GO TO statement with a variable statement number. The form is

GO TO I, $(s_1, s_2, \ldots, s_n)$

where

I	is a simple integer variable
$s_1, s_2, \ldots, s_n$	is a list of statement numbers, which must be integer numbers; this list gives all the possible statement numbers to which the statement might branch

This statement means GO TO statement I, where I is one of the statement numbers in the list. Before executing this statement, some value must be assigned to I. This is not done by the usual assignment statement; that is, the following is *incorrect*:

```
IWRONG = 10
GO TO IWRONG, (10, 20, 25)
```

A special **ASSIGN** statement must be used to assign a value to a variable to be used in an assigned GO TO. The ASSIGN statement has the form:

ASSIGN n TO I

where

n	is an integer constant representing a statement number
I	is a simple integer variable

After this assignment has taken place, the variable I may be used in an assigned GO TO.

Thus,

```
      ASSIGN 122 TO JUMP
      GO TO JUMP, (100, 5, 122, 99)
```

will transfer to statement 122. The reason the ASSIGN statement is required is that the value stored in JUMP is not really the integer value 122, but some address representing the location of statement 122. For this reason, the value of JUMP should not be modified in the program except by assigning a different value through another ASSIGN statement.

The STOP *n* and PAUSE *n* Statements

An alternate form of the STOP statement is the statement

STOP *n*

where *n* is an octal number of four or fewer digits. An octal number is a number in base 8. For the purpose of this statement, it is just a number that does not contain the digits 8 or 9. So, 1125 is correct but 93 is not, since it contains the digit 9.

The **STOP n** statement does exactly the same thing as a STOP statement. The only difference is that the number *n* will be displayed on the program listing when the STOP *n* statement is executed. If the program uses several STOP *n* statements with different values of *n*, this allows the programmer to determine where the program stopped. For instance, suppose you are dividing Y by X to give A. X should never be zero; but just in case, you might include the statement

```
      IF (X .EQ. 0.0) STOP 3
```

If X were, in fact, equal to zero, the number 3 would be displayed in the output; and you would be able to go back and find the trouble in the program.

The **PAUSE** and **PAUSE n** statements do almost the same thing as the STOP and STOP *n* statement. The difference is that the computer operator can restart the program manually. Suppose that in some program you want the computer operator to mount a magnetic tape on unit 3. You then want to read this tape. The program might include the statements

```
      PRINT, 25
   25 FORMAT('MOUNT TAPE 3')
      PAUSE
```

When the PAUSE statement is executed, the program will pause and wait for the operator to take some manual action. When the operator restarts the program, the next statement is executed.

Some versions of FORTRAN, including WATFIV, allow a PAUSE statement with a message in it, enclosed in quotes. The form is

PAUSE '*message*'

This causes the program to pause, and the message will be displayed for the operator. This is an easy way to provide simple error checking in a program.

INTEGER and REAL Statements

FORTRAN determines whether a variable is integer or real by the first letter of the variable name. To depart from the usual naming convention, we can use the **INTEGER** and **REAL** statements. The first of these has the form

INTEGER $name_1, name_2, \ldots, name_n$

All the variables named in the list will be treated as integer variables throughout the program. For instance, if a program contains the declaration

```
INTEGER A, B, C
```

then the variables A, B, and C will be used as integer variables in the program although they would normally be real variables. Similarly, the statement

REAL $name_1, name_2, \ldots, name_n$

would cause the variables named to be treated as real variables throughout the program, regardless of the usual naming conventions.

As with other types of declaration statements, these statements, if used, must come at the beginning of the program, before the first executable statement. They may also give dimension information. For instance, the statement

```
REAL I(10, 5)
```

would cause I to be set up as a 10 by 5 real array in the program.

The IMPLICIT Statement

Some FORTRAN compilers, including WATFIV, allow an **IMPLICIT** statement which can be used to implicitly define the types of variables. Instead of explicitly naming the variables that are to be of a certain type, the IMPLICIT statement declares that all variables beginning with a certain letter be of a certain type. For example, the declaration

```
IMPLICIT INTEGER(A), REAL(P – S)
```

means that all variable names which begin with the letter A will be integer variables, and all variable names which begin with letters P through S (i.e., P, Q, R, and S) will be real variables.

In general, the IMPLICIT statement has the form

$$\text{IMPLICIT } type_1\,(A_1, A_2, A_3, \ldots),\, type_2\,(B_1, B_2, B_3, \ldots), \ldots$$

where

$type_i$	is the type of variable (e.g., INTEGER or REAL)
A_i, B_i	is either a single letter, or two letters separated by a hyphen (minus sign) to indicate a range of letters

The IMPLICIT statement must come at the beginning of a program before any other declarative statements. The effect of the IMPLICIT statement may be overridden by explicit declaration of type. For example, if the following two statements appear in the beginning of a program, then all variables will be integer variables, except for the variable MASS and any variables beginning with the letters A or Z which are real variables:

```
IMPLICIT INTEGER (B – Y), REAL(A, Z)
REAL MASS
```

The DATA Statement

We have covered two ways to initialize a variable. One is to read in values for the variable. The other is to assign a value to the variable with an assignment statement. The **DATA** statement is also used for initializing variables. When the DATA statement is used, the variable is initialized when the program is *compiled*, rather than when it is executed. This is a subtle but very important difference. As an example, the following DATA statement initializes the variable PI with a value 3.1416.

```
DATA PI / 3.1416 /
```

The following statement also accomplishes this:

```
PI = 3.1416
```

The assignment statement is an executable statement which causes something to happen when the program runs. A variable PI has been set up in the computer memory and a number 3.1416 has also been stored somewhere in the computer memory. The statement

```
PI = 3.1416
```

fetches the value of the number and moves this value to the variable PI.

On the other hand, the DATA statement is nonexecutable. It causes no action to occur when the program is run. When the program is compiled it sets up a memory location PI containing the value 3.1416. This value may be changed during execution of the program, but initially the variable PI will have the value 3.1416.

The form of the DATA statement is

DATA $name_1, \ldots, name_n/value_1, \ldots, value_n/, name_{n+1}, \ldots / value_{n+1}, \ldots /$

where

$name_i$	is a variable name
$value_i$	is the corresponding initial value

For example,

```
DATA A, B, N / 5.1, 5.2, 0 /
```

has the same effect as

```
A = 5.1
B = 5.2
N = 0
```

except that it initializes these variables during compilation.

To initialize several variables to the same value, a repetition factor may be used. This consists of an integer number followed by an asterisk. It can precede any value in the DATA statement to specify a sequence of identical values. For example,

```
DATA A, B, C, D / 1.0, 1.0, 1.0, 2.0 /
```

could be written as

```
DATA A, B, C, D / 3*1.0, 2.0 /
```

The 3*1.0 means three values of 1.0.

Most versions of FORTRAN, including WATFIV, allow implied DO loops in a DATA statement as well as an array name. The statements

```
DIMENSION X(10), Y(10)
DATA (X(I), I = 1, 10, 2) / 5*1.0 /
DATA (X(I), I = 2, 10, 2) / 5* -1.0 /
DATA Y / 10*0.0 /
```

will initialize X(1) = 1., X(2) = −1., X(3) = 1., and so on, and will set all of Y to zeros.

Unlike the assignment statement

```
N = 3.2
```

the DATA statement

```
DATA N / 3.2 /
```

does *not* perform any conversion from real to integer. Thus, it stores the real number 3.2 in the integer variable N. This will almost certainly lead to incorrect results. To avoid this problem, observe the following rule when using DATA statements:

Rule for Type Agreement in DATA Statement

Rule: The type of the value in the DATA statement must agree with the type of the corresponding variable.

Character data may be stored in a variable of any type using a DATA statement. The statement

```
DIMENSION A(3)
DATA A(1), A(2), A(3) / '+', '-', '*' /
```

stores the characters '+', '−', and '*' in the array A.

The DATA statements must come at the beginning of the program unit. They must come after other declarative statements (COMMON, DIMENSION, etc.) and before the first executable statement.

Exponential Form

Scientific notation is a way of writing numbers which is especially useful for expressing numbers that are very large or very small. Some examples are given in Table B.1. As the table shows, in scientific notation a number is written as a regular decimal number multiplied by a power of 10. The decimal number can be written as a number between 1 and 10. The exponent of 10 tells how many places to move the decimal point. For example, in $365.0 = 3.65 \times 10^2$, the 2 in the exponent means to move the decimal point two places to the right.

Table B.1 Examples of Scientific Notation

Number	*Scientific Notation*	
365	3.65×10^2	(days in a year)
86,400	8.64×10^4	(seconds in a day)
31,536,000	3.1536×10^7	(seconds in a year)
0.0022	2.20×10^{-3}	(pounds in a gram)
0.000001	1.0×10^{-6}	(meters in a micron)
0.0000000667	6.67×10^{-8}	(gravity constant in centimeter-gram-second system)

Scientific notation makes it possible to work with numbers whose values are not precisely known. For example, the mass of the earth may be written as 5.975×10^{27} grams. This does not imply that the figure is accurate to within 1 gram. It does imply that the true mass is between 5.974×10^{27} grams and 5.976×10^{27} grams. We say that 5.975×10^{27} represents the mass of the earth to four **significant digits**.

There is a method of representing real numbers in FORTRAN, which is similar to scientific notation. This is called **exponential form** or **E form**. Instead of a power of 10 multiplier, the letter E is used, followed by the exponent. Table B.2 gives some examples.

In general, a real number in E form is written according to the following rules.

Rules for Exponential Form

Rule 1: The first part of the number is a regular FORTRAN real number that follows the rules given previously. If it is a whole number, the decimal point may be omitted.

Rule 2: Next, write the letter E.

Rule 3: After the E, write an integer number of one or two digits. This number is the exponent of 10 by which the number is multiplied. The exponent has the effect of shifting the decimal point to the right or to the left. If it is positive, it tells how many places to shift to the right; if it is negative, it tells how many places to shift to the left.

Rule 4: Blank spaces and leading zeros do not affect the value of the number.

Table B.2 Exponential Form of Real Numbers in FORTRAN

FORTRAN Number	*Scientific Notation*	*Value*
2.0E4	2.0×10^4	20,000
2.E4	2.0×10^4	20,000
2E4	2.0×10^4	20,000
2 E 4	2.0×10^4	20,000
+02.00E + 4	2.0×10^4	20,000
2.0E04	2.0×10^4	20,000
1.63E1	1.63×10^1	16.3
1.63E − 1	1.63×10^{-1}	0.163
.163E0	0.163×10^0	0.163
163.0E − 3	163.0×10^{-3}	0.163
1.0E − 6	1.0×10^{-6}	0.000001
7.E13	7.0×10^{13}	70,000,000,000,000

The E Field Descriptor

In Chapter 6, you saw that the F field descriptor is used for output (and input) of real numbers. The **E field descriptor** is an alternate way to specify output of real numbers. The difference is that the E field descriptor will print numbers in exponential form. Numbers appear as a decimal fraction followed by the letter E followed by an exponent, which is the power of 10 by which the number is to be multiplied.

The form of the E field descriptor is

En.m

The *n* tells how wide the field is, that is, how many columns to use to print the number. The *m* tells how many digits to the right of the decimal point to print. The number output will have a decimal point followed by *m* digits, followed by the letter E, followed by a plus or minus sign, followed by a two-digit exponent. For example,

```
      PI = 3.1416
      PRINT 10, PI
10    FORMAT(1X, E10.4)
```

will print

```
0.3142E + 01
```

(the blank caused by the 1X carriage control is not indicated). The 4 in E10.4 means to print four places after the decimal point (note that the number is rounded). The 10 in E10.4 means the field is ten columns wide. Since nine columns were required to print the number, the leftmost column is blank. In general, the number will be output right justified with blanks on the left. Thus, the statements

```
      PI = 3.1416
      PRINT 10, PI
10    FORMAT(1X, E15.4)
```

will print

```
bbbbb0.3142E + 01
```

The b means blank; again, the carriage control character is not shown. If the number is negative, a minus sign will precede the decimal point. Thus,

```
      X = -1.0
      PRINT 5, X
5     FORMAT(1X, E10.2)
```

prints

$$b - 0.10E + 01$$

When using E*n*.*m* output, *n* must always be greater than or equal to $m + 7$. This is because one space is required for the possible minus sign, one space for a leading zero, one space for the decimal point, one space for the letter E, and three spaces for the exponent, including its sign. A field description of E5.2 would be too small to print any number. Printing a number with this field would result in five asterisks being printed, indicating the number would not fit in five spaces.

Double Precision and Complex Data

All floating-point arithmetic contains an inherent error because of the limited number of digits that a memory location can contain. In many cases, this error is not significant. Sometimes, however, you may need more precision than is provided by ordinary floating-point arithmetic. For such cases, you can use **double precision** arithmetic.

The **DOUBLE PRECISION** statement can be used to declare variables to be of double precision type. There are special forms for double precision constants and double precision field descriptors, and there are special FORTRAN-supplied functions for use with double precision data.

Another kind of data that is useful in certain applications is **complex data**. A **complex number** in algebra is a number of the form $a + bi$, where i is the square root of -1, the base of the so-called imaginary numbers. In FORTRAN, a complex number is written as a pair of numbers. For example, the number $1 + 2i$ is written in FORTRAN as (1.0, 2.0).

The **COMPLEX** statement declares variables to be of complex type. There are special rules for reading and printing complex values, and there are special FORTRAN-supplied functions for use with complex data.

Double precision and complex data are not difficult to use in FORTRAN, but the details are beyond the scope of this book.

APPENDIX C

Suggested Projects

Now that you know the basics of FORTRAN, an excellent way to increase your programming skills is to undertake a more challenging project. The following list will give you some ideas to get you started. The best project is one you're interested in, so feel free to branch off in your own direction.

You might want to try an application related to your other courses. (Perhaps an instructor will let you work on a computer project for credit in another class.) If you are taking math or engineering courses, you can find many interesting problems requiring numerical calculation. If you've ever done an experiment in a social science course, you may want to find out how to get the computer to do the statistical analysis and graphing of data that is often required. Even in the fine arts, applications abound: Many serious artists today work not in oils but in computer graphics displays.

Game playing is a delightful way to learn programming, especially if you have access to a timesharing system where you can play against the machine. A good chess player can still beat the best computer program, but people have been trying for years to make a machine that can checkmate the masters. (Besides being fun, these efforts yield insights into human intelligence and artificial intelligence.)

Just how difficult a problem is will depend on how much you want to do with it. For example, a program to play tic-tac-toe can be very simple. You can type in a number corresponding to some square on the board and have the computer print a number for its move corresponding to some empty square. You can easily program the computer to pick a random empty square. Of course, the program will be easy to beat if done this way, so you might try incorporate a more intelligent strategy for the computer. You might also have the program print a pattern of Xs and Os to show the moves. You might also have the machine vary its play, just to keep the game interesting. You could spend anywhere from an hour to several weeks on this project, depending on your interest.

A good plan is to begin with a simple version of the problem, get a program working, then add more features one step at a time. This approach will let you develop an understanding of the program before spending too much time on it, and it will let you debug the program in stages. It will also keep you from getting discouraged by trying a problem that is too difficult.

The Calendar

Write a program that reads a year and the day of the week of January 1st and prints a calendar for the year. For example, if January 1 falls on a Wednesday, the month of January can be printed as shown in Figure C.1.

```
         JANUARY
 S  M  T  W  T  F  S
---------------------
          1  2  3  4
 5  6  7  8  9 10 11
12 13 14 15 16 17 18
19 20 21 22 23 24 25
26 27 28 29 30 31
---------------------
```

Figure C.1 Sample output from a calendar program.

A simple version of this program can print the months one after another. A fancier version can print two or three columns of six or four months. As another enhancement, have the program compute the day of the week of January 1 given only the year.

Graphing a Function

There are many special devices used for computer graphics applications: special terminals with a plotting mode of operation, plotters that move an ink pen over a sheet of paper, and cathode ray tube displays, to name a few. You probably don't have access to any of these, but you can learn the techniques involved using only a line printer.

Given a mathematical function, such as $y = x^3$, you can plot its graph for a range of x values and display the graph as a set of x and y values and print a character on the printer page corresponding to each (x, y) pair. Figure C.2 shows a graph plotted in this way.

To make the problem simple, assume that the function to be graphed has values between 1 and 100 as the X values range from 0 to 100. To make the program more general, have it read the maximum and minimum X values and compute the maximum and minimum Y values; then scale the graph so that it fits nicely on one page of output. You can also have the program print labels and values on the X and Y axes. You might try printing grid lines on the plot to make it easier to read the X and Y values. Additionally, you can have the program plot several functions on one graph.

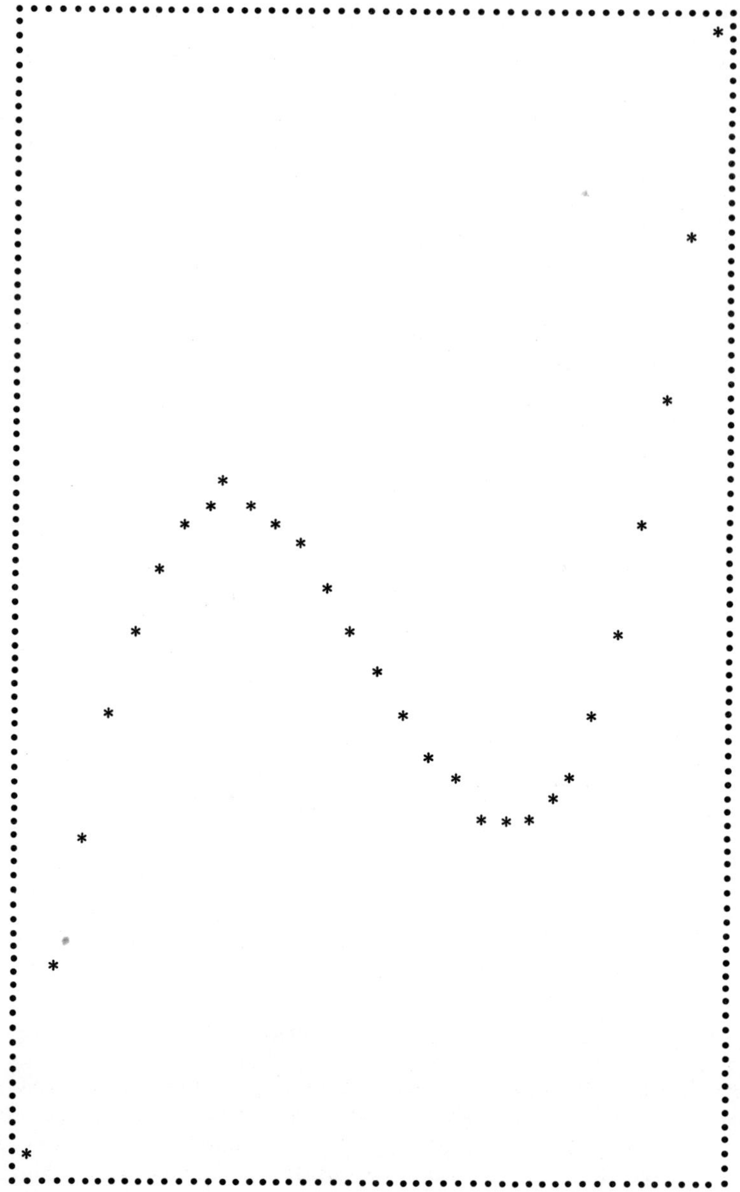

GRAPH OF Y = X*(X − 3)*(X − 5)
OVER THE RANGE −1 TO 6

Figure C.2 A computer-generated graph.

Morse Code

The international Morse code uses a sequence of dots and dashes to represent each letter of the alphabet. Figure C.3 shows these codes represented by asterisks and equal signs. Write a program that reads a message from a card and prints it in Morse code.

A	*=	J	*===	S	***
B	=***	K	=*=	T	=
C	=*=*	L	*=**	U	**=
D	=**	M	==	V	***=
E	*	N	=*	W	*==
F	**=*	O	===	X	=**=
G	==*	P	*==*	Y	=*==
H	****	Q	==*=	Z	==**
I	**	R	*=*		

Figure C.3 The Morse code for the alphabet.

This program can be fairly easy if you always print four characters for each letter (and four blank characters for a space). A prettier output, which is a bit harder to program, is to print one space between letters and an extra space between words.

You could also write a program to do the reverse: Translate a message from Morse code into alphabetic text.

Cryptography

Write a program that will encipher a message you read in, or decipher a previously enciphered message. An easy way to do this is by letter substitution. Instead of the letter A, for example substitute the letter Q. This is easy to program, but unfortunately it is an easy code to crack. For more devious ciphers, consult an encyclopedia article on cryptology, or see *The Codebreakers* by David Kahn (New York: New American Library, 1973).

Computer Art

If you're artistically inclined, try your hand at printing something attractive on the line printer. It is fairly easy to make a checkerboard pattern on a page of output. With a little more effort, you can make a program print patterns of rectangles of various sizes. An interesting effect can be achieved by printing rectangles of random sizes in random parts of the page. You can experiment with the number and sizes of rectangles, and with the total area of the rectangles. You may get a pattern resembling some of the work of the Dutch artist Piet Mondrian.

Circles are harder than rectangles, but not too much so. Experiment with patterns of overlapping or concentric rings or disks made of different characters.

Another idea is to print a replica of your favorite cartoon character. It would probably be difficult to rely on mathematics for describing the picture. You may want to sketch the picture on a sheet of printer layout paper, then keypunch cards with each card representing one line or part of one line of the picture. A program can print the cards to reproduce your sketch.

If you have access to a plotter, you can do some really fancy drawings. Start with simple geometric patterns and go on from there. Figures C.4 and C.5 show some examples.

Figure C.4 This drawing may seem complicated, but it was quite easy to program. It is made entirely of straight lines, drawn in a pattern of squares within squares within squares.

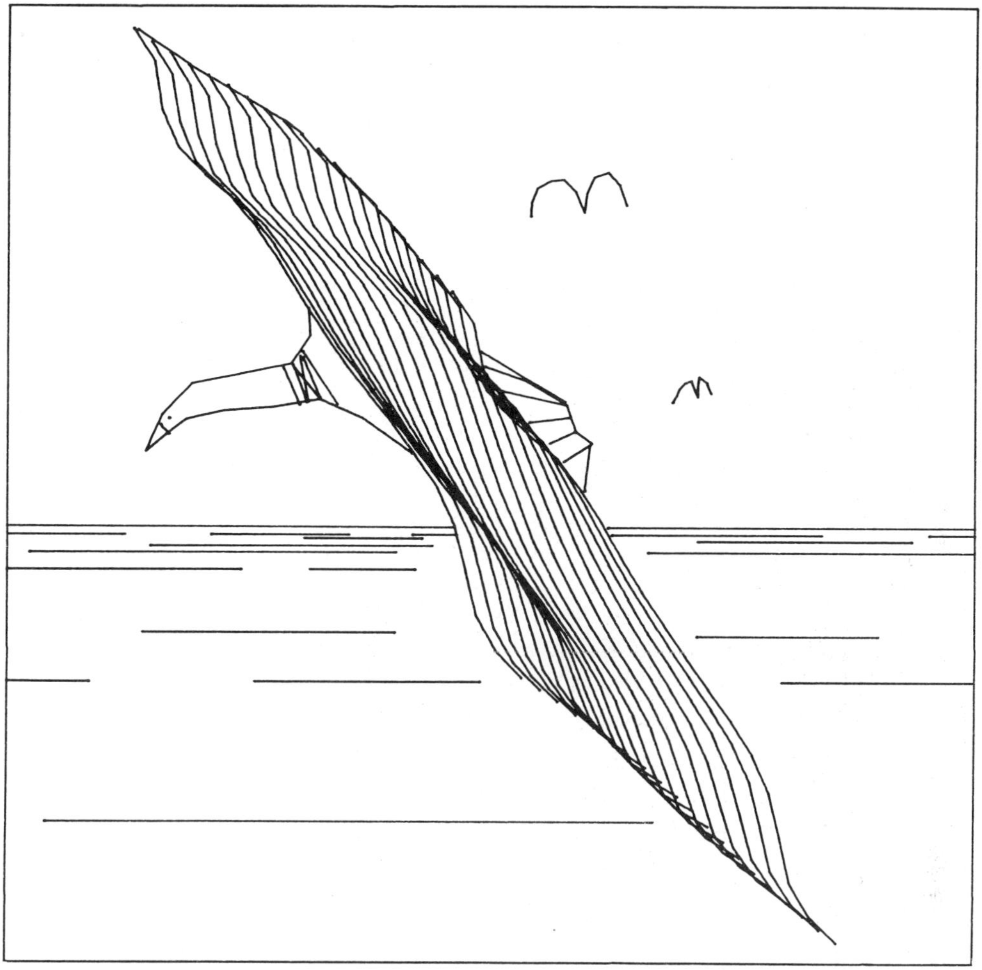

Figure C.5 This picture was programmed by Jack Schoof at the University of Arizona, and drawn on a Tektronix 4662 plotter.

Tic Tac Toe

Write a program that plays Tic Tac Toe. Consider that the cells on the tic tac toe board are numbered as shown in Figure C.6. The computer goes first and types the number of its move. The person then enters the number of his or her move. If this move is illegal, the machine types "illegal move" and asks for another move. Otherwise, the machine computes its move according to some strategy. The machine and the player continue to alternate moves until the game is over, at which time the program prints "I win," "You win," or "A draw."

1	2	3
4	5	6
7	8	9

Figure C.6 Numbering system for tic tac toe.

You can make this problem easy if you have the machine simply move in any vacant cell. Write the "strategy" part, which determines the machine's move, as a separate subroutine so that it will be easy to modify.

When you have a simple version working, try making the machine play according to the following strategy:

Tic Tac Toe Strategy

On the first move, the machine moves in the center.

If the machine can get three in a row, it does so and wins.
Otherwise, if the person has two in a row in which there is a vacant cell, the machine blocks by moving in the vacant cell.

Otherwise, if the machine has a move in a row where the other two cells are vacant, the machine moves in the lowest numbered vacant cell in that row.

Otherwise, the machine moves in the lowest numbered vacant cell.

Played this way, the machine is unbeatable; if the person plays well, the game will always be a draw. You can try other strategies, too, to make the game more interesting to play. The machine can always ensure a draw, even if the person is allowed to move first.

You can print the tic tac toe board after each of the machine's moves, using Xs and Os, as shown in Figure C.7.

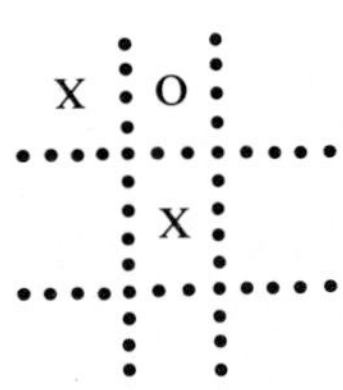

Figure C.7 Suggested output from a tic tac toe program.

Random Numbers

If you roll a die, it comes up showing a number from 1 to 6. The number is "random" in the sense that all six numbers are equally probable, and there is no way of knowing in advance what number will come up.

Most computer installations provide a FORTRAN function to generate random numbers. The function RAN(X), shown as follows, is typical. The argument of this function is ignored (any value will do). The subroutine SETRAN must be called once to initialize the RAN function. After you call SETRAN, you can reference the function RAN and it will return a different value between 0 and 1 each time it is called. Here are the FORTRAN statements for the RAN function.

```
      FUNCTION RAN(DUMMY)
C-----------------------------------------------------------------------
C
C   RAN(X) IS A RANDOM NUMBER GREATER THAN 0, AND
C       LESS THAN 1. THE VALUE OF THE ARGUMENT
C       DOES NOT MAKE ANY DIFFERENCE.
C
C-----------------------------------------------------------------------
C
C   CAUTION: YOU MUST CALL THE SUBROUTINE SETRAN
C       ONCE BEFORE THIS FUNCTION IS CALLED.
C
C-----------------------------------------------------------------------
C
      COMMON I, J, K, M
      I = MOD(I * J + K, M)
      RAN = FLOAT(I)/FLOAT(M)
      RETURN
      END

      SUBROUTINE SETRAN
C-----------------------------------------------------------------------
C
C   INITIALIZE THE RANDOM NUMBER GENERATOR.
C
C-----------------------------------------------------------------------
C
      COMMON I, J, K, M
      I = 0
      J = 3612
      K = 5701
      M = 566927
      RETURN
      END
```

As an example, the following program prints 20 random numbers.

```
C   PRINT A LIST OF RANDOM NUMBERS.
C
      N = 20
      CALL SETRAN
      DO 10 I = 1, N
          X = RAN (0.0)
          PRINT 20, X
10        CONTINUE
```

```
20      FORMAT(F20.8)
        STOP
        END
```

You may wonder how a program can generate random numbers using just simple arithmetic. The answer is that the numbers are not *really* random in the sense of a roll of die. The FORTRAN function generates what we call **pseudorandom** numbers. All the real numbers between 0 and 1 are equally probable, and the sequence of numbers generated is in a seemingly random order. We will not go into the theory of pseudorandom numbers. A complete discussion can be found in *The Art of Computer Programming*, vol. 2, 2nd ed., by Donald E. Knuth (Reading, Mass.: Addison-Wesley, 1973).

Using the RAN function, write and test a FORTRAN function NRAND(I, J) that returns a random integer between I and J, inclusive. Simulate the rolls of a die by generating a a sequence of random integers from 1 to 6.

Try generating 1000 random integers from 1 to 10. Count how many of them are equal to 1, how many are equal to 2, and so on.

Poker Hands

A deck of cards can be represented in a program by the numbers 1 to 52. The numbers 1–13 can represent spades, 14–26 can represent hearts, and so on. Using the letters A, J, Q, K for face cards, and using the letters S, H, C, D to represent the four suits, write a program that prints all the cards in a deck:

```
A S
2 S
 :
Q S
K S
A H
 :
```

To represent a five-card poker hand, you can choose at random five *different* numbers between 1 and 52. Using the NRAND function from the previous project, write a program that prints a series of randomly chosen five-card poker hands.

This kind of program is called a *simulation*: The computer is simulating a random occurence. Simulation can be used to compute probabilities that are difficult to compute otherwise. As a simple example, generate 1000 random poker hands and see what percentage of the hands form a flush (all cards are of the same suit).

A rather difficult example of the same kind of simulation is this: Compute the probability of winning at the game of solitaire.

Sign Maker

Write a program that reads a card containing up to 80 letters, and prints a sign with the letters from the card printed as large letters like the example in Figure C.8. You will probably have to keypunch codes for the letters, then read them into an array.

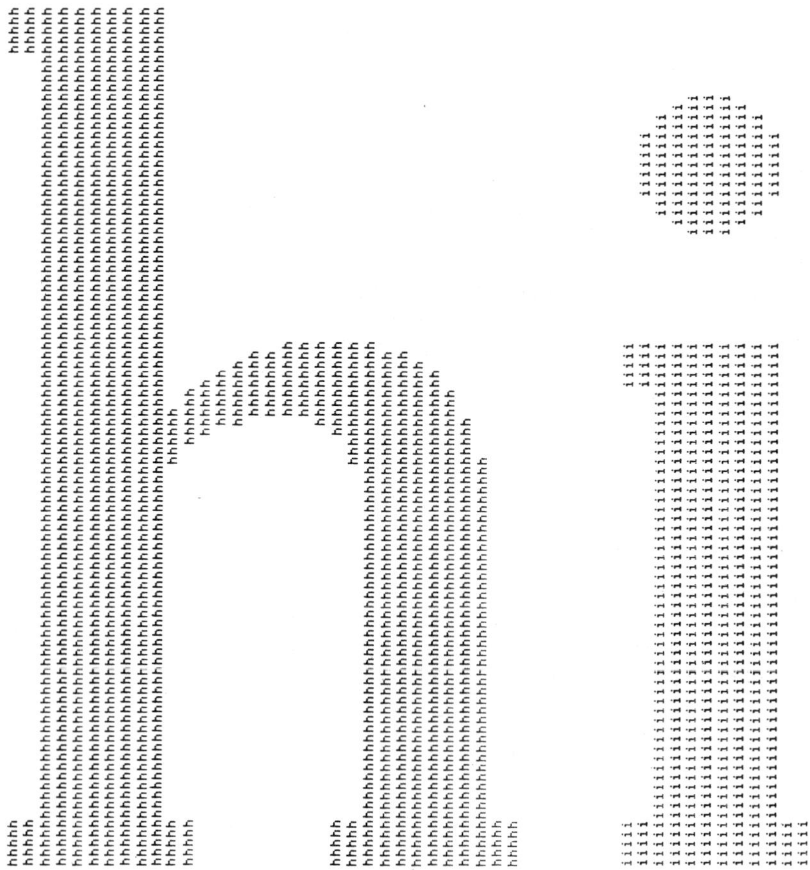

Figure C.8 Output from a sign-making program.

Sorting Alphabetic Data

Chapter 9 explained a way to sort numbers. Sorting alphabetic data is trickier, because the character strings may be longer than can be contained in a single word. Write a program that reads a set of cards and prints them in alphabetical order.

Address Book

Most people keep a book of some sort with the names, addresses, and phone numbers of their friends. But friends move, phone numbers change, and address books are usually out of date. Computerize your personal address book and see if that makes it easier to maintain.

A simple version of this program could just list a set of data, formatting it in an attractive way. A more ambitious project would be to have the program alphabetize the entries by name. You might also include a facility to update the book by simply adding correction cards for new information, rather than manually replacing the cards for information that has changed.

Calculator Program

If you have access to a timesharing system, write a program that will let you use it as a calculator, so that you can type in numbers and symbols and have it perform the computations you give it.

A simple way to approach this job is to type in a number on the first line, type in another number on the second line, then type in an operator on the third line: +, −, *, or /. That is, if you want to compute 10 − 3, you enter

```
10.0
3.0
-
```

You could also have your program save the result of one computation for further use. For instance, to compute (10 − 3)*5, you would type

```
10.0
3.0
-
5
*
```

If you want to try a difficult version of this problem, write a program that will compute the value of an expression such as

```
(3 + (4/(5 + 6) - 1))/(7 - 8)**3
```

Personal Finance

In Chapter 1 we drew a flowchart for a simple procedure to balance a checkbook. There are numerous enhancements you could make to such a program. You might write a program to balance your checkbook and simultaneously produce a listing of whom the checks were written to. You might include categories of expenditures and list the amount spent in each category, either for budgeting or tax preparation purposes. You might include a record of credit card expenditures, calculating the interest and service charges. You might include an automatic method of recording outstanding checks. In general, design and implement a computerized system to manage your personal finances. Try using it for a month or two and see if you can think of ways to make it more convenient to use.

Permutations

A permutation of a set of numbers or letters means a rearrangement of them. There are six different permutations of the numbers 1, 2, and 3:

```
1 2 3
1 3 2
2 1 3
2 3 1
3 1 2
3 2 1
```

Write a program that will read a number *n* and print out all the permutations of the numbers 1 through *n*. (*Note*: This is a tricky problem, although it can be done with a very short program.)

Cryptarithmetic

A well-known problem in cryptarithmetic is the following:

```
  SEND
+MORE
MONEY
```

Each letter stands for a digit 1 through 9. The same letter always stands for the same digit, and different letters stand for different digits. Also, leading digits (the M and the S) cannot be zero. Surprisingly, there is only one way of assigning digits to these letters that will make the sum come out right.

You might enjoy working this puzzle with a pencil and paper. An entirely different kind of challenge is to write a program to solve the puzzle. You could do this by trying out all the different ways of assigning digits to the above letters until you find one that makes the sum correct. (*Hint*: Begin by working the project on permutations.)

For some more problems of this type, see 150 Puzzles in Cryptarithmetic by Maxey Brooke (New York: Dover, 1972).

Document Preparation

If you do any writing—program documentation, memos, term papers, or whatnot—you will find it very helpful to have a document preparation system available. You can type your document on cards and have the computer produce the listing. A simple program for this job can simply list the cards. There are many desirable features you can add, however.

You might adopt the convention that any card having an asterisk in the first column is a control card. For example, a card with *P in the first columns might mean to skip to the top of a new page before printing the next line. A card with *T in the first columns might contain a title to be listed at the top of each page. A *SKIP 10 directive might skip ten lines in the document to leave room for a figure. Design and implement a document preparation program of this sort.

A somewhat tricky but very useful feature is to have the program *justify* the text for you. That is, instead of having the program list each card on a separate line, have the program list as many words as will fit on one line, regardless of how they are prepared on the input. You can add a directive to begin a new paragraph and have the program generate the correct indentation. You may also want a directive to turn off the justification feature, so that you can include tables (or programs, and so forth) in the text.

If your printer can produce listings in upper-case and lower-case letters, you might implement a feature to transform your input to upper and lower case. For example, you could type your input card as:

+JOHN AND + MARY LIVE IN + OHIO.

and have the program transform this to:

John and Mary live in Ohio.

APPENDIX D

Answers to Selected Exercises

Chapter 1, page 31

1.

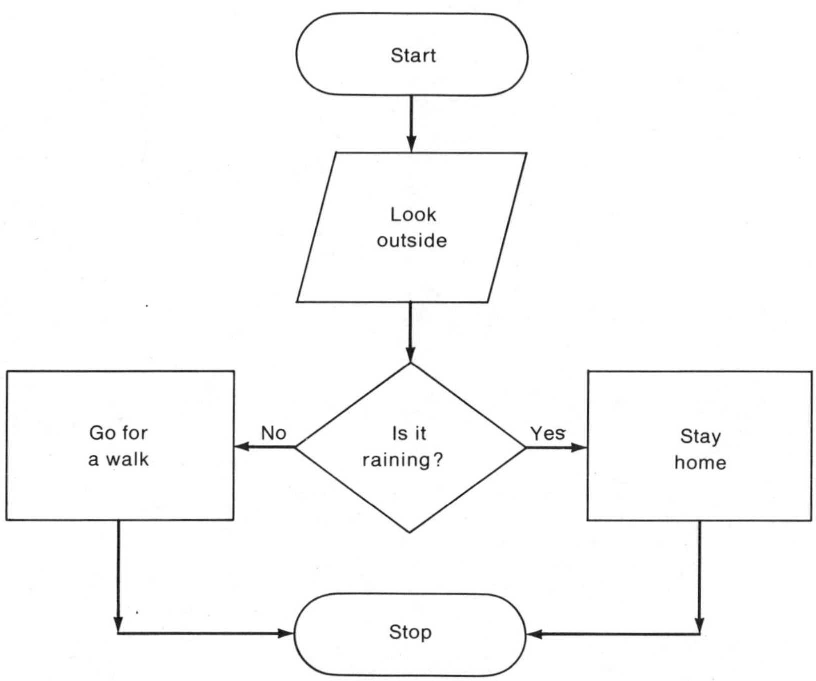

3.

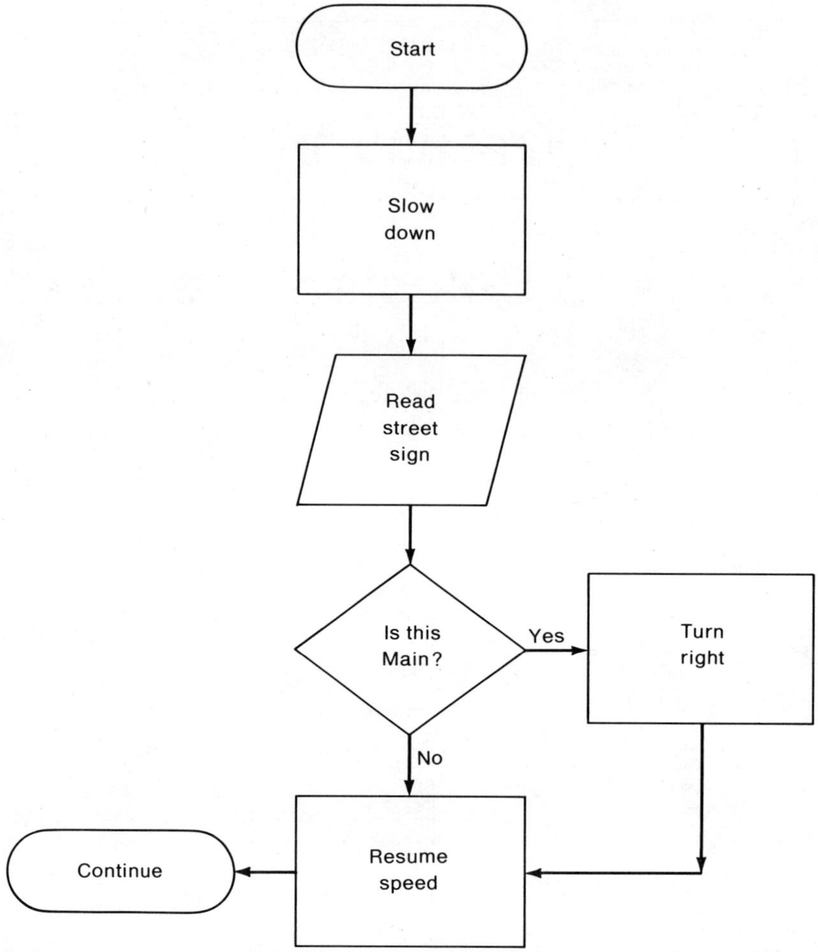
Start
Slow down
Read street sign
Is this Main?
Yes
Turn right
No
Resume speed
Continue

5.

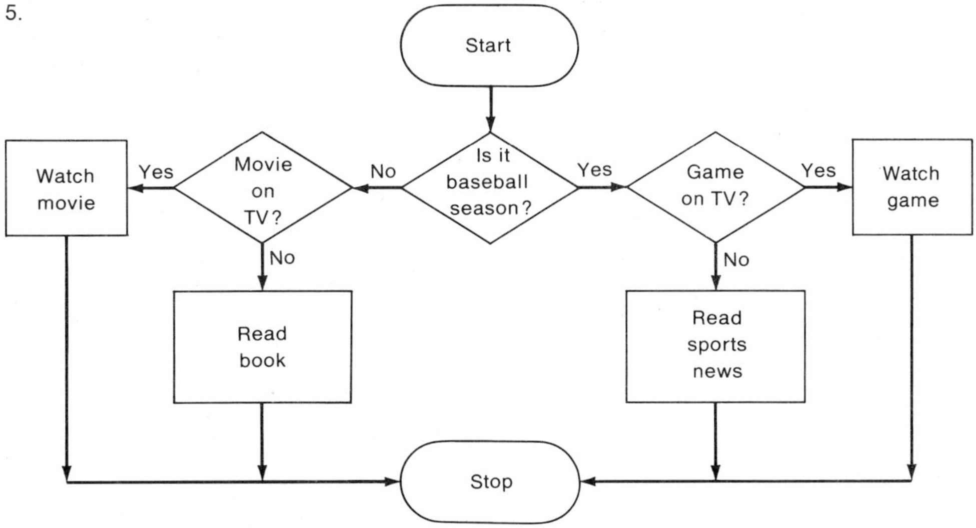
Start
Is it baseball season?
No
Yes
Movie on TV?
Game on TV?
Yes
Yes
Watch movie
Watch game
No
No
Read book
Read sports news
Stop

7.

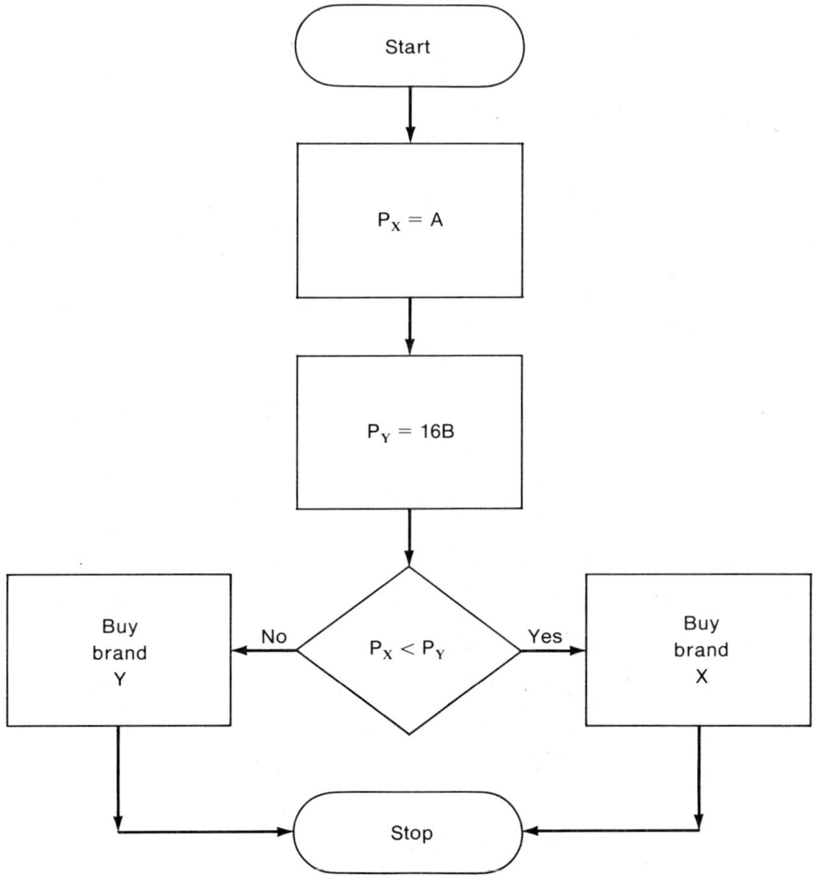
Start
$P_X = A$
$P_Y = 16B$
$P_X < P_Y$
No
Yes
Buy brand Y
Buy brand X
Stop

9.

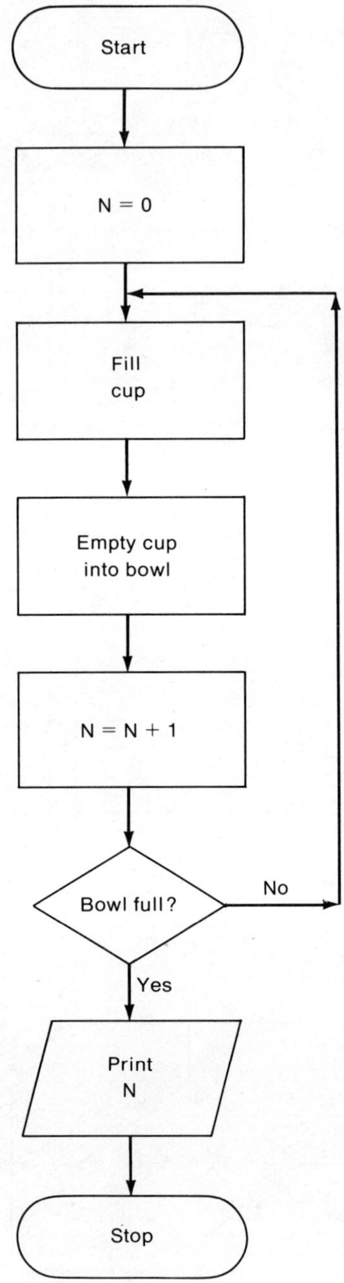
Start
N = 0
Fill cup
Empty cup into bowl
N = N + 1
Bowl full?
No
Yes
Print N
Stop

11.

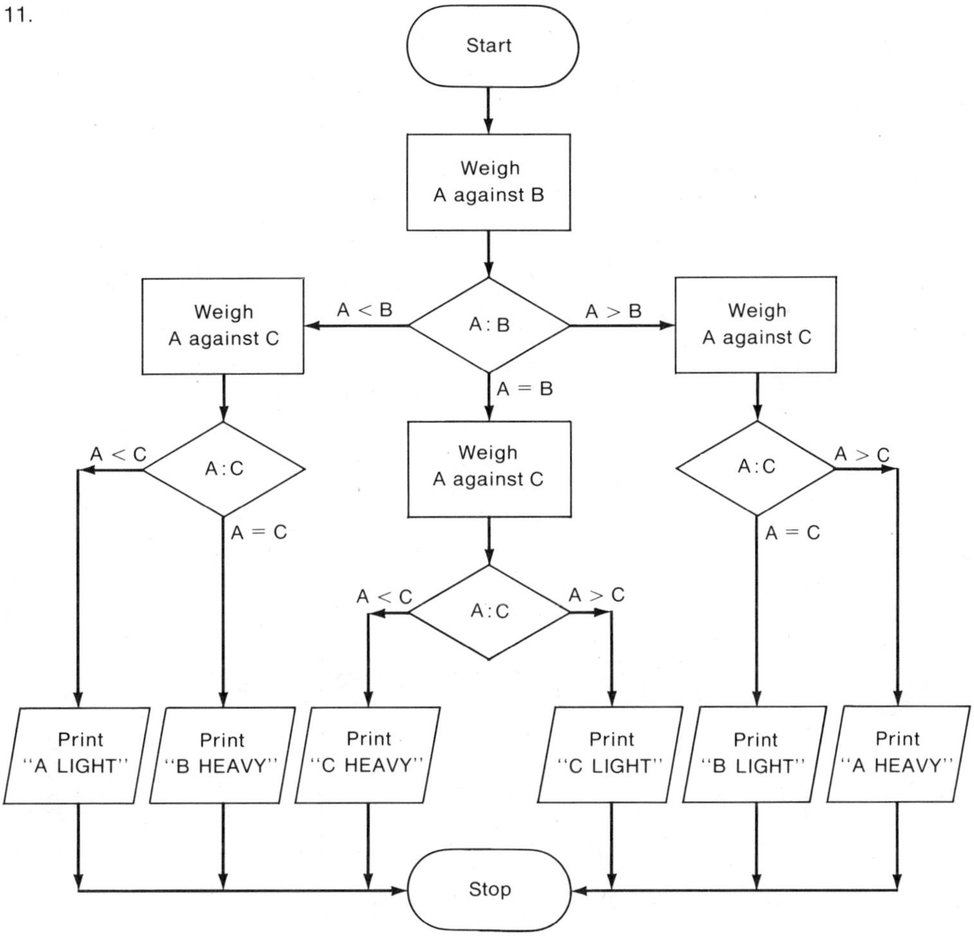
Start
Weigh
A against B
A : B
A < B
A > B
A = B
Weigh
A against C
Weigh
A against C
Weigh
A against C
A : C
A < C
A = C
A : C
A < C
A > C
A : C
A > C
A = C
Print
"A LIGHT"
Print
"B HEAVY"
Print
"C HEAVY"
Print
"C LIGHT"
Print
"B LIGHT"
Print
"A HEAVY"
Stop

13.

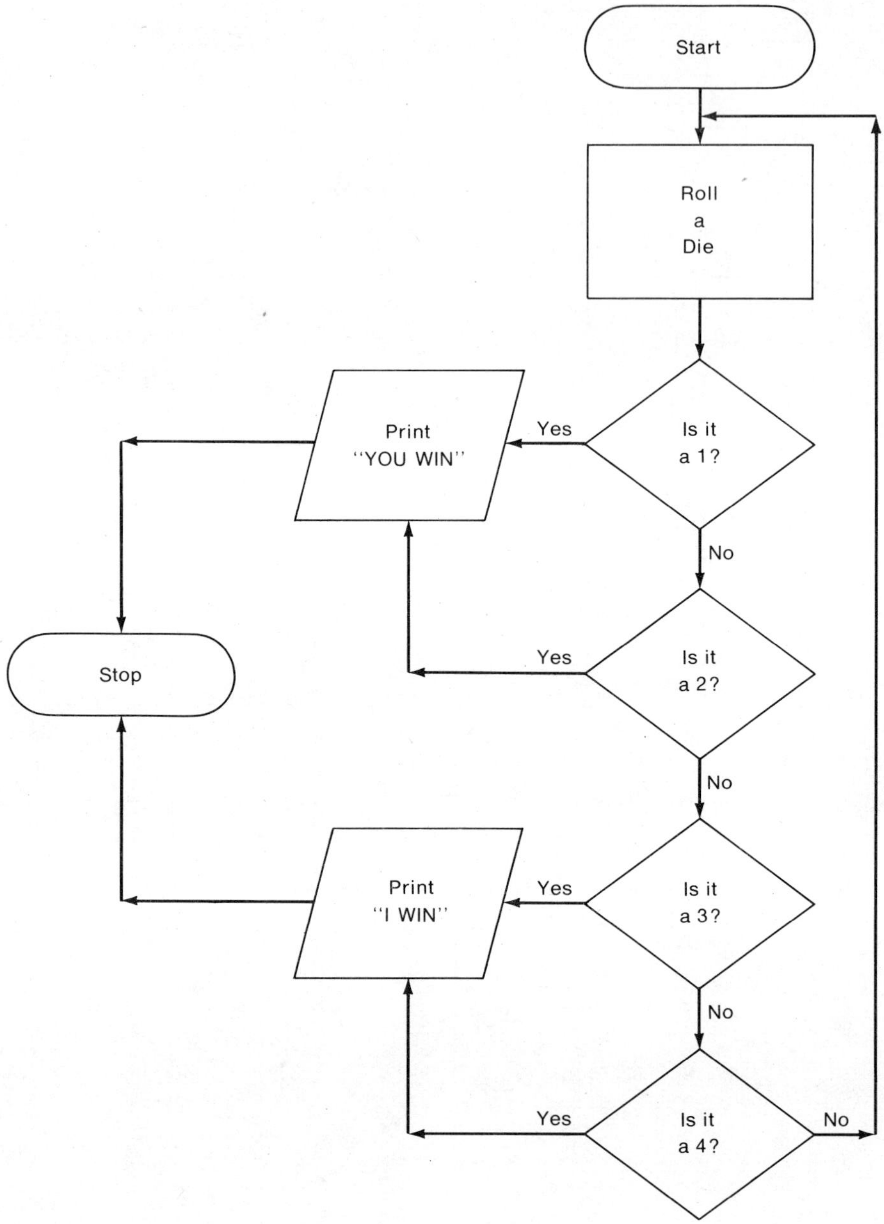
Start
Roll
a
Die
Is it
a 1?
Yes
Print
"YOU WIN"
No
Is it
a 2?
Yes
Stop
No
Is it
a 3?
Yes
Print
"I WIN"
No
Is it
a 4?
Yes
No

15.

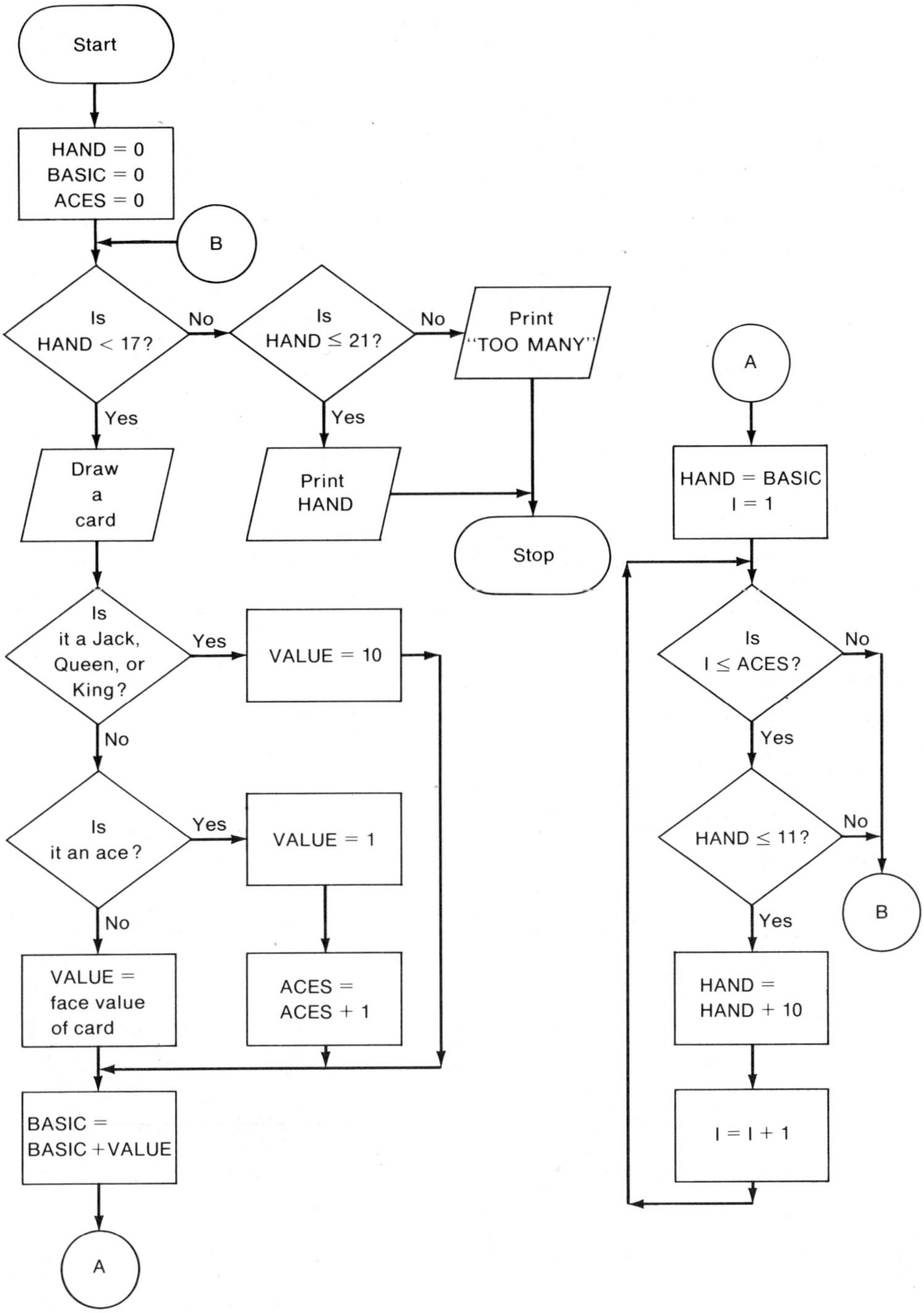
Start
HAND = 0
BASIC = 0
ACES = 0
B
Is
HAND < 17?
No
Yes
Is
HAND ≤ 21?
No
Yes
Print
"TOO MANY"
Print
HAND
Stop
Draw
a
card
Is
it a Jack,
Queen, or
King?
Yes
No
VALUE = 10
Is
it an ace?
Yes
No
VALUE = 1
ACES =
ACES + 1
VALUE =
face value
of card
BASIC =
BASIC + VALUE
A
A
HAND = BASIC
I = 1
Is
I ≤ ACES?
No
Yes
HAND ≤ 11?
No
Yes
B
HAND =
HAND + 10
I = I + 1

17. $$X = \sum_{N=1}^{5} N$$

This can be generalized to

$$X = \sum_{N=1}^{L} N$$

by changing the decision box and adding an input box to read L.

19. This prints the positive even numbers less than or equal to 10. If I is initially 0, the first value printed is 0; then the other values are printed as before. If the decision is changed to $I \leq 10$, the last value printed is 22.

21. For A = 1, B = 3, C = 2.5, output is 1.
For A = 1, B = 1, C = 2, output is 2.

23. For input of X = 5, the output is 4, 3, 2, 1, 0, "the end."
For input of X = 3.6, the algorithm never stops; it is stuck in a loop.

25. N is increased whenever $I < J$ where $1 \leq I \leq 5$ and $1 \leq J \leq 5$. Thus, N is increased for (I, J) = (1, 2), (1, 3), (1, 4), (1, 5), (2, 3), (2, 4), (2, 5), (3, 4), (3, 5), and (4, 5). The final output is 10.

27. See page 335.

29. See page 336.

The output is all the positive odd numbers less than N. (If $N < 1$, the output is the single number 1.)

Chapter 2, page 57

1. a. Valid.
   b. Not valid (the variable must go on the left of the equal sign).
   c. Not valid; multiplication must be denoted by an asterisk (*).
   d. Valid.
   e. Not valid; instead of the equal sign, it should have the symbol .EQ.

3.
```
IF (X .LT. 0.0) STOP
```

5. There can be more than one STOP statement—you can use a STOP statement anywhere in the program. But there can be only one END statement—this is required as the last statement in any program.

7. See page 337.

9. On each iteration of the loop, the statement

```
SUM = SUM + X
```

adds the value of the number read to SUM, which is a running total of all the numbers read so far. The statement

```
COUNT = 0.0
```

is necessary to initialize COUNT. If this statement were omitted, you could not be sure that COUNT is equal to 0 on the first time through the loop. For the given input, the variable SUM will be the sum of the numbers: 30, just before statement 20 is executed. The output will be the numbers 5 and 6.

27.

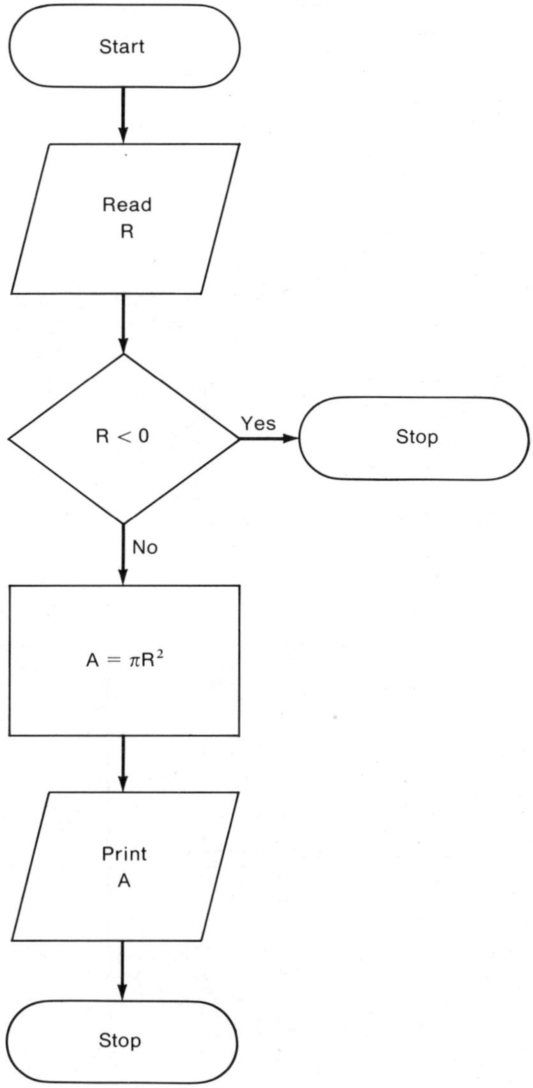

Flowchart for Chapter 1: Answer 27

29.

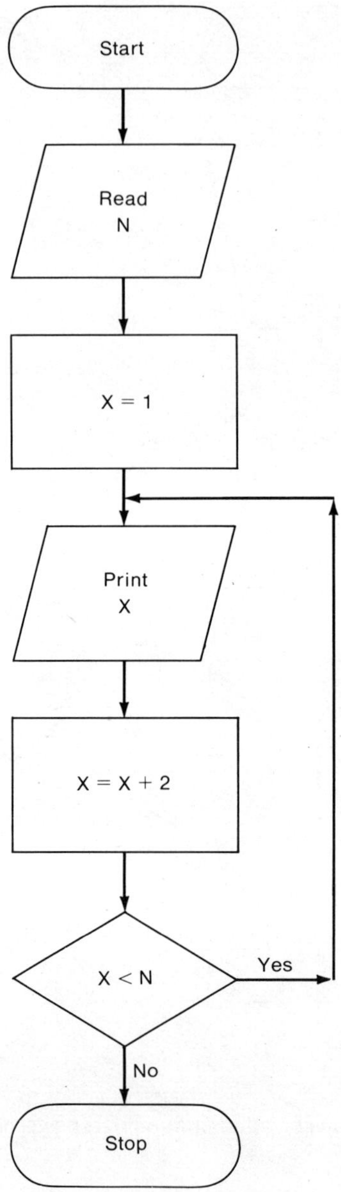

Flowchart for Chapter 1: Answer 29

7.

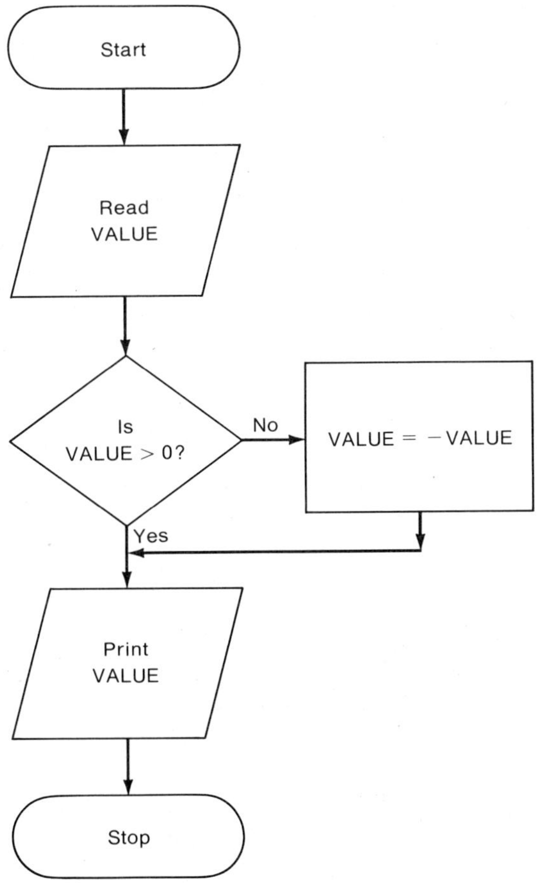

Flowchart for Chapter 2: Answer 7

Chapter 3, page 69

3. John Van Winkle will have $57, 444, 797.43 when he wakes up. (This is before taxes, of course.)
6. You owe $10,737,418.24.

Chapter 4, page 89

1. 0.1
3. 1000000.0
5. 0.333333

7. −1.0

9. 1000

11. −1

13. Use "/", not "÷" for division.

15. Needs parentheses: R * * (−2).

17. Needs multiplication operator: 2 * (N + 1).

19. Missing parenthesis.

21. Invalid, begins with number.

23. Invalid, begins with number.

25. Valid, integer.

27. Valid, real.

29. Valid, real.

31. Valid, real.

33. Valid, integer.

35. Valid, real.

37. $\dfrac{\dfrac{a}{b}}{c}$

39. $a + \dfrac{b}{c} + d$

41. $a^b c + 1$

43. $\dfrac{1}{1 + x}$

45. $\sqrt{ad - bc}$

47. W = (X2 − X1) * Y * * 2

49. A = B* (D/4.0)/3.0

51.

```
      READ, AMOUNT, RATE, N
      PRINT, AMOUNT, RATE, N
      PRINCE = AMOUNT/(1.0 + RATE)**N
      PRINT, PRINCE
      STOP
      END
```

53.

```
      NPAIR = (52*3*48*44*40)/(2*6)
      NTHREE = (52*3*2*48*44)/(2*2*3)
      NHANDS = (52*51*50*49*48)/(5*4*3*2)
      PRINT, NPAIR, NTHREE, NHANDS
      PPAIR = FLOAT(NPAIR)/FLOAT(NHANDS)
      PTHREE = FLOAT(NTHREE)/FLOAT(NHANDS)
      PRINT, PPAIR, PTHREE
      STOP
      END
```

55.
```
          READ, SCALE
   10     READ, DIMEN
          IF (DIMEN .EQ. 0.0) STOP
          DNEW = DIMEN/SCALE * 12.0
          PRINT, DIMEN, DNEW
          GO TO 10
          END
```

57. The output is zero for *any* value of F because the fraction $\frac{5}{9}$ is written as the quotient of integer numbers, so it is truncated to zero before multiplying by (F − 32). The formula should be written:

```
          C = 5.0/9.0 * (F - 32.0)
```

Chapter 5, page 105

1.
```
          IF (I .NE. 10) I = 0
```

3.
```
          IF (A .LT. B) GO TO 10
             A = 0
             GO TO 15
   10     A = A - B
   15     PRINT, A
```

5.
```
          IF (T .GE. TZERO) GO TO 10
             I = 1
             T = 0.0
             GO TO 15
   10     T = T + 1.0
   15     next statement
```

7.
```
    5     J = J - K
          IF (J .GT. 0) GO TO 5
          I = -J
```

9.
```
   10     N = N - 1
          IF (N .EQ. 0) STOP
          Y = Y + 1.0/FLOAT (N)
          GO TO 10
```

11.
```
  100     READ, X
          IF (X .GE. 1000.0) STOP
          Y = X**2 + 7.21*X + 160.4
          PRINT, X, Y
          GO TO 100
          END
```

13.
```
          M = 0
          READ, N
          I = 1
    5     IF (I .GT. N) GO TO 10
             M = M + I**2
             I = I + 1
             GO TO 5
   10     PRINT, M
          STOP
          END
```

Module I, page 142

1.

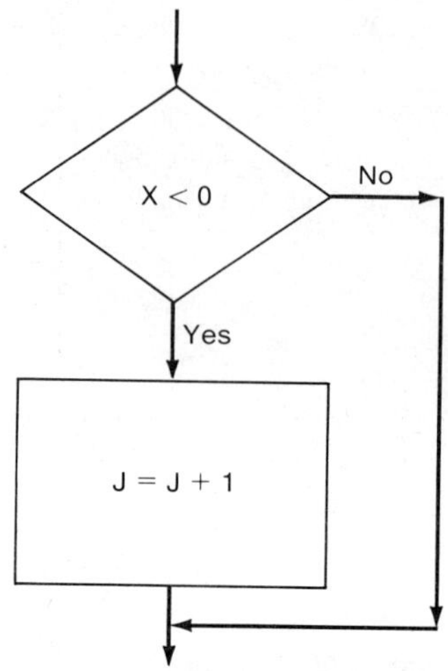

IF (X .LT. 0.0) J = J + 1

3.

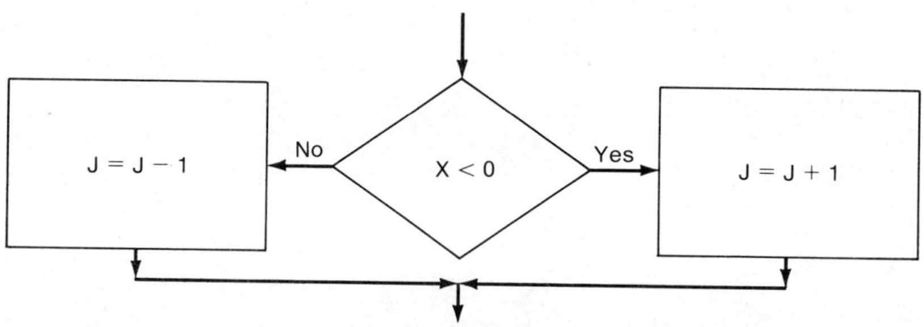

IF (X .LT. 0.0) J = J + 1
IF (X .GE. 0.0) J = J − 1

5.

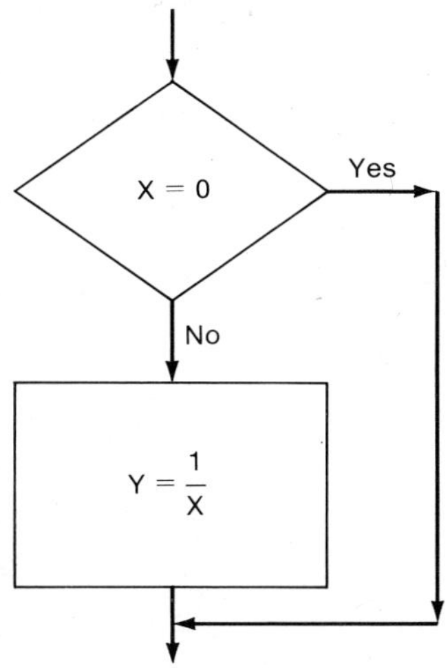


```
IF (X .NE. 0.0) Y = 1.0/X
```

7.

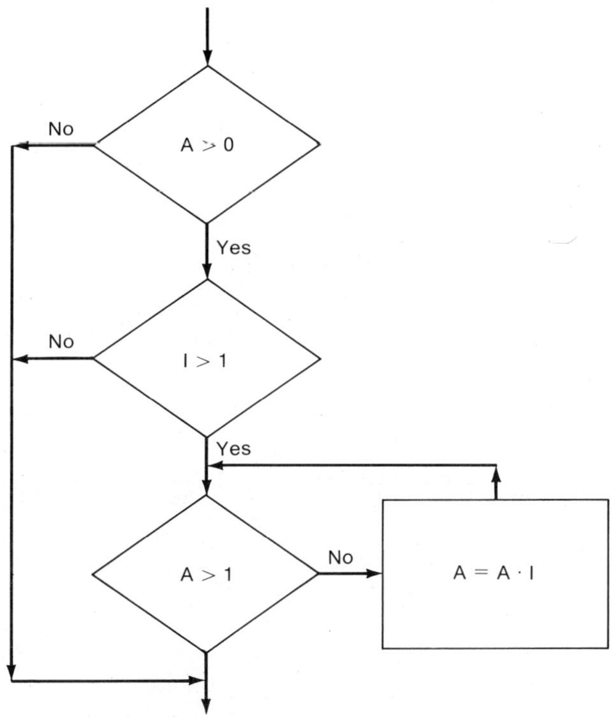


```
        IF (.NOT. (A .GT. 0.0 .AND. I .GT. 1)) GO TO 20
10      IF (A .GT. 1.0) GO TO 20
            A = A * FLOAT(I)
            GO TO 10
20      next statement
```

9.

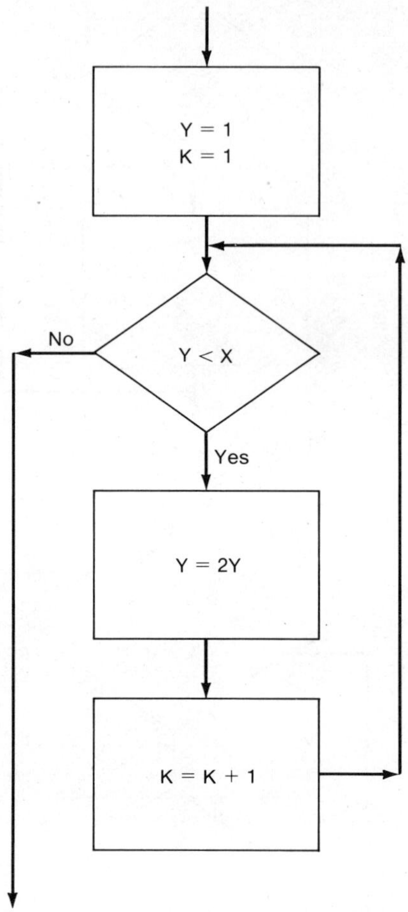


```
          Y = 1.0
          K = 1
10        IF (Y .GE. X) GO TO 20
             Y = 2.0*Y
             K = K + 1
             GO TO 10
20        next statement
```

11.

```
  1       READ, T
          IF (.NOT. (10.0 .LT. T .AND. T .LT. 45.0)) GO TO 10
  C   T IS CELSIUS
          TNEW = (9.0/5.0)*T + 32.0
          GO TO 20
  10      IF (.NOT. (50.0 .LT. T .AND. T .LT. 115.0)) GO TO 30
  C   T IS FAHRENHEIT
```

```
      TNEW = (5.0/9.0) * (T - 32.0)
20    PRINT, T, TNEW
      GO TO 1
30    STOP
      END
```

13.

```
C  ITEM = IDENTIFICATION NUMBER FOR THE ITEM
C         (ZERO INDICATES END OF DATA CARDS)
C  NUNITS = NUMBER OF UNITS
C  PRICE = PRICE PAID PER UNIT
C  CPRICE = CURRENT MARKET PRICE PER UNIT
C  VALUE = INVENTORY VALUE FOR THIS ITEM
C  TVALUE = TOTAL VALUE OF THE INVENTORY
      TVALUE = 0.0
10    READ, ITEM, NUNITS, PRICE, CPRICE
      IF (ITEM .EQ. 0) GO TO 20
      IF (PRICE .LE. CPRICE) VALUE = NUNITS * PRICE
      IF (PRICE .GT. CPRICE) VALUE = NUNITS * CPRICE
      TVALUE = TVALUE + VALUE
      PRINT, ITEM, NUNITS, VALUE
      GO TO 10
20    PRINT, TVALUE
      STOP
      END
```

17.

```
C  PRINT ALL COMBINATIONS OF DIFFERENT INTEGERS
C  BETWEEN 1 AND N.
      READ, N
      I = 1
10    IF (.NOT. I .LE. N - 1) GO TO 30
        J = I + 1
20      IF (.NOT. J .LE. N) GO TO 25
          PRINT, I, J
          J = J + 1
          GO TO 20
25      I = I + 1
        GO TO 10
30    STOP
      END
```

19.

```
C  EUCLIDS ALGORITHM FOR FINDING THE
C  GREATEST COMMON DIVISOR
      READ, M, N
      PRINT, M, N
10    IF (N .EQ. 0) GO TO 20
        KREM = MOD(M, N)
        M = N
        N = KREM
        GO TO 10
20    PRINT, M
      STOP
      END
```

Chapter 6, page 177

1.
```
          I = 1
          PRINT 11, I
          PRINT 13, I, I, I
          PRINT 15, I, I, I, I, I
          PRINT 17, I, I, I, I, I, I, I
          PRINT 19, I, I, I, I, I, I, I, I, I
          STOP
   11     FORMAT(5X, I1)
   13     FORMAT(4X, 3I1)
   15     FORMAT(3X, 5I1)
   17     FORMAT(2X, 7I1)
   19     FORMAT(1X, 9I1)
          END
```

3.
```
          N = 0
          TDIST = 200.0
          H = TDIST
    5     PRINT 10, N, H
   10     FORMAT(1X, 'BOUNCE', I3, 5X, 'HEIGHT', F6.1)
          N = N + 1
          H = 0.75 * H
          TDIST = TDIST + 2.0 * H
          IF (H .GE. 1.0/12.0) GO TO 5
          PRINT 15, TDIST
   15     FORMAT('0', 5X, 'TOTAL DISTANCE', F10.2)
          STOP
          END
```

5.
```
   C   MAN1 = MAN NUMBER FROM CARD 1
   C   MAN2 = MAN NUMBER FROM CARD 2
   C   SOLD1, SOLD2, SOLD3 = SALES FROM LAST QUARTER
   C   SELL1, SELL2, SELL3 = SALES FROM THIS QUARTER
   C   TOTOLD, TOTNEW = TOTAL SALES
   C   PCTINC = PERCENT INCREASE
   C
   100    READ 510, MAN1, SOLD1, SOLD2, SOLD3
          IF (MAN1 .EQ. 0) GO TO 200
   C          STOP WHEN A ZERO EMPLOYEE NUMBER READ
          READ 510, MAN2, SELL1, SELL2, SELL3
          IF (MAN2 .EQ. 0) GO TO 200
          IF (MAN1 .EQ. MAN2) GO TO 110
              PRINT 520, MAN1, MAN2
              STOP
   110    TOTOLD = SOLD1 + SOLD2 + SOLD3
          TOTNEW = SELL1 + SELL2 + SELL3
          IF (TOTOLD .NE. 0.0)
         $    PCTINC = 100.0 * (TOTNEW-TOTOLD)/TOTOLD
          IF (TOTOLD .EQ. 0.0) PCTINC = 100.0
              PRINT 530, MAN1, SELL1, SELL2, SELL3
```

```
            PRINT 540, TOTNEW, PCTINC
            GO TO 100
C
200         STOP
C
510      FORMAT (I3, 1X, 6X, F8.2, 2X, F8.2, 2X, F8.2)
520      FORMAT (1X, 'UNMATCHED EMPLOYEE NO.', 2I6)
530      FORMAT (1X, 'SALESMAN', I4, 5X,
      $     'SALES THIS QUARTER', 3F12.2)
540      FORMAT (1X, 'TOTAL SALES', F12.2, 5X,
      $     'PERCENT INCREASE', F5.1)
         END
```

7.

```
         LINE = 1000
20       READ 105, ID, SEX, HT, WT, CLASS, RANK
         IF (ID .EQ. 0) STOP
         IF (SEX .NE. 1.) GO TO 20
         IF (HT .LE. 60.) GO TO 20
         IF (WT .LE. 180.) GO TO 20
         IF (CLASS .EQ. 1.) GO TO 20
         IF (RANK .LT. 85.) GO TO 20
         LINE = LINE + 2
         IF (LINE .LE. 55) GO TO 30
         LINE = 1
         PRINT 100
100      FORMAT('1', 5X, 'ID', 3X, 'SEX', 2X,
      $        'HEIGHT', 2X, 'WEIGHT', 2X, 'CLASS', 2X, 'RANK')
         LINE = LINE + 2
30       PRINT 110, ID, SEX, HT, WT, CLASS, RANK
105      FORMAT(I5, F1.0, F2.0, F3.0, F1.0, F2.0)
110      FORMAT('0', 5X, I5, F3.0, 2X, F6.0, 2X, F6.0,
      $     2X, F5.0, 2X, F4.0)
         GO TO 20
         END
```

Chapter 7, page 193

2. a. Invalid; DO loop cannot end with GO TO.
   b. Valid.
   c. Invalid; GO TO statement branches to within a DO loop.

3.

```
C   TABLE OF FACTORIALS
         NFACT = 1
         DO 10 I = 1, 10
            NFACT = NFACT * I
            PRINT 5, NFACT
5           FORMAT (1X, I15)
10          CONTINUE
         STOP
         END
```

5.

```
C   Q = (364/365) * (363/365) * . . .
C   P = 1 - Q
```

```
C
       TOP = 365
       Q = 1
       DO 20 N = 2, 50
          TOP = TOP - 1.0
          Q = Q * (TOP/365.0)
          P = 1.0 - Q
          PRINT 100, N, P
20        CONTINUE
       STOP
100    FORMAT (1X, I10, F10.6)
       END
```

7.

```
       DO 10 N = 1, 100
          H = N
          D = SQRT(1.5 * H)
          PRINT 20, N, D
10        CONTINUE
20     FORMAT (1X, I10, F10.1)
       STOP
       END
```

9.

```
       H = 0
       P = 29.9
       PRINT 500, H, P
       DO 100 N = 400, 20000, 400
          H = N
          P = 29.9 * (10.0) * * ( - 0.93 * H)
          PRINT 500, H, P
100       CONTINUE
       STOP
500    FORMAT (1X, F7.0, F15.3)
       END
```

11.

```
       READ 200, NGRPS, NPERGP
       PRINT 210
       DO 100 NG = 1, NGRPS
          AVHT = 0
          DO 50 N = 1, NPERGP
             READ 215, NP, NGG, NDATE, HEIGHT
             IF (NGG .EQ. NG) GO TO 40
                PRINT 220
                STOP
40           PRINT 225, NGG, NP, NDATE, HEIGHT
             AVHT = AVHT + HEIGHT
50           CONTINUE
          AVHT = AVHT/NPERGP
          PRINT 230, AVHT
100       CONTINUE
       STOP
200    FORMAT (2I5)
210    FORMAT (1X, 'GROUP NO. PLANT NO. DATE PLANTED HEIGHT')
215    FORMAT (3I5, F5.0)
220    FORMAT (1X, 'CARDS OUT OF ORDER')
```

```
225      FORMAT (1X, 3I10, F10.1)
230      FORMAT (1X, 'AVERAGE HEIGHT', F10.2)
         END
```

13.

```
         US = 210
         CANADA = 25
         DO 10 I = 1, 50
            US = 1.011 * US
            CANADA = 1.0475 * CANADA
            PRINT 100, US, CANADA
            IF (CANADA .GT. US) PRINT 110
10          CONTINUE
         STOP
100      FORMAT (10X, 'US', F10.0, 5X, 'CANADA', F10.0)
110      FORMAT (10X, 'CANADA IS LARGER')
         END
```

15.

```
C   MILES TO KILOMETER CONVERSION
C
         C = 1.609344
         DO 10 MILES = 1, 50
            XMILES = MILES
            XKM = C * XMILES
            PRINT 50, MILES, XKM
10          CONTINUE
         STOP
50       FORMAT (10X, 'MILES', I3, 5X, 'KM', F8.2)
         END
```

Chapter 8, page 225

1.

```
         DIMENSION X(100)
         MAX = 100
         XSTOP = 9999.0
         I = 1
10       READ 500, X(I)
         IF (X(I) .EQ. XSTOP) GO TO 20
         I = I + 1
         IF (I .LE. MAX) GO TO 10
20       I = I - 1
         IF (I .EQ. 0) STOP
         PRINT 500, X(I)
         GO TO 20
500      FORMAT (F10.3)
         END
```

3.

```
C   FIND THE AVERAGE AND VARIANCE OF N NUMBERS.
         DIMENSION X(200)
         S = 0.0
         Q = 0.0
         READ 500, N
         IF (N .LT. 2 .OR. N .GT. 200) STOP
         DO 10 I = 1, N
            READ 510, X(I)
```

```
10        CONTINUE
       DO 20 I = 1, N
          S = S + X(I)
          Q - Q + X(I) * * 2
20        CONTINUE
       AV = S/FLOAT(N)
       VAR = (Q - AV)/FLOAT(N - 1)
       PRINT 520, AV, VAR
       STOP
500    FORMAT(I5)
510    FORMAT(F10.0)
520    FORMAT(10X, 'AVERAGE = ', F12.4, 5X, 'VAR = ', F12.4)
       END
```

7.

```
       DIMENSION A(11, 5)
C   READ, WINS, LOSSES
       N = 0
10     N = N + 1
       IF (N .GT. 11) STOP
       READ (A(N, J), J = 1, 3)
       IF (A(N, 1) .NE. 0.0) GO TO 10
       N = N - 1
C   COMPUTE PCT
       DO 20 I = 1, N
          A(I, 4) = A(I, 2)/(A(I, 2) + A(I, 3))
20     CONTINUE
C   FIND BEST TEAM (THIS SECTION IS UNNECESSARY IF
C   THE BEST TEAM IS THE FIRST INPUT)
       IBEST = 1
       ABEST = A(1, 4)
       DO 30 I = 1, N
          IF (A(I, 4) .LT. ABEST) GO TO 30
             IBEST = I
             ABEST = A(I, 4)
30     CONTINUE
C   COMPUTE GAMES BEHIND
       I = IBEST
       DO 40 J = 1, N
          A(J, 5) = ((A(I, 2) - A(I, 3)) - (A(J, 2) - A(J, 3)))/2.0
40     CONTINUE
C   OUTPUT
       PRINT, 'TEAM, WINS, LOSSES, PCT, GAMES BEHIND'
       DO 60 I = 1, N
          PRINT, (A(I, J), J = 1, 5)
60     CONTINUE
       STOP
       END
```

9.

```
       DIMENSION NVALID(10), NQUAN(10)
       DO 10 I = I, 10
          READ, NVALID(I)
          NQUAN(I) = 0
```

```
10      CONTINUE
20      READ, NPART, NUMBER
            IF (NPART .EQ. 0) GO TO 50
            DO 30 I = 1, 10
                IF (NPART .EQ. NVALID(I)) GO TO 40
30      CONTINUE
            PRINT, 'INVALID DATA', NPART, NUMBER
            GO TO 20
40          NQUAN(I) = NQUAN(I) + NUMBER
        GO TO 20
C-- AT END OF INPUT
50      DO 60 I = 1, 10
            PRINT, 'PART', NVALID(I), 'QTY.', NQUAN(I)
60      CONTINUE
        STOP
        END
```

11.

```
C   BELLEMORTE INSURANCE COMPANY
        DIMENSION AGE(7), PREM(7)
        N = 6
        AGE(1) = 0
        AGE(2) = 20
        PREM(2) = 2
        AGE(3) = 30
        PREM(3) = 5
        AGE(4) = 40
        PREM(4) = 12
        AGE(5) = 60
        PREM(5) = 17
        AGE(6) = 1000
        PREM(6) = 25
        READ, A, C
        DO 10 I = 1, N
            IF (AGE(I) .LE. A .AND. A .LT. AGE(I + 1))
     $          AP = C*PREM(I + 1)*12.0
10          CONTINUE
        PRINT, A, C, AP
        STOP
        END
```

13.

```
        DIMENSION A(1000), B(1000)
C-- CREATE A MATRIX
C   SELECT ITEMS BETWEEN ALOW AND AHIGH
        M = 0
        DO 100 I = 1, N
            IF(.NOT.(A(I) .GT. ALOW .AND. A(I) .LT. AHIGH)) GO TO 100
                M = M + 1
                B(M) = A(I)
100     CONTINUE
        PRINT, (B(J), J = 1, M)
        STOP
        END
```

14.
```
      DIMENSION A(1000)
C-- CREATE THE ARRAY A
C   SELECT ITEMS BETWEEN ALOW AND AHIGH
      M = 0
      DO 100 I = 1, N
         IF (.NOT.(A(I) .GT. ALOW .AND. A(I) .LT. AHIGH)) GO TO 100
            M = M + 1
            A(M) = A(I)
100   CONTINUE
      PRINT, (A(I), I = 1, M)
      STOP
      END
```

Chapter 9, page 258

1.
```
      SUBROUTINE NEXT(X, N)
      DIMENSION X(6)
10    READ, (X(J), J = 1, 6), NCODE
      IF (NCODE .EQ. N) RETURN
      IF (NCODE .EQ. 1000) STOP
      GO TO 10
      END
```

3.
```
      SUBROUTINE CHK(NCODE, NVALID, NSIZE)
      DIMENSION NVALID(NSIZE)
      DO 10 I = 1, SIZE
         IF (NCODE .EQ. NVALID(I)) RETURN
10    CONTINUE
      PRINT, 'INVALID CODE', NCODE
      STOP
      END
```

5.
```
      SUBROUTINE REVERS(A, N)
C   REVERSE THE ARRAY A
      DIMENSION A(N)
      I = 1
      J = N
10    IF (I .GE. J) RETURN
         TEMP = A(I)
         A(I) = A(J)
         A(J) = TEMP
         I = I + 1
         J = J - 1
      GO TO 10
      END
```

7. Since the argument of the subroutine when called is integer type, while the argument when defined is real type, the results are undefined. On many systems, no error would be detected, but the value printed would be 0.00.

9.
```
      FUNCTION P(X, A)
      IF (X .GT. 0.0) P = X ** A
      IF (X .EQ. 0.0) P = 0.0
      IF (X .LT. 0.0) P = -ABS(X) ** A
```

```
      RETURN
      END
```

11. The function GEOM should return the value N if R = 1. You can rewrite the function as follows.

```
      FUNCTION GEOM(R, N)
      IF (R .EQ. 1.0) GEOM = N
      IF (R .NE. 1.0) GEOM = (1.0 - R**(N + 1))/(1.0 - R)
      RETURN
      END
```

13.

```
      FUNCTION NGCD(I, J)
C     NGCD IS THE GREATEST COMMON DIVISOR OF I AND J.
      M = I
      N = J
C     NOTE--COPY THE DUMMY ARGUMENTS SO THAT WE CAN
C     SAFELY CHANGE THEIR VALUES.
10    IF (N .EQ. 0) GO TO 20
         NR = MOD(M, N)
         M = N
         N = NR
         GO TO 10
20    NGCD = M
      RETURN
      END
```

15.

```
      FUNCTION NC(N, KK)
      K = MIN 0 (KK, N-KK)
      NUM = 1
      LIMIT = K + 1
      IF (LIMIT .GT. N) GO TO 20
      DO 10 J = LIMIT, N
         NUM = NUM * J
10    CONTINUE
20    NDENOM = 1
      IF (K .LT. 1) GO TO 40
      DO 30 J = 1, K
         NDENOM = NDENOM * J
30    CONTINUE
40    CONTINUE
      NC = NUM/NDENOM
      RETURN
      END
```

17.

```
      SUBROUTINE SORT(A, N, NPTR)
C     THIS IS AN INDIRECT SORT. INSTEAD OF SORTING THE
C     ARRAY A, IT SORTS AN ARRAY NPTR OF POINTERS TO THE
C     ARRAY ELEMENTS. A IS UNCHANGED.
C
C     ON RETURN, NPTR IS AN ARRAY OF INTEGERS SUCH THAT
C     NPTR(1) IS THE SUBSCRIPT OF THE SMALLEST ELEMENT OF THE
C     ARRAY A, NPTR(2) IS THE SUBSCRIPT OF THE NEXT SMALLEST
C     ELEMENT, AND SO FORTH.
```

```
C
      DIMENSION A(N), NPTR(N)
      DO 5 I = 1, N
         NPTR(I) = I
5        CONTINUE
      IF (N .LE. 1) RETURN
C
      LAST = N - 1
      DO 20 I = 1, LAST
         JMIN = I
         JFIRST = I + 1
         DO 10 J = JFIRST, N
            JMPTR = NPTR(JMIN)
            JPTR = NPTR(J)
            IF (A(JMPTR) .LT. A(JPTR)) JMIN = J
10          CONTINUE
         CALL SWAP(NPTR(JMIN), NPTR(I))
20       CONTINUE
      RETURN
      END

      SUBROUTINE SWAP(N, M)
      NTEMP = N
      N = M
      M = NTEMP
      RETURN
      END
```

Chapter 10, page 297

1.

```
      CHARACTER*30 LINES(6), FLAG*4
      L = 0
10    DO 20 I = 1, 6
         LINES(I) = ' '
20    CONTINUE
      I = 0
30    I = I + 1
      IF (I .LE. 6) GO TO 40
         PRINT, 'TOO MANY LINES IN THIS LABEL'
         I = 1
40    READ 45, LINES(I), FLAG
45    FORMAT(A30, A4)
      IF (FLAG .NE. ' ') GO TO 30
      L = L + 1
      IF (MOD(L, 5) .NE. 1) GO TO 50
      PRINT 60, LINES (I), I = 1, 6
         GO TO 10
50    PRINT 55, LINES (I), I = 1, 6
      GO TO 10
55    FORMAT(6(A30/)//)
60    FORMAT('1', 6(A30/)//)
```

```
100     STOP
        END
```

3.

```
        B = ' '
        X = 'X'
        PRINT 5
5       FORMAT('1' /////)
        DO 100 LINE = 1, 54
           T = FLOAT(LINE - 1)/27.0 - 1.0
           S = SQRT(1.0 - T**2)
           N1 = 11.0 + 44.5*(1.0 - S)
           N2 = 11.0 + 44.5 * (1.0 + S)
           NO = N1 - 1
           PRINT 10, (B, I = 1, NO), (X, I = N1, N2)
10         FORMAT(1X, 110A1)
100     CONTINUE
        STOP
        END
```

5.

```
        CHARACTER * 4 A(21)
10      READ 15, (A(I), I = 1, 21)
15      FORMAT(A1, A3, 19A4)
        IF (A(1) .EQ. '*') STOP
        IF (A(1) .NE. 'C') GO TO 10
        PRINT 20, (A(I), I = 1, 21)
20      FORMAT(10X, A1, A3, 19A4)
        GO TO 10
100     STOP
        END
```

Index

Notes